THE MIRAMICHI FIRE

McGILL-QUEEN'S RURAL, WILDLAND, AND RESOURCE STUDIES SERIES

Series editors: Colin A.M. Duncan, James Murton, and R.W. Sandwell

The Rural, Wildland, and Resource Studies Series includes monographs, thematically unified edited collections, and rare out-of-print classics. It is inspired by Canadian Papers in Rural History, Donald H. Akenson's influential occasional papers series, and seeks to catalyze reconsideration of communities and places lying beyond city limits, outside centres of urban political and cultural power, and located at past and present sites of resource procurement and environmental change. Scholarly and popular interest in the environment, climate change, food, and a seemingly deepening divide between city and country is drawing non-urban places back into the mainstream. The series seeks to present the best environmentally contextualized research on topics such as agriculture, cottage living, fishing, the gathering of wild foods, mining, power generation, and rural commerce, within and beyond Canada's borders.

1 How Agriculture Made Canada
Farming in the Nineteenth Century
Peter A. Russell

2 The Once and Future Great Lakes
Country
An Ecological History
John L. Riley

3 Consumers in the Bush
Shopping in Rural Upper Canada
Douglas McCalla

4 Subsistence under Capitalism
Nature and Economy in Historical
and Contemporary Perspectives
Edited by *James Murton, Dean
Bavington, and Carly Dokis*

5 Time and a Place
An Environmental History
of Prince Edward Island
Edited by *Edward MacDonald,
Joshua MacFadyen, and Irené
Novaczek*

6 Powering Up Canada
A History of Power, Fuel,
and Energy from 1600
Edited by R.W. Sandwell

7 Permanent Weekend
Nature, Leisure, and Rural
Gentrification
John Michels

8 Nature, Place, and Story
Rethinking Historic Sites in Canada
Claire Elizabeth Campbell

9 The Subjugation of Canadian
Wildlife
Failures of Principle and Policy
Max Foran

10 Flax Americana
A History of the Fibre and Oil
That Covered a Continent
Joshua MacFadyen

11 At the Wilderness Edge
The Rise of the Antidevelopment
Movement on Canada's West Coast
J.I. Little

12 The Greater Gulf
Essays on the Environmental History
of the Gulf of St Lawrence
Edited by *Claire E. Campbell,
Edward MacDonald, and Brian
Payne*

13 The Miramichi Fire
A History
Alan MacEachern

The Miramichi Fire

A History

ALAN MACEACHERN

McGill-Queen's University Press
Montreal & Kingston • London • Chicago

© McGill-Queen's University Press 2020

ISBN 978-0-2280-0148-5 (cloth)
ISBN 978-0-2280-0149-2 (paper)
ISBN 978-0-2280-0284-0 (ePDF)
ISBN 978-0-2280-0285-7 (ePUB)

Legal deposit second quarter 2020
Bibliothèque nationale du Québec

Printed in Canada on acid-free paper that is 100% ancient forest free (100% post-consumer recycled), processed chlorine free

This book has been published with the help of a grant from the Canadian Federation for the Humanities and Social Sciences, through the Awards to Scholarly Publications Program, using funds provided by the Social Sciences and Humanities Research Council of Canada. Funding was also received from the J.B. Smallman Publication Fund and the Faculty of Social Science, the University of Western Ontario.

We acknowledge the support of the Canada Council for the Arts.

Nous remercions le Conseil des arts du Canada de son soutien.

Library and Archives Canada Cataloguing in Publication

Title: The Miramichi fire: a history / Alan MacEachern.

Names: MacEachern, Alan, 1966– author.

Series: McGill-Queen's rural, wildland, and resource studies series; 13.

Description: Series statement: McGill-Queen's rural, wildland, and resource studies series; 13 | Includes bibliographical references and index.

Identifiers: Canadiana (print) 20200206370 | Canadiana (ebook) 20200206389 | ISBN 9780228001485 (cloth) | ISBN 9780228001492 (paper) | ISBN 9780228002840 (ePDF) | ISBN 9780228002857 (ePUB)

Subjects: LCSH: Wildfires—New Brunswick—Miramichi River Region—History—19th century. | LCSH: Forest fires—New Brunswick—Miramichi River Region—History—19th century. | LCSH: Miramichi River Region (N.B.)—Environmental conditions—19th century | LCSH: Miramichi River Region (N.B.)—History—19th century | LCSH: Collective memory.

Classification: LCC FC2495.M56 M33 2020 | DDC 971.5/2102—dc23

This book was typeset by Marquis Interscript in 10.5/13 Sabon.

To Genevieve and Sadie

Contents

Figures ix

Prologue xi

1 Introduction 3

2 The Timber Boom 14

3 Leafs vs Flames 50

4 The Phoenix 96

5 The Barrens and the Birches 134

6 Conclusion 177

Acknowledgments 185

Appendix: Some of the Dead 187

Notes 193

Bibliography 247

Index 277

Figures

0.1 Jackson family gravestone. Photograph by Alan MacEachern. xii

1.1 Northeastern North America and the Miramichi region, 1825. Maps by Eric Leinberger. 5

2.1 *The Largest Ship Ever Built, THE BARON [of] RENFREW, Capt'n Matt'w Walker*, 1825. Lithograph by M. Young and S. Vowles, Peter Winkworth Collection of Canadiana, R9266–3280, Library and Archives Canada. 15

2.2 The Miramichi watershed. Map by Eric Leinberger. 18

2.3 The ecoregions of the Miramichi. Map by Eric Leinberger, from Vincent Frank Zelazyny, *Our Landscape Heritage: The Story of Ecological Land Classification in New Brunswick* (Fredericton, NB: New Brunswick Department of Natural Resources, 2007). 19

2.4 New Brunswick population distribution, 1803 and 1824. Maps by Paul Jance, in Graeme Wynn, "Population Patterns in Pre-Confederation New Brunswick," *Acadiensis* 10, no. 2 (1981): 133–4. 30

2.5 *View of Beaubear's Island, Miramichi – The Commercial Establishment of John and Alexander Fraser and Co.*, c. 1825. Oil painting by R. Thresher, Heritage Branch, New Brunswick, GH 996.9.1. 32

3.1 Forest fires across the Northeast, 1825. Map by Eric Leinberger. 79

3.2 Reported forest fires in Maine, 1825. Map by Eric Leinberger, overlain on Moses Greenleaf, *Map of the Inhabited Part of the State of Maine* (Portland, ME: Shirley & Hyde, 1829). Courtesy of David Rumsey Map Collection. 86

Figures

4.1 Cover of *A Narrative of the Late Fires at Miramichi, New-Brunswick* (Halifax: P.J. Holland, 1825). 106

5.1 "View on the Miramichi," 1849. Sketch in James Edward Alexander, *L'Acadie, or Seven Years' Explorations in North America*, vol. 2 (London: H. Colburn, 1849), 162. 149

5.2 Robert Chalmers's estimate of the Miramichi Fire zone, 1888. Map by Robert Chalmers, in *Report on the Surface Geology of North-Eastern New Brunswick* (Montreal: Dawson Brothers, 1888). 158

5.3 *Salmon Fishing on Miramichi River, NB*, c. 1908. Photograph by William Notman & Son, McCord Museum, view-4371. 163

5.4 *Dr. William Francis Ganong, Renous River Region, Northumberland County, New Brunswick*, 1904. Photograph by Arthur Henry Pierce, W.F. Ganong photo collection, 1987.17.1219.187, New Brunswick Museum. 164

5.5 William Francis Ganong, "Map to Illustrate the Limits of the Great Fire of Miramichi of 1825," in "Note 90: On the Limits of the Great Fire of Miramichi of 1825," *Bulletin of the Natural History Society of New Brunswick*, no. 24 (1906): 418–19. 169

5.6 *Dr. William Francis Ganong, Banksian [Jack] Pine, Portage Road along Portage Brook, Northumberland County, New Brunswick*, 1906. Photograph by Mauran I. Furbish, W.F. Ganong photo collection, 1987.17.1218.202, New Brunswick Museum. 173

5.7 American Red Cross map of the Miramichi Fire, c. 2000. Disasterrelief.org. 176

6.1 Tree core sampling project by Chris Norfolk and Alan MacEachern. Georeferenced rendering of William Francis Ganong's 1906 map (see figure 5.5) by Eric Leinberger. 179

Prologue

A family grave – Volcano, verse, vegetation – The planet and the stubble

The graveyard at St Paul's Anglican Church in Miramichi, New Brunswick, is two centuries old but smaller than you would expect – a fact that speaks less to the durability of Anglicans than to demographics. For one thing, the French Catholic and Irish Catholic majority in the area have long favoured nearby St Michael's Basilica. (There is now also a Miramichi Islamic Centre right down the street.) For another, the population of the area has stayed small. St Paul's was born when northeastern New Brunswick was booming thanks to the part it played in the international timber trade. The Miramichi region of the early nineteenth century was not unlike today's Fort McMurray, Alberta, a thriving place on the periphery, its name recognized and respected for the natural resource it provided the imperial centre. But the region slowed down and has languished since then, to the point that its population is not much more than it was two centuries ago. Indeed, within what geographers call Canada's ecumene – its core, well-settled area – the interiors of northern New Brunswick and Gaspé constitute the nation's largest "non-ecumene pocket" of low population density.[1] Miramichi (pronounced MEER-ah-ma-SHEE) is a name that always referred simultaneously to the watershed, the major river that runs through it, the region generally, and even to Northumberland County, of which it was a part. And in the mid-1990s it also became the name of the region's major town, formed by the amalgamation of Newcastle, Chatham, and other communities along the river – small, longstanding rival towns finally succumbing to the need to lean on one another.[2] Given this history, the nineteenth century figures heavily on the grounds of St Paul's. Father of Confederation John M. Johnson

Figure 0.1 Jackson family gravestone, St Paul's Anglican Church Cemetery, Miramichi, New Brunswick.

is buried here. So is Dr John Vondy, who died treating typhus victims fleeing the Irish famine. So are the infant children of timber patriarch Joseph Cunard; the trunk of a tree has grown round their gravestone, hugging it tight.

One simple, slab gravestone, stained and darkened by almost two centuries of lichen and acid rain – but unlike many of its neighbours still standing straight – is conspicuous because of its size. It is big, and needs to be, to bear all the inscription it does and to shelter all the dead it does. It reads,

Prologue xiii

Sacred to the Memory of
Ann
Wife of John Jackson & six of their children

The mother aged 41 years with three of her children
John aged 13 years,
Margaret aged 6 years, & Anthony aged 10 months,
perished together in the flames
on the memorable night of the 7th of Oct 1825.
The others died in consequence of the injuries
they sustained by the Fire.
Robert died on the 11th Oct aged 12 years,
William died on the 14th of Oct aged 15 years,
and
Joseph died on the 25th of Oct aged 9 years.

John Jackson was the sexton of St Paul's Anglican Church on that memorable night of 7 October 1825, when a massive fire swept through a curtain of forest and down upon communities along the Miramichi River. Jackson is said to have saved the church that evening by draping wet blankets across its roof, only to return home and discover his family dead.[3] The Jacksons were among an estimated 160 killed; thousands more were left homeless. When the smoke cleared, the true scale of the blaze became known. Early reports estimated that the fire burned 6,000 square miles (15,500 square kilometres) of New Brunswick, one-fifth of the colony, and virtually every account over the following generation confirmed this estimate. It was, at the time, the largest forest fire ever recorded. What's more, 1,300 square miles (3,400 square kilometres) burned in neighbouring Maine the same day, making this what is still the most extensive fire in that state's history.

At the base of the Jacksons' stone, just above the grass, the inscription has a brief coda:

Forests were set on fire – but hour by hour
They fell and faded – and the crackling trunks
Extinguish'd with a crash – and all was black
All earth was but one thought – and that was death.

The lines are from Lord Byron's apocalyptic poem "Darkness," composed in Geneva in July 1816. Byron was stranded there during a

xiv *Prologue*

patch of miserably cold weather, and he would later recall writing the poem on "a celebrated dark day, on which the fowls went to roost at noon, and the candles were lighted as at midnight."[4] He could not know that the gloom that inspired him was the result of the eruption of Mount Tambora in Indonesia a year earlier, which had subsequently spread a cloud of ash and dust around the globe. In Europe, the cool, wet weather over the next several years killed harvests, threatened famine, and encouraged emigration – including of people such as the Jacksons, who left England for New Brunswick in this era. Meanwhile, in northeastern North America, the same cool, wet weather checked forest fires and allowed combustible vegetation to accumulate, producing the conditions for an eventual conflagration, the magnitude of which new immigrants to the region were completely unprepared for. Byron's poem was unknowingly prescient, and the Jacksons' epitaph unknowingly acknowledged that fact.

The book that follows is about rediscovering such forgotten connections and considering how they were forgotten in the first place. In 1825 Great Britain ruled the largest empire in the world and relied heavily on the importation of timber. Of all its timber sources, British North America produced the most. Within these colonies, New Brunswick produced the most. Within this colony, the Miramichi region produced the most. So when trees in the Miramichi burned down before they could be cut down, it was of significance on both sides of the Atlantic. Yet whether and how individual trees burned was the result of exceptionally local circumstances, involving climate, geology, topography, botany, and land use, among other things. A poet, in the words of Henry David Thoreau, must "weave into his verse the planet and the stubble."[5] I extend that obligation to the historian. A history of the Miramichi Fire must be open to the possibility that a volcanic eruption on one continent connects to the writing of a poem on another and to the growth of vegetation on still another and that they together connect to the death of a family. Such a history is necessarily intensely global and intensely local – because all histories are.

THE MIRAMICHI FIRE

I

Introduction

Remembering and forgetting the great fire – Official versus vernacular history – Stalking the dreaded lacuna – Environmental history – Social memory – Spoilers – Of fire, wood, paper, and cloud – My debt to digital

Whatever happened to the Miramichi Fire? I first came across it in George Perkins Marsh's groundbreaking 1864 *Man and Nature*, the first modern treatise on humans' effects on nature. He recalled it in these terms: "The great fire of Miramichi in 1825, probably the most extensive and terrific conflagration recorded in authentic history, spread its ravages over nearly six thousand square miles, chiefly of woodland, and was of such intensity that it seemed to consume the very soil itself."[1] Marsh had been living in Burlington, Vermont, when the fire took place and surely breathed its smoke, but even without that sensory memory, it is not surprising that the fire came to his mind four decades later: it was one of the most famous natural disasters of the nineteenth century.

The fire's occurrence generated not only substantial press but also a substantial relief effort across the Western world. Subscriptions were gathered in London coffeehouses, a ballad was composed and sold in Wales to raise funds, and there was an informal rivalry between American cities over who would give the most. A generation later, a Scottish historian sought to convey the widespread fascination with the disaster at the time:

The celebrated fire in Miramichi at once horrified and astonished all the civilised world; and perhaps, for the first time, conveyed an adequate notion of the vastness and compactness of the North American forests. When first recorded in the newspapers, it appeared like some wild fiction. People were accustomed to hear of tenements being burned down before their unfortunate inhabitants could escape, and of several thus perishing in some great city conflagration; but that the fire should literally travel over a province – that its influence should be felt for days before it actually reached its victims – and that they should find, with both the land and the water before them, no means of escape from its devastating approach, seemed something incomprehensible.[2]

For an increasingly literate public aided by an expanding public press, it was the first forest fire to capture the Western imagination. It made people consider that the bounty of the new world might not actually be inexhaustible, as people could inadvertently lay it all to waste. It was, in the words of historian Stephen J. Pyne, the "first historic holocaust of the reclamation."[3] When foresters or forest historians compile lists of historic forest fires, the 1825 Miramichi Fire is almost always the first one cited.[4]

The fire retained its notoriety throughout the nineteenth century, flaring up time and again in literary discussion. In 1838, for example, in the course of arguing that we should attempt contact with the estimated 4.2 billion aliens on the moon – of the some 22 trillion in the solar system – Scottish astronomer Thomas Dick mused that they may already suspect our existence: a fire such as the Miramichi one would look like "luminous specks" to them.[5] When in the 1860s naturalist Henry David Thoreau debated newspaperman Horace Greeley on the theory that forests spontaneously regenerate after fire, Greeley used the example of the inferno that had swept the pine woods of "Maine, New-Brunswick, &c." and left birches in their place.[6] The Peshtigo Fire, which burned across Wisconsin on 8 October 1871 and killed perhaps ten times as many people as the Miramichi Fire, certainly overshadowed the 1825 blaze, but the earlier fire continued to be remembered. Norman MacLeod's 1861 essay "Fire in the Woods," which argued that "no such fire as that which devastated Miramichi ever visited any of our colonies before or since," became a staple in British and Canadian school primers for the remainder of the century.[7] The fire was considered of sufficient significance to Canadian history that the final exam in that subject at Dalhousie University in 1885 asked students to "Write a brief account of the Miramichi Fire. Give date."[8] Maritime writer John MacKinnon was likely right in 1915 when

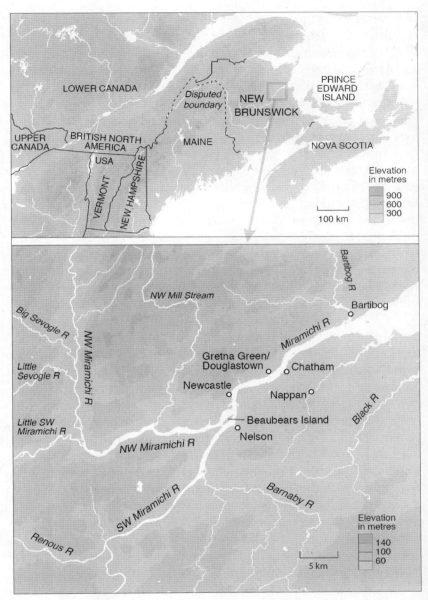

Figure 1.1 Northeastern North America and the Miramichi region, 1825.

6 *The Miramichi Fire*

he opened a short piece on "The Greatest Conflagration on Record" by noting that in the nineteenth century the Miramichi region was more widely known than the colony of which it was a part.[9] The Miramichi Fire is still arguably the most famous historical event to have taken place in New Brunswick. It is also the largest wildfire to have occurred within the British Empire, one of the largest in North American history, and the largest ever recorded along the Eastern Seaboard.

Having come across the fire in Marsh's *Man and Nature*, I looked forward to reading more about it. But that turned out to be difficult: there has been very little historical writing on it. Not only has the fire never merited its own book; it has all but disappeared from provincial and regional histories written during the twentieth and twenty-first centuries. It receives just two sentences in both W.S. MacNutt's 1963 *New Brunswick, a History: 1784–1867* and Philip Buckner and John Reid's 1994 *The Atlantic Region to Confederation* – and, in the latter case, the wrong year is given. Graeme Wynn's 1981 *Timber Colony* remains by far the most authoritative analysis of the relationship between people, forests, and forestry in colonial New Brunswick, and it certainly served as both reference work and inspiration when I was writing the present book, but it devotes just a single paragraph to the fire. Famed New Brunswick botanist and historical geographer William Francis Ganong's 1906 essay "On the Limits of the Great Fire of Miramichi of 1825" remains the most sustained historical analysis of the disaster, at nine pages.[10] That is strange.

This is not to say that the fire has been utterly extinguished. As noted, it still shows up in the media when historic forest fires are discussed, typically when an inferno is raging somewhere. It persists in local folk memory, too. Shortly after the fire, John Jardine, who lived just south of Chatham, wrote a long ballad chronicling the disaster, which began,

> This is the truth, that I now tell you
> For mine eyes in part did see
> What did happen to the people
> On the banks of the Miramichi.

Jardine set the poem to music, and "The Miramichi Fire" soon became one of the best-known fiddle tunes throughout the Maritimes and New England. It is still played today, usually without the accompanying lyrics.[11] The story of the Miramichi Fire is also often told in museums

Introduction

and at heritage sites across the region, such as the Beaubears Island National Historic Site and the Central New Brunswick Woodmen's Museum. It has been recounted repeatedly in fiction, most notably this century in Pulitzer Prize–winning author Annie Proulx's *Barkskins* and in Valerie Sherrard's young adult book *Three Million Acres of Flame*. It is a staple in local histories, too – and this present book, as the endnotes will attest, has benefited greatly from the work of local authors such as W.D. Hamilton and William R. MacKinnon Jr. But even the local histories and sites, hardly less than the fictionalized accounts, tend to rely on a few well-known early sources and otherwise repeat a long string of secondary sources and legend. Folklorist Sandy Ives once wrote of Jardine's ballad that many people "had a clipping or even a handwritten copy around somewhere, but very few people could sing more than a few stanzas from memory. It was a song well known *about* but not well *known*."[12] Much the same could be said of the Miramichi Fire itself.

I was motivated to write a history of the great fire, then, in part by the fact that none had been written. That may raise red flags with some readers, and rightly so: I know that whenever I hear the word "lacuna," I reach for my pistol. I would say, however, that I was attracted to the topic not by the notion of filling a gap in the literature – of imagining my scholarship as grout – but by a curiosity as to *why*, even as the fire has more or less survived in vernacular history, it has almost entirely disappeared from more formal history.

The book that follows is in many ways a very traditional work of Canadian history. It tells a nineteenth-century story complete with sailing ships, white settlers, a staples crop, and a natural disaster, all presented in chronological, narrative form. There is even an apology for the inadequate reclaiming of an Indigenous perspective. A dead white pine view of history, if ever there was one. Yet it is also steeped in, and in turn contributes to, two of the most innovative and important subfields in historical scholarship this century: environmental history, or the study of the relationship between humans and nature through time; and social memory, or the study of how a group's historical memory is created and fostered.[13]

How these two intersect can begin to be understood by way of Henry David Thoreau's explanation for writing about the weather in his daily journal: "That which was so important at the time cannot be unimportant to remember."[14] To the slim degree that traditional histories, Canadian or otherwise, would treat a forest fire as an apt subject for consideration, they would see it as a discrete event in which nature suddenly and unexpectedly was involved in human affairs. Environmental history, by comparison, recognizes that human affairs are always tightly bound with nature, that there may well be no subject more central than our means of gaining subsistence and the relations we develop with nature to do so. The Miramichi was a forested region whose settlement was predicated on – and whose significance to the colony and motherland was based on – its forest economy, so a major forest fire was certain to have profound social, political, economic, and demographic effects. Moreover, the fire itself was in essence a product of that forest, just as much as the forest in turn became a product of the fire. Rather than treating the Miramichi Fire as a discrete event, then, this book examines it in the larger context of the changing relations between humans and nature in colonial New Brunswick, a process in which both parties played active and symbiotic roles. Writing such a history requires understanding how not just society but also nature worked, and so this book delves as needed into climatology, forest ecology, and dendrochronology as often as it delves into political, economic, or art history.

But, recalling Thoreau, if nature was so important at the time, how did it become unimportant to remember? The study of social memory offers an answer. French historian Pierre Nora argues that modernity has witnessed the passing of *milieux de mémoire*, or "real" collective memory shared daily and organically within premodern communities, and its replacement by *lieux de mémoire*, or "sites of memory" such as monuments, songs, fields of battle, and anything else vested with popular historical significance.[15] Like water beading on a surface, the past consolidates into histories that are more defined, compartmentalized, and tractable – and so more easily nation-, state-, and capital-controlled – and ultimately more easily forgotten. The Miramichi Fire may usefully be considered a *lieu de mémoire* in that although it was a disaster of undetermined – and, in many ways, undeterminable – duration, range, and environmental and human toll, it nevertheless acquired greater definition over time. Little wonder that local, vernacular understanding of the disaster increasingly deviated from more distant, formal histories of it or that by the turn of the twentieth century the distance between the two was great enough to offer opportunity for a wholesale reinterpretation of it. But if the case of the Miramichi Fire exemplifies a *lieu de mémoire*, it also demonstrates how difficult it is for an environmental topic to become one,

Introduction

for although the Miramichi forests were the ultimate "site of memory" of the Miramichi Fire, they comprised a living site, one that was constantly regenerating, and reburning, a moving target on which to build a history. Many environmental topics such as the Miramichi Fire have been lost to history – lost *by* history – because they were easier to forget than to know.

***

This book traces a history of the Miramichi Fire from the years preceding it, which would determine the manner in which it occurred, through to its curious position today, preserved in public memory but largely forgotten in formal history. Chapter 2 introduces the fire's geographical and temporal contexts, concentrating on the Miramichi region of New Brunswick, which would experience the worst of the fire's destruction, and on the development of a timber trade just reaching its peak there in 1825. The Miramichi was a healthy, diverse ecosystem but never a static one, in part because of its millennia-long use by Mi'gmaq people.[16] The limited degree of early Acadian and then British settlement meant that dramatic change, when it finally did come after 1815, was even more environmentally and culturally destabilizing than it would have been otherwise. In the decade prior to the great fire, the Miramichi suddenly boomed with a lucrative international timber trade – timber moving out and British settlers moving in with the speed and consistency of a crosscut saw. The chapter's key argument is that the settler population that experienced the Miramichi Fire in 1825 consisted largely of recent immigrants who possessed little knowledge of North America's forests and fires, let alone New Brunswick's, and they had arrived during a period of unusual coolness and low fire activity. Their unfamiliarity with local conditions may not have caused the fire, but it certainly exacerbated the fire and defined their reactions to it.

In tracing the life of what might be called the Miramichi Fire proper – the fire as it burned – chapter 3 slows down and methodically describes a disaster defined by its ephemerality. Historical descriptions of the fire have relied largely, when not on local legend, on a few well-worn secondary accounts peppered with the most sensational eyewitness testimony available. My strategy, by contrast, is to tell the most broad-based and comprehensive history of the fire possible, giving preference to newspaper accounts, diary entries, government debates and petitions, and other sources written immediately or shortly after it. The chapter's most important contribution is in mapping the fire, demonstrating the degree to which this was not strictly a "Miramichi" fire at all but rather part of a fire complex burning throughout northeastern North America that fall – not only in Maine but also in Lower Canada. This geography and the fact that all contemporary accounts (but one) in the generation following the fire accepted that its range was on the order of 6,000 square miles suggest that the Miramichi Fire complex actually was one of the largest forest fires in recorded history. Chapter 3 ends by considering the fire's cause. Since it is ultimately impossible to know whether, not to mention where and when, a white settler farmer or lumberman or a Mi'gmaw – or nature via lightning or spontaneous combustion – ignited the spark that would become the Miramichi Fire, the changing nature of blame in the nineteenth century spoke more to changing attitudes about these groups than to changing information about the fire itself.

Chapters 4 and 5 examine the social and environmental effects of the fire respectively. In both cases, dire predictions in the aftermath of the disaster did not come to pass, which would later shape how Miramichi citizens and more distant observers came to assess the fire's meaning. Chapter 4 opens with survivors caring for the injured and the dead and proceeds with subsequent attempts to determine the fire's death toll. The scale of devastation made many Miramichiers initially fear, or even assume, their society's collapse, whether from anarchy, outmigration, starvation, or the persistence of fire-related illness and mortality. But the international relief effort that the disaster generated that autumn not only provided for the survivors' physical needs but also helped to preserve social hierarchies and convinced the people of the region that they were still connected to and valued by a wider world. Tangibly and psychologically, charity laid the groundwork for reconstruction. But of what form? Colonial leaders urged the people of the Miramichi region to take the opportunity, when rebuilding, to correct fundamental problems within its society – its lack of attention to agriculture and the rivalry between communities on the north and south sides of the river – but these problems, too, were reconstructed.

Unstated in chapter 4 is why, on the heels of a massive forest fire, reconstruction seemed feasible to a society built within a forest region and reliant on a forest industry. This matter is taken up in chapter 5, which deals with the anticipated and actual effects of the great fire on the forests (and waters and wildlife) of the Miramichi region.

Introduction 11

Although the conflagration did destroy a great many trees that would otherwise have been available for timber, it left many more unscathed or still marketable. Time and ecological succession took over from there. The forest economy and the forests themselves rebounded quickly – which to many distant observers suggested that the original reports about the fire's destruction must have been exaggerated. Yet as the fire retreated into the past, other authors of the late nineteenth century decided that the developing myth demanded long-term devastation as well as initial tragedy, so they wrote as though the fire had left the Miramichi forests permanently barren. It was this growing dissonance that led botanist and geographer William Francis Ganong to reconstruct the Miramichi Fire in the early twentieth century. His solution – an attempt to conform the historical record to the extensive forests he saw around him – has shaped, or rather misshaped, understanding of the great fire to the present day.

✳✳✳

A few words about sources are in order. A forest fire is about wood, but it is also about paper: if a fire burned in a forest and no one wrote about it, did it actually burn? (Well, yes.) My research relied heavily on primary-source written accounts, the closer in time and place to the disaster the better. My thinking was that those written after the smoke cleared but within the subsequent generation would tend to be the most reliable, particularly when written by local authors for a local audience who would know whether the information given was wrong or embroidered. Yet my affection for and reliance on documentary sources from the early to mid-nineteenth century raise their own problems. Such sources skew toward accounts that are male, white, middle-age or older, middle-class or richer, urban, official, and beyond the Miramichi. Although this was Mi'gmaw territory and the fire undoubtedly took Mi'gmaw lives and affected Mi'gmaw livelihoods, Mi'gmaw people are glaringly absent from the written sources, both as authors and as subjects. I can think of only one primary written source that claims to offer a direct Indigenous perspective related to the fire, and this source is a newspaper transcription in pidgin English.[17] Although I have worked to tease out how Mi'gmaq and other underrepresented populations experienced the fire, I cannot pretend this narrative gives them sufficient weight.

What I could not know when my research started was the degree to which paper would drift away and turn to … cloud. This book would not exist without the proliferation this century of digital tools and sources, which have gone from being relatively obscure to utterly pervasive. While researching, I constantly updated a Google map showing where sources mentioned that the great fire had burned, which allowed me simultaneously to compile, organize, and analyze spatial data. But it was the digitization of textual sources and the creation of online databases, including the Internet Archive, Canadiana Online, the Google Newspaper Archive, the HathiTrust Digital Library, the *Dictionary of Canadian Biography*, Our Roots, Ancestry, the Biodiversity Heritage Library, and many others, that were absolutely indispensable to this work.[18] Such databases, some available only through library subscriptions but most open-access, allowed me to uncover things no one had noticed before. For example, when researching the Gale database of nineteenth-century British newspapers, I learned that some would-be British immigrants sailed to the Miramichi region in early October 1825, found it in flames, and sailed right back, reporting what they had seen in local British newspapers. No one writing about the Miramichi Fire on this side of the Atlantic had ever noticed these eyewitness accounts, either at the time or in the two centuries since. I will admit how fortunate I was to be doing digital research on an event that not only took place on a single precise day but was also associated with an unusual place name. If the fire had become known as the "Newcastle Fire," for example, keyword-based searching would have been much more difficult.

The proliferation of digital databases has been a curse as well as a blessing, of course. I first learned of the Gale database when visiting Britain, and I scrambled to gather notes from it while free-riding a library's subscription there. Shortly after I returned to Canada, my own university library bought a subscription, and when Gale released part 2 of the collection, I waited for the library to buy access to that, too. I see just now that parts 3 and 4 have since been produced but are not available through my university. So I am left with the gnawing sense that there may well be more material out in the universe that I have missed.[19] Historian Barbara Tuchman counselled young scholars to determine when to stop their research by applying the same principle that her mother had counselled her as a teenager to apply when ending a date: a half-hour before she wanted to. I have wantonly contravened that rule. Having come to a topic under-researched and newly researchable, I have thoroughly over-researched it. Perhaps a

Introduction 13

part of me was hoping to create a work so definitive that it would preclude anyone ever writing on it again.

But I also sought to wrestle the fire to the ground as a means of demonstrating the significance of contemporary digital research. It was only because of such research that I could take a topic that had never permitted ten pages of description and analysis and write almost two hundred pages on it. Although this book chronicles an event that has been well known for the past two centuries, I estimate that more than 90 per cent of the references have never before been cited anywhere in any historical work related to the fire – or to anything else. That is remarkable, like finding a lost city in the forest. New ways of researching and communicating history mean that in the twenty-first century, historians are essentially starting over, reinventing every historical topic that has ever been of interest, even as we dream up new ones. My desire to share these nineteenth-century sources convinced me to provide in the endnotes and bibliography links to open-access (that is, not subscription-based) digital versions of them, wherever available. (And if you are reading the ebook, all the better: many of the endnotes take you directly to the page in question.) I encourage you to visit these digital repositories. A history is like a tree in that the above-ground text thrives only thanks to a healthy root system. Beyond that, there is simply the joy – like the joy of mixing metaphors – in enticing a reader to the edge of a rabbit hole and offering them easy opportunity, if they choose, to jump in.[20]

2

The Timber Boom

Wood's floating castle – Introducing the Miramichi region – Its forests, classified – A stage of forest, not a forest as stage – Mi'gma'gi and Mi'gmagiji'j – Early European settlement – The Mi'gmaq and fire – The colonial preference – Napoleon, Gilmour, and Rankin – And Cunard – Forest workers new to forests and to forest fires – The Year Without a Summer – The decade without fire – Let us join and hail the pine – How the timber trade worked – Profits and perils – The timber bubble – The Wild East – The days of Duffy Gillis – Welcome to the boomtown – The Baron *arrives in Britain*

On 18 June 1825 one of the largest wooden ships that has ever been built was to be launched in Quebec City, and history's best witness to the event was a young man who happened to have arrived in port the night before. "P. Finan" – his first name is unknown – was an Irishman who had lived in Upper Canada a decade earlier when his soldier father had fought in the War of 1812, and he was now returning to Canada out of what he called a "fondness for travelling which is natural to an enquiring mind." In an account published three years later, Finan would tell of his ship anchoring near to where a giant timber ship sat in its stocks. This ship, to be christened the *Baron of Renfrew*, was, in Finan's words, "an immense floating castle." More than 100 yards long, 20 wide, and 10 deep, the four-masted barque possessed a ridiculously huge tonnage of not less than 5,880 tons. It was built to carry a timber cargo equal to ten standard ships.[1]

The *Baron of Renfrew* epitomized the scale and the pace of the timber trade then under way between British North America and Great Britain. Over the previous fifteen years, the British North American colonies had been transformed from inconsequential to indispensable suppliers of the wood that was feeding Britain's

Figure 2.1 *The Largest Ship Ever Built*, THE BARON [of] RENFREW, *Capt'n Matt'w Walker*, 1825, by M. Young and S. Vowles.

Industrial Revolution. Quebec City in 1825 was, in the words of one historian, "the greatest timber port the world had ever known."[2] The *Baron of Renfrew*'s builder, the aptly named Charles Wood, had dreamed up this monster ship as a means of getting the most timber from Canada to Britain as quickly and as profitably as possible. Not only would he dramatically undercut his competitors' shipping costs by the sheer volume of timber his vessel could carry, but he would also dismantle the ship on arrival and sell its timber – and in doing so evade the duty of 10 shillings per load on that timber's sale.[3] Wood's scheme was technically lawful, but whether the British government, which did not comment on public reports about the vessel, would actually allow such a blatant circumvention of its regulations was unclear. For P. Finan, gazing up at the ship in Quebec City's harbour and aware of how it blurred the lines between carrier and cargo, the sheer woodenness of the wooden ship was inescapable. He was struck "on observing the trees that were growing very near, and remembering that, but a short time before, it was, like them, growing in the forest."[4]

The morning after landing, Finan joined the people of Quebec City in watching the *Baron of Renfrew* being launched. The river was jammed with small boats crammed with spectators. On some of the boats, military bands played away. But when the *Baron* was set loose to slip into the water, its great weight produced so much friction that the grease on the slideway caught fire. The ship ground to a halt.[5] "[T]he hands that were half raised to the hats, in order to wave them 'high in air,' in triumph, fell motionless by the side."[6] The dejected throngs dispersed.

A second attempt was made to set the ship afloat a week later. The crowd was much smaller on this occasion, but Finan was again a part of it, and he was able to draw closer and describe the *Baron of Renfrew* in finer detail. It was wall-sided, flat-bottomed, and built entirely of logs rather than worked planks.[7] It was so immense that a team of four horses, hoisting in cargo, walked the roomy decks easily. The ship's bottom was left plain, not tarred or painted, and the masts were just trees – huge trunks, their branches lopped off and bark stripped away. "She is constructed," Finan concluded, "in the roughest manner possible." Yet he was admiring of the *Baron*'s lunkish form, and when the ship launched successfully this time, he felt fortunate to be present at such a historic moment: "The event was very interesting and important; the largest ship of modern times was committed to her native element … If it should answer to employ her constantly, it would prove a great blow to the shipping interest engaged in trade."[8] We will leave Finan here and let him return to his travels.

Now that the *Baron of Renfrew* was afloat, men spent the next two months filling it with timber. An estimated 4,000 tons of pine logs and 2,600 tons of deals were put aboard, along with pieces, staves, spars, rafters, lathwood, treenails, and what were reportedly the largest masts ever sent from Canada. Timber was even piled on deck, although this was known to be a dangerous practice. By the time it was fully loaded, the vessel carried 9,500 tons of timber beyond its base weight of about 600 tons.[9] When the *Baron of Renfrew*, as much raft as ship, finally set sail in late August for its maiden voyage across the Atlantic, it was said to bear the equivalent of seventy years' growth of more than 300 acres (120 hectares) of Canadian forests.[10]

✳✳✳

The *Baron of Renfrew* and all of the other timber vessels sailing out of Quebec City were helping to make the British North American colonies Great Britain's leading source of timber in 1825. However, it was not Lower Canada but New Brunswick that provided the most wood that year. And within New Brunswick, it was the Miramichi region that supplied the most. This was an extraordinary transformation: even a decade earlier, the Miramichi was a virtually undeveloped, unsettled unknown. Eighteenth-century cartographers of northeastern North America had left it a big, blank space, a convenient place to drop a cartouche or an inset map of Quebec City.[11] But in retrospect, the area's advantages for a transatlantic timber trade, in terms of location, accessibility, and a veritable forest of forests, seem self-evident. They certainly did to British North America's surveyor general, Joseph Bouchette, when he wrote of the area a few years later. Describing Northumberland County, of which the Miramichi was a part, in 1831 he stated,

> [T]he mind is struck no less by its extent than by the number and grandeur of the rivers by which it is watered, and the length of coast it occupies. Of the rivers, the Miramichi, opening into a spacious bay of the Gulf of St. Lawrence, and stretching through the county to its south-western extremity, and communicating by easy portages with the St. John, is the most remarkable ... It is navigable for large ships for more than thirty miles. There is a sand-bar off the entrance, but it is at all times covered with a sufficient depth of water to float the vessels entering its mouth, which have rarely been either destroyed or injured. Near the sea the land is low, and covered only with dwarf trees; but as we advance into the country, we soon find tracts of heavy timber.[12]

Advancing into the country was relatively easy to do. Beginning 25 kilometres into Miramichi Bay on the province's east coast, the Miramichi River separates into two main branches, the Northwest and the Southwest, which in turn fan into many smaller rivers and streams that run more than 200 kilometres into the province's interior. The extent of this branching is evident in the Lower North Branch Little Southwest Miramichi River, a stream only marginally longer than its name – the longest geographical name in Canada.[13] The Miramichi watershed all told covers almost 14,000 square kilometres, draining one-fifth of New Brunswick.[14] The land is a planation surface, a low-relief plain that climbs slowly and steadily through this part of the province from the southeast to the northwest, peaking at an

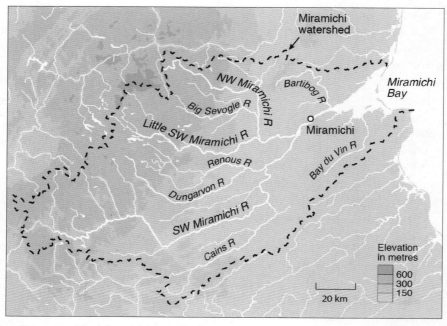

Figure 2.2 The Miramichi watershed.

elevation of 800 metres deep in the province's north-central interior. This slow rise meant that one could paddle to the headwaters of many parts of the river system without a carry. It made the downstream transport of logs straightforward, too.

Although New Brunswick has spent the past two centuries as a timber colony and a timber province, it is still 85 per cent forested today. With the exception of a small area of boreal forest in the province's interior highlands and on its northwestern edge, it is almost entirely part of the Acadian Forest Region, as are almost all of the Maritime provinces. This is a geographic zone whose characteristic feature today is the red spruce, with other common species being the balsam fir, eastern hemlock, eastern white pine, yellow birch, sugar maple, and American beech.[15] As this mix of deciduous and coniferous species suggests, the Acadian Forest Region is a transition zone between the boreal forest of more northern latitudes and the hardwood forests of the northeastern United States. There is significant

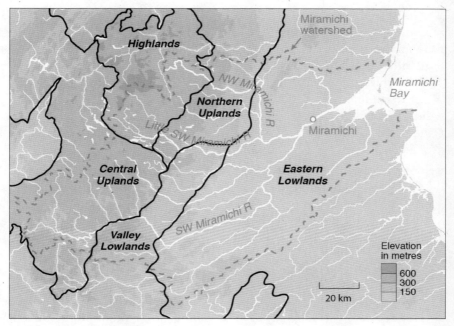

Figure 2.3 The ecoregions of the Miramichi.

variation within this forest region, of course. In 1962 ecologist Orie Loucks produced a classification system for subdividing the Maritime forests into seven of what he called "ecoregions" – the first use of the term, which has since been adopted widely in the field of ecology. Loucks's system was refined in the decades that followed – taking into greater account biodiversity and land-use issues, for example – such that by the mid-1990s the New Brunswick Department of Natural Resources and Energy had produced its own Ecological Land Classification (ELC), breaking the one province into seven ecoregions, subdivided further into thirty-four ecodistricts.[16]

The immensity of the Miramichi Fire's purported range is indicated by the fact that it stretches across as many as five of the ELC's seven bioregions. Both of the main branches of the Miramichi River lie mostly within the Eastern Lowlands, an immense triangle covering much of the eastern half of the province, with vertices at Bathurst, Sackville, and almost as far inland as Fredericton. Constituted as a zone of red spruce, hemlock, and pine, it produces what may be considered a distinctively Maritime forest, with stunted spruce and tamarack amid the extensive peatland near the coast and with fire-adapted species such as jack, red, and white pine as well as trembling aspen throughout. Fir, spruce, hemlock, and others are typical on gently rolling land, and tolerant hardwoods are to be found along ridges and in hilly areas. The Northern Uplands ecoregion runs from the north coast of the province down through the middle. It is a zone of sugar maple, hemlock, and pine, with yellow birch and hemlock also abundant, but extensive areas are exclusively coniferous. The Central Uplands ecoregion is concentrated in the province's northwest, and the Valley Lowlands ecoregion predominates in the west and southwest, but a strand of each runs up the province's centre to the westernmost part of the Miramichi watershed. Both are transition zones and as such have truly mixed forests, with hemlock, cedar, and red spruce common as well as hardwood forests along their hills. The Highlands ecoregion (more particularly, its Ganong ecodistrict) in the north-central heart of the province is a zone of fir, pine, and birch. Its elevation and cold, wet climate mean that it produces boreal-like forests more akin to those located a few degrees of latitude north.[17]

We might assume that the forests of today generally resemble those of two centuries ago since the amount of forested land in New Brunswick has not declined significantly in the interim, since the soils, terrain, and climate that determine which species will thrive in what locations have not changed drastically either, and since the point of a classification scheme such as Loucks's or the ELC is presumably its constancy. But the forests have changed dramatically. They are most certainly not made up of the same trees: it is thought that less than 2 per cent of the province's stands are more than a century old.[18] That in itself is indicative of a broader change. Today's forests are dominated by younger, early-successional species – opportunistic species that thrive in the wake of habitat disturbance such as fire, logging, or land clearing. But two centuries ago, these species made up only a negligible percentage of the forests. Besides widespread mid-successional species, an estimated half of forests were comprised of late-successional, "climax" species (that is, those likely to remain indefinitely, short of habitat disturbance) and old-growth trees (with stands possessing dominant trees at least 150 years old).[19] "Add the fact that late-successional forests can self-replace indefinitely," notes ecologist Donna Crossland in reference to the Eastern Lowlands, "and the possibility that such forests were perhaps thousands of years old must be considered."[20] These forests were composed of old trees of great height and diameter. There was considerably more diversity of species, both within individual stands and in the overall forests, than there is today. Some species that now exist only at a remnant level, such as beech and eastern hemlock, were common or even dominant in the early 1800s. A few species common today, notably jack pine, were essentially nonexistent. The forests of the past were more disease-resistant, more windfirm, and less fire-prone than those that have replaced them, so a walk through one would have meant a walk through a relatively open understory with a closed canopy above; there would have been little or no fallen, windthrown, or dead standing timber.[21] We can scarcely conceive how much more healthy and biodiverse the Miramichi forests of two centuries ago were than those of today[22] – and, as a result, how much more lucrative they were to those who would evaluate them in terms of timber. There were more big trees and more marketable trees of more marketable species: more hemlock and red pine, more yellow birch and elm, and above all more white pine, the most sought-after timber species.[23]

Describing New Brunswick's forests, to set the stage for the fire to come, necessarily means calling attention to the extent to which there was never really a "stage" at all. Or if there was, it was not a stage in the sense of a solid, static foundation on which humans acted but rather a stage in the sense of a step in a process. Loucks's classification system, for example, is a product of its time given that, like all such systems, it drew on existing knowledge and embodied the biases of its time as to what was important and unimportant, but more than that, his system describes forests today that are somewhat different from when he described them and that were far more different two centuries ago. Pollen records indicate that late-successional forests dominated the Maritimes for the past 5,000 years, but the extensive and intensive human activity over the past 200 years has irrevocably altered that.[24]

✳✳✳

What are now the Maritime provinces of Canada have been home to Indigenous people for at least 9,000 years. Paleo-Indians who were descended from the original peoples to reach the Americas from Asia arrived first and were joined thousands of years later by Proto-Eastern Algonquin. Eventually, they merged and became a unique cultural group, the Mi'gmaq. Present-day northeastern New Brunswick and Gaspé together constituted one of the seven districts within Mi'gma'gi, the Mi'gmaq homeland, and was called Gespe'gewa'gi (or Kespe'kewek) – "the last land." Some have interpreted the name in historical terms as the last part of Mi'gma'gi to be occupied, but it could just as easily be interpreted in geographical terms as the beginning of the easternmost part of the continent south of the Saint Lawrence River.[25] The Mi'gmaq referred to the Miramichi River as Welastuguji'j, "the yet smaller Welastuk," signalling that it was named later than both the Welastuk River (i.e., the Saint John River, which runs through west and south New Brunswick) and the smaller Welastuk River (i.e., the Restigouche River in the northwest). One might suppose from this ordering that the Mi'gmaq regarded the Miramichi region – a late-named place in the last land – as a backwater, but in fact it was of considerable importance to them. Especially its waters. In summer, a small population of a few hundred Mi'gmaq fished the Miramichi River for salmon, and in winter they headed upriver to hunt moose, caribou, and deer. The river's generous branching permitted canoe travel far into the district's interior and, from the other direction, meant that the river's mouth served as an important Mi'gmaq meeting place. The Miramichi region's forests were also utilized, of course, but largely to the degree that they were in proximity to water. Beyond material value, the forests also retained great spiritual significance – and the deeper the forest, the greater the significance. In both its waters and forests, then, the Miramichi region was a paradigmatic Mi'gmaq homeland. The word Miramichi is in fact now believed to be a French mispronunciation of Mi'gmagiji'j – a new, or smaller, Mi'gma'gi.[26]

European people and politics insinuated themselves into Mi'gma'gi in the 1500s and 1600s, but Mi'gmagiji'j itself was largely overlooked. Although the greater region had become the French colony of Acadia by the early 1600s, it was not until the 1740s that a tiny Acadian village arose in the Miramichi. In the run-up to the Seven Years' War (1756–63), the British expelled Acadians from all parts of Acadia in 1755, and for a brief moment Beaubears Island at the mouth of the Miramichi River became a refuge for thousands. Short on provisions and susceptible to disease, hundreds of Acadians died there, and the survivors soon drifted away. Although some Acadians did return to live along the east coast of the colony, the Miramichi settlements were not rebuilt. But at war's end, the British colony of

Nova Scotia, of which the Miramichi was now a part, sought to encourage settlement there.

In 1765, on the promise to recruit settlers, Scotsmen William Davidson and John Cort were granted 100,000 acres of land, about 400 square kilometres, that extended deep into the region along both the Northwest and Southwest branches of the Miramichi River. The partners worked diligently in the years that followed to develop a business selling salmon and furs to Europe – and they made the initial foray into selling timber, too. What they did not do was attract much settlement. With the outbreak of the American Revolution (1765–83), Davidson quit the Miramichi; Cort died sometime after. Davidson returned when the conflict had ceased, only to find that Nova Scotia had awarded the Mi'gmaw *saqamaw* (chief) John Julien 20,000 acres on the Northwest branch of the Miramichi River in appreciation of his people's support during the Revolution – not noticing or caring that the parcel overlapped Davidson's.[27] The government's awarding of land to the Mi'gmaq and the ultimate decision to revoke Davidson's claim outright in 1785 speak to the bounded nature of British imperial power around the world in the late 1700s. Still feeling its way in dealing with Indigenous peoples (and British colonists, for that matter) throughout the realm, Britain was still open to fair dealing with them.[28] But it would be a serious mistake to overstate the significance of this predisposition. For one thing, Britain's granting of land to the Mi'gmaq assumed that the land was its to grant. For another, the Crown revoked Davidson's claim less to lawfully accommodate the Mi'gmaq than to bodily accommodate the Loyalists. These American colonists loyal to the Crown, who had fled the Revolution and settled in what, as of 1784, was the new, separate colony of New Brunswick, were lobbying to have the colony's land-granting process rebooted. Few of the Loyalists, however, chose to settle in the Miramichi, and the region's population stayed low for the remainder of the 1700s.

Compelled by the loss of its American colonies, Great Britain turned to British North America in search of timber sources. Surveyor General of the King's Woods John Wentworth, who travelled through the colonies in the 1780s to assess the state of the forests, raved about the conditions he found in the Miramichi region. "Great quantities of pine timber were found and marked for the King's Service ... The pine timber was found still better as one advanced up the river." At one point, he came across the largest tree he had ever seen. He wrote in summary, "The river of Miramichi, and its immense branches, is greatly extended; the soil everywhere good, and covered with forests of the largest Timber; probably the best of it not yet discovered." Wentworth's only caveat was that the Mi'gmaq set fire to meadows to kill off scrub and produce better feed for moose and deer. The fires frequently spread – although "lightly," he said – to the forests and scorched some trees, weakening them and so lessening their value for timber. Even this mild criticism was likely exaggeration or error: like Indigenous peoples throughout northeast North America, the Mi'gmaq had little reason to burn forests extensively. As Alex Mosseler and colleagues state, within the Acadian Forest Region prior to European settlement, "there was probably only a slight increase in fire frequency above levels caused by lightning that can be attributed to aboriginal activities."[29] But in any case, Wentworth stated that the problem of Mi'gmaw fires was on the decline because the Mi'gmaq themselves were: "The Indians have been decreasing many years, and are fast retiring into Canada; their remaining numbers are inconsiderable, so that the practice of annual fires has ceased, and I am convinced Pine Timber will every year be found larger and sounder in these Provinces."[30] Wentworth may not have had all the details right: it is unclear whether the Mi'gmaq population dropped much in the late 1700s or whether that decline awaited the greater pressure of European settlement in the early 1800s. But he accurately assessed the timber trade's promise and recognized that the waning of the Mi'gmaq would simplify matters with respect to both forests and a forest industry.

Yet the promise of the timber trade in the Miramichi region – and, indeed, in all of British North America – continued to outstrip the reality. Masts, spars, and square timber were cut from Miramichi woods for the first time in the early 1790s, but when France declared war against Britain, shipping costs rose to the point that it took years to bring this wood to market, and then only for a very low price.[31] New Brunswick as a whole did somewhat better, but it was a slow beginning: by 1800 the colony was exporting only 2,000 tons of timber and 4 million feet of lumber annually to Great Britain.[32] British North America overall still shipped only an average of 6,000 loads of squared timber to Britain each year. Britain instead depended heavily, as it had for the past two centuries, on the Baltic and Scandinavian countries, which annually shipped 200,000 loads its way.[33] The trade patterns were too well established, the product's quality too assured, and the costs too reasonable to turn to a new, unknown supplier three times as far away, even if it was part of the imperial family. Economics trumped empire.

The Timber Boom 25

But then the economics changed. Beginning in 1806, Napoleon Bonaparte made a concerted effort to close Baltic ports to British shipping. Although some timber did trickle through, its price rose dramatically. Since the duty paid on colonial timber was lower than that from foreign nations, the higher costs of shipping from British North America were suddenly offset. By the end of the decade, Britain was importing as much wood from the colonies as from northern Europe. Then, in 1810 and 1811, Britain raised its timber tariffs but did so differentially, greatly favouring the colonial market.[34] British North America would be Britain's foremost supplier of timber for the next forty years.

The colonial preference on timber – or "protection," as it was often called – infuriated elements in Great Britain. Some resented the extra cost to consumers. Others were philosophically opposed to protectionism. Still others were engaged in the Baltic trade themselves. And others, as we will see, simply deemed the colonial product inferior.[35] Not surprisingly, the colonies just as strongly supported the duty and jealously guarded its retention. The 465-page *Report from the Select Committee on Timber Duties*, a transcript of British governmental committee hearings in 1835 on whether to narrow the gap between colonial and foreign duties, is the single most informative document on the Canadian timber trade of the early nineteenth century because the hearing required both opponents and advocates of the colonial preference to defend their positions, which necessitated describing the particulars of the industry in great detail. An exchange between the committee and Henry Bliss, the provincial agent for New Brunswick, may be said to be the précis of the entire hearings. The committee asked Bliss point blank, "What, besides ashes and wood, do you think the British North American Colonies will ever be able to pay to this country for the enormous amount this country has sacrificed by forcing the import of [North] American instead of Baltic timber?" Bliss was a great supporter of the colonial preference and replied dryly, "I cannot answer that question without denying that this country has ever sacrificed anything by this trade; on the contrary, I think this country has gained enormously by it." The preferential duty helped to keep the forestry revenue and freight costs within the empire. And it helped the colonies to thrive. Recalling the years immediately preceding the introduction of the colonial preference, Bliss said, "Never were Colonies more depressed than they were at that moment."[36]

The Napoleonic Wars (1803–15) stimulated New Brunswick's timber trade even before the imposition of dramatically preferential tariffs. Exports rose from 6,000 to almost 100,000 tons of timber between 1805 and 1812.[37] But very little of this wood came from the Miramichi: the region languished a little longer. In 1832 historian Robert Cooney blamed these doldrums on "every pamphleteer and scribbler" who out of ignorance or mischief had long misrepresented the region: "Altho' possessing a valuable sea coast, and a fertile soil; enriched with large forests; blest with a salubrious climate; and inhabited by British subjects; it has been almost universally represented, as a country covered with swamps, enveloped in fogs, as cold as the arctic circle, and peopled by savages."[38] There were only perhaps 2,000 people living along the Miramichi River and its tributaries in 1815.

✳✳✳

A few months after the 1825 Miramichi Fire, the new Chatham newspaper, the *Mercury*, ran "The Life and Adventures of a Pine Tree, Written by Itself," a serial that presented the history of the region from the tree's perspective. The turning point was the arrival of the white man. "[E]ven the Richibuctos and Micmacs," it opined, "although they scalped and murdered each other, never made us the objects of their warfare, but these christians and civilized men, had no sooner got among us, than the 'axe was laid to the root of the tree,' and we were destroyed without mercy." But this protagonist pine was providentially passed over and had the opportunity to observe the white man's manners and habits. "I soon found," it reported, "that they were composed of men from different countries – Englishmen, Irishmen, Scotchmen, and some of the native Sons of New-Brunswick."[39] That French Acadians did not even rate a mention indicates just how contemporary this pine's history was. In the previous decade, immigration from Great Britain had transformed the settlements and the forests of the Miramichi.

In 1811 Allan Gilmour Sr had sailed from Scotland to British North America to assess its timber potential in the express hope of exploiting the new era of colonial preference. Seven years earlier, he had co-founded a Glasgow-based lumber company, Gilmour, Pollok, & Co., with a pair of his childhood friends; by 1835 it would be the largest timber company in Europe.[40] During his North American circuit, Gilmour was particularly taken with the Miramichi region. It required a shorter sailing time than places along the Saint Lawrence River, a factor that would soon influence masses of immigrants as

The Timber Boom

well. It was underdeveloped, and the two principal settlements – the small towns of Chatham on the south bank and Newcastle, little more than a few buildings almost 10 kilometres upriver, on the north bank – consisted mostly of Scots, many of whom had moved up from New Brunswick's Saint John River Valley.[41] Gilmour's men returned the following year and put down stakes on the northern shore of the river halfway between Chatham and Newcastle. They dubbed the new settlement Gretna Green, after the famed picturesque village back home in Scotland, also on the north bank of a river just in from the coast.[42]

The new timber operation was named Gilmour, Rankin & Co. and soon commonly called Gilmour and Rankin. It was managed by Alexander Rankin, an employee from the Scottish head office. Like Gilmour and the two Pollok partners, Rankin hailed from the village of Mearns southwest of Glasgow. In fact, they were all related.[43] Such clannishness hints at how self-reinforcing the early Miramichi timber trade would become. Young Scotsmen, with or without their families, sailed westward in company vessels to cut the timber that would fill the ship's hold on the return voyage. And because the timber cargo necessarily took up more space than the human cargo, there was always the opportunity to fill more timber ships and in turn transport more workers until the supply of trees or people dried up or stopped being profitable.[44] The growth of Scottish settlements along the Miramichi River encouraged the growth of others. In 1815, for example, Robert Doak of Ayrshire was on a ship bound for Kentucky when bad weather forced it into the Port of Miramichi. Doak stayed and, having experience running a sawmill, soon moved to the Southwest branch of the river to set up a milling operation. The Scottish community that developed there became Doaktown.[45]

The scale of immigration to the Miramichi region, and to North America generally, rose dramatically upon the end of the Napoleonic Wars in 1815. Britain experienced a severe economic downturn, which increased desire both to migrate and to exploit the colonial timber preference. Henry Bliss would argue before the 1835 Select Committee on Timber Duties that the timber trade encouraged migration in three ways: by giving migrants many ports to sail from, by letting them do so cheaply, and by giving them work when they arrived.[46] Even by the time Gilmour and Rankin was established, Glasgow companies had all but run out of North America–bound passengers along the River Clyde, so westbound ships stopped off at the Highlands and

28   *The Miramichi Fire*

Western Isles. After 1815 ports all across Scotland were thrown open to accommodate regular Atlantic crossings, which meant that immigrants came from across the country.[47] And the poor of Ireland began to leave there in great numbers. By the late 1810s hundreds of Irish were coming to the Miramichi each year, from Cork and Tipperary in particular. Many were on their way to the United States, but they paid less if they booked passage only as far as New Brunswick. Some stayed in the region, by necessity or choice, their first paying job in the new world being to load lumber aboard the ship that had carried them there. The lots along the main branch of the Miramichi River had all been claimed by 1820, so Irish communities grew along tributaries farther up the Southwest branch on the Bartibog, Barnaby, Bartholemew, Renous, and Sevogle Rivers.[48] By the time of the great fire, the Irish greatly outnumbered the Scottish on the Miramichi River and likely outnumbered all other groups together.[49] Settlement encouraged more lumbering, and lumbering encouraged more settlement. Immigrants from Wales and England joined those from Scotland and Ireland. Americans moved in as well. Thomas Boies of Maine erected a sawmill far up the Southwest branch, considerably closer to Fredericton than to the mouth of the Miramichi, and within a few years American expatriates had formed a community called Boiestown around it.[50] Workers from Prince Edward Island, Nova Scotia, and throughout New Brunswick itself also flooded into the Miramichi region as its timber industry expanded in the late 1810s. And still the demand for labourers could not be met. Miramichi lumbermen began travelling to Gaspé to entice farmers and fishermen to come work for them in the woods.[51]

   The Miramichi timber trade, already bustling, rose to yet another level in 1820 when Joseph Cunard moved from Halifax with his brother to open a Chatham branch of the family's timber and mercantile business. Cunard was just twenty-one years old, but he was big, brash, and ambitious, and he quickly became a patriarch in the region, a position he would maintain for the next quarter-century. His firm bought a wharf and was soon involved in cutting, milling, and shipping timber, as well as shipbuilding. Just as Newcastle (supplanting Gretna Green) had become a company town for Gilmour and Rankin on the north side of the river, Chatham became one for Cunard on the south side. Although Cunard concentrated his forestry efforts on the Northwest branch of the Miramichi, leaving the Southwest branch largely to the well-established Gilmour and Rankin,

The Timber Boom 29

an intense rivalry for regional dominance was born. The two firms and the two towns faced each other across the river like squabbling siblings. Cunard later explained his firm's low, relatively unprofitable prices by saying, "We don't give a damn so long as we sell more deals than Gilmour, Rankin & Co."[52] What the colony's lieutenant governor, Howard Douglas, called "those killer rival feelings" between Newcastle and Chatham would soon become evident in their response to the Miramichi Fire.

***

Thanks to the timber boom happening along the Miramichi River, the population of the region roughly quadrupled to 8,500 in the decade before the great fire. Northumberland County – constituting almost 40 per cent of New Brunswick's land area, a fact that in itself indicates the degree to which it was the colony's hinterland – went from being one of the least populated counties to the most populated.[53] Given that the great majority of the recent settlers were new to North America and given that they had moved into a forested area dominated by a forest economy, it is reasonable to wonder what knowledge they brought with them. Employment in the timber trade did not demand experience or training, after all. Handed an axe and pointed to a tree, workers could be expected to figure out what to do.[54]

Over the course of centuries, Great Britain had depleted most of its woodland, and its remnant forests were nothing like the seemingly boundless ones of New Brunswick. Just 2 per cent of Ireland was still wooded. Although there were lots of Irish towns whose names ended in "derry," meaning "oak," the oak forests themselves were long gone.[55] Scotland was more forested but not by much: a liberal estimate has it that 8 per cent was treed.[56] The late-eighteenth-century English landscape theorist William Gilpin, famous for critiquing landscapes with all the acidity of a modern-day fashion critic, pronounced, "A *Poverty of landscape* from a want of objects, particularly of wood, is another striking characteristic in the views of Scotland."[57] People and cattle had over the centuries put more and more strain on the Scottish forests, and the large-scale sheep farming that followed enclosure all but broke the forests' backs.[58] Men such as Alexander Rankin and Robert Doak had acquired timber industry expertise that they imported to the Miramichi, teaching new immigrants the trade, but most of their knowledge was based on the wood they imported from the Baltic to Scotland. Indeed, the absence of a homegrown Scottish

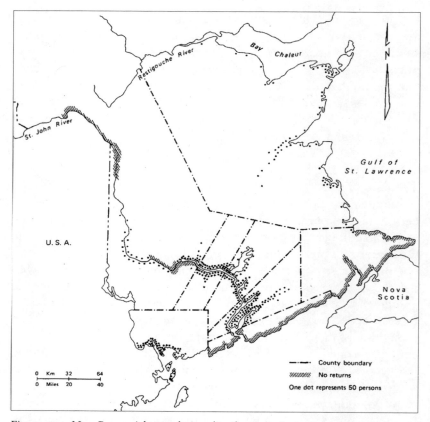

Figure 2.4a New Brunswick population distribution, 1803.

timber industry was blamed on the long-time low price of Baltic wood.[59] The vast majority of immigrants who came to the Miramichi in the decade before the great fire had never seen such immense, untamed forests, let alone worked in them.

If most of the people living along the Miramichi River in 1825 had only a newly acquired knowledge of North American forests, they had still less familiarity with North American forest fires. In both Scotland and Ireland, there was a long folk history of burning fields to recycle nutrients back into the soil for the purpose of growing crops or improving pasture. But there was also a long history of landowner and government opposition to such burning. Fires could get out of control, and even when they did not, the notion that it enriched the soil was thought to be nothing more than peasant

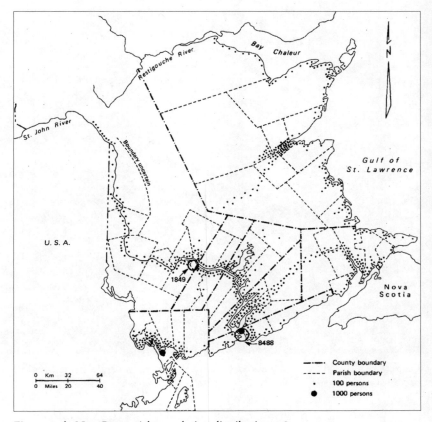

Figure 2.4b New Brunswick population distribution, 1824.

superstition. The Irish Parliament banned the burning of agricultural land outright in the mid-1700s.[60] But later in the century, setting such fires became more socially acceptable across Great Britain. Out of Devonshire came the practice of "denshiring," based on the peasant custom of paring and burning peat to improve the soil but now given a scientific stamp of approval.[61] In Ireland burning also grew more reputable when it was found to be beneficial for the growing of potatoes.[62] Historian Stephen J. Pyne notes that the 1814 "Year of the Burnings," in which Scottish landowners set ablaze the huts of evicted crofters, was part and parcel of their more extensive burning of the landscape to make way for sheep herds. As fire became more respectable, whether for clearing off vegetation or peasants, it was applied more casually, resembling "English style burning without its social

Figure 2.5 *View of Beaubear's Island, Miramichi – The Commercial Establishment of John and Alexander Fraser and Co.*, c. 1825, by R. Thresher.

restraints," in Pyne's words.[63] The people who settled the Miramichi after the Napoleonic Wars – even those Highland crofters fleeing the smoke of the clearances – were conditioned by a combination of long-time custom and the latest fashion to believe not only that fire helped in clearing land but also that in doing so it improved the soil for agriculture.

What's more, whereas an out-of-control forest fire in the old country might engulf tens of hectares, in North America it could consume hundreds or thousands of them or more. But large fires were uncommon in the decade prior to 1825, a fact that made the people of the Miramichi region even more unprepared for the great fire. The 1810s are believed to have been the coldest decade of the past 500 years. One reason was low sunspot activity, which is connected to cooler weather. Another reason was a series of major volcanic eruptions around the globe, starting with the second largest of the past two centuries, which occurred somewhere in South America in 1808–09.[64] Then the *largest* occurred – in fact, the largest in recorded history. In April 1815 the Mount Tambora volcano in Indonesia erupted, spewing an estimated 40 to 60 cubic kilometres of rock, ash, and dust high into the air. Aerosols spread throughout the global atmosphere, lessening the solar radiation that could reach the earth and cooling the planet measurably.[65] The resulting harvest failures in 1816 triggered what historian J.D. Post has called "the last great subsistence crisis in the Western world," marked by bread riots, famine, and disease in Europe and beyond. In eastern North America, a snowstorm in June 1816 heralded the onset of what became known as the Year Without a Summer.[66] The New Brunswick legislature put £6,000 toward emergency food and provisions, advancing credit to those in need, and the lieutenant governor outlawed exporting grain or distilling it into liquor.[67] The years that followed 1816 were just as cold across northeastern North America. At Quebec City, for example, the ice bridge that some winters formed across the Saint Lawrence River did so for four consecutive winters beginning in 1816 and extended to its largest size ever in 1817.[68] The second half of the 1810s ended up being the single coldest segment of the Little Ice Age, the three-century period of relative cold across the globe that would draw to a close in mid-century.[69] It was only in the early 1820s that the climate in the Northeast returned to something resembling normalcy, but there was no particularly hot year prior to 1825.

What happened on a mountain in Indonesia not only spread outward spatially to influence New Brunswick but also rippled forward temporally, yielding effect upon effect. The cool climate likely encouraged some in the colony to turn to the timber trade. A local history of Houlton, Maine, on the border with New Brunswick, claimed that after 1816, "[f]rom the signal failure of crops, the farmers, as an alternative, changed their occupation for a time" to lumbering.[70] But if the weather discouraged agriculture at the individual level, it may also have encouraged it at the societal level, both because crop shortages demonstrated the need for personal and societal food security and because it was widely understood that people helped to moderate climate themselves by clearing forests and cultivating fields. Trees, particularly evergreens, were believed to actively produce cold air, making North America colder than Europe only because so much of it was still forested.[71] It was thought that a positive feedback loop was already well underway in recent centuries in North America, with more settlers clearing more land and so producing more moderate temperatures and encouraging more settlers.[72] In 1825 New Brunswick historian Peter Fisher would report, "For a few years back the seasons have been more favourable to agriculture."[73] In the Miramichi region, the fact that a moderating climate coincided with more land clearing, itself the result of intense population growth, may have seemed proof that one was the result of the other.

Still, people had difficulty understanding the dramatic change in the weather in the decade before the fire. Writing of New Brunswick in 1831, British North America Surveyor General Bouchette observed that "the climate of New Brunswick has been gradually ameliorating for some years past, as the thermometrical tables will show; the excesses both of heat and cold having generally considerably moderated. In 1816 the weather was excessive, and it has been gradually improving since that time." But he could not figure out why: "The clearing of land indubitably tends to moderate the excess of cold, as observation has abundantly proved; ... but this operation has not been carried on in New Brunswick to a sufficient extent to account for any general alteration in the climate of the province."[74] Bouchette was well educated and quite familiar with New Brunswick, yet even well after the fact he could not explain the colony's fluctuating weather. Ordinary residents of the Miramichi region, many of them recently arrived, could hardly be expected to understand it at the time – or even to realize how unusual that weather was.

The cool weather of the late 1810s slowed vegetation growth across North America: tree rings tend to be narrower in this period.[75] But it also created poor conditions for forest fires, which meant that more vegetation accumulated, available to combust. The summer of 1821 was the only fire season of any significance in New Brunswick in the years prior to the Miramichi Fire, with fires ranging through the woods on the Maine–New Brunswick coast and along the Tobique and Etienne (Cains) Rivers in the colony's centre. But the populated settlements at the mouth of the Miramichi River were spared; there is no record of forest fires striking the region in the decade before 1825.[76] The new British settlers who had arrived in that period gained no experience of just how catastrophic a North American forest fire could be.

In the wake of the Miramichi Fire, the most confounding thing to many commentators was how slowly the populace had been to react. How could people living along the bank of a river at the edge of an

The Timber Boom 35

immense forest not interpret cinders and smoke blowing in from the woods on hurricane-force wind as anything other than harbingers of an impending disaster? But this Canadian natural disaster cannot be understood without remembering that most of its victims were barely Canadian at all. What they knew of forests and fire had in large measure been learned elsewhere based on conditions elsewhere. And what knowledge they had of the local climate and fire regimes was gained during uncharacteristically cool years, ill-preparing them for what, as we will see, was an uncharacteristically hot one. It is an added irony that some of the victims were undoubtedly what today would be called "climate refugees." They had come to New Brunswick to escape the Tambora-triggered subsistence crisis in Europe, only to have traces of Tambora's influence follow them.[77] They had jumped from the frying pan into the fire.

✳✳✳

The Miramichi forests were highly diverse, considerably more so than today, with red, black, and white spruce, eastern hemlock, larch, yellow birch, balsam fir, and beech all common and a sprinkling of other species, including red oak, hornbeam, American elm, and Indian pear trees, also to be found.[78] But one tree rose literally and figuratively above all the others and so is worthy of more fixed attention. At a public dinner on the Miramichi River in 1825, the assembled sang a song of thanks to their benefactor:

Old England boasts her beauteous rose,
Her leek see Cambria rearing,
The fearless thistle Scotia shows,
And the Shamrock's dear to Erin.
To Miramichi; an emblem fine,
By nature's self was given –
Then let us join and hail the PINE
And bless the land we live in.[79]

Specifically, the white pine. Beginning the natural history chapter of his 1832 history of northern New Brunswick, Robert Cooney asserted, "The White Pine is the sovereign of our forests."[80] It was not that white pine was the dominant forest species; it made up a relatively small percentage of the trees in eastern forests.[81] Nor was it, as might be thought, that white pine was famous for supplying the masts of the British Navy; by the time the Miramichi developed in the 1810s, the mast trade had largely moved on from New Brunswick to Upper Canada.[82] Besides, as Henry Bliss noted in his 1831 *On the Timber Trade*, "not one tree in 10,000 is fit for a mast," so masts on their own could never sustain a forest industry.[83] Rather, white pine was far and away the dominant commercial species. In 1825 alone, perhaps 100,000 Miramichi white pines were cut down for export.[84] It was so intrinsic a part of the economy that it was sometimes accepted as a unit of currency.[85] It was the basis of industry and so of society in the Miramichi.

But white pine transcended the role of resource to become symbol because of its size and grace. It rose as much as 50 metres into the air, far surpassing its neighbours. And it grew straight and true, a metre or more in diameter, with few branches along the way that would require the lumberman's lopping – until the very top, where the branches burst out horizontally, ostentatious above the surrounding canopy.[86] There is a passage in John S. Singer's 1851 *Forest Life and Forest Trees* in which he describes the lumberman climbing to the top of a spruce to search for white pine, "like a mariner at a masthead upon the 'look-out' for whales (for indeed the Pine is the whale of the forest) … They are the object of his search, his treasure, his *El Dorado*."[87] Yet this was a treasure within the reach of Miramichi lumbermen. Using square timber harvest records of the early nineteenth century, historical ecologist Donna Crossland concludes that eastern New Brunswick produced a higher volume of white pine timber per hectare than did subsequent timber areas in Maine and Upper Canada, suggesting that the colony enjoyed a higher concentration of the trees, or larger ones, or both.[88] White pines were to be found in nearly pure stands in both wet and dry soils but particularly on flat land along the rivers, "as if growing there on purpose to be handy for rafting," as a later writer put it.[89] They seemed to be there for the taking.

White pine was also known as yellow pine or pumpkin pine, which alluded to both its colour and its soft, mealy wood.[90] It was almost delicate: when cutting it down, one had to be careful how it fell because it could so easily shatter.[91] The tree's softness was what allowed it to be used more, and more diversely, than any other North American tree. The wood was light, flexible, easy to work with, and free of knots. Because the tree grew to a great height, it furnished wide boards and large timber – yet it was abundant enough to be cheap.[92] What's more, according to British politician and merchant Henry Warburton in an address to the 1835 Select Committee on Timber Duties, "That of Miramichi is the lightest and most spongy, and the least fibrous of all. It is exceedingly *mellow*, to use the joiner's word, has no tendency to warp, and preserves the form that the workman gives it." Warburton recalled having been willing, in 1824, to pay 50 per cent more for pine from the Miramichi than from Quebec. Nevertheless, Warburton ended with something of a warning about the possible side effects of using Canadian pine: "Yellow pine timber ought not to be used for rafters, joists, girders, or plates, in any building; for no purpose, in short, and in no situation, where strength and stiffness are required, and where the ends or any part of the timber come in contact with brickwork or masonry, or are liable to damp."[93]

Such as the damp island nation of Great Britain, perhaps. Although Warburton praised some characteristics of white pine, he believed it utterly unsuitable for the construction of buildings and ships, for which most timber was needed. Moreover, the longstanding British complaint against North American pine was that it was prone to dry rot; Britain had gone so far as to ban the use of this timber in its navy until the situation was better understood.[94] The substandard quality of North American pine would be a common chorus during the 1835 Select Committee. Warburton even accused white pine of spreading dry rot to red pine if the two were in the same ship's hold.[95] It rankled free traders such as Warburton, then, that the colonies received a preferential tariff to inflict such a shoddy product on the British market. Scottish politician James Stuart summarized this resentment when describing Canada as "a country which not only makes us no return, but has the address to impose on us a bad article at a greatly increased price."[96]

Those who profited by a healthy British North American timber trade – that is, all British North Americans – played down criticism of their pine as being prejudiced and politically motivated. New Brunswick agent Bliss noted that white pine was discussed as though it were the only possible construction material, and so it "suits the purposes of the anti-colonial party, at one time to depreciate as worthless, at another to represent as indispensable."[97] Men like Bliss emphasized the many products for which British North American pine was unrivalled. It was considered the very best wood for interior panelling, mouldings, picture frames, blinds, and – as was often mentioned – musical instruments. More than one witness at the Select Committee hearings summarized that North American timber was best for interior work, Baltic timber being preferred for exteriors.[98] According to Henry Warburton, ships filled with Miramichi pine were often unloaded into three piles: the largest, straightest pieces would go to the making of musical instruments and be sold at 80 shillings per load; smaller, clean timber for interior materials went for 70 shillings; and rougher pieces for the builder went for 55 shillings.[99] Bliss did concede that there were purposes for which British North America's white pine was "undoubtedly unfit" – but in such cases its red pine was readily available.[100]

✳✳✳

When Peter Fisher penned the first history of New Brunswick in 1825, the Miramichi was so young that it hardly had a history at all. Yet Fisher believed it had already gone badly astray. Yes, the "great lumbering country" was booming, and each year upward of 300 ships sailed from the mouth of the river filled with timber that would be traded for cash or goods from Great Britain and the West Indies. But the firm foundations of a society were not being built. "A stranger would naturally suppose," Fisher wrote, "that such a trade must produce great riches to the country; and that great and rapid improvements would be made … But here he would not only be disappointed, but astonished at the rugged and uncouth appearance of most part of this extensive county." There were few improved farms or public buildings, and there was no town yet worthy of the name. Instead, "the forests are stripped and nothing left in prospect, but the gloomy apprehension when the timber is gone, of sinking into insignificance and poverty."[101] That Fisher himself was a lumber merchant who had turned to farming added weight to his indictment.

The Miramichi had experienced an economic and demographic transformation in the decade prior to Fisher's writing thanks entirely to the timber trade. It had gone from almost no timber activity at the end of the Napoleonic Wars to loading almost one-fifth of the British vessels employed in the British North American trade just four years later.[102] And that was before the flood of immigrants from Ireland and elsewhere, the intense exploitation of the river's Northwest branch by Cunard's firm, and a boom in the British construction trade in the early 1820s. The timber trade provided migrants with the means of passage, it gave them immediate work on landing, and it gave them

The Timber Boom

the means to invest and export a needed and valuable resource. Yet the nature of the industry was such that it was still considered detrimental to the development of a healthy society. It was accused of encouraging the migration of individual male workers rather than families and of giving those workers too much opportunity to focus on short-term earnings rather than on a transition toward the long-term pursuit thought most appropriate for settlers: agriculture. To an observer like Fisher, what had given birth to Miramichi society also threatened to be the death of it.

The wellsprings for the Miramichi's development were a seemingly endless supply of forests, an extensive web of waterways that allowed them to be reached and extracted, and a legislative and commercial system that made doing so straightforward and profitable. Access to forest land began at the unit of the household. All British subjects could receive 100 free acres (40 hectares) of Crown land, plus 50 acres per child, so long as they committed to clearing for cultivation a modest 3 acres of every 50 acres received.[103] This was a down payment on a life: it gave colonists a place to settle down, the materials to build a home, fuel for warmth, and even a resource – timber – that they could take to market in the process of readying the land for agriculture. Settlers could also obtain licences to cut timber commercially beyond their own property by contacting the Halifax-based Office of the Surveyor General of the King's Woods up to 1817 and the New Brunswick government directly thereafter; it was largely a matter of asking. Some lumbermen avoided even this simple step and just started cutting. Only beginning in 1819 did timber cruisers have to state precisely where and how much they proposed to cut and have to pay a duty on the timber of a shilling per ton.[104] In this early era of timber exploitation, the licences themselves were extremely straightforward, often defining the berth strictly in relation to an existing one and directing the licensee to "extend up stream," or beyond the previous licence, and "to the rear a sufficient distance," or as far back from the river as it took to obtain the amount of timber for which one was licensed (usually between 1 and 2 kilometres).[105] Since the most desirable property for both lumbermen and agriculturally minded settlers was river frontage as close to the mouth of the Miramichi River as possible, this land along the river and then its tributaries got snapped up quickly. This fact, and that many Irish immigrants in this era only stopped in the region for a period of indentured labour before moving on, meant that a blotchy settlement pattern developed, with isolated farms being surrounded by tracts of forests that were either awaiting the axe or had been cut down and left.[106]

The timber trade was low-tech, low-skill, and eminently scalable – which would greatly affect how Miramichi society developed. Whether you were a settler clearing a corner of your property and selling the wood or a timber operator with a licence to cut a substantial berth, the process was essentially the same.[107] Work parties were relatively small: settlers tended to work together in small teams, both for safety's sake and because the size of logs required it, and even commercial work parties were rarely more than ten men so that they would not get in each other's way.[108] In the fall, parties would clear trails in preparation for the winter's work; if the parties were large enough and the work distant enough, they would build camps, too. The lumbering began with the snow, when the wet covering on frozen ground allowed sleighs to travel smoothly. The trees were felled, their limbs removed, and the remaining logs hewn roughly square for ease of transport. Any of these steps might be performed by any of the men, with a broadaxe their primary tool. The squared logs, perhaps 12 metres long and almost half a metre in diameter, would then be moved by horse and sleigh over the rough frozen ground to landings near the river, where they awaited the ice breakup in the spring. At that point, the logs were driven down the river system to Chatham or Newcastle, each work team delivering perhaps 100 to 500 tons of timber. A relatively small percentage of that was then milled into deals and boards in this era. The Miramichi was decidedly behind the more established parts of the colony in setting up sawmills; in 1823, although almost twice as much timber was exported out of the Miramichi than the Port of Saint John, it sent only one-tenth as much in pine boards and planks.[109] Instead, most of the Miramichi timber was simply rehewn neater, sold to a shipping merchant, and loaded for England. The timber year was thus a full three seasons long – and it was in this respect that the experiences of the settler and the hired labourer engaged in the trade were most different. To the settler, the trade meant the chance to earn additional money on one's property while working around agriculture's schedule. To the hired labourer, it could mean as much as three-quarters of the year living in a work camp distant from family and the broader society.

The Timber Boom

That the demand for timber rose in the 1810s and 1820s, with prices rising in turn, became in the eyes of many observers exactly the problem: the trade grew too financially seductive for the good of those engaged in it. Settlers found themselves lured deeper into the timber trade as a means of augmenting their farming income. For some, it was a matter of joining with other farmers and committing their time, effort, and capital to running a lumber operation as a sideline. For others, it was a matter of hiring onto an existing operation, often at piecework. In either case, since farmers worked away from their own property and since, with nearby stands cut first, the berths being licensed inevitably lay farther and farther away, it became increasingly difficult for settlers to return home each evening and engage fully in farming. John McGregor, a Prince Edward Islander who had become an analyst on British North America, told the 1835 Select Committee on Timber Duties that settlers drew one another into temptation, the result bad for all. "[A] man does not go into the distant woods to cut timber for himself," McGregor said, "for the timber business is such that men must go in bodies; and the general rule appears to me to be, that if they go in bodies they generally involve themselves, and all others connected with them, in some difficulty."[110] Individual labourers hired onto a timber operation could earn £25 or more for a timber season. This attracted not only young men from throughout the Maritimes and Maine but also recent immigrants. In McGregor's estimation, Irish immigrants in particular appreciated the opportunity of employment immediately upon arrival but as a result ended up in a "much worse condition" than those English or Scottish settlers who "place themselves at once on a piece of land, and apply themselves to clear the wood and cultivate the soil."[111]

The timber business grew even more enticing in the early 1820s, when – in the view of hindsight – a full-blown "timber mania" occurred. New Brunswick timber exports rose from 255,000 tons in 1822 to 417,000 tons three years later, the bulk of the increase being taken from the Miramichi region and from the nearby Tobique and Richibucto watersheds.[112] The entire tenor of the trade changed. The author of the 1829 *Letters from Nova Scotia and New Brunswick* had a gentleman from the latter colony state,

For many years there was an extensive demand for our timber; but in 1823, 1824 and 1825, the timber trade had attained a

climax of prosperity unknown to any previous time ...
Thousands of fresh hands were employed in the business. Money
flowed abundantly ... Credit was boundless ... Men, who, in
reality were not worth a dollar, had a dozen or score of vessels
upon the stocks at the same time ... But the old and the prudent,
as well as the young and the raw, were led away by this combination of delusions ...Wages were also enormous. Apprentices
could easily obtain two or three dollars a day for their services,
and master workmen, who were skillful and sober, almost whatever their consciences allowed them to demand.[113]

The availability of credit from timber merchants such as Cunard or
Rankin was seen as particularly perilous because it allowed the poor
to live and dream beyond their means. In a letter to the local newspaper in 1829, "Civis" – journalist and soon-to-be historian Robert
Cooney – recalled the time before the great fire as one in which a man
with "no other property than a lying tongue" could get as much credit
as he wanted on his promise of having found "'a d___d fine grove,
or a *capital* chance.'" Even "Raw Emigrants," Cooney noted, were
being fully stocked to head into the woods![114] McGregor told the
1835 Select Committee of one lumberman who, having built up a
debt of £25,000 to Gilmour and Rankin, quietly borrowed close to
the same amount from another merchant on the river, likely Cunard.[115]
   By 1825 there was growing concern on the part of many New
Brunswick observers that what was supposed to be an agriculture-
based society was turning into a timber-based one, particularly as a
result of the boom happening in the colony's northeast. Lumbering
was thought to be especially pernicious because, unlike fishing or
mining, it stole away landowners who would otherwise farm full-
time.[116] Looking back on this era from the early 1850s, agricultural
chemist James F.W. Johnston wrote,

The lumberer, fond as the Indian of the free air and untrammeled
life of the woods, receiving high wages, living on the finest flour,
and enjoying long seasons of holiday, looked down upon the
slavish agricultural drudge who toiled the year long on his few
acres of land, with little beyond his comfortable maintenance to
show as the fruit of his yearly labour. The young and adventur-
ous among the province-born were tempted into what was considered a higher and more manly, as well as a more remunerative

The Timber Boom

43

line of life; many of the hardiest of the emigrants, as they arrived, followed their example: and thus not only was the progress of farming discouraged and retarded, but a belief began to prevail that the colony was unfitted for agricultural pursuits.[117]

As Johnston's complaint suggests, the purported problems of a timber-based economy extended beyond the economic. Lumbering produced a misshapen society – first and foremost, because it was a society that was predominantly male. The work unit was the lumber team, isolated in a camp in the woods for months at a time, which discouraged families from immigrating specifically for the timber trade, while encouraging single, male workers to do so instead. As a result, the Miramichi had a high male to female ratio. According to the 1824 census, whereas in the colony's most established towns of Fredericton and Saint John there were 1.1 males to every female, in Northumberland County the ratio was 1.5 to 1, and in North Esk Parish, located in prime timberland to the west and northwest of Newcastle, the ratio was the highest in New Brunswick, almost 5 to 1. The discrepancy was even larger among the adult population: North Esk had 921 men and just 119 women over the age of sixteen.[118] Little wonder that "The Lumberer's Song" in the Chatham newspaper in 1826 proclaimed,

No Wives have we here to disturb or perplex us,
And bother our brains with their scolding and cries,
Nor Brats, with their Bawling, to worry and vex us,
Nor Sweethearts to teaze us with smiles and with sighs.[119]

The reputation of the Miramichi grew based on young men with money in their pockets doing what young men with money in their pockets have always done. For one, they spent it. "Civis" wrote of Miramichi lumber merchants' horses "richly caparisoned with handsome dray collars, fancy reins, and initialed winkers; in short they were attired almost as splendidly as Whitbread's dray horses."[120] John McGregor claimed of timber workers throughout British North America generally that "the epithet 'lumberer' is considered synonymous with a character of spendthrift habits, and villainous and vagabond principles. After selling and delivering up their rafts, they pass some weeks in idle indulgence; drinking; smoaking; and *dashing off*, in a long coat, flashy waistcoat and trowsers, Wellington or hessian boots, a handkerchief *of many colours* round the neck, a watch

44 *The Miramichi Fire*

with a long tinsel chain and numberless brass seals, and an *umbrella*."[121] Only a leopardskin pillbox hat was needed to complete the Dylanesque ensemble.

Miramichi lumbermen also drank hard, like lumbermen everywhere were said to. (A contemporary worker on the Saint Croix River between New Brunswick and Maine called rum the one essential provision: "In all our movements, from the stump in the swamp to the ship's hold, it was Rum! Rum!")[122] McGregor simultaneously perpetuated and excused the stereotype when he stated, "Being exposed to every variety of weather, to the cold of winter, and the snow water of the freshets, and to a hot sun, while rafting down the timber, he very naturally indulges more than others in drinking spirituous liquors."[123] Goaded by these spirituous liquors, the lumbermen fought. The Miramichi saw periodic rioting throughout the early 1820s, inflamed by testosterone, by the rivalry that pitted the Rankinites and Newcastle on the north side of the Miramichi River against the Cunardites and Chatham on the south side, and by competing ethnic groups, particularly after the arrival of waves of Irish immigrants. A riot in the summer of 1822, for example, resulted in sentences against fifty-nine participants.[124] Governor Howard Douglas complained that with civil authorities unable to maintain law and order, he was constantly required to deploy a military force to the Miramichi to keep the peace. Douglas ultimately decided to visit Northumberland County himself in 1824, as much as anything to make civil authority known to the inhabitants, "by far the greater part of which had never been visited by any Person in the administration of the Government, or in Command of the Province."[125] The early Miramichi was the Wild East, always only a step or two from utter lawlessness, and its lumbermen gained a reputation for hardness that they never surrendered. "I was born on the Miramichi," a woodsman is quoted as saying in 1962's *The American Lumberjack*. "The further up you go, the tougher they get, and I was raised on the headwater."[126]

The wild nature of the Miramichi lumbermen was evident not only in how they comported themselves in society but also in how they went about their work in the woods. They were frequently accused of wasting much of the trees they cut down and leaving behind a mess of branches, bark, and chips. The hero of "The Life and Adventures of a Pine Tree, Written by Itself" told of neighbour trees being "hacked and hewed most unmercifully, until instead of being round, as nature made them, they became square and unsightly, and lost not only their limbs but at least one fourth of the original bulk of their bodies."[127] This was a generous estimate. Lumbermen cut trees at breast height, often while standing on depths of snow, which meant that the trunk left behind might be several metres high. Add to that the unused top portion of the trunk, and a modern estimate has it that only 45 per cent of a tree was actually floated down the river. And as much as 20 per cent of *that* was removed in a final rehewing at port.[128] Such wastefulness was said to speak to the lumberman's character, but it also spoke to the ubiquity of trees and so to their marginal individual value and significance. Only a few years later, it would be noted that all the timber necessary to build a New Brunswick house, including floors, doors, and window frames, could be purchased for just £6 sterling.[129] The recent British immigrants who made up the bulk of the Miramichi population in 1825 arrived with little to no knowledge of vast forests such as those that surrounded them, but they soon learned to take them for granted.

Drunken. Riotous. Profligate. Neglectful of agriculture. Villainous and vagabond. Miramichi society, however, did have its defenders. Before the Select Committee on Timber Duties, both Henry Bliss and Allan Gilmour stated that lumbering in the colonies was no more likely to degrade men or to attract degraded men than was industry in Great Britain itself. Bliss did not think that lumbering was any more "demoralizing" than any other employment, "certainly not more than any other employment that brings people of that class together," and that its workers ended up "more moral than the labourers in towns."[130] Likewise, Gilmour spoke of having entrusted his own nephews to work in the Canadian woods, knowing that they would be safer there than "with our cotton-spinners in this country, people much more vicious."[131] Faint praise, admittedly.

The negative portrait of Miramichi timber society was never entirely disinterested. Criticism of the timber industry and its participants was often an excuse for condemnation of the colonial tariff preference or an expression of the commitment to agriculture as society's true foundation. Nor was the portrait entirely accurate. Only about half the adult men on the Miramichi River were directly engaged in the timber trade, or little more than one-quarter of the overall population.[132] Many families were farming full-time, and it was still widely expected that agriculture would eventually become the mainstay of the region. Moreover, many people accepted that the timber trade was facilitating agriculture (by clearing the ground for cultivation)

46   *The Miramichi Fire*

and financing it (by supporting farmers as they started out on new land). It was therefore not so strange that when the Northumberland Agricultural and Emigrant Society was founded in 1825, three-fifths of the executive were the prominent lumber merchants James Gilmour, William Abrams, and Alexander Rankin.[133] Even a critic such as John McGregor, who warned against the danger of farmers getting drawn into forestry, admitted that "young men of steady habits," upon coming to the Miramichi from elsewhere in British North America "for the express purpose of making money, have joined the lumbering parties for two or three years; and, after saving their earnings, returned and purchased lands, &c. on which they now live very comfortably."[134] Young men and their families were not lured into the timber trade: they entered it having made rational decisions based on the availability of work and trees and on the complementary seasonality of farming and lumbering. And over the course of the nineteenth century, it would become clearer to many in the Miramichi, and in many other parts of New Brunswick, that the soil was simply not well suited to agriculture and that trees might well be the crop most appropriate to local conditions. When engaged in the timber trade, the Miramichi might well be performing to its peak potential.

Nevertheless, the negative portrait of Miramichi lumbering and lumbermen at the time of the great fire mattered. It biased the colonial and imperial governments against a region that was at that very moment, and might be for some time, the empire's leading source of a critical resource. And as we will see, once the fire struck, the region's reputation influenced the responses of governments, charity benefactors, and even residents themselves. A Nova Scotian preacher told a surely apocryphal story of visiting the Miramichi and testing a small boy's knowledge of Christian teaching by asking whether he knew where the bad people go. The child replied, "To the Miramichi."[135] Many would look on the Miramichi Fire and suggest that lumbermen had contributed not only the need for divine retribution, and not only the ironically appropriate form of retribution, but also, by virtue of the masses of flammable slash they left lying in the woods, the means of retribution itself.

✳✳✳

Those early glory days of the Miramichi timber trade are occasionally still referred to locally as "the days of Duffy Gillis," after a come-all-ye ballad of the late nineteenth century. It opens,

The Timber Boom 47

Come all you jolly lumbermen,
Whose better years have fled,
And I will sing of halcyon days,
Before we had Confed.
When two logs made a thousand,
Our country at its best,
In the days of Duffy Gillis
From the Sou-ou-West.

There really had been a Duffy Gillis, but he was not, as the song would have it, a lumberman so much as a land speculator. He may well have been best known in his day for setting a net across the Little Southwest branch of the Miramichi River to secure all its salmon – and choosing a traditional Mi'gmaw burial site as the spot from which to do so.[136] From the Mi'gmaw perspective, then, "the days of Duffy Gillis" is an apt name for this era. The conditions of their existence declined precipitously in the region – and, indeed, throughout Mi'gma'gi – across the late eighteenth and early nineteenth centuries.[137] The 20,000 acres granted Chief John Julien in the 1780s had been broken up and replaced with four smaller reserves, together possessing considerably less river frontage, along the Northwest branch of the Miramichi River. White settlers competed for food as well as land. Mi'gmaq were forced to expand their hunting areas, leading to conflicts with more distant Indigenous people. Colonists such as Duffy Gillis depleted salmon stocks, and logging and lumbering also killed fish in the rivers. Their land dispossessed and their ability to feed themselves disrupted, the Mi'gmaq people saw their numbers in the entire Miramichi watershed decline to a matter of hundreds, less than 5 per cent of the region's total population.[138] And the British state, which in the mid to late 1700s had felt some obligation to act conciliatorily in its dealings with Indigenous peoples across its empire, no longer felt the same need to do so – and so didn't. New Brunswick's 1824 banning of traditional Indigenous fishing practices, particularly salmon spearing, signalled that a more aggressive, unapologetic settler colonialism was well under way.[139]

But for white settlers, the Miramichi in October 1825 was showing every sign of being home to a viable, thriving community. Timber constituted two-thirds of New Brunswick's exports, and the timber being drawn out of the Miramichi River system not only represented a full one-third of that amount but was also returning the best prices

48   *The Miramichi Fire*

in the colony.[140] The year 1825 saw the best timber season ever. More than 200,000 tons – enough to fill the *Baron of Renfrew* twenty times – had shipped that summer and was on its way to Great Britain.[141] And a reported 3,000 men were in lumbering parties in the backwoods once again, prepared to make 1826 another record year. As evidence of the region's increasing importance to New Brunswick, Lieutenant Governor Howard Douglas proposed that a planned road to connect Halifax to Quebec City swing northeast through the colony, passing through the Miramichi settlements.[142]

Signs of the community's development were everywhere. Houses were going up; there were one and a half times as many under construction in Northumberland County as in any other county in the colony.[143] A twenty-one-year-old journalist, James Pierce, arrived in the Miramichi to launch a local newspaper that October; having some of his type stolen and more thrown into the harbour delayed but did not discourage him.[144] The Chatham Fire Company was established, and Pierce became one of its first volunteers.[145] Chatham also appointed twenty-year-old James Caie as its first postmaster, on the very day of the great fire.[146] The frame of a new Roman Catholic chapel was raised in the community of Nelson, its foundation having been dedicated in a ceremony by Governor Douglas a few months earlier. The good citizens of Gretna Green had honoured the governor's visit by renaming their settlement Douglastown. In the governor's words, all in the Miramichi was "prosperity, plenty, and comfort."[147]

Even Robert Cooney, who in his 1832 history would decry the timber bubble that the region experienced until the very day of the fire, admitted that in the months preceding it, "we were happy and cheerful. Our trade was looking up; and brightening were our prospects ... Our Wharfs and Warehouses groaned under the weight of the wealth they contained; the market was well stocked with its staple commodity; ships clustered on our sea board; commerce flourished in our towns; and plenty filled our hamlets. Health sat on every cheek; gladness beamed in every eye."[148] This was, for Cooney as it is for me, a narrative device, a means of making a quiet moment ominous by virtue of the knowledge of what would come next. But for Cooney as for me, it had the advantage of being true. On 7 October 1825 the Miramichi was more prosperous than it had ever been and more prosperous than it would ever be again.

✳✳✳

The Timber Boom

Meanwhile, the *Baron of Renfrew* sailed across the Atlantic. Anticipating that the mammoth timber ship would fail, newspapers published reports that it sank off Newfoundland.[149] But on it lumbered – was there ever a more fitting word? – beset by heavy weather,[150] leaking, and continually threatening to come apart, before arriving safely off the south coast of England in early October 1825. Two pilots were brought onboard to take it up the Thames River. But they were inexperienced at guiding a vessel of anything resembling its size and, when manoeuvring though the outer Thames Estuary, ran the ship aground on Long Sand. Boats were allowed to pick away at its cargo in hopes of lightening its load so that the sea would lift it, but to no avail. When the ship began breaking apart, the crew was removed, and the *Baron of Renfrew* drifted toward the coast of France. It smashed ashore and scattered along a 20-kilometre swath between Dunkirk and Gravelines. The locals are said to have fared well for timber for the next few years.[151]

3

Leafs vs Flames

*The American agents – Ignition – Telling a fast story slowly –
Too darn hot – Fire weather – When the wind blows through the
piney wood – Here comes the story of the hurricane? – Arrival –
At the eye – Flight – The monsters of the deep and the tenants
of the forest – Of biblical proportions – Folk tales – Measuring
fire – Speed and duration – Height and breadth – Fire(s) – Where's
the fire? – Smoke on the water – To inhale the upturned earth –
Size – Mapping the fire in the Miramichi – Bringing the fire's
borders into focus – * – Mapping the fire beyond the Miramichi –
Montreal's Miramichi Fire – The burning Pine Tree State – The
known unknown – A "blood of flame," a flood of blame – A call
for social media – A bad star – Finger-pointing – Wilful fire raising – The one and only named suspect – Captain Chase, in the
backwoods, with negligence*

The travel journals of George Coffin and James Irish offer a rare
portrait of the Miramichi Fire season, although they never passed
within 100 kilometres of the Miramichi region itself. The two men
were land agents – Coffin for Massachusetts and Irish for Maine – and
were directed by their states to team up and travel to Fredericton in
the fall of 1825. They were to discuss with officials there the ongoing
dispute over the location of the Maine–New Brunswick border, which
had just led Maine to ban lumbering in the area. Coffin and Irish in
effect were to find out whether the New Brunswick government was
aware of – and maybe even complicit in – its citizens' ongoing cutting of timber on what the Americans considered American land. The
two land agents were then to head to the disputed land to investigate
settlers' claims and bring offenders to justice.

When Coffin and Irish set off from Massachusetts in early September, it was during one of the most extreme heat waves eastern North America had ever known. In fact, according to a charity pamphlet published and distributed internationally in the wake of the great fire, "The summer of 1825 was unusually warm in both hemispheres."[1] The hot weather had begun in mid-June, and the July that followed was the hottest month ever recorded in New England prior to the establishment of the US weather service in 1870.[2] The temperature climbed to over 100 degrees Fahrenheit repeatedly in American cities, with newspapers reporting that recently arrived Irish labourers were dying in droves from drinking cold water.[3] (Who knew?) British North America faced the same conditions. According to Montreal weather observer John Siveright, the mercury had reached 90 degrees Fahrenheit by noon eleven times that July.[4] In Woodstock, New Brunswick, 200 kilometres from the Miramichi region, Rev. Frederick Dibblee recorded in his diary on 17 September that since mid-June the weather had been continuously warm, "never the like before in this country."[5] And it was not only hot but also dry: the Northeast saw less precipitation that year than in almost any other in the first half of the nineteenth century.[6] For North America as a whole, 1825 would end up being one of the hottest years, if not the very hottest, of the entire century.

This weather made for summer-like fall travel for Coffin and Irish. The days were warm and dry as they made their way along the coast to Saint John, where they witnessed twenty large British ships loading timber for Europe. They journeyed on from there to Fredericton, and on 22 September, Coffin enjoyed a "very pleasant morning and a delightful air" as he walked around town before his appointment with the commissioner of Crown lands and forests and the surveyor general of New Brunswick, Thomas Baillie. His contentment turned to annoyance, however, when Baillie refused to let him see documents related to timber licences in the disputed borderland in the absence of Governor Howard Douglas. The governor had been called away – perhaps on a matter related to his home having burned down a week earlier. With nothing more to do, Coffin and Irish departed the capital and headed up the Saint John River on their way to the disputed territory. According to Coffin, they experienced a "fine pleasant morning" while travelling to Grand Falls on 1 October and "uncommonly warm and pleasant" weather on arrival there. This turned to

52 *The Miramichi Fire*

"extreme summer heat" and "full summer heat" on 4 and 5 October as they camped along the Saint John River.[7]

Such weather made travel more comfortable, but it also hampered navigation. The water in the river was low – "much more so than was ever known before, and diminishing daily," Irish stated in his official report.[8] Even before reaching Fredericton, Coffin and Irish's boat had run aground on a sandbar. By 4 October they realized that not only smaller tributaries but even the sizable Aroostook River leading into Maine would be impassable. So they dispatched their two boatmen, Ezekiel Chase and John Fowle, into the Maine interior on foot while they turned back down the Saint John. Coffin and Irish made it almost as far as Hartland, New Brunswick, on 7 October, a day Coffin called "very pleasant and extreme warm." But at 4:00 P.M., he wrote in his journal, "the wind came suddenly round to the northwest, and in the Evening it increased almost to a hurricane. We could see the woods in a southwesterly direction, all on fire, for a great extent, we supposed the fire to be in the neighbourhood of Houlton Plantation" – that is, over the border in Maine. As they gazed toward that fire, they did not know that at their backs, far away to the northeast, a much larger fire was pouring down on the Miramichi.[9]

✳✳✳

Somewhere deep in the Miramichi interior, or well beyond it, a fire was set burning. A heat source was applied to organic matter. Moisture fled the matter's surface to the point that the surface began to break down chemically, releasing smoke and gases. When the gases heated to a certain point, they burst into flame. Once ignited, the fire heated the surface of the matter all the more, allowing a more established beachhead for smouldering or glowing combustion while encouraging the preheating of adjacent matter. This process repeated itself endless times. The history of the Miramichi Fire is a history of its consolidation into a single, cataclysmic event of a defined range and duration, but the fire was also no more than a composite of these miniscule biochemical events happening over and over and over again. If one had measured the temperature of the massive wildfire that burned through the communities on the Miramichi River, it would not have been much greater than the temperature of that original little flame.[10]

The ignition of what would become the Miramichi Fire seems the natural starting point of its story, but it is in fact a void in that story because we don't know where and when the fire originated. We don't know if it was set alight by a lumberman clearing slash or by a farmer clearing land for settlement. We don't know if it was ignited by a Mi'gmaq or a European settler or if it was the product of miscalculation or sheer carelessness. We don't know if it was started by lightning. We don't know if the fire was born somewhere within the Miramichi watershed just a day or two earlier or if it was a long tendril of a fire that had been burning in Maine or Lower Canada for weeks before travelling northeast, east, or southeast on prevailing winds, the gradual topographical descent it faced in New Brunswick slowing its progress to the sea. And we will never know. There is no smoking gun. All that is known about the fire's origins was written in the days and years after it became the Miramichi Fire, and so this knowledge is as much a product of the fire as were scorched bodies and blueberry patches.

Indeed, the same could be said of all parts of the fire's history. It is remarkable how often new details about the blaze were reported by distant authors long after the fact throughout the nineteenth century, almost always without citation, let alone supporting, corroborable evidence. It is even more remarkable how often this information has been repeated uncritically by historians in the twentieth and twenty-first centuries and still more remarkable how often they have added new, uncited information of their own. Although some of these later details may well be accurate, it is difficult to determine which ones. The fire's cause, for example, tends to become tied up with the commentator's pre-existing biases, whether against Mi'gmaq, lumbermen, farmers, or nature itself. Likewise, the fire's origins in terms of place and time become tied up with the commentator's desire to illustrate its great range and speed or alternately to minimize its significance.

This chapter sifts through the ashes of these accounts to piece together the history of what might be considered the Miramichi Fire proper, from the anonymous, unobserved moment of its ignition to the anonymous, unobserved moment of its exhaustion. Beyond telling a narrative of the fire, it seeks to measure the fire's direction, speed, height, width, and duration and then doubles back to explore the fire's presumed range and cause. Sources are valued more highly to the degree that they were written soon after the fire by survivors or locals and for (or available to) a local audience.[11] Having said that, sources distant from the Miramichi Fire in time and space often prove valuable in a different way given that they show what spiritual, economic, or environmental lessons the greater society took from it.

The chapter, then, is like the fire itself: a single unit composed of countless miniscule events. It is the product of many hours scribbling away and snapping photos in archives, squinting before microfilm,

54 *The Miramichi Fire*

poring over books and articles of biography, local history, and fire ecology, scouring online databases, and comparing, collating, cross-checking, and dismissing information. To say that this is the most comprehensive description of the Miramichi Fire ever offered is more an admission of obsession than a declaration of accomplishment. I do not regret any of the hours spent, even the unproductive ones, because I believe the fire to have been an event deserving such a detailed analysis, particularly given its effects on nineteenth-century New Brunswick's economy, demography, and ecology. What worries me is that historical methodology and the historical genre itself seem bound to distort the historical event under examination. The Miramichi Fire was defined by and experienced in terms of its suddenness, its swiftness, its ubiquity, and its ephemerality. It would be foolish to imagine that the fire can be imagined as a finite number of discrete instances, slowed down to a crawl, dissected, and then reassembled out of the comments and contentions of primary and secondary sources without a resulting loss of integrity. But this is a fast story that I cannot possibly tell fast. When writing this chapter, I felt simultaneously closer to history and more distant from the past than I ever had before.

✳✳✳

The almanac called for cool weather, but Friday, 7 October 1825, was just as hot as the days, weeks, and months that preceded it.[12] Just a day earlier, the *Montreal Herald* had noted that it was "as hot as it generally is in the month of June. Every day of the present month has been extremely warm[,] the thermometer rising above 80°." This part of the world was living "under the burning sun of a second summer."[13] In southern New Brunswick, weather diarist Benjamin Crawford noted that 5 October was "very warm or hot."[14] New Brunswick governor Howard Douglas's biography asserts, implausibly, that the thermometer reached 126 degrees Fahrenheit in the first week of October, but the claim that it read 86 degrees in the shade is more reasonable.[15]

Although over time there would be hundreds of accounts of the Miramichi Fire, almost all of which mentioned how hot that summer was, surprisingly few spoke directly to Miramichiers' experience of it. The two most evocative reports appeared seven decades later, in the 1890s, which in itself makes their reminiscences suspect. An old, unnamed man who had been eight years old in 1825 recalled the drought that preceded the fire and how hard it was for the family to water and pasture their cattle.[16] And according to a Louis Bubier, potatoes had grown no larger than hens' eggs that year, and the woods were "so dry" that "every little twig would snap and dust fly up under one's feet."[17] For those living on the Miramichi River, the weather was particularly intense because the region kept missing out on the occasional rain that was offering some relief to places not all that distant. Whereas the diarist Crawford mentioned at least some rain falling in the south of the colony on 9, 14, 17, and 23 September and the land agent Coffin mentioned it in eastern Maine and western New Brunswick on 14, 17, 23, and 30 September, no rain whatsoever seems to have fallen on the Miramichi region between June and October.[18] The soil and forests were about as parched as they could possibly be.

New Brunswick deputy land surveyor George N. Smith arrived at the Miramichi settlements on 6 October, saying that when he travelled down the Southwest branch of the river, the smoke was so heavy it obscured the opposite bank.[19] From reports such as this one, and from their own senses, the people of the Miramichi were well aware that fire was blazing somewhere in the backwoods. October may seem late in the year for forest fires, but it is in fact a very common time for them – after summer heat has dried out vegetation and before cool and wet seasonal weather has begun. Conifer forests are especially vulnerable because their trees' moisture content, already lower than that of deciduous trees, dips still lower over the course of the year.

One of the most often asked questions in the wake of the Miramichi Fire was why residents did not show more concern about its approach, let alone take precaution against it. The author of the charity pamphlet put the blame squarely on their unfamiliarity with forest fire: people's indifference "can hardly be accounted for except from the circum-stances of their never having experienced the sad effects of fires in any former instance, and their not estimating properly the great aridity of the forests that followed the extraordinary, and long-protracted heat of the past summer."[20] Whether the author meant that recent immigrants were ignorant of local conditions, or that the local condi-tions themselves had been unusual in recent years, or that both were the case is unclear. Local historian Robert Cooney, by contrast, traced the residents' lethargy to the fire itself: "The atmosphere was over-loaded; an irresistible lassitude seized the people."[21] A still relatively distant fire could not really have had such an effect. But this inter-pretation was constructive in that it implicitly suggested that those who suffered or died were not responsible for their fate, so later writers made that argument explicitly.[22] At the time, Smith offered a more prosaic explanation for people's inaction: they assessed the potential risk and misread it. The fire was burning somewhere in the backwoods, and when 7 October brought a moderate wind from the southwest, Smith stated, "hopes were entertained of its moving parallel to the course of the river, and that the buildings and clearances would escape its ravages; the only anxiety which was intensely felt, was therefore on account of the back settlement."[23] Experience is a cruel teacher. When Governor Douglas reported on the disaster to the secretary of the Colonial Office ten days afterward, he still seemed dazed that "however incredible it may then have appeared," the fire had jumped from the woods to the town.[24]

On the afternoon of 7 October, an immense pillar of black smoke arose to the northwest of the communities along the Miramichi River.[25] In a first-hand account that merchant Isaac Paley wrote to his father and was then reprinted in the *London Times*, he reckoned that this cloud "covering half the heavens" was 20 to 30 miles away.[26] A man who returned to Scotland immediately after the fire told a newspaper there that it was the largest smoke cloud he had ever seen, and he had once witnessed 400 houses afire.[27] To the people of the Miramichi, the cloud's presence may have seemed a good omen: the wind had dropped, and the fire had slowed, to the point that smoke was now accumulating in one place. But this is the condition in which a firestorm can occur. When a fire slows down, it has more time to heat up, so a column of warm smoke – a convection column – accumulates and rises. As it does, it pulls warm air up with it, so cool air rushes in to replace it, creating an indraft and the potential for a whirlwind.[28] The weather helps to make the fire, but then the fire can help to make the weather. By 7:00 P.M. or so, the cloud had blotted out the sky, such that, in Smith's words, "everything was enveloped in total darkness, so black and horrific, that to a person in the open air there appeared a void nonentity."[29] It being so dark, many along the Miramichi River went to bed.[30]

As the sky darkened, the wind turned. The wind's course through these hours is critical to understanding the Miramichi Fire because it suggests not only from which direction the fire had been travelling and therefore which forests had already been burned – a matter to be picked up later in the chapter – but also why the blaze then blew up as it did. The earliest accounts recognized the wind's significance, although they could not agree as to its exact path. The charity pamphlet, for example, had the wind starting from the north until "a smart breeze" sprung up from the northwest, whereas Isaac Paley stated that it began blowing from the northwest and then increased as it came from the north.[31] George N. Smith mentioned the wind blowing hard only from the north, whereas Governor Douglas and several other early reports had it coming only from the northwest.[32] Basing its opinion on a first-hand account, the *Edinburgh Weekly Journal* stated that the wind shifted three times during the calamity, adding that it was because of this factor that all points around Chatham ended up charred.[33] Some individuals could not make up their mind. Describing the fire in 1828, author John McGregor claimed that the wind "came on to blow furiously from the north-west," but in another book four years later, in what reads like a correction, he stated that it "came on to blow furiously from the westward."[34] Despite such variation, these accounts share a basic trajectory: the wind that had been blowing moderately from the southwest earlier in the day (or not blowing enough to merit mention at all) shifted in the evening to blow hard from the west, northwest, and/or north. This trajectory is perfectly consistent with the passage of a cold front, a condition associated with over three-quarters of all large forest fires on the Eastern Seaboard. Ahead of the front, winds come from the southwest. As the front passes, the winds pick up and shift, coming in from the northwest. Since forest fires tend to burn in an ellipse – driven by the wind to be longer than they are wide – when the wind direction changes, the long flank of the fire becomes the long front of it. A fire 2 kilometres wide can suddenly become 10 kilometres wide, with stronger winds urging it along.[35] A large fire burning behind the Miramichi settlements was suddenly an enormous one bearing down on them.

The wind began blowing what Smith and Paley each called "a perfect hurricane."[36] Although "Fire and Hurricane" was the title of three of the most reprinted newspaper accounts of the Miramichi disaster, it took me many readings to realize that the word "hurricane" was meant literally and that witnesses believed an actual hurricane had swept through, multiplying the fire's ferocity.[37] Certainly, it was understood that the fire would never have created the damage it did if not for the accompanying wind, which stoked the flames, carrying them from woods to town and driving them faster than people could run. Confusing the issue was that the term "hurricane" was often used figuratively, as in the charity pamphlet's claim that "the wind blew a hurricane,"[38] and also used to describe the cyclonic winds that the fire itself generated, as in Joseph Bouchette's 1831 description of a fire's working: "the rarefaction of the air produced by the heat occasions a rush of air from all quarters, which constitutes a hurricane."[39] But had all early accounts of the Miramichi Fire used the term in such fashion? It *was* hurricane season. Since telegraphs and meteorological services did not exist in 1825, no one knew where weather came from or where it went, so newspapers wrote about weather strictly in local terms. But it is possible to stitch together these local references to track a storm. Although there is no record of a major hurricane hitting the Eastern Seaboard that October, one of undetermined strength did strike Cuba on the first day of the month. It then made landfall around St Augustine, Florida, on 2 October before heading up the Georgia coast. A hurricane's remnants could well have taken five more days to wander up the Eastern Seaboard, reaching eastern New Brunswick at the most inopportune time imaginable and amplifying the impact of a conflagration.[40]

There is also compelling evidence from well after the fact. In 1828 the Miramichi businesses of Gilmour, Rankin & Co. and William Abrams petitioned the colonial government for a refund of duties paid on goods destroyed during the great fire. They argued that it was only reasonable that the public purse not profit from their loss, especially given that they had relinquished all claim to relief from the post-fire charity effort. "Your petitioners take leave to mention," they wrote, "that the peculiar character of the calamity occasioned a relaxation of the rules in the Insurance Associations in Britain by means whereof your petitioners received immediate payment of the Small amounts insured, notwithstanding a clause in the policies which would exonerate the Underwriters in case of loss by hurricane, an exception being taken it was immediately Said 'this has been a Sweeping desolation the assured have lost every thing, and we must act liberally.'"[41] In other words, insurance firms apparently decided that although the devastation may have been worsened by a hurricane, the fire was its underlying cause, so they would treat the hurricane's role as essentially beside the point. Perhaps we should do the same.

Cinders, ashes, and flaming debris began raining down on the communities along the Miramichi River. This phenomenon, called spotting, occurs when the hot air of a fire draws materials upward and the prevailing wind flings them forward, sometimes kilometres forward,

Leafs vs Flames

as forerunners of the coming fire. Spot fires do not tend to increase a fire's range because typically by the time they develop sufficient intensity to do damage they are overtaken by the fire's front.[42] In 1838, New Brunswick historian Peter Fisher recalled that on the night of the Miramichi Fire, "[f]lying atoms, and burning bark ... was carried to a distance out to sea, to the great danger of the shipping."[43] A Scottish chronicler claimed later that "the ashes of the fire fell thick on the streets of Halifax, St. John's, Newfoundland, and Quebec, and that some were carried as far as the Bermudas, while the smoke darkened the air hundreds of miles off."[44] We might write off this entire statement but for the fact that, as we will see, smoke did subsequently cover the entire Northeast.

Still, the people of the Miramichi were not sure what was happening. A group headed north into the woods to see what they could see, "and they ran back as fast as they could, and before they got down two minutes, the fire was at their heels."[45] A man in Newcastle walked 200 yards from his house to find the cause of the tremendous roaring he heard in the woods, only to be turned back by the smoke and ashes. By the time he made it back to his house and grabbed what he could, his roof and the town were on fire.[46] All who wrote of the Miramichi Fire told of the speed of its arrival and how quickly it washed over the region. Many commentators worked backward from there to suggest that the fire had moved that fast for its entire life. In 1851 James F.W. Johnston stated, "It travelled eighty-five miles in nine hours, so that scarcely on a fleet horse could a man have escaped from it."[47] And the fire grew only faster in the years to come. Louise Manny and James Wilson in the 1960s and Wayne Curtis in the 1980s clocked it at 1 mile (1.6 kilometres) per minute for its entire run.[48] In reality, even in the optimal conditions of a closed-canopy conifer forest, a wildfire is likely to travel no more than 3 to 6 kilometres per *hour*, with occasional bursts up to 10 or 15 kilometres per hour.[49] But it was probably inevitable that the fire was remembered as having moved much faster. To the people of the Miramichi, all of the woods – whether 1 kilometre behind the settlements or 20 – served equally as backdrop, and only when the flames pushed through the final row of trees did the real danger of the situation present itself.

The final word on the fire's arrival must be given to Robert Cooney, who witnessed the disaster first-hand. His 1832 account exhibits all his talent for dramatic journalism and so offers an immediacy and universality that has made it the most quoted description of the fire

60 · *The Miramichi Fire*

over the past two centuries. Cooney devoted three full pages to mounting omens of disaster and then concluded with a flourish:

> The tremendous bellowing became more and more terrific. The earth seemed to stagger as if it had reeled from its ancient foundations. The harmony of creation appeared to have been deranged; and about to revert into original chaos. *Earth*, *Air*, *Sea*, and *Sky*; all visible creation seemed to conspire against man; and to totter under the weight of some dreadful commission they were charged to execute. The river, tortured into violence by the hurricane, foamed with rage, and flung its boiling spray upon the land. The thunder pealed along the vault of Heaven; the lightning rent the firmament in pieces. For a moment, and all was still, a deep and awful silence reigned over everything. All nature appeared to be *hushed* into *dumbness*; – when – suddenly a lengthened and sullen roar came booming through the forest, and driving a thousand massive and devouring flames before it. Then Newcastle and Douglastown, and the whole Northern side of the river, extending from Bartibog to the Nashwaak, a distance of more than 100 miles in length, became enveloped in an immense sheet of flame, that spread over nearly 6,000 square miles.[50]

✳✳✳

The fire's destruction of communities on the Miramichi River is the very crux of this history yet the moment least suited to history because it seems to occur entirely outside time. According to a number of sources, houses were ablaze within three minutes of the fire's arrival, and all of the devastation occurred within just fifteen.[51] The events of those few minutes cannot be assembled and made orderly as having happened first here and then there or before this and after that. They are just a jumble of observations obscured by incomprehension, panic, and haze. One could say the same about the challenge of chronicling a historical battle, but at least in a battle there are sides, with advances and retreats, and so there is an inherent narrative. Here, there are only instances of comprehensibility – and fewer instances than one would expect. Among the many contemporary accounts of the Miramichi Fire, there are relatively few anecdotes involving specific people at specific places here in the heart of it.

In Newcastle that night, some citizens were enjoying the novelty of a sermon being delivered by a black preacher named Preston – presumably the Halifax-based minister and abolitionist Richard Preston. Outside, the loud beating of a drum began, and the congregation assumed that it was intended to disrupt the service. But it was an alarm being raised by a William Wright, who is said to have come from the woods and witnessed the fire sweeping through the country there.[52] Some Miramichiers heeded the alarm and filled fire buckets with water, but that was about the extent of preparation. Many more stayed in their beds, some sick from a yellow fever outbreak in the region.[53] When the fire arrived – around 8:00 P.M. according to the charity pamphlet and 9:00 P.M. according to Paley and Cooney[54] – it was an active crown fire, meaning it was burning both at the forest's surface and in its canopy, each plane feeding off the other. It bore down on Newcastle and Douglastown on the north side of the river. It also jumped the Southwest branch of the river somewhere and snaked behind Chatham to rage only a couple of kilometres behind it. The flames, "unlike the fires of this world," set buildings ablaze seemingly instantaneously.[55] Sound thrived at the expense of sight: whereas thick black smoke and raining cinder reduced visibility to nil, the night was filled with the roaring of the flames and the screams of animals and people. "Perhaps the center of a volcano during an eruption may be the best comparison," wrote Paley.[56] Any thought of fighting the fire evaporated.

Those on the north side of the river fled for their lives. As many as 1,000 people from Newcastle took refuge in Strawberry Marsh, less than a kilometre to the southwest of the town; its lack of combustible vegetation, as much as its marshiness, saved them.[57] Many more took to the river. Some people – especially those working in the backwoods along the Miramichi's smaller branches – survived simply by submerging themselves as fully into the water of the dried-up rivers as possible; exposed skin got badly burned.[58] On the main Miramichi River, people scrambled aboard boats or canoes or rafts or sticks of timber and pushed off toward Chatham. Some had brought bags and boxes of their money and valuables. One young Irish immigrant couple are remembered for having stood neck-deep in the Miramichi River, their doubloons in their hands, until the fire passed over.[59] Many others were obliged to abandon their valuables, which were in subsequent days found in molten lumps along the shore.[60] Making it onto the river did not guarantee safety. Rafts fell apart and passengers drowned, and windthrown burning trees and buildings flew into the river and overturned boats and rafts.[61] Amid the turmoil, there were undoubtedly acts of human weakness. A Scottish newspaper, relying on a first-hand account, reported that once the ferries that traversed the river had made it to the south shore, no one was willing to sail back and pick up others.[62] There were undoubtedly acts of heroism, too. Two parents spent the night on the north bank with their four children, "keeping them continually wet, the father with his hat, and the mother with her shoes, until morning, when they were taken aboard the shipping."[63]

A running thread in descriptions of the fire was its effects on fish and animals. In fact, the single most common element in contemporary accounts of the fire, after discussion of the people it left dead, dying, and homeless, may well be mention of the fish it killed. Salmon and other fish were said to have suffocated, to have been struck by burning wood, to have boiled in the water, to have been poisoned by ashes that leached into the water, or to have been driven or flung themselves on shore.[64] For whatever reason, the image of fried and floating fish resonated. This was expressed most vividly by George Manners, the British consul in Massachusetts, whose dreadful long poem "The Conflagration" was sold with the aim of raising funds to aid (human) victims of the fire. Eight pages into the poem, he declaimed,

> Not e'en the natives of the flood were spared,
> The stifled shoals the gen'ral havoc shared;
> Lifeless they float among the neighb'ring strand,
> Or lie, in putrid myriads, on the sand;*

The asterisk denotes that, not satisfied with the lines – and who would be? – Manners appended a footnote apologizing that "[t]o describe this circumstance, with any degree of poetical effect, I found extremely difficult: Fish, save 'the enormous Monsters of the Deep,' are by no means *a subject of the Sublime.*"[65] The editors of the *Boston Patriot* admired the sentiment behind the consul's poem, but of the work itself the best they could say was that it was "a handsome specimen of typography."[66]

Manners acknowledged the difficulty of making the death of fish a subject of the sublime, but at least he tried; he ignored livestock and wildlife altogether. This omission was not all that unusual in that descriptions of the fire's effect on animals were surprisingly perfunctory. It was noted that many cows, horses, and pigs were afterward seen floating down the river, having perished seeking safety from the flames.[67] The "tenants of the forests" – including bear, moose, deer, snakes, "lucifee" (lynx or bobcat), and foxes – were observed, both living and dead, during and after the fires in New Brunswick and Maine.[68] Birds were said to have been drawn to the flames by confusion or fascination, but it is more likely they were incapacitated by the thick smoke, fierce winds, and ferocious heat.[69] Nor was the fire always the direct cause of death. Flocks of owls flew to southern New Brunswick to escape the flames, only to be shot there in great number.[70] I have been working on this book for a long time, and not a month goes by that I don't think of those owls.

The best vantage point, if you can call it that, for witnessing the great fire as it wreaked its full destruction was the deck of one of the estimated 150 timber and fishing vessels anchored in the river.[71] As a result, the most clear-eyed and vivid contemporary accounts were from ships' captains, although even these descriptions were relatively brief. "The fire flakes came off the land on board thicker and faster than ever I saw a snow-storm in my life," reported Captain Walton of the *James*.[72] John Redpath, aboard the *Canada*, wrote to his mother of going aloft with a member of his crew in hopes of extinguishing fires in the sails. They were unsuccessful, the ship burned, and he and his crew were left with "not a second shirt to our backs."[73] The captain of a small shallop worked continually wetting its sails. Having witnessed horrors he could not put to words, he eventually retreated to his cabin "and taking out his prayer book read the account of the last day; and such a resemblance had the river around him to the description he then read, that he could not but believe, the final destruction of the world, as is predicted in holy writ, was then in the act of accomplishment."[74]

Given that this was a culture steeped in Christian imagery, it is hardly surprising that a number of commentators joined this captain in interpreting the fire as apocalyptic, both because that was the way they understood it and because that was a way they knew they would be understood. Shortly after the inferno, John Jardine of Black River, just southeast of Chatham, wrote the words and perhaps the music of the ballad "The Miramichi Fire." According to Jardine,

Many that did see the fire,
Thought it was the Judgement Day.[75]

64 *The Miramichi Fire*

As we will see, such thinking led Jardine and many later commentators to work backward in order to determine what the people of the Miramichi had done to merit such punishment from God. But the apocalyptic imagery seems often to have served simply as a means to position the fire in world-historical terms. In Wales, Dafydd Amos wrote a song to elicit charity there, in which he claimed,

> There is no one on the face of the earth who had ever seen such
> a fire,
> Everyone believed that the last day had come upon them.[76]

Isaac Paley likewise wrote, "I am persuaded ... that never since the destruction of Sodom and Gomorrah has the world witnessed a scene so terrific and appalling; for only a country such as this (the face of which is one interminable forest) could produce a conflagration so great and so awful."[77] There is a whiff of pride in Paley's statement: it required the great forests of the Miramichi region to fuel such a cataclysm. Robert Cooney again merits the last word for the skill with which he defined the fire as a natural force so great that it could be comprehended only in supernatural terms: "A greater calamity ... never befell any forest country, and has been rarely excelled in the annals of any other: and the general character of the scene was such, that all it required, to complete a picture of the GENERAL JUDGMENT, was the blast of a TRUMPET, the voice of the ARCHANGEL, and the resurrection of the DEAD."[78]

Notwithstanding such grandiosity, most contemporary accounts tended to be matter-of-fact, grounded, and literal. But as the decades passed, new stories continued to appear, many of them more maudlin, fantastic, and symbolic.[79] The occasional report of a child being born during the fire grew until, according to twentieth-century folklorist Louise Manny, "It is said that thirteen babies were born that night on the marsh and rafts."[80] It is worth noting, however, that whereas sixteen children were baptized at St Paul's Anglican Church in Chatham in the first two weeks after the fire, none of them were newborns.[81] The tale was told of a young woman who almost slipped off a raft but was saved "by the superhuman efforts of her lover," who grabbed her hair and pulled her to safety. "[N]eedless to say they were shortly after wed."[82] Needless to say. My favourite anecdote is of a cow having carried a two-year-old girl on its back across the Miramichi River to safety.[83] The story is from 1897, a generation after the Great Chicago Fire had been attributed to Mrs O'Leary's cow kicking over a lantern, so it reads as a case of bovine redemption, a species' reputation cleansed by fire. My inclination is to give greater weight to accounts contemporary with the fire, but, of course, some of the stories found in newspapers, diaries, and correspondence of the day were inaccurate or fanciful, too. What's more, it may well be that some events came to light after the smoke had cleared, were shared orally over the years, and emerged in print only much later. Still, the dearth of well-attributed accounts of the Miramichi Fire as it passed through the Miramichi is striking. But maybe not so surprising. As the charity pamphlet puts it, "The suddenness of the calamity at Miramichi prevented that cool and collected observation of facts, so desirable to form the ground-work of a correct narration."[84] Or as Norman MacLean writes in *Young Men and Fire*, "Throughout history, blowups have been seen almost entirely by survivors of big forest fires, who would not have survived if they had stopped to observe them."[85]

✳✳✳

The Miramichi had been overwhelmed, according to the author of the charity pamphlet, by "an ocean of fire that we may conclude to be unparalleled in the history of forest countries, and perhaps not surpassed in horrific sublimity by any natural calamity from this element, that has ever been recorded."[86] This account hints at another reason why there were relatively few contemporary anecdotes about specific people: humans were not the story's central characters – the forest fire was – even in a pamphlet published to raise money for its victims. Writers sought to describe and even to make sense of the fire, and they did so primarily by attempting to measure it.

Some early writers, and many who have followed, told of the fire's short life, noting that it did its entire damage during the day and night of 7 October. In his ballad John Jardine stated plainly,

Forty-two miles by one hundred
This great fire did extend;
All was done within eight hours,
Not exceeding over ten.[87]

The charity pamphlet was likewise insistent on the point: "Mistakes have been made as to the fires raging after the conflagration. This was not the case – All the damage that the fire could produce in the woods, particularly on the point above Chatham, and on the northern banks of the river, was effected on the night of the calamity, as on the following morning, it was nearly all extinguished without the agency of rain – for after the light stuff had been burnt, the strength of the wind and flying sand, &c. tended to repress the influence of the fire, and hardly any materials were left for consumption."[88] If accurate, this is an important concession as to the fire's effects: the author essentially states that the fire's speed worked against the fire, causing it to burn itself out quickly and so limiting the damage it could inflict. Large, fast-moving fires by their nature do indeed leave lots of forest fuel untouched. Yet the charity pamphlet elsewhere refuted its own claim that the fire lasted only one night, quoting a report that a man just returned from the scene of devastation said the flames still raged, as well as stating that cinders rained down on Chatham on 9 October, clear evidence that fire persisted somewhere.[89] (The fire was also said to have burned after 7 October well beyond the Miramichi region. A report from Fredericton on 10 October, for example, spoke of "a frightful conflagration" still burning in the surrounding woods: "We see nothing but dreadful loneliness from our windows, and the smoke of the adjacent woods envelopes the city in almost total darkness.")[90] A contradiction is at work here. If the main fire travelled so fast over such a large area that it left vegetation unburnt, how likely is it that it burned itself out entirely with so much vegetation still there to feed it? For that matter, how could anyone know that all the points within a fire that was being measured in the thousands of square miles had not only died out entirely but also died out quickly? Perhaps it is only natural that those in the burned communities assumed that the fire was finished everywhere when it was finished with them. Perhaps it is also natural that they, and indeed everyone, conceived of the fire as a single entity, a single enemy, that had overturned existence in a single sweep.

Witnesses and later commentators invariably described the fire that arrived on the Miramichi River as a giant wall or wave of flame. Although, or because, it was the very model of ephemerality, many sought to bear witness to its vast dimensions. John McGregor wrote in 1828 of "the flames ascending more than a hundred feet above the tops of the loftiest trees," but four years later, in a nearly identical passage, he wrote of "the flames ascending from one to two hundred feet above the loftiest trees." By the time James Alexander borrowed liberally from McGregor's work in 1849, the flames were "a couple of hundred feet above the loftiest pines."[91] They rose no higher than that in later years. In reality, a fire's height might simultaneously be called its most important and its most misleading measure. On the one hand, it is flame height that determines whether the fire affects atmospheric processes, so it is the fire's height, rather than its range, that governs whether fire ecologists and managers consider a blaze "small" or "large." On the other hand, the height may distract from where the real action in a forest fire is occurring: on the forest floor. Research of recent decades has proven that fire generally burns too slowly in trunks and canopy to be carried from tree to tree. Fire spreads across a large area by feasting on the dry, decaying duff and slash on the ground. The monstrous grows out of the miniscule.[92]

Recording the flame's breadth, like its height, similarly served to document the unprecedented, even unnatural, nature of the Miramichi cataclysm. As noted, Cooney claimed that the "immense sheet of flame" was 100 miles (160 kilometres) long when it burst from the woods. It is as though the fire's sudden appearance at Newcastle was made all the more dramatic by having it appear everywhere at once. In 1861 Johnston estimated the fire's front to be 25 miles across, whereas Cooke in 1963 said 100 miles, Manny and Wilson in 1968 said 30 miles, and Curtis in 1988 said 20 miles.[93] No writer cites evidence for the figure given or explains why it differs from earlier estimates. Nor does any writer explain how an individual could have taken in 20 to 100 miles at once, amid deep smoke, at the very moment when hell was breaking out all around. In reality, it is only in little or no wind that a fire maintains a wide front. Even if, as discussed earlier, the changing wind direction turned a long fire into a wide one, the wind would straightaway have begun narrowing the fire's front once again. For that reason, it is all but impossible for a fire to be both superfast and superwide for any amount of time. The Miramichi Fire may have been 160 kilometres wide over the course of its life, but there is no reason to suppose that it burned that breadth in a single swath.

This understanding leads to an obvious but key point: a fire is not a flood. It does not blanket all points within its range with equal intensity. Instead, it burns in an irregular pattern, a mosaic, with distinct patches sustaining distinct damage based on varying fire intensities, themselves based on such factors as slope, wind, humidity (itself the product of many factors, including time of day), and, of course, availability of fuels. Significant portions of a fire's burn area

68 *The Miramichi Fire*

can escape entirely untouched. In fact, only about one-third of the vegetation within the perimeter of a large fire typically burns.[94] Moreover, a large wildland fire typically consists of separate fires that may join, separate, and rejoin over time and space. These characteristics of fire behaviour lead to a whole series of pyro-metaphysical questions. When should an amalgam of fires be considered a single fire (and when a Fire)? If two discrete fires with two discrete ignitions touch, are they forever one? Is a fire defined by its perimeter, regardless of how much area burns within, or is it defined strictly by those areas themselves?

Early accounts of the Miramichi Fire grappled with such questions, particularly as to whether the 7 October disaster was to be blamed on a fire or fires. The charity pamphlet is entitled *A Narrative of the Late Fires at Miramichi, New Brunswick*, after all. John McGregor exemplifies the difficulty that writers had in simultaneously describing and explaining the disaster. And he was in a better position to discuss it than many: he lived on nearby Prince Edward Island during the disaster and visited the Miramichi in 1828. That year, he wrote, "In October, 1825, upwards of a hundred miles of the country, on the north side of Miramichi river, became a scene of the most dreadful conflagration that has perhaps ever occurred in the history of the world." But in 1832, without having revisited the Miramichi in the interim, he began, "In October 1825, about a hundred and forty miles of extent, and a vast breadth of the country on the north, and from sixty to seventy miles on the south side of Miramichi River became a scene."[95] The fire had grown considerably bigger. McGregor was a conscientious reporter, so we may surmise that this revision was due to him having been apprised of more distant damage and having expanded the fire's size accordingly. Yet the same author, in the very same editions, changed "[t]he ravages of the fire extended as far as Fredericton, on the River St. John ...; and to the northward, as far as the Bay de Chaleur" to "[g]reat fires raged about the same time in the forests of the River St. John ... Fires raged also at the same time in the northern parts of the province, as far as the Bay de Chaleur."[96] "Fire" had become "fires." McGregor had apparently decided that the peripheral burning should not be included in defining the fire proper – although he himself had incorporated peripheral burning in enlarging the size of the overall conflagration. Ultimately, in assessing the Miramichi Fire in historical terms, all one can do is hold it to the same standards, if you will, of other forest fires. Every fire that becomes

Leafs vs Flames

historic enough to be given a name becomes defined by distinct borders. The Miramichi Fire was no less of a fire because it left large patches within its borders unburnt; that is true of every fire. Likewise, it was no less a single fire because it was composed of smaller fires; that is also true of every fire. What makes the Miramichi Fire case unusual, as we will see, is the way that the definition of its physical borders was mutated by political borders. Fires that burned across New Brunswick, Maine, and Lower Canada in October 1825 ended up taking the name of the New Brunswick site of greatest death and damage, even while the discreteness of the jurisdictions meant that the fires drew apart and consolidated separately, such that few people thought them physically joined.

✳✳✳

The single most important measurement of the Miramichi Fire, apart from the number of people it killed, was its size. The scale of the fire's destruction was what made it historically significant, and so every account of the past two centuries has sought to define the fire's range. But in truth, its size has always been impossible to determine. In early 1826 the Miramichi-based relief committee calculated that 30,000 acres of private property had burned,[97] yet this represents just $1/_{128}$ of what became the standard estimation of the fire's New Brunswick range. The vast majority of the presumed burn area was beyond what Europeans had settled. Or even knew. Seven years after the fire, New Brunswick's commissioner of Crown lands and forests, Thomas Baillie, published a map of the colony on which the land less than 100 kilometres due west of the Miramichi communities was labelled "Country very little known."[98] A half-century further on, famed New Brunswick forestry official Edward Jack travelled through that area and lamented that it was still largely unsurveyed: "We rely on our timber lands to pay our debts, and here is a country of which we absolutely know nothing."[99]

Accounts from the time of the fire can help to stitch together a map of all known Miramichi Fire damage. Having said that, some of the early statements are undoubtedly inaccurate, so the fire cannot simply be assumed to be the cumulative product of all accounts of it: some places said to have burned may not have, just as some that did burn may have escaped attention. Focusing on the fire's boundaries, as most sources do, may also lead to mistakenly measuring the fire's size simply by multiplying its length by width, ignoring the fact that large

70   *The Miramichi Fire*

areas within did not burn. What is noteworthy about the Miramichi Fire's size in the first half of the nineteenth century, however, is that it essentially did not change. It did not get larger, either from embellishment or as subsequent evidence of burned areas appeared. Nor did it get smaller once the smoke cleared and people had the chance to see whether the devastation to communities in the Miramichi had exaggerated the fire's impact on a broader region. Rather, understanding of the fire's presumed size and shape solidified in popular and historical memory quite quickly and retained that form throughout much of the remainder of the century.

But before wading into the fire, it is worth considering smoke. It is a mistake to assume that where there's smoke, there's fire – the two need not be commensurate – but the range of one may be indicative of the other. Northeastern North America was shrouded in smoke during the Miramichi Fire. In fact, the smoke began in some places before 7 October, then intensified afterward, dispersed, and returned again, supporting the premise that fires were burning far beyond the Miramichi. On 5 and 6 October the haze around Quebec City was already so thick that from 100 yards "large lofty woods could not be distinguished."[100] Brockville in Upper Canada likewise reported there being smoke "impregnated with a smell, similar to that of burning turf," early on 7 October.[101] But along the Eastern Seaboard, there are no reports of widespread smoke on the day with which the fire is associated or on the day following. The wind – or the hurricane – seems to have scattered it. Even on 8 October, Massachusetts land agent George Coffin wrote in his diary of "the weather continuing pleasant all the day" while staying at Woodstock, New Brunswick, 200 kilometres from the mouth of the Miramichi River.[102]

But on 9 October, Coffin awoke to a "very foggy morning," and when travelling that day, he encountered smoke that "came upon us from the burning woods, so astonishingly dense, and suffocating."[103] Unknown to him, a dense smoke had settled that day over much of British North America, New England, and even beyond. Things were most dire on the Miramichi River itself. On the morning of 9 October, the smoke was already so thick in Chatham that nothing was visible at a distance of 30 yards. By noon, according to the charity pamphlet, "the alarm was given that cattle had suffocated, and the wretched inhabitants expecting it soon to be their own doom (a heavy pressure upon the breast being already felt) prepared themselves the last alternative, by digging holes in the ground, to inhale the fresh turned up earth."[104]

"Digging holes in the ground, to inhale the fresh turned up earth." There are moments in reading material from the past when we are reminded just how alien, how not-me, those people were. I knew that people had long believed places were capable of giving off bad air and making them sick. But I had never encountered the idea that the ground could be a moderating influence, storing good air when the air above was bad, as oceans moderate the temperature of the lands they surround. The image nicely captures how people of the time understood the parts of nature to be interconnected. And it helps to explain why, as will later be discussed, in the wake of the great fire, people assumed that the soil as much as the forests had been destroyed.

Cinders began raining down on Chatham at 4:00 P.M. on 9 October, evidence that the fire was continuing to burn somewhere nearby. The people made ready to flee the fire when it came, but it never did, and by the morning of 10 October, the smoke, and the suspense, had subsided.[105]

Nowhere else experienced such a terrifying scene, but at least the people of the Miramichi understood what was happening. People elsewhere were mystified by the thick smoke – or fog, as it was often referred to[106] – and much more so when it became evident how widespread the phenomenon was.[107] With visibility approaching nil, navigation ground to a halt on both the Saint Lawrence River at Montreal and the Potomac River at Washington, DC, 800 kilometres apart.[108] There were reports of smoke on the Mississippi River and far out into the Atlantic.[109] (And might it have travelled farther still? The Gosport Observatory near Portsmouth, England, noted a "thick haze" to the southwest on 14 October. Decades later, a Quebec newspaper recalled that five days after the Miramichi Fire, smoke darkened the atmosphere of Great Britain.[110] If it seems farfetched to suggest that the smoke crossed the Atlantic, know that this is exactly what happened in 1950, when smoke from the Chinchaga Fire in western Canada reached England within three days.)[111] Ferrymen on the Penobscot River in Maine resorted to using a compass and also claimed that "a phenomenon, much resembling a *mirage*, was observed. People with lanterns, saw their images distinctly reflected from the fog surrounding them; the likeness produced was so perfect as to be known." Others reported that the smoke was of "a peculiar hue," adding a surreal element to the scene.[112] An American editor noted that the nights were "*as dark as Egypt*" and compared the days to New England's famous "Dark Day" of 19 May 1780 (which also likely involved a forest fire) – except that, in this case, the smoke affected the eyes more.[113] People on both sides of the international border complained that their eyes stung, as did their lungs. "It is extremely penetrating, affecting the eyes with an inflammatory sensation, and is quite disagreeable to the organs of respiration," one newspaper said.[114] An editor in Portland, Maine, initially attributed the smoke simply to "fires running in the woods" nearby but concluded that this was impossible when word arrived of more and more distant places experiencing the same conditions. "Where," he asked, "did all this smoke come from?"[115]

And then the smoke dissipated. And then it returned, or at least in Upper and Lower Canada it did. On 12 and 13 October, Montreal and Quebec City were blanketed by smoke as thick as that of a few days earlier. There was concern that fire was raging on the north side of the Saint Lawrence River.[116] Yet there was not even consensus in the press that this smoky fog or foggy smoke or whatever it was could be blamed on a forest fire – or even on fire. "If it be really the effect of fire," a Montreal newspaper stated, "the fire must not only be very great, but of a most alarming nature."[117] The smoke soon dissipated from the pages of newspapers, too, replaced by the accounts that began to appear about the Miramichi Fire – accounts that would have arrived sooner if the mails had not been delayed by the smoke.[118]

The first reports of the Miramichi Fire paid no attention to its size: authors sought help for the burned settlements and neither knew nor cared how far the fire had travelled. An early account dated 11 October, published as "Fire and Hurricane" a week later in the *Fredericton New Brunswick Royal Gazette* and subsequently reprinted all across North America and Great Britain, was said to be written by the Gilmour and Rankin lumber company.[119] It focused on the destruction of Newcastle and Douglastown, but it also mentioned further destruction on the Miramichi River's Northwest branch, as well as on the Bartibog River to the northeast of the main Miramichi settlements and the Nappan River to the southeast. A first-hand account by a "spectator and sufferer" published – coincidentally, also as "Fire and Hurricane" – in the *Halifax Novascotian* the following day confirmed that the Bartibog and Nappan areas had burned, added the Black River southeast of Chatham to the scene of destruction, and also estimated that the fire had burned 89 miles along the Miramichi River.[120]

As the embers cooled, it became clearer that the fire had burned wantonly throughout northeastern New Brunswick, and more accounts attempted to map its path or at least its footprint. *A Narrative of the Late Fires at Miramichi, New Brunswick*, the charity pamphlet published out of Halifax that November, claimed that the conflagration had travelled north-south a distance of 85 miles from the Bay of Chaleur, "where two cottages in the forest were consumed," to Richibucto and a west-east distance of 100 miles, putting its total area at around 8,000 square miles.[121] Based on a report coming out of Chatham on 10 October, a Maine newspaper put the New Brunswick fire at half that – 40 by 100 miles – and this figure became widely circulated in the press.[122] As mentioned, John Jardine's song has the fire's dimensions as 42 by 100 miles, whereas the charity song by Welshman Dafydd Amos gauges its length in one stanza at 200 miles and in another at 100 miles.[123]

Remarkably, whereas North Americans learned about the great fire by way of a small number of newspaper articles widely reprinted, people in Great Britain had access to more and different accounts. Eyewitnesses from the Miramichi region arriving aboard timber ships told of the fire when they landed in Britain, and their reports were published in local newspapers across the country. It was often crew members making such reports, but there were also cases of would-be immigrants having arrived in New Brunswick to what seemed like an entire colony ablaze and sailing back to Great Britain. Perhaps next year would be better. These newspaper reports went unnoticed by historians for the next two centuries, awaiting the advent of Internet databases. Captain Walton of the *James* admitted that no one yet knew how far the fire extended into the forest: "some say eighty, some say 200 miles back." For 20 miles along the shore, nothing remained but chimneys.[124] A man arriving in Scotland claimed that the fire had burned from the southwest to northeast a distance of 16 miles and had extended a full 50 miles to the top of the colony at Restigouche.[125]

The 1866 memoir of William Butterfield of Maine, who wrote in detail of a trip through the Miramichi to trap beaver in September 1825, is not strictly of the day, but it is credible and detailed enough that it merits shoehorning in here. Butterfield started off from the American Thomas Boies's place in what became Boiestown on the Southwest branch of the Miramichi River. "From thence," he wrote, "we went East over on to Canes [Cains] River, found a family of Beaver but it was to early to citch them and we returned back to the southwest Branch. Traveled up that branch about 10 miles to Salmon Brook and found Beaver on that stream. Thence we past on North about 20 miles" before returning to Boies's around 1 October. In other words, Butterfield had travelled counterclockwise around an oval of a few hundred square kilometres, with Boiestown its westernmost point. He was just heading back to the Cains River when "[t]he Great Fire Commenced that burnt the most of the Maremachee Took place and that country where we had lately left was all burned over and our labour was lost and our prospect ruined for that season."[126]

One might assume that time would bring clarity to the question of the fire's size – that after dealing with the immediate disaster and getting through the winter, the people of the Miramichi and elsewhere in New Brunswick would in 1826, just in the course of living, ascertain the fire's exact boundaries. But that did not happen. For one thing, there was no pressing need to; the curiosity of future historians was not even taken into account. For another, great portions of the presumed fire area were thinly populated and inaccessible, and those travelling there were unlikely to report to distant newspapers. What's more, as will be discussed later, forest fires burned in the Miramichi interior again in the summer of 1826, alarming the survivors of the 1825 fire and muddying forever the precise boundaries of the earlier blaze.[127] The Provincial Archives of New Brunswick contain many 1830s cadastral maps of Northumberland County bearing reference to "burnt land," but there is no way of knowing if any or all of them reference the Miramichi Fire.[128]

Nevertheless, some credible local reports as to the fire's dimensions did accumulate in the years that followed. There is, for example, an 1827 map of the Great Road that ran between the Miramichi region and the town of Bathurst, about 65 kilometres to the north, which put the fire's boundary about 27 kilometres north of the Miramichi settlements. A road superintendent effectively corroborated this finding a year later in stating that, when heading south from Bathurst, one reached the "Burnt Woods" 20 miles (35 kilometres) south of Bathurst. "Roots of Large Trees," he wrote, "that was blowen down at the time of the Great Fire are left on the Road, but enough is cleared so that Sleighs can pass."[129]

An 1831 report by "W" in the *Chatham Gleaner and Northumberland Schediasma* offers particularly compelling testimony. "W" – almost certainly Robert Cooney, then working at the newspaper – documented the fire's path of destruction more fully than had any previous writer. Just as importantly, he did so for a local audience who would know if he was being inaccurate. "W" had the Miramichi component of the fire commence in the woods at the source of Burnt Land Brook (so named prior to 1825), a tributary of the Southwest branch of the Miramichi River, and then travel northeast "with an instantaneousness resembling a train of gunpowder," wiping out the villages along the north side of the river. The settlements farther back from the Miramichi River, in the rear of Douglastown and along the Bartibog and Nappan Rivers, were "the great theatre of suffering" because their waters were so low that summer that they offered no means of escape. Although he noted that some damage occurred east of the Bartibog River, "W" drew the fire's main boundaries as being from the source of the Northwest branch of the Miramichi River in the west to the Nepisiguit River in the north and to the Bartibog River in the east; he made no mention of its boundary south of the Miramichi settlements. Within this region, all "buildings, goods, and fences of man" were consumed, and the standing timber formed "a vast amphitheatre of blackened, dead, and useless forest trees – daily falling, encumbering the land, and rendering it almost impassable for man or beast."[130] What Cooney's accounting of the fire's size in *A Compendious History* a year later lacked in the way of new detail (although he did add Ludlow Parish, home of Boiestown, to the sites of destruction), he made up for in concision, concluding that the fire had burned almost 6,000 square miles. (In an autobiography decades later, Cooney confirmed this figure and added the Cains River area to the path of destruction.)[131] The evocative nature of Cooney's writing and the authority he held from having been on the scene for the disaster meant that his description was reproduced widely. An area of 6,000 square miles – and its rough equivalent of 4 million acres – became the standard reference for the fire's size in the nineteenth century and beyond.[132]

But even as the Miramichi Fire's size and shape became solidified, a few reports from knowledgeable mid-century travellers, appraising the New Brunswick colony with a critical eye to its mining, agricultural, and forestry potential, added additional information about the fire's shape. The Nova Scotian geologist and inventor of kerosene Abraham Gesner affirmed Cooney's figure, but when travelling along tributaries of the Upper Tobique River, near the western edge of the colony, he stated that this area had been overrun by the 1825 fire, too.[133] Surveyor James Alexander wrote in 1849 of coming across the fire's aftermath when he reached the Gaspereau and Cains Rivers, the southernmost mention within the region to date.[134] In 1855 agricultural chemist James F.W. Johnston extended the fire 20 kilometres farther east, as far as the Burnt Church River, based on information provided to him by "Mr. Rankin" while in the Miramichi.[135] Finally, surveyor Alexander Monro in 1855 came up with the same figure as Cooney had a generation earlier as to the fire's size but offered – without any accompanying evidence – more precision as to its outer boundaries: "[A]lmost the entire country, from within a short distance of the Gulf shore, and the head of the Tabusintac river, thence nearly to the Falls of the Nipissiquit, and from the vicinity in the direction of the Tobique River, and near to its head, and in another direction, beginning at the mouth of the Miramichi River, embracing both its banks, and extending in some places, beyond the present limits of the county to the Nashwaak river, in the county of York, thus comprehending in the whole, nearly 4,000,000 acres of the best lumbering region of the Province."[136]

I engage in this cataloguing to give greater definition to the Miramichi Fire. However, some of the reports, by survivors too close to the action or writers too far from it, are undoubtedly exaggerated or in error. A worse mistake would be to assume that the accounts are cumulative, that wallpapering a map of New Brunswick with all of the reports on top of one another will reveal an accurate portrait of the fire. (One could as easily make a cumulative map of where the fire *didn't* burn and conclude that the fire never happened.) It is nevertheless worth noting that everyone who wrote about the fire within the first generation of it – during the time when people were best able to dispute others' accounts – were in general agreement as to the fire's range and ferocity. Everyone who discussed its range accepted that it burned over a rectangle roughly 60 by 100 miles (95 by 160 kilometres), or roughly 6,000 square miles (15,500 square kilometres), which was roughly one-fifth of New Brunswick. No accounts dispute this assessment.

Except one.

On 31 October 1825, Thomas Baillie, the commissioner of Crown lands and forests and the surveyor general for the colony, wrote to his superior, Earl Bathurst, secretary of the Colonial Office, saying that if Bathurst had received word of a recent forest fire, not to worry: "An exaggerate statement, would most probably be too freely promulgated in the United Kingdom, which would reduce the entries in the several ports of this Province by deterring those merchants who are in the habit of trading for Timber, from sending their vessels for the usual supply. It however gives me great pleasure to be able to inform your Lordship that but a small proportion of Timber has been destroyed; and even that, where the wood has formerly been worked, the groves having been rendered more open; and quantities of chips and Pine Tops lying in all directions served to conduct the flame." Not only had the forest fire not burned many trees; it had actually cleaned up the forest, readying it for more forestry! Baillie went on to say that although the fire had burned along the Miramichi River's Northwest branch, "the great body of Pine remains yet untouched" along the headwaters of the Northwest and Southwest branches. He even enclosed a map (which has since disappeared). Baillie concluded his letter, "The fire has appeared in different parts of the Province, but the injury done to the Timber is so trifling that I will not trouble your Lordship with a further detail."[137]

"Untouched." "Trifling." Such was the on-the-ground opinion of the person most responsible for New Brunswick's forests just weeks after the great fire. What is the opposite of a smoking gun – a dripping hose?

But there is good reason to doubt the accuracy, and even sincerity, of Baillie's letter. Thomas Baillie had earned his government position the old-fashioned way: through patronage. His father, William, was tight in British political circles, and his older brother, George, was head clerk in the North American department of the Colonial Office in London when the twenty-eight-year-old Thomas was hired there as a clerk in 1824. Within a few months, Thomas received the New Brunswick appointment at ten times his previous salary.[138] So he was new to the colony and to the job in 1825, making it unlikely that he visited the Miramichi at all before the great fire. And it is unlikely that he did so immediately afterward. There are reports of him being in Fredericton on 11 and 21 October, so even if he somehow did visit the Miramichi by river or road before writing the Colonial Office on 31 October, he could not possibly have made a survey of the backwoods.[139] The commissioner of Crown lands and forests instead relied on reports by public servants such as Deputy Land Surveyor George N. Smith, whose 20 October letter to him began, "An immense tract of the County of Northumberland & its settlements have been laid waste by a destructive fire."[140]

Thomas Baillie's letter downplaying the fire was clearly written to ensure that the timber trade kept moving. The Colonial Office could use the letter to reassure British timber merchants that the colony still had wood, that the wood was available, and that it was still in their interests to sail across the Atlantic and get it. Indeed, George Baillie wrote Governor Howard Douglas two months later saying that his brother Thomas's letter "has greatly relieved us as to the future Trade of the Province, as a Commissary in Nova Scotia ... wrote to the Treasury, saying that the Province would not be able to *export any Lumber for many years*. I shall therefore make an intimation by and bye to prevent the absurd reports on this head from being credited and perhaps preventing some of the Merchants from sending their ships as usual."[141] Thomas Baillie's letter had done its job. When Baillie wrote in reference to the Miramichi Fire in later years, he never again said that its destruction was overstated.[142]

✴✴✴

Thomas Baillie very nearly became a victim of forest fire himself on 7 October 1825. That afternoon, his newly built home a mile outside Fredericton was threatened by fire from the nearby woods. The town's fire engines were called into action, and many of Fredericton's inhabitants rushed to the scene, led by garrison troops and Governor Douglas, whose own residence, Government House, had succumbed to flames barely two weeks earlier. Baillie's house was saved, but then word came that fire had broken out back in town. The citizens hurried back to the capital, but in the hours it took to defeat the blaze as it raged through York and Queen Streets, forty-one houses – one-third of the town – were destroyed. No one was killed, at least.[143]

Of course, it is hardly coincidental that Fredericton burned on the same day as the Miramichi settlements. The two locations are only 150 kilometres apart, and the capital is only about 70 kilometres from what would become accepted as the fire's southwest corner, the forests along the Southwest branch of the Miramichi River. Fuels had been building up in the forests of both areas for years because of everything from spruce budworm infestation to the extended cold spell of the 1810s. The areas also shared the same fire season throughout that summer – right up to the day itself. Those fighting the Fredericton blaze grew exhausted, it was said, from "the weather then being intensely and unseasonably hot, and the wind blowing with great violence" – the same conditions occurring in the Miramichi that evening.[144] For much the same reasons, it is also not coincidental that a forest fire destroyed fifteen houses on 7 October 1825 along the

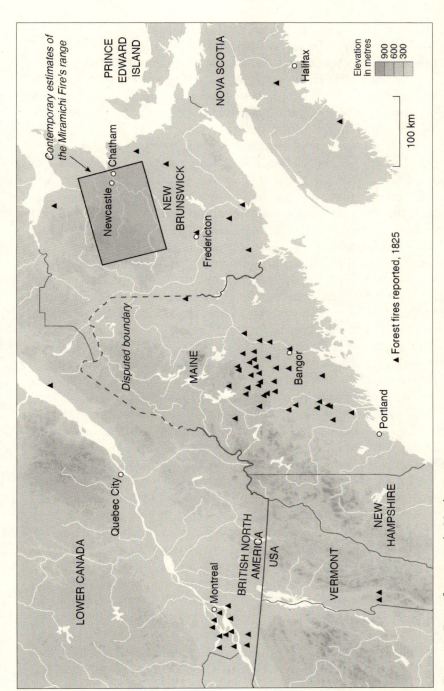

Figure 3.1 Forest fires across the Northeast, 1825.

Oromocto River, 40 kilometres south of Fredericton.[145] Or that fires burned that day in Charlotte County in the very southwest corner of the colony.[146] Or that they burned that day or that season in Nova Scotia, and in Gaspé, and around Montreal, and in Vermont.[147] Or that they burned in Maine, where the fires of 1825 are still the most extensive in the state's history, estimated to have covered approximately 3,400 square kilometres.

The Miramichi Fire's presumed range came into focus and consolidated in the months and years after the disaster to the point that it was understood to have covered a rough rectangle of 15,500 square kilometres in northeastern New Brunswick. But setting this area as its limits was itself something of a consolidation because fire burned throughout other parts of northeastern North America that day and that season – and, as we will see, some commentators believed these blazes to be joined. Although it might be assumed that fires beyond the Miramichi region are not within the scope of a book on the Miramichi Fire, they are, for four reasons. First, they provide necessary context about the broader fire season and so improve understanding of the fire that burned in the Miramichi itself. Second, they underscore the significance of the charitable efforts made by people in places such as Lower Canada and Maine to assist the people of the Miramichi region, although they experienced forest fires of their own. Third, they demonstrate how historical memory of the largest fire complex ever on the Eastern Seaboard has been distorted: the fire in the Miramichi overshadowed and ultimately subsumed others throughout the Northeast that fall, such that "Miramichi Fire" has become shorthand for all the fires that season, even though burning that occurred beyond the Miramichi region has been largely forgotten. And fourth, since fires smoulder and flare up, divide and unite, it may well be that one or more of these fires distant in time from 7 October or distant in space from the Miramichi ultimately *did* become part of the Miramichi Fire. Understanding the Miramichi Fire demands understanding the fires beyond the Miramichi.

The charity pamphlet described the 7 October fire as "desolating various parts of America, from Brockville [Upper Canada] to Miramichi, and from the Saint Lawrence to the Penobscot" River of southern Maine, but it would be more accurate to say that fire was ubiquitous across northeastern North America that summer and fall.[148] Within New Brunswick itself, the fire that day was just the

Leafs vs Flames

capstone of a season of fires. Smoke had been seen rising in the province's interior throughout the summer – which calls into question, of course, how long what became the Miramichi Fire had been blazing. Looking back from 1832, Robert Cooney told of fires not only on the Gaspé Peninsula but also along the entire eastern coast of New Brunswick from the Bay of Chaleur toward Westmorland County. These fires, he was quick to say, were of "rather ordinary circumstances" compared to what would befall the Miramichi.[149] Fire also raged through the woods of peninsular Nova Scotia for two months, extinguished only by rain that fall.[150]

Lower Canada also had an intense fire season. Montreal was particularly hard hit, dealing not just with the threat from forest fires nearby but also with the ordinary urban fires common to wooden colonial towns. In the heat of early September, a fire broke out in Montreal's east-end "Quebec suburbs" and spread quickly, destroying upward of sixty houses. Citizens were said to be "in a very frightened condition, from the entire want of engines, of water in many places, and of any organized institution" responsible for fighting the flames.[151] They grew more frightened when a rash of fires in Laprairie, across the river from the Island of Montreal, was blamed on arson. Newspapers whipped up hysteria about "the Laprairie incendiaries," which made even fires in the forest seem suspicious that flammable season.[152] But given the weather conditions and the sheer number of fires that were burning in the woods, the more likely culprit was careless land clearing for either forestry or agriculture; call it accidental arson. Fires blazed all around Montreal, on both sides of the Ottawa and Saint Lawrence Rivers, from the woodlands between Lac des Deux Montagnes and Saint-Eustache to the west, at Vaudreuil and Les Cèdres (The Cedars) in the southwest, at Beauharnois and Chateauguay in the south, and on Île Jésus and the Island of Montreal itself.[153] A newspaper from Potsdam, New York, warned that forest fires were burning along the 50 miles from Pointe-des-Cascades west of Montreal to Glengarry in Upper Canada and 50 miles back from the Saint Lawrence River all that way, "making 2,500 square miles of land on fire!"[154] This was surely an exaggeration and was suggestive of how easily the press could stoke a fire's size and significance. But it was not an exaggeration when a Montreal newspaper concluded in late October, "We believe that it is not in the recollection of any person now alive, when fires were so frequent in the forests of America as they have been during the last and present months."[155]

The simultaneity of the fires in Montreal and the Miramichi region meant that in Montrealers' public memory, the two became joined. Incredibly, Montrealers came to refer to the local blazes as the Miramichi Fire, as though the beast that threatened their town had shambled eastward and eventually wiped out communities 600 kilometres away. (And, of course, although it is unlikely, that may be exactly what happened.) The fire that passed through the Beauharnois and Chateauguay seigniories on the south side of the Saint Lawrence River that year and the longstanding visible damage it left in the Teafield cedar swamps just north of Huntingdon made it easy for that area to remain associated with 1825 and so with the most famous fire of that year. "Upon the upper side of this immense swamp, stretching over many thousand acres," the *Montreal Courier* wrote in 1843, "[T]here yet remains terrible evidences of the Miramichi fire. This tract of country is called the 'Pine Plains,' and its name to those who have ever looked upon it is synonymous with desolation in its most hideous form."[156] As late as the 1880s, when newspaperman Robert Sellar interviewed 300 settlers of the region about times past, the term "Miramichi" still came up repeatedly in reference to the Montreal-area fires of 1825. One man, for example, recalled that "[t]he fall we came was that of the Miramichi fires. The largest [fire] was behind the village and along the creek." Sellar's book contains one of the most arresting accounts of a settler's encounter with fire during that "fall of Miramichi fires," as he called it. W.C. Roberts recounted,

> I was ... coming down Covey hill [close to the US border] with
> a load of corn, when I saw the fire darting from the west.
> Unhitching the oxen, I ran with them and just got across in time.
> Although there was little wind, the fire passed like lightning over
> the ground, the extreme dryness of the soil from great drouth
> and the thick covering of fallen leaves being favorable. You may
> suppose how quick the fire ran, from hens dropping dead into
> it from their roosts on fences and trees. Where the sled was left
> happened to be a hollow, and being moist around it, the fire did
> not touch it or the corn. Many settlers had outbuildings burned
> and the smoke from the mucky land to the north was so pungent
> that we were like to be suffocated. The low ground was badly
> burned, and long tracks of blackened trees channelled the forest.

Sellar also remarked that the smoke in Huntingdon that autumn was "afterwards believed to have come from New Brunswick," but it is unclear whether residents really believed that the fire they experienced and the one in New Brunswick were one and the same.[157] What is clear is that they found the term "Miramichi Fire" sufficiently expressive and the fire itself sufficiently expansive that they were comfortable adopting it as their own.

As significant as the fire season was in Nova Scotia and Lower Canada, it was much more severe in Maine. The Pine Tree State was as dominated by forests and forest cutting as neighbouring New Brunswick and as susceptible to combustion that sizzling-dry year. Reports of fire throughout the south-central part of the state began to appear in late August, touching Bowdointown (Bowdoinham), Hallowell, and Augusta to the west as well as Sebec and Bangor farther east.[158] From Norridgewock in Somerset County, it was said, "In every town and on almost every farm for some weeks past the woods have presented one continued sheet of fire and devastation."[159] Because there was somewhat earlier and more settlement in Maine's interior than in New Brunswick's, its rural folk were more familiar with forest fires, and so inhabitants of threatened regions seem to have taken more precautions against them. Wooden fences were torn down. Swabs were tied to long poles, ready to blot out fires on the roofs of cabins. Barrels of water were stationed outside homes. Spare clothes and bedding were buried just in case.[160] The Norridgewock article noted that such safeguards had so far prevented the invader from doing much damage to property, but it added, "The danger still continues, however, and nothing can remove it but (what we have not seen for a long time) a good wholesome, soaking rain." That did not come, and on 8 September a Bangor reporter – writing as fire ran within his town – told of a 30-mile "sea of fire" burning along both sides of the Penobscot River. The roaring of the flames was like thunder and could be heard 15 miles away.[161] Newspapers reported that fires blazed around the communities of Williamsburg, Brownville, Sebec, Atkinson, Blakesburg (Bradford), Milo, Kilmarnock (Medford), and Sebois in Penobscot and Somerset Counties, centred in what is now Piscataquis County.[162] Although fires were said to be "more extensive than ever known before,"[163] they were defined almost exclusively in terms of the towns they threatened, not a more general range. Regardless, the fire season then went quiet for a time.

"The light rains in September checked the fires," a Maine newspaper would report a month later, "but the hot weather since has dried the

84 *The Miramichi Fire*

ground, and the strong wind on Friday night last [7 October] sent them raging as severely as ever." The state was hit by the same storm system as New Brunswick – or a stronger version of it since it was likely weakening as it headed northeastward up the coast. Smouldering wildfires flared up all over. On the evening of 7 October, a Captain Loring sailing off Portland – that is, off the southwest corner of Maine – saw the "reflection of a large fire upon the sky" extending to the north toward Penobscot.[164] There was news out of Hallowell, in Kennebec County, that the whole country was on fire for more than 100 miles and that flames travelling northeast from Belgrade and Sidney had thrived in the lowland peat and burned to a depth of 10 feet.[165] Communities in Somerset and Penobscot Counties in the centre of the state, particularly Guilford, Ripley, Parkman (Parkham), Harmony, Dover, and Moorstown (Abbot), were listed repeatedly in the press as having suffered on 7 October.[166] Yet the nature of that suffering was fundamentally different from that faced in New Brunswick. Consider a newspaper account of how the fire entered Bangor that day. After describing circumstances so similar to those experienced in the Miramichi that they might be lifted from an article about it – wind shifting from the southwest to northwest-north, flames bursting suddenly out of the woods – the author concluded, "But the most distressing part of our relation is yet to come. Twelve buildings with most of their content were totally destroyed."[167] The Maine fires resulted in the loss of pines and property, not persons, so when word arrived of the more extravagant disaster in the Miramichi, the Maine ones were quickly eclipsed. As a result, there was actually less in the press that fall about Maine's 7 October fires than there had been about the almost certainly smaller ones earlier in the summer. In public memory, however, the two distinct fire periods merged, making it all the more difficult to determine what had burned on 7 October.

Once it was understood that Maine and New Brunswick had each experienced historic fire events on the very same day, it is little wonder that many assumed that the fires were connected – that they were not, in effect, fires at all, but a single fire. "This devastating element," in the words of a newspaper article reprinted in the charity pamphlet, "hurried through the wildernesses of Maine on the Atlantic and swept onwards on the blast of the hurricane, until stayed by the waters of the Gulf of St. Lawrence."[168] It became routine in early accounts to mention the fires in Maine when describing the 1825 conflagration as a means of showing the scope of the disaster, but the death and destruction on the Miramichi River utterly overshadowed what happened elsewhere. As a result, no writer of the day attempted to map the fire's path between Maine and New Brunswick – for example, to see whether the fire that Massachusetts land agent George Coffin witnessed near the international border on 7 October actually crossed it.[169] The closest anyone came to trying was when "W," in the *Chatham Gleaner and Northumberland Schediasma* in 1831, tracked the fire's advance across New Brunswick – starting at the colony's extreme southwest corner, right on the border with Maine. "Commencing in the County of Charlotte," he wrote, "on the left bank of the Maguaguadavic, embracing both sides of the Piskehagan, sweeping over the rocky heights to the sources of the South West branch of the Oromocto, and descending that river to near its confluence with the St. John, the fire can be traced in a broad and dreary zone, extending in width on the right bank of the river towards the mountains bounding the Black Creek" and then on toward Fredericton and the Miramichi.[170] As mentioned, "W" was almost certainly the *Gleaner*'s own Robert Cooney, who would publish *A Compendious History* the following year. In that book, he provided none of this detail; he was focusing on the Miramichi component of the blaze so as to position it as the defining event in the region's history. He would be successful, and so the writer who most carefully mapped the fire in New Brunswick beyond the Miramichi became the writer who, more than anyone, solidified its range as principally in the Miramichi. After Cooney, the 1825 fires of Maine and New Brunswick only moved farther apart.

There is a lovely 1829 map by Maine cartographer Moses Greenleaf showing the northeastward progress of colonization of the state since the American Revolution. Superimposing reported 1825 fire locations on this map reveals that most of the burns occurred in newly settled territory and that there were relatively few reports of fires beyond.[171] These findings are only to be expected, for two reasons. For one thing, land clearing, timber cutting, wood heating, cooking, and other trappings of human settlement all increase the potential for fires that get out of hand; generally speaking, where there are fewer people, there are fewer fires. But for another thing, places that are more settled, particularly those with newspapers, are more likely to record their experiences; where there are fewer people, there are fewer reports of fire. There is ample evidence that fires burned in populated areas around Montreal, in southern Maine, and in eastern New Brunswick

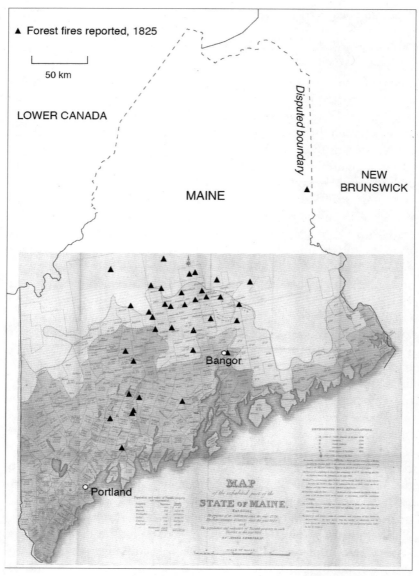

Figure 3.2 Reported forest fires in Maine, 1825. Overlain on Moses Greenleaf's *Map of the Inhabited Part of the State of Maine* (1829). Greenleaf's map shows the northward spread of settlement, the lightest shaded band representing land settled in 1800–20.

in the summer and fall of 1825. But if you draw a straight line on a map from Montreal through northern Maine to the Miramichi, it passes through some of the least populated parts of northeastern North America – then and now. Fires could well have burned there and gone unreported. Of course, this possibility is in no way evidence that fire *did* burn anywhere along that line. Rather, it is an acknowledgment that some things can never be known. And that is worth knowing.

***

There had been so much criticism of the Miramichi timber trade before the fire, on the grounds that it ruined society and souls, that one would expect that in the wake of the great fire the I-told-you-sos must have rained down as swiftly and steadily as spotting. But early accounts were more restrained than that. Although survivors and writers did, of course, speculate as to the fire's cause, the focus was on the suffering. Governor Douglas, for example, who had warned the region about focusing on lumbering to the detriment of agriculture, said only that fires had "burst in a blood of flame upon the devoted settlements on the Miramichi river, and have occasioned ruin, desolation, death, and misery, where late I witnessed prosperity, plenty, and comfort."[172] There were lessons to be learned from the fire, but they could be learned later. It would take years for the "blood of flame" to become a flood of blame.

Many of the earliest accounts interpreted the fire as having a purely natural cause. Some thought lightning was responsible. It was noted that the ship *George Canning* had been struck by lightning on the night of the blaze as it sailed into the Miramichi: a mast had been shivered, and a crewman had either been killed or "palsied."[173] But it is actually surprising how rarely the fire was, and has been, blamed on lightning – surprising in that it would have been a reasonable, untraceable cause of a fire that started distant from human settlements and so would have saved pinning the blame on humans.[174] Others believed that combustion had occurred spontaneously, the product of a hot summer and forests as dry as tinder. This was the opinion, for example, of Dafydd Amos in the Welsh folksong he produced.[175] John McGregor noted that northeastern New Brunswick contained "boundless fir forests, every tree of which contains, in its trunk, bark, branches and leaves, vast quantities of the most inflammable resins."[176] Conifers have naturally lower moisture content than do deciduous

88   *The Miramichi Fire*

trees, and this level dips still lower in the course of the year when they, as James Alexander stated, "full of resin, are dried up by intense heat of the summer sun."[177] But combustion, let alone spontaneous combustion, was too imperfectly understood for any commentator of the era to speak with authority as to when it might occur. In 1838 New Brunswick historian Peter Fisher admitted that some blamed the great fire on spontaneous combustion, but he saw no reason to make that leap, whereas three years later Cornish journalist James Silk Buckingham concluded that it could not be ruled out.[178]

One newspaper in the fall of 1825 identified the Miramichi Fire as offering an exceptional opportunity to better understand nature's workings. "It is perfectly evident," stated the *Montreal Herald*, "that this fire, like that which lately ravaged Upper and Lower Canada, must have been occasioned by the rays of the Sun, operating on some inflamable matter on the surface of the Earth during an unparalleled hot and dry summer." The editor argued that this process was not merely of abstract concern but of real importance for people living in eastern North America. There were many hotter places on the globe, but there may not "be a spot on earth covered with so much combustible matter as there is to be found in these regions." The *Herald* therefore called on citizens to share everything they had observed about the fire and the events surrounding it:

> This is a phenomenon well worthy of the attention of naturalists; and it appears to us, that to collect all the information that can be obtained relating to an event so alarming and devastating, would be a matter of curiosity, if not of real utility. We should therefore suggest to all gentlemen living in the country, who have had personal demonstration of the destructive effects of the late fires, the propriety of communicating to the public, through the Newspapers, all that may have come under their observation regarding so unusual an occurrence. By this means it might be possible ... to trace the manner in which the great heat of last summer operated in producing the fires which have spread such alarm and devastation through the northern continent.[179]

This proposal – that newspapers could serve as conduits for the transmission and compilation of ordinary citizens' knowledge of the world – was revolutionary and would have made them truly social media. If it had been implemented, this book would have been written

Leafs vs Flames

a century ago. But the idea was so forward-thinking that no one, not even the *Herald* itself, followed up on it. The *Quebec City Gazette* mocked its rival for supposing that fire may have burned spontaneously – in effect, for tracing the fire back to environmental conditions rather than a human agent. The *Gazette* wrote that "a courier from the planet Mercury which called in at the principal towns of Venus and the Moon" had informed it that these locales had been on fire that summer, too, "which we attribute to their 'combustible matter.'"[180]

These journalists' thoughts had likely turned skyward because some commentators hazarded that the Miramichi Fire's cause was celestial. An extremely bright and long-visible comet – Comet Pons, C/1825 N1 – attracted attention across North America all that fall; the *Montreal Gazette* attributed the heat wave of early October, and indeed all that summer, to its passage.[181] After news of the fire, it was natural to link the comet to the disaster – a word that comes, after all, from the Italian *disastro*, "bad star." Baltimore's *Niles' Weekly Register* noted that a writer in a New York paper "ventures the opinion that comets are bodies of *fire*, and that the earth will be brushed by the *tail* of one now visible" – and immediately below this account printed an article about the wildfires in Maine.[182]

Whereas some people looked to the sky for answers, most assumed that the Miramichi Fire had been caused by people back on earth. Exactly who, however, was up for debate. The November 1825 issue of Montreal's *La bibliothèque canadienne* magazine began a series of reports about the fire with a passage from Virgil: "Nam sæ incautis pastoribus excidit ignis" – "Since often fire is left behind by a careless shepherd." But the editor's translation was more inclusive: "Il arrive quelquefois qu'un berger imprudent, un bucheron, un chasseur, met le feu" – adding to the shepherd (i.e., the farmer), the lumberer and the hunter as the possible incendiary.[183]

Lumberers seemed the most obvious suspects: they had means, motive, and opportunity. They were capable of setting fires (admittedly, like all humans). They had reason to set fires. As Joseph Bouchette noted in 1831, "It is not an uncommon thing for fires to be lighted in the woods, sometimes for the protection which the smoke affords from muskitoes and flies, and sometimes for the assistance it affords the lumberers in clearing the brushwood."[184] Clearing logging sites of slash was a commonplace cause of wildfires in this era; in 1821 such fires were already said to have taken a "heavy toll" on forests up the Saint Croix River along the Maine–New Brunswick border.[185] And the lumberers were in great numbers in the backwoods, where the fire had presumably begun. Underlying the belief that lumbermen caused the fire was the opinion that they were instruments of their own God-ordained punishment. An old woodsman told Scottish author James Alexander in the 1840s, "We wanted that fire; from the Tobique to the Miramichi, the lumberers were very wicked; they gloried in their lumber, in their pine forests, and led very bad lives in their camps; an when they came into the settlements, they drank, gambled, and swore, and fought. Saturday and Sunday were all the same to them, and they cared for neither God, man, nor devil. The fire was a judgment on the land."[186] To many observers, lumbermen had caused the fire one way or another.

But as much as lumbermen seemed both potential and apt culprits, it was universally agreed that the land-clearing practices of settlers were just as likely to have caused the fire. Commissioner of Crown Lands and Forests Thomas Baillie described the cut-and-burn process of clearing land in an 1832 emigrants guide: the settler felled 4 or 5 acres of woodland, waited until the wood was dry, set fire to the clearing, and – since this fire would consume only brush – rolled the logs into piles and set fire to that, repeating the process over and over until all was ashes.[187] This was a routine part of the settler's work year: Upper Canadian farmer Benjamin Smith wrote in his diary of devoting sixteen full days between June and November 1825 to piling and burning brush and logs.[188] There was no help for it: in such circumstances, fire occasionally got out of hand. The charity pamphlet pointed responsibility squarely in that direction. Miramichi residents had observed flames in the distance, it noted, "but fires in the woods are usual every summer in the British provinces, being the mode of clearing the soil adopted by the farmers, and no damage was anticipated nor the slightest apprehension." The pamphlet was also the first to draw a lesson from the fire, suggesting that more caution was needed in clearing woodland. "That settlements should never be made until a sufficient extent of country be cleared to protect them from fires in the woods, seems also an object of the first importance."[189] Of course, there was a catch-22 here: to make a settlement safe from fire, the land around it had to be cleared, but clearing it meant setting fire. In 1830 Scottish forest theorist Thomas Cruickshank warned the people of his country against "tampering with that element in the neighbourhood of plantations" and used the Miramichi Fire example as an object lesson. Immigrants to New

Brunswick had been conditioned by British forest practice, and now the favour was being returned.[190]

A few writers accused the Mi'gmaq of having caused the Miramichi Fire – conspicuously, the sole time that contemporary white sources mentioned the Indigenous population in reference to the fire at all. Discussing the blaze in the context of North American forest fires generally, the *London Examiner* noted, "Sometimes they occurred in consequence of the carelessness of the Indians, over which the colonist had no control."[191] New Brunswick historian Peter Fisher, after describing the great fire in his 1838 *Notitia*, suggested that it was surprising such fire in the forests did not happen more often given "the numerous classes of persons such as Indians, lumberers, and others, who roam through the wilderness, and light up fires where they encamp, or shake the embers out of their pipes among dry leaves and other combustibles, and pass on unheedful of the evils of their thoughtlessness."[192] Ironically, by the end of the nineteenth century, forest conservationists had rebranded Indigenous people as stewards of the forests said to be more careful with fire than were lumbermen and especially settlers.[193]

Whether pointing to lumberers or settlers or Mi'gmaq, many writers traced the great fire back to carelessness. It had long been recognized as a problem in well-forested North America. Indeed, New Brunswick's first forest conservation law had been the 1786 Act to Prevent the Burning Woods, by Carelessly or Wantonly Firing the Same, which was still on the books in 1825. Anyone who left a fire they had set without securing it was liable for a £3 fine plus damages.[194] But carelessness implies that it was within people's capacity to wholly manage fire, and it is not at all obvious that this was the case. Clearing land for agriculture or as preparation for lumbering necessitated fires of significant size, and the forests of northeastern New Brunswick were dense enough and the population sparse enough that there was no realistic hope of containing every single blaze. Moreover, until the invention of the friction match – in 1826, actually – the common method for fire starting was striking flint with steel to ignite tinder, a process that could take half an hour.[195] Once you had gotten a fire burning, there was significant motivation to keep it burning.

Moreover, North Americans of the day simply did not think about trees or forests – and therefore about forest fires – as we do today. Colonists had moved from places where forests were scarce to a place where they were seemingly inexhaustible, and they had quickly come to take them for granted. "Trees in England ... are statistics, as it were – so many trees, *ergo*, so many owners so rich," stated the popular American writer Nathaniel P. Willis. "In America, on the contrary, trees grow, and waters run, as the stars shine, quite unmeaningly."[196] Trees were, if anything, in the way, so there was nothing like the stigma that is felt today when someone sets fire to woods accidentally. Or on purpose. Elizabeth Simcoe, wife of the first lieutenant governor of Upper Canada, so enjoyed taking walks along the Saint Lawrence River while settlers' land-clearing fires burned that she told her diary, "Perhaps you have no idea of the pleasure of walking in a burning wood, but I found it so great that I think I shall have some woods set on fire for my evening walks. The smoke arising from it keeps the mosquitoes at a distance, and when the fire has caught the hollow trunk of a lofty tree, the flame issuing from the top has a fine effect."[197] That was in 1792, but such attitudes endured through many decades and many forest fires. In 1851 agricultural chemist James F.W. Johnston was in New Brunswick making his way toward the Miramichi when his party "amused ourselves by setting fire to the bark of the birch-trees," taking pleasure in the "very beautiful sight ... It destroys the trees, of course; but, in these forests, trees are of no value; and it is to the making of such experiments that, in very warm and arid weather, the firing of whole tracts of forest are often to be ascribed."[198] He was lighting his fires in October – too late in the season, he believed, for them to spread. Birch is an early-successional species that thrives in a post-fire environment, so it is possible Johnston was burning trees that had grown up in the ashes of an October 1825 fire.

It is little wonder, in retrospect, that most early accounts of the Miramichi Fire paid little attention to what might have caused the blaze. It was not merely that commentators did not possess the necessary information to offer an opinion; this deficit did not stop them from estimating the fire's size or death toll, for example. Rather, they felt there was little to be gained by knowing. Fires were the car crashes of the nineteenth century, being ubiquitous and sufficiently random as to seem inevitable by-products of society's healthy operation. It would have been productive for New Brunswickers of the time to consider not causes but *factors*. How much of the fire's severity was due to the summer's heat? Or to migrants' unfamiliarity with forest fire? Or to spruce budworm having killed so many trees a few years earlier? But such analysis was largely beyond them. Later in the nineteenth century and throughout the twentieth, writers would be

Leafs vs Flames

more open to taking lessons from and so laying blame for the Miramichi Fire, but at the time fire in the forest was simply too familiar and too foreign.

✳✳✳

After witnessing a forest fire rage at the Maine–New Brunswick border on 7 October, the Massachusetts and Maine land agents George Coffin and James Irish continued on toward Fredericton, arriving three days later. There, they found the people "all in confusion" from the fire that had destroyed a section of the town, causing an estimated £35,000 in damages. Coffin and Irish again tried to meet with Commissioner of Crown Lands and Forests Thomas Baillie but were told that although he wished to speak with them more about the timber licensing issue, he was out of the office dealing with a fire in the woods raging near his house.[199] They waited two days at the Fredericton Hotel, but he never got back to them. James Irish would grumble in his official report that they were unsure whether Baillie had really been saving his home or just avoiding them, but they thought that it was likely the latter.[200] The two land agents returned, uneventfully, to the United States.

Coffin's and Irish's accounts of their mission to New Brunswick would be nothing more than an interesting perspective on the 1825 fire season except for an order they gave during their journey. When on 4 October they dispatched their boatmen Ezekiel Chase and John Fowle to make for the headwaters of the Aroostook River, and from there down the Penobscot River to Bangor, they directed the two "to examine the rivers, streams, lakes, mountains, & also ascertain, if any timber was cutting by trespassers, & mark the same if any MxM, also if they found any Hay cut on the undivided land, to put fire to it, & burn the whole."[201] Meadow hay served as fodder for the draft animals employed in unlicensed timber operations and was a commodity in its own right, selling for a dollar per ton, but its portability meant government officials could not simply impound it as they could timber. Irish recounted in his report an incident earlier that year when his men had been turned back by timber thieves in the interior who – in the style of the Boston Tea Party – "blacked themselves," "called themselves Mohawks," and threatened to kill them. Irish wrote that when an unnamed sheriff under his direction subsequently came upon cut hay in a deserted illegal timber operation, "the only means left to protect the timber, was to destroy the hay" – that is, burn it – so "joint

94   *The Miramichi Fire*

orders were given with great caution, to destroy the hay. This being the only alternative. The hay was accordingly destroyed; and the Agent is happy to say, without occasioning any damage, or loss, to public, or private property."[202]

If it sounds as though Irish doth protest too much, that is because by the time he wrote his report, he and Coffin were being blamed for having ordered the setting of fires that had swept across Maine that summer. The accusations had started while they were still in New Brunswick. A letter appeared in a Bangor newspaper in mid-September, purportedly from Penobscot Indian leader John Neptune, accusing Irish and his man Chase, a captain in the Revolutionary War, not merely of starting the fires but of having done so on purpose: "What meanum states agent send Captain Chase to burnum hay when everything so dry – Indian two township all burn up before rane come – Indian lossum all timber and hay … When indian havum all timber and hay nobody burnum hay – now state gettum all indian land but two township, then he settum fire to drive all indian off."[203] This suspicion then spread to include the 7 October fire, although Chase and Fowle in fact had an airtight alibi: they had left Grand Falls, New Brunswick, on foot on 4 October, and so had not been in a position to set fires that burned west to east across Maine three days later. Nevertheless, white squatters in eastern Maine complained that "Collin" and Irish had purposely burned them out.[204] Newspapers were undecided as to whether the land agents were actually responsible for the fires – and those who said they were assumed that their motivation was to disrupt illegal timber operations rather than displace Indigenous people. But it is a statement as to the perceived inevitability of fire in the nineteenth century that even these newspapers were not all that upset about it.[205]

The idea that the state's own officials had caused the state's worst fires was so delicious that it became woven into public memory. A good example is the sprawling and strange 1882 *History of Penobscot County, Maine*, a book written by numerous anonymous contributors whose entries often utterly contradict one another. One author republished John Neptune's letter, although rejecting its accusation.[206] Others defended Irish directly, suggesting that Neptune had been the dupe of unlicensed lumberers seeking to discredit the land agent. "It is very certain that, if it had not been for the lawless acts of the timber and hay thieves, there would have been no occasion of complaint against the Land Agent for burning their hay," it was said. And regardless, "[t]he utmost care was enjoined."[207] Another claimed that Ezekiel Chase was just going about his business as an agent of the state when "[t]he great fire of that year in the north woods came upon him while thus engaged, and he had to flee with the utmost dispatch."[208] He found safety on the slopes of a nearby mountain that, two centuries on, is still named Mount Chase. The story's details continued to blur. In 1899 the *New York Times* précised the 1825 Maine fire as a latter-day expulsion of Acadians: "two special constables" were bent on evicting "French Canadians" and, "after turning the families out, set fire to the houses and haystack." Soon, "the biggest forest fire ever known in the State was sweeping north, burning off more than fifty townships of old-growth pine and doing more than $10,000,000 damage to the State lands."[209]

Like so much about the Miramichi Fire, it is impossible to know for sure whether a small fire set by the agents' men caused or contributed to the fires that bedevilled Maine – and New Brunswick? – that year. But also, like so much about the Miramichi Fire, this uncertainty did not stop people such as James Irish or John Neptune from speaking with absolute conviction. The very fact that the fire's cause was unknown, that its existence was ephemeral, and that its range was unclear meant that it was open for interpretation, able to serve the arguments of whoever needed it. But the fire's effects were real, and it had a profound influence on the people and nature of the Miramichi region and beyond.

4

The Phoenix

Survivors and sufferers – The phoenix effect – The morning after – The dead and their toll – Anarchy avoided – Relief and embarrassment – Help from all over – American charity – Britain is heard from – Poyais and panic – An unexpected visitor – A man, a plan, a ship, a town: Douglas – The call to farm – Let no man quit the country – A rivalry arises from the ashes – When a disaster seems insufficiently disastrous – Dispensing relief – How the sufferers fared – Disaster's long memory – A nobler town arose? – The lessons of the day

Just four months after the great fire, a newspaper was launched in the Miramichi region. In the inaugural issue, publisher and editor James Pierce elected not to describe the event that had decimated so much of northeastern New Brunswick, saying that enough had already been written, and "we must pronounce those accounts correct, or if failing in any thing, only coming short of the real loss and actual suffering of this afflicted settlement."[1] One might have expected Pierce to call his newspaper the *Phoenix*, the Greek bird born out of its own ashes, but instead he named it the *Mercury*, after the Roman god of commerce. He wanted to define the Miramichi in terms not of the past disaster but of future prosperity. In the course of broadening the newspaper's reach in the years that followed, Pierce renamed it repeatedly, until it became the superinclusive *Gleaner and Northumberland, Kent, Gloucester and Restigouche Agricultural and Commercial Journal*.

William and Sarah Abrams were survivors of the Miramichi Fire, but they were also, in the parlance, sufferers. They were Scots who had come to the Miramichi in 1819 and had bought two expensive, well-situated properties in Rosebank, midway between Newcastle and Douglastown.[2] William Abrams & Co. quickly became one of the region's major lumber and shipbuilding firms. Both properties were levelled on 7 October, as were two unchristened ships the firm had on the stocks in the harbour. The Abrams's monetary losses were estimated at £40,000, but their losses were more than monetary. Their family had fled the flames, "some of them with nothing but their linen on," it was said, and their son William Harvey, aged two and a half, and their daughter Ann, aged eleven months, were both badly burned. Both died six weeks later.[3] With the Abrams family diminished and their business and the industry underlying it in ashes, one might expect them to have moved back to Scotland or to have moved on. Instead, they lodged in John Williston's store in Chatham while they rebuilt their home and business in Rosebank.[4] William Abrams & Co. was soon up and running once again, advertising in the *Mercury* that it was selling insurance on behalf of the West of Scotland Fire Insurance Company of Glasgow "on *Dwelling Houses, Stores, Goods, Vessels on the Stocks*, and other Property against Loss or Damage by Fire."[5] The advertisement ran for years. In June 1826 the resurrected Abrams shipbuilding firm launched a 386-ton vessel on the same spot on the river that it had lost the others. The new ship was called the *Phoenix*.[6]

James Ledden was a member of one the Miramichi's founding families, his father having settled in Newcastle in the late 1770s. It speaks to the ubiquity of fire in that world – where people were dependent on wood-fire heating, lived in wooden houses, and were surrounded by trees – that the store that Ledden and his brother-in-law James Abbott owned was damaged by fire in 1823, again in 1824, and then again in 1825 by the Miramichi Fire.[7] Cursed or blessed, it survived, one of only two stores on the north side of the river left standing after the great fire. The other was W. Ledden's, belonging to James's father or brother, but in July 1826 it was struck by lightning, and when "the electric fluid, passing through the roof, communicated instantaneously with the rum, of which fifteen puncheons were laying, in the lower part of the building," the rum burst into flame.[8] James Ledden and Abbott's store was also destroyed by fire that year, with Ledden himself almost losing his life by re-entering the store to save his company's ledger. Legend would later have it that the Leddens had gouged the survivors in the wake of the Miramichi Fire and that the 1826 fires they suffered were God's punishment. But the Leddens, like the Abrams, remained in the Miramichi. James was in fact appointed as a local fireward in 1828, and he continued in that position through the 1840s.[9]

The Miramichi Fire did not destroy Miramichi society, as many distant observers originally assumed it would. Even the obliterated communities on the north bank of the river began to rebuild. This restoration in turn raised questions about whether initial reports of the fire had been exaggerated. But of course it is perfectly natural for survivors of disaster to rebuild. Indeed, they frequently come to interpret the disaster as an opportunity to prove the content of their character by creating a community even better than the one that was lost. In disaster studies, this is called the "phoenix effect."[10] The most sustained and appreciative exploration of this phenomenon is Rebecca Solnit's *A Paradise Built in Hell: The Extraordinary Communities that Arise in Disaster*. "The prevalent human nature in disaster," she suggests, "is resilient, resourceful, generous, empathic, and brave." If only in the immediate wake of catastrophe – before the established social order comes flooding back in – survivors get "a glimpse of who else we ourselves may be and what else our society could become."[11] Other scholars have been decidedly more wary of the phoenix effect. Christof Mauch believes that North Americans' post-catastrophe optimism has historically helped survivors to justify the soundness of decisions that had put them in the path of disaster in the first place, thus making them more likely to both accept risk and fail to plan for further trouble.[12] The responses of Miramichi residents to the great fire has much to say, then, not only about what kind of society they wanted but also about why it had become the society it was in the first place.

Natural disasters, it must be said, are the low-hanging fruit of environmental history. The field's goal of illuminating the interplay between nature and culture is made easier when we study a disaster because this interplay is suddenly right at the surface, with people producing sources that explicitly discuss natural surroundings and processes and their relationship to them. As will be discussed in chapter 5, the Miramichi Fire had profound effects on the forests and forest industry of northeastern New Brunswick without wiping out either one. How governments, the forest industry, burgeoning forest and fire science, and ordinary New Brunswickers interpreted and reacted both to the effects and to the limits of those effects tells us a great deal about how nature was understood in the nineteenth century. But historians' long neglect of environmental topics such as the Miramichi Fire has done more than forego an opportunity to study past nature-culture relationships because missing these stories has also meant missing the stories that spiralled out from them.

Whereas chapter 5 focuses on the fire's environmental effects, this chapter concentrates on the fire's cultural effects – such as its role in producing an early international relief effort and in shifting the demography of colonial New Brunswick. Not all the effects were so dramatic, and in fact an important strand of this chapter is not resiliency but complacency, or people's tendency to restore things just as they were before, right down to the civic rivalry between Chatham and a new Newcastle. But as the lives of James Ledden and the Abrams demonstrate, even the most fortunate of survivors were touched by the fire.

***

Having carefully chronicled the hours leading to the fire's arrival at the Miramichi settlements, contemporary accounts shifted to a pointillist depiction of moments of horror. And then these accounts jumped forward in time. We know little about how people, unable to fight the flames, spent the night of 7 October. Gathered in Chatham, huddled in Strawberry Marsh, floating on the river or cowering beside it, survivors just survived and helped others to survive. In accounts, evening is suddenly morning, and the sun rose upon a scene of utter devastation. Here is how the charity pamphlet described it: "Where villages, houses and improvements had existed on the previous day, blackened heaps of ruins met the view. Tall chimneys standing alone or in clusters, marked the sites of the large and elegant wooden buildings, of which they were the sole remnants. Vessels on shore, logs of timber adrift and scattered on the shores, with fragments of household utensils. The lofty pines stripped of their verdure and beauty, and standing scathed monuments of the devastation."[13]

All the bridges and most of the fences in the county were gone. The ships *Canada* and *Concord* and the brig *Jane* lay burned and sunk in the harbour. Although Chatham did not bear the brunt of the firestorm, a number of houses there had been destroyed, whereas other buildings, including St Paul's Anglican Church, had caught fire but been saved. Its sister church in Moorefield, across the river, had not been so fortunate. In fact, the communities on the north side of the Miramichi River were so devastated that, in the words of merchant Isaac Paley, "it will be easier to name those that have escaped."[14] Of the some 250 houses and stores in Newcastle, only fourteen remained standing. In Douglastown, there were just three left. One of these was the home of Alexander Rankin, head of Gilmour, Rankin

& Co., and it was being used as a field hospital where a reported 100 people lay maimed.[15] (In time, legend would have it – whether Mi'gmaw legend or settler legend is unclear – that Rankin's house had been spared because he had always treated the Mi'gmaq well.)[16] Most businesses had been unable to save their ledgers and papers – no small thing when it was their only evidence of debts owed them.[17] A Madras school that had been spearheaded by Englishman John Smith was gone, as was a private hospital built by Scotsman Dr James Petrie.[18] So was the new Church of Scotland, which its congregation had just spent £800 to build.[19] So was the Roman Catholic chapel, which Governor Howard Douglas had dedicated just a few months earlier by placing coins and inscriptions under the foundation, as he said, "to convey to remote ages, how long that edifice stood." It stood no longer.[20]

And everywhere there were bodies. The charity pamphlet gave extended, graphic detail of the scene, both to arouse the pity of potential donors and simply because nineteenth-century readers expected it:

> The bodies of the burned were to be seen in some instances, so horribly mangled that nature recoiled at the spectacle. Some that when touched fell to pieces in almost a pulverized state, others mutilated. Of some the heads were partially destroyed and the brains bursting out of the integuments; in others, the entrails were bared. Many were so disfigured that they could not be recognized. In every direction such horrible objects were to be seen, frequently in the convulsed posture in which their distracted tortures had terminated existence. The bodies of the drowned were cast on the shore, partially burned or otherwise mangled. The horses, oxen, sheep, dogs, and in fine all kinds of domestic animals had shared with their protector, man, the miseries and destruction of the horrible night, and were scattered around dead or dying on the land and the waters.[21]

The survivors were in shock; it would later be said that, for the next two days, they did not have the presence of mind to respond to what had befallen them.[22] Perhaps they were waiting for the fire, still burning in the woods, to return and finish what it had started. But the rain that fell on 10 October – and the cold weather and wet snow that arrived some days after – awoke Miramichiers to the realization that the immediate danger was over and that much needed to be done to survive the coming winter.[23]

A priority for the living was finding and burying the dead. Many of the survivors were injured or tending to the injured and were homeless or housing the homeless, so the circumstances demanded that the dead be attended to quickly and with little ceremony. Some were taken away in box carts, placed in the ground, and covered.[24] There was often little to recover. In one case, the dead were shovelled into coffins, as many as six to a coffin.[25] The tallying was also made difficult by the fact that more people kept dying: from burns, from respiratory or cardiovascular issues, or from the fire's ancillary effects. In the short term, this meant that, as a Miramichi man wrote to his brother on 10 October, "numbers have expired with cold and hunger; and many poor, sick people, just rescued from the [yellow] fever, have perished from the effects of fatigue."[26]

In the longer term, it meant that there would be Miramichiers dying prematurely from the fire for weeks, months, and even years to come. Consider the burial register of St Paul's Anglican Church. In the twelve months prior to the fire, only thirteen deaths were listed. The average age (of those whose age was given) was twenty-seven and a half. In the twelve months after the fire, forty-three were buried in the church cemetery, their average age just eighteen. What's more, a full twenty of those forty-three died more than six months after the fire; nine of them were under the age of twenty. Although there is nothing to say that all of these deaths were related to the fire, the numbers suggest that its effects persisted.[27] But as revealing as St Paul's burial register is, its baptism register offers an even more unexpected and unsettling glimpse of the tragedy. On Friday, 7 October – presumably that night – Rector Samuel Bacon baptized eight children, aged from one month to six years. He baptized another eight through the remainder of the month and continued to baptize children at a heightened rate well into 1826. These baptisms, particularly those on 7 October, may have been of children gravely injured in the blaze. Yet these were *not* the children who subsequently died; William Ryan was the sole child to appear in both of St Paul's registers in the year after the fire. It may be that the fire prompted more parents to ensure their surviving children's eternal salvation.[28]

Just as the sparsely populated nature of the fire's area made it difficult to determine exactly how immense that area was, so the immense distances made it impossible to know exactly how many the fire had killed. A cohort of 3,000 men were widely believed to have been working in lumbering parties in the Miramichi backwoods when the fire struck.[29] It was the size of this contingent more than anything that made those who first wrote about the fire warn that the number of dead was sure to rise, even to what might be catastrophic levels. "It is most melancholy," stated one, "to think that some thousands of persons have perished in the flames in different parts of the woods."[30] But by the end of October, there was somewhat better news: "That many of the lumbering parties supposed to have perished, survive without injury – from 100 to 120 lost their lives on the night of the conflagration and from thirty to forty have since died, a number for want of medical aid and nourishment."[31] The majority of reports gravitated to a range of between 100 and 200 total dead, probably closer to the latter.[32] But there were credible outliers. The charity pamphlet claimed that no fewer than 250 had perished.[33] And Governor Douglas himself, reporting on a visit to the scene of destruction in late October, concluded that at least 300 had died along the north shore of the river.[34]

There was no systematic attempt within or between contemporary accounts to discern or describe exactly how many died where. Some articles just listed what dead they could: "David Lockhart, his father, mother, sister, and two children; William Kilpatrick, sen. his wife, son, and daughter; this is the old man whose mill Mr. Gilmour turned, and whose cleanly house he admired so much; Robert Scob, wife and four children, next adjoining him; James Lyon's wife and child; ... David Goodfellow, wife, and daughter; old Newlands and nephew, who lived in a cot of ours at Mill Creek." Even as eighteen of this group were being interred, another eight bodies were being carried out of the woods.[35] Other witnesses described the hardest hit places. John Jardine's song "The Miramichi Fire" is actually the most orderly of all accounts in that it alone matches principal scenes of destruction with how many died there: twenty-two men on the Northwest branch of the Miramichi River, twelve more in Newcastle and five below it, twenty-five more in the river, thirteen families in Douglastown, and sixty individuals in Black River.[36] Whether these numbers were accurate is another matter, of course. Most commentators described just one location as suggestive of the scale of devastation. Twenty-seven people, including a family of seven, were said to have perished in a settlement behind Douglastown.[37] The charity pamphlet claimed that "[t]he back settlements suffered severely," stating that sixty to seventy

The Phoenix 103

"at Baltibogue [Bartibog] and Nappan alone" burned to death and that another fifty there subsequently died of their injuries. An eyewitness who had returned to Scotland similarly believed that the deaths were "mostly in the second tier" of properties.[38] These repeated references to people in the back settlements suffering the most casualties is noteworthy but not altogether surprising: these properties were newer – built only after riverfront land was taken – and so less cleared, closer to the forest, and farther from the river. The concentration of suffering in these back settlements may also mean that, as one source noted, a disproportionate number of the victims were Irish immigrants. Although it was determined that lumbering parties overall had not suffered as heavy casualties as had been originally supposed, individual parties were annihilated, with seven of eight dying in one party, four of twenty in another, and sixteen of eighteen in yet another.[39]

Early in 1826 a death toll for the Miramichi Fire was calculated that would become the standard one, right down to the present day. The local committee that had been set up on 1 February to administer relief (which will be discussed later in the chapter) published its findings of how many lives and how much property had been lost in the fire. The committee concluded that 160 people had been killed: 130 burned, 10 drowned, and 20 "from injury received by the fire, not before reported." Of those killed, 108 had died in Newcastle Parish (19 in the upper district – that is, farthest up the river, to the west – 52 in the middle, and 37 in the lower), 22 in North Esk, Ludlow, and Nelson Parishes combined, and 10 in Chatham Parish (8 in the upper district and 2 in the middle).[40] This tally places the great majority of deaths in and just to the north of Newcastle, with a smattering of deaths in communities to the west, southwest, and south. This accounting obviously carries a great deal of authority, having been assembled shortly after the disaster by a group of leading citizens tasked with determining exactly what had happened; if nothing else, their neighbours would have known whether they had gotten details wrong. Still, it is worth flagging the real limitations of this inventory. The report was written by, for, and about Miramichiers, and it involved no research beyond the Miramichi communities. It did not pretend to determine how many people, if any, had died in the fires in Maine or greater New Brunswick – such as the wife and seven children of Calvin Camp, said to have died on the Oromocto River south of Fredericton.[41] What's more, the focus of the report on Miramichiers' property damage as the basis for determining relief may mean that it missed deaths among the thousands of new immigrants and transient lumbermen from Maine, the Maritimes, and Lower Canada who were working in the backwoods.

The inventory was also silent on whether any Mi'gmaq were killed, whether on the reserves along the Northwest branch of the Miramichi River, or in the backwoods, or even in settler communities. Since it is difficult to imagine the relief committee lumping Indigenous victims in with white victims without at least drawing attention to their specific numbers, it may well be that no Mi'gmaq were known to have died – or that their deaths were deemed not worth mentioning or even counting.[42] The Mi'gmaq population's absence from white society's accounts of the Miramichi Fire is almost absolute – except, as has been noted, in suggestions that Mi'gmaq may have caused the fire by their carelessness. Nor have I found any Mi'gmaw sources that speak of any Mi'gmaq dead.[43]

The relief committee's calculation of the fire's death toll is also weakened by the fact that it produced its results so quickly that it could not take into account those who died of their injuries later, such as those in the St Paul's burial register. Nor could it include those dead who were discovered only later. In April 1826 a corpse floated down the Miramichi River on the spring freshet and out into the Gulf of Saint Lawrence. It was later regretted that no attempt had been made to bring it ashore.[44] This was the first of a series of bodies that the river returned that spring. There was John F. Corbett, whose family of seven was believed to have died the night of the fire. His body was found in June alongside the ship *Briton*; the bodies of a daughter and a son were subsequently found. There was Thomas Miller, who was known to have drowned that night. There was Richard Rimmer, identified as perhaps a ship's carpenter by the gimlets found in his pockets.[45] Although the Miramichi relief committee surely knew that the body count had ticked upward, it never reopened its numbers, and so when it published its final report two years later, the fire's death toll was still given as 160, more firmly entrenched than ever.[46] But it was always recognized that a precise number was something of a fiction anyway. "Numbers must have perished, of whom no account will probably be ever obtained," a Halifax newspaper noted shortly after the fire, "and many persons who have been mutilated, and otherwise personally injured, will continue from time to time to be discovered in remote situations, or will perish through want, in distant and retired parts of the country."[47]

The Phoenix   105

* * *

Three days after the great fire, a group of Chatham's leading men formed a Miramichi relief committee, agreeing to meet every subsequent day at 10:00 A.M. The committee's composition evidently upset those living on the north side of the river – the side far worse hit by the fire and in far greater need of charity – because within weeks a new, re-formed committee with members from both sides of the river had been created. In any case, the Chatham group was the first halfway-official response to the disaster, and its very first statement was as follows: "Resolved that it is the opinion of the undersigned petitioners that the distress occasioned by the late calamity has exposed … private property, and want of a place of confinement wherein to secure defenders, is likely to be productive of great disorder, and that an additional military force will be necessary to enable the magistrates to enforce the laws and to protect the property which has escaped destruction."[48] They requested law and order. Then, and only then, did they call for relief to prevent the famine that would occur if emergency food supplies did not arrive before navigation closed for the season.

There was concern in the Miramichi – and then, once word of the conflagration spread, far beyond it – that the fire would turn out to be a leveller of society as much as it had been a leveller of buildings. It had been indiscriminate in its effect on well-to-do lumbermen and indentured labourers.[49] People from all strands of society were left without homes, possessions, food, or, in the short term at least, the resources to regain any of these things. What's more, three of the principal sites of public order – the courthouse, the jail, and the military barracks – had all burned down.[50] A fourth – the churches – also suffered, with the new Catholic chapel in Nelson and the Presbyterian churches in both Newcastle and Moorefield lost. Newspapers exhibited and fed societal fears, assuming that the fire had brought out humanity's worst. The charity pamphlet, for example, recounted the tale of "a creature in the shape of a human being" who, the morning after the fire, robbed his aged mother-in-law of the only £50 she possessed.[51] There were scattered reports of looting, even a claim that those who, fearful of the approaching fire, had hauled their belongings out of their homes had lost more to theft than if they had left things where they were.[52] When word of the fire reached London, England, the colony's agent, Henry Bliss, gravely warned at a charity event that

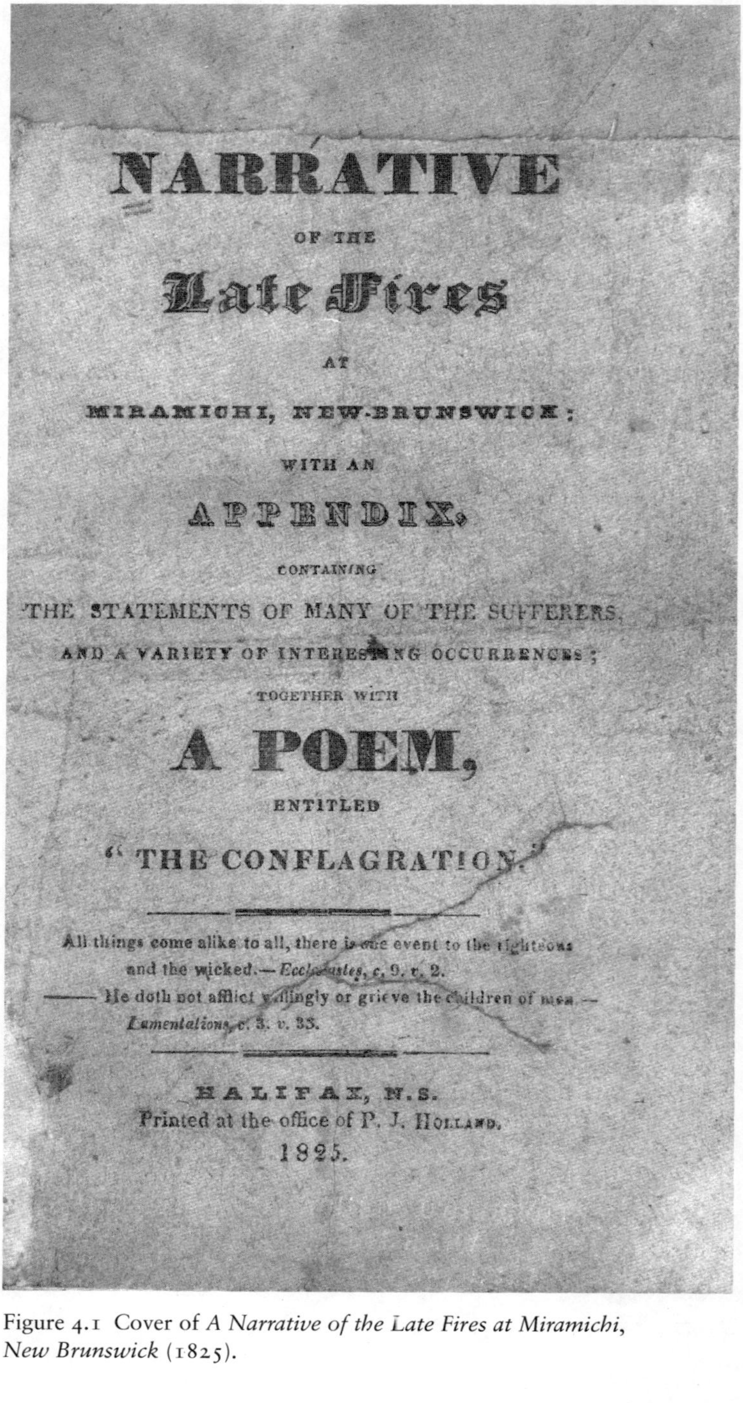

NARRATIVE

OF THE

Late Fires

AT

MIRAMICHI, NEW-BRUNSWICK:

WITH AN

APPENDIX,

CONTAINING

THE STATEMENTS OF MANY OF THE SUFFERERS,

AND A VARIETY OF INTERESTING OCCURRENCES;

TOGETHER WITH

A POEM,

ENTITLED

"THE CONFLAGRATION."

All things come alike to all, there is one event to the righteous
and the wicked.—*Ecclesiastes, c. 9. v. 2.*
—— He doth not afflict willingly or grieve the children of men.—
Lamentations, c. 3. v. 33.

HALIFAX, N.S.
Printed at the office of P. J. HOLLAND.
1825.

Figure 4.1 Cover of *A Narrative of the Late Fires at Miramichi,
New Brunswick* (1825).

"the number of those who still had property left in the colony would hardly be sufficient to protect it from the attacks of the sufferers, rendered desperate by hunger and privation."[53] In the days following the fire, men took turns guarding stores to make sure they were not broken into. There was talk of imposing a curfew (from the French *couvre-feu* – to cover or extinguish the fires for the night).

But fears of anarchy went unrealized. Social order did not collapse. In fact, the few references to cases of looting appear decidedly overstated. A thief was said to have stolen considerable sums of money from the burned-out shells of Newcastle houses – but eventually to have returned it.[54] A gentleman was forced to watch over his store because it was "threatened by the hungry poor" – who presumably meant to eat, not profit by, his food. And to his credit, the gentleman seemed most worried that if the food was taken, it would not be fairly distributed.[55] There is just as much evidence (i.e., not very much) that stores price-gouged survivors as there is that the poor plundered stores. A British publication claimed that merchants on the Miramichi River, "taking advantage of the universal necessity," sold single-weave blankets at the inflated price of 3 shillings per pair, and pork at 7 shillings and 10 pence per barrel.[56] When in the spring of 1826 lumberman Thomas Boies advertised that he had boards available for rebuilding, he went out of his way to note that he was selling at pre-fire prices, implying that others were not.[57] But even if so, the larger point was that Boies represented the great majority of the citizenry, whose behaviour did not change in the wake of the fire. A Nova Scotia newspaper in late October reported that the Miramichi was taking its first steps toward rebuilding and noted that "perfect tranquility, and obedience to the laws, has been restored upon the River. No destruction of property, no thefts, no violence had been committed at Chatham; and in Newcastle they had already commenced the erection of temporary buildings for the winter."[58]

The people of the Miramichi were already witnessing a better side of human nature. That autumn, the news of the conflagration and the fact that it had left hundreds dead and thousands homeless on the eve of a Canadian winter excited sympathy and generosity all across the Western world. The international relief effort that would flower after the Miramichi Fire was not without precedent: Great Britain had a long tradition of providing disaster relief within its own borders, for example, and by the mid-eighteenth century this practice had spread to assisting its colonies. Nor was the scale of the 1825 drive unmatched: for example, the British Parliament donated a huge sum to victims of an 1831 hurricane in the colonial West Indies, whereas it made no direct allocation to the Miramichi sufferers whatsoever.[59] But the Miramichi case is apparently the largest disaster relief effort in pre-Confederation Canada. This fact is particularly remarkable in that the fire was not an urban disaster, where victims are more plentiful and donors more prosperous.

The formation of a local relief committee on 10 October signals that people on the Miramichi River knew of previous charity efforts in response to previous disasters. But no specific case was ever mentioned as a model or comparator. Regardless, the committee members clearly recognized the importance of communicating the direness of the situation. So not only did they send letters describing people's plight via ships bound for Halifax, Quebec City, Fredericton, Saint John, Pictou, and Charlottetown, but they also issued a handbill to be distributed widely. It began,

> Fire and Hurricane!
> Amidst confusion and distress, the inevitable consequences of
> the dreadful dispensation of Providence, which has befallen our
> devoted colony, it is altogether impossible to calculate or describe
> the extent of its destructive effects, but to awaken the sympathy
> of those who under the Divine Protection of Almighty God,
> have escaped the awful calamity, it will be sufficient thus briefly
> to state, that more than a Hundred Miles of the shores of
> Miramichi are laid waste; independent of the North west Branch,
> the Bartibogue, and the Nappan Settlements, from one or
> two hundred people have perished within immediate observa-
> tion, and thrice that number are miserably burnt or otherwise
> wounded; and at least two thousand of our fellow creatures are
> left destitute of the means of subsistence, and thrown at present
> upon the humanity of the Province of New Brunswick.[60]

The committee dispatched Justice of the Peace William Joplin to Fredericton to notify New Brunswick governor Howard Douglas of the fire; once there, Douglas sent Joplin on to Quebec. A Fredericton-based relief committee had already been established on 8 October to assist the sufferers of the fire that burned around the capital, and when that committee learned of the fire's extended reach, it extended its reach too.

The nature of the tragedy was sure to captivate. Here were small
communities of British settlers living on the edge of a vast wilderness

Word of the fire spread. The express ship arrived in Halifax on
15 October, and within a day £1,200 in relief was raised, increasing
within two days to £2,000.[61] In Quebec, Governor General of British
North America the Earl of Dalhousie wrote in his diary of receiving a
Mr "Hoplin" from New Brunswick and granting "such blankets and
woolen cloaths as could be spared, with six months Provisions for
1,000 people, in flour & Pork &&&."[62] Joplin provided the Quebec
newspapers with what was fast becoming the standard account of
the fire, an article beginning, "On the night of the 7th inst [instant;
i.e., the current month] this place exhibited the terrible spectacle of a
general conflagration."[63] This article and a few others were reprinted
broadly throughout the English-speaking world that fall. In Halifax
the forty-eight-page *A Narrative of the Late Fires at Miramichi, New
Brunswick* went on sale at the price of 2 shillings each, or twelve for
20 shillings, with the express purpose of encouraging aid. Although
the *Halifax Novascotian* mentioned at the time that the pamphlet
was "under the direction of a person who was an eyewitness to the
scene," the pamphlet is generally credited to Halifax publisher and
historian Beamish Murdoch.[64]

The nature of the tragedy was sure to captivate. Here were small
communities of British settlers living on the edge of a vast wilderness
who had experienced a holocaust of apparently unprecedented size
and ferocity and who, having survived, looked forward only to the
loss of home and livelihood and to a cold Canadian winter. It had the
elements of the domestic, the imperial, and the apocalyptic. Although
it is difficult to know how readers responded to reports of the fire –
the relief effort itself is the best barometer – there can be little doubt
that the reports resonated. Donations were raised wherever news of
the fire reached. The Government of Lower Canada granted £2,500,
Upper Canada and Nova Scotia £1,000 each, and New Brunswick
itself £5,000. Governor Douglas personally contributed £110. A gold
ring was donated at a Halifax Baptist meeting. The Quebec Bible
Society dispatched fifty Bibles, twenty-five in English and twenty-five
in French. There were charity sermons in Montreal and Halifax, a
theatrical production in Fredericton, and a concert by the Saint John
Phil-Harmonic Society. The Nova Scotia towns of Pictou, Liverpool,
and Chester raised £700 between them and donated 900 bushels of
potatoes and 50 bushels of wheat. Ships were dispatched to the
Miramichi with food, clothing, bedding, and other supplies. Newspaper
reports of the day listed the largest subscriptions, but much of the

relief effort was the product of countless small acts of charity that were individual and anonymous.[65]

Generosity flowed just as freely from the United States. Historian Robert H. Bremner has noted that although many encouragements existed in the young republic to make money, there were few encouragements to spend it, and so Americans tended to give generously to foreign relief.[66] Thomas Dixon of New York stepped forward early and offered $5,000 (about £1,000) to the Miramichi effort in advance of donations that he was confident would come.[67] Spurred by newspapers' publication of subscription lists, there arose a competition to see which city would give the most. "Boston had done most nobly," and "Philadelphia has at length taken the field," a New York paper noted, but it was happy to report that its own city had raised $3,884 in a single day.[68] Boston's noble response may have been a result of its long-time connection to the Maritimes, particularly to New Brunswick Loyalists. Thirty-five Boston churches collected money for the Miramichi, and the schooner *Billows* sailed twice to Halifax with provisions.[69]

The *Billows* did not stop in Maine to help sufferers there, it should be noted. There was essentially no American charity drive to help victims of the Maine fires. The American Insurance Office in Boston announced that it would collect money, provisions, and clothing for Maine sufferers, but this relief effort is the only one that I have come across.[70] One US newspaper, after describing aid to the Miramichi, asked tentatively "whether assistance is not more needed by the sufferers in Maine," but this suggestion was the closest anyone came to saying that Americans should care for Americans first.[71] The scope of the disaster in the Miramichi simply overshadowed that in Maine. Even residents of Eastport, Maine, well aware that forest fires had wreaked havoc in their own state, raised $400 to help the New Brunswick survivors.[72]

The American aid to the British colony is especially impressive given that the nations had fought the War of 1812 only a decade earlier and were still disputing the Maine–New Brunswick border. The relief effort in the United States was frequently promoted as a way to confirm and fortify America's close relationship with Great Britain and its colonies. A Boston circular reminded readers of "the good principles which ought to regulate international friendliness and courtesy of neighbouring countries."[73] Such thinking was framed most vividly by George Manners, the British consul in Massachusetts, in his poem

The Phoenix III

"The Conflagration." Manners presented the fire as a God-given opportunity to overcome past British and American differences, ending the poem,

> Of Nature – O, may thy bland influence bind
> In one vast family all human kind,
> Soften asperities of kindred States,
> Blot out all traces of unnat'ral hates,
> Conciliate feelings lib'ral, just and kind,
> And re-unite the ties by feuds disjoin'd![74]

British North American commentators shared such sentiments. Halifax personages Enos Collins and Brenton Halliburton sent a thank-you to Boston, saying that although American generosity would undoubtedly have been on display if the victims had been "the African, the Asiatics, or the American Savage," they were confident that it had been increased by the knowledge "that we are all descended from Common Forefathers."[75] Likewise, in a letter republished in US papers, a Miramichi man wrote to a Boston friend that American aid demonstrated that "the late hostile and unpleasant feelings" between the two nations were gone and that "good and friendly feeling" now reigned "between the two greatest and I trust one day will be the most firmly allied nations in the world."[76] By the time the charity pamphlet was published, its author was able to praise "the flame of sympathy" that had already raised £25,000 in subscriptions – even before Great Britain had been heard from.[77]

Word of the fire reached Britain on 10 November, when the *Lydia* arrived in Liverpool from the Miramichi; the *London Times* carried its first article about the fire the next day.[78] Rather than relying on the few early descriptions that were circulated and then recirculated in newspapers across eastern North America, the British press published a considerable number of eyewitness reports. There were New Brunswickers who wrote letters to reassure family members and business partners in Britain. There were ship's captains who shared what they had witnessed. There were also recent immigrants to New Brunswick who lost everything in the fire and returned to the mother country on the first ship that would take them. The *Diana*, for example, carried back to Scotland twenty-eight people for whom "the prospect of a long and dreary winter, with the anticipated scarcity of provisions in the colony, made them all eagerly embrace the opportunity of returning to a home where they knew they would meet with sympathetic friends."[79] The stories of such survivors and witnesses swirled throughout the British press for the next month.

The charity effort began in London the same day as the first *Times* story appeared, with a public meeting organized by New Brunswick's agents in Great Britain, John Bainbridge and Henry Bliss. "Appeals to the charity of the British nation were, it was well known, not infrequent," Bliss admitted, "but never was there a more pitiable ground for an appeal of such a nature than that which had lately come to the public knowledge." He spoke of the nature of fire in such a wooded land, how it wiped out anything and everything in its path, leaving all equally bereft. The *Times* reported that Bliss further motivated his countrymen by noting that Americans were sure to be helping already: "The unfortunate event would not fail to excite commiseration in the United States. He really felt jealous of the liberality of that country to a British colony" and urged British generosity to redeem itself. A committee was formed and £2,600 committed at that first meeting, including £50 from Bliss and £100 from Colonial Secretary Earl Bathurst.[80] For the next month, the *Times* ran almost daily notices of the campaign, complete with names of new donors and more firsthand accounts as they appeared.

The disaster was of special interest in Great Britain because it had struck a British colony with which the mother country had significant interaction. It is little wonder that the Welshman Dafydd Amos wrote a song to raise money for Welsh sufferers of the fire: how could the people of Wales not be moved upon hearing of Welsh immigrants who had been killed or displaced by a fire that was, by some estimates, as large as Wales itself?[81] The City of Liverpool voted to donate £300 and in the course of deliberations raised the sum to £500.[82] In its discussion of a meeting held to explore how best to help the sufferers, an Aberdeen newspaper referred to "the Miramichi" without further geographical reference, indicating both that the region was assumed to be well known to Scottish readers and that the New Brunswick fires were becoming defined strictly in terms of that region.[83] Utterly absent from British discussion of the fire and the subsequent relief effort was what effect the presumed loss of a leading timber supplier might have on Great Britain itself.

The British relief effort ultimately raised about £10,000 for the people of the Miramichi. This was more than any other jurisdiction, but given Britain's size, wealth, and status as the colony's mother country, the

The Phoenix

amount was a disappointment, if not an outright failure. The nation had forty-five times the population of Lower Canada, for example, yet had given less than twice as much. In London, after the £2,600 donated at the initial 11 November meeting, less than that amount again was raised through the remainder of the year. The London relief committee publicly blamed this apparent parsimoniousness on the fact that the New Brunswick government had been unable to send word about the fire with the first mail packet, with result that the early, unofficial accounts were thought by some to be embellished.[84]

Privately, however, it was understood that the shortfall occurred because Britain was at that very moment undergoing a crisis of its own. "You have read of bubbles," wrote Victorian novelist Charles Reade in *Hard Cash*. "Well, in the year 1825, it was not one bubble but a thousand."[85] Throughout the early 1820s, British investors had speculated heavily in bonds issued by the fragmented, independent states formed from the collapse of the Spanish Empire in the Americas. Many of these bonds were of dubious value, none more so than those associated with the Republic of Poyais on Honduras's Mosquito Coast, because Poyais, as it turned out, did not exist. It was a land invented by Scottish adventurer Gregor MacGregor as a means to attract British investors.[86] The bubble burst in the autumn of 1825 due to the failure of many British country banks in October and November and the collapse of a raft of London banks in December.[87] It is surely a bad economic indicator when a nation's leading newspaper publishes an article on the "Origin of the Term Panic."[88] The blame pointed everywhere and nowhere. A Scottish newspaper defended the director of the Bank of England, saying that he was no more at fault for this economic calamity than for "producing the Burmese war, or setting fire to the woods of Miramichi."[89]

That the economic calamity was at fault in weakening the relief effort to help the victims of the fire was not in doubt. George Baillie, head clerk in the Colonial Office (and brother of Thomas), wrote New Brunswick governor Douglas that the aid effort had been largely unsuccessful "from the most extraordinary convulsion in the Money Market (which I trust is only temporary) ... [P]eople who would have given £50 or £100 a few months ago are now content with a subscription of £5."[90] Early in the new year of 1826, when members of the London-based relief committee called upon the city's mayor with the subscriptions "very much on the decline," the mayor said that "he did not at all wonder at the low condition of the funds for relief ...

when there were all around us such evidence of distress." The public was naturally focused on "domestic calamities."[91] The phrase is revealing: the fact that disaster had befallen a British colony did not make it a domestic matter. Britain's interests were so extensive and diverse that the fate of an imaginary republic in Honduras could figure just as prominently as that of its real, foremost timber colony.

In the fall of 1825, Great Britain's economy went into a tailspin that would last into the 1830s, pulling its colonies' economies and indeed the global economy down with it. As will be discussed further in chapter 5, this economic collapse more than anything is what makes it impossible to calculate the exact effect that the Miramichi Fire had on the economy of New Brunswick or even of the Miramichi. Even before the onset of the financial crisis, Great Britain had begun measures to reduce its spending on all its colonies. On 8 October 1825, unaware of the catastrophe that had struck New Brunswick the day before, Colonial Secretary Earl Bathurst wrote Governor Douglas with instructions to have the legislative assembly henceforth fund the colonial government itself. Douglas objected when he received this instruction, pointing out that Britain's £5,000 annual investment helped to produce a healthy colony that cleared 1,100 ships, most of them bound for Britain. Bathurst relented, citing the colony's extraordinary expenses associated with the Miramichi Fire, but in the longer term colonies such as New Brunswick would receive less support from the mother country.[92] The financial crisis robbed the Miramichi Fire of some of its oxygen, reducing what its impact might otherwise have been perceived to be. In subsequent discussion of the forest trade in New Brunswick, even in the Miramichi, it soon became common to discuss the early 1820s timber speculation and then turn to the depression without factoring in the fire at all.[93] In describing New Brunswick's economic situation at the end of the decade, author John McGregor stated that "the effects of the romantic projects of 1824" still lingered, employing a lovely turn of phrase to describe a dismal reality. His reference seems to have been to British financial speculation as much as to the colony's timber speculation – one being but a local manifestation of the other.[94]

But all these matters lay ahead. In the fall of 1825, although the British organizers of the Miramichi relief effort expressed disappointment with the amount of money raised, if anyone in New Brunswick thought the amount tepid, there is no record of it. The people of the colony were instead overwhelmingly appreciative, even moved by

The Phoenix 115

the sympathy and support the drive had generated across North America and Great Britain. Those on the ground took it as a great responsibility to ensure that the aid would be distributed in a just and Christian fashion.

***

On 27 October the people of the Miramichi were "literally astonished to find their beloved and most excellent Governor among them."[95] Without notice, Governor Howard Douglas had ridden the more than 200 kilometres from Fredericton by horse. According to his biographer, his appearance was treated with almost religious awe: "Simultaneously the whole crowd went forward, and every one uncovered as they met, receiving him with a silence more eloquent than cheers."[96] And on the third day (really), Douglas addressed the assembled communities. His theme was reconstruction. He commiserated on their having "experienced one of the most dreadful visitations, that ever fell upon the earth," and although he could not restrain himself from restating the weaknesses in Miramichi society that he had identified to the communities earlier in the year, his focus was on the future: "This ... is a crisis which should be taken advantage of." Simply put, it was a chance to consolidate the society and expand its economy. Douglas noted that during his previous visit, "I was forcibly struck with the inconvenient, disadvantageous, and greatly scattered condition of Miramichi." The population lived on haphazardly lain lots that stretched along many miles on both sides of the river, such that no church, no school, no doctor, and no business could accommodate the whole area, which ensured that every element of civilization was small and insignificant. "At the extremes of these scattered hamlets stood two rival towns." Douglas did not deign to tell the people of the Miramichi how to solve their problems – but given that Newcastle and the other communities on the north bank were in ashes, it was obvious that he hoped the people would resolve their differences and settle together around Chatham on the south bank. Douglas also saw the fire as an opportunity for the region to move beyond just timbering: "I have always told you, that this is a trade which must terminate some time or other from exhaustion of the material, and which shall change its seat of business by migrating in the province to ports situated in the next vicinity of the next progressive forests; and which besides, is exposed at any time to injury or cessation from external circumstances, over which we have [no] control. Were any or either of these circumstances to happen in the present condition of Miramichi, I can conceive nothing more ruinous than your situation would be." What is extraordinary here, of course, is that in Douglas's mind the great fire did not in itself constitute a circumstance beyond control that had exposed the timber trade to injury or cessation. "The pine stands unhurt in the vast forests of our country," he stated, having just ridden from the capital to the coast. But, he continued, "the other fields for exertion, the natural resources of the country, which I have so often recommended you to cultivate more industriously, are open to you." As with any society, agriculture was where the people should start.[97]

Douglas's address, or at least his visit, was by all accounts very well received. He toured the burnt-over communities and headed back to Fredericton. A month later, a newborn in Ludlow was christened Howard Douglas Price, and the following summer, a new ship built on the Miramichi River was christened the *Governor Douglas*.[98] In the initial issue of the *Chatham Mercury*, editor James Pierce noted, "Every individual in Miramichi, while the stream of life flows in his veins, will remember with the liveliest emotions of gratitude, the condescending, kind, humane, and fatherly attention of His Excellency Sir HOWARD DOUGLAS, our beloved Governor, in visiting us in our deepest distress. His presence raised our hopes, and dispelled our fears."[99] Douglas may have taken some pride in these tributes, but he must have felt more mixed emotions to learn that Douglastown, the village renamed in his honour prior to the fire, was being rebuilt on the north side of the Miramichi River. The people along the river appreciated the governor's attention, but whether they would follow his advice was another matter.

Effort was made to implement one of his principal suggestions, namely that the Miramichi should devote more attention to agriculture. To many people on the river and far beyond, the fire – and the collapse of the economy shortly thereafter – was proof of the timber trade's ultimate unsuitability as the foundation of a society because of its vulnerability to nature, market forces, or God's judgment – take your pick.[100] But the fire had also opened up land for cultivation, and there was believed to be a serious ecological reason for turning to agriculture right away. "It is a well known fact," according to the Northumberland Agricultural and Emigrant Society, "that lands which have been burnt over, become every year worse and worse." This body urged people, if they could not plant grain or potatoes, to at least sow grass seed, "both to cover the land from the scorching heat of the sun, and furnish an abundance of pasture where, otherwise, there would be nothing but sterility."[101] A difficulty was that the forest fire had also burned seed supplies and farming implements. As a result, and as a way of nudging Miramichiers toward agriculture, a considerable part of the charity effort was directed to providing these necessities. The Scottish town of Alloa subscribed £90 specifically for the purchase of ploughs; the Fredericton relief commission gave £400 to Miramichi sufferers for the purchase of seed; and at the initial London charity meeting, Chair John Bainbridge asked that some funds assist agricultural activity.[102] Although the Miramichi's economy had been built on a timber trade and the region's value to Britain was principally in terms of timber, the expectation nevertheless was that it was both necessary and appropriate that it move toward agriculture.

But the region did not rapidly, radically transform. Although somewhat more attention than usual was paid to agriculture in the spring of 1826, according to a resigned *Chatham Mercury*, "the unintelligent observer may soon see that there are other occupations which still preeminently aggrandize attention to the exclusion of this foundation of all public wealth." The early trials to scatter grass seed on the lands burned by fire were almost entirely unsuccessful, the seeds germinating only in a few low, wet spots. "Our hopes," said the newspaper, "of a little good coming out of the great evil, are at an end, and we shall have to wait the usual slow operations of the axe, hoe and harrow, to produce pastures."[103] But at least these slow operations were under way. The New Brunswick Agricultural and Emigrant Society reported that even in 1826 more land was going into cultivation in Northumberland and York Counties, places typically reliant on lumbering. It credited the shift to the slump in the timber economy, making no mention whatsoever of the Miramichi Fire.[104]

Governor Douglas had exhorted his Miramichi audience, "Let no man ... yielding to groundless despondency, quit the country."[105] There was a real fear that with the fire having wiped out properties and the economy that sustained them, there would be a mass exodus from the region. There was an exodus but not as great as feared. Some Miramichiers did as Governor Douglas had hoped and moved to Chatham, whereas others set up new communities on the Miramichi River and its tributaries, such as the group of Irish and English settlers who relocated along the Cains River.[106] But other displaced or not-yet-settled emigrants moved on. Itinerant labourers headed back to their homes elsewhere in the Maritimes, Lower Canada, or Maine.[107] Local historian and genealogist W.D. Hamilton notes that the names of even some well-established Miramichi lumbermen "simply vanished from the record." But he has been able to trace a considerable number to locations on both sides of the Bay of Chaleur: Bonaventure County on the south shore of Gaspé, Quebec, and the Bathurst and Pokemouche areas of northern New Brunswick.[108] An unknown number of families seeking the next timber frontier headed west, travelling up the Ottawa Valley on the border between Upper and Lower Canada. They named their new home "Miramichi." It became Pembroke a generation later, but even now, two centuries on, the town's long-term care facility is the Miramichi Lodge.[109]

In its February 1826 inventory of losses sustained, the relief committee listed "Sufferers who left Miramichi immediately after the fire: 300."[110] But in its final report two years later, it clarified that it had been referring specifically to members of the labouring class who had received assistance to move to a neighbouring port. No official attempt was ever made to tally how many people left the Miramichi on their own or at a later date; if they were no longer part of the community, what was the point of counting them? Nor was any attempt made to calculate how many people went missing after the fire. And the committee claimed that most of the 300 it counted had returned the following spring.[111]

There were good reasons to return. For one thing, the governor had decreed that no aid would go to persons quitting New Brunswick – a strong incentive for people who had lost everything.[112] But more fundamentally, the Miramichi was rebuilding, and what had drawn settlers there before the fire drew some of them, and others like them, back afterward. Despite getting international attention for the worst possible reason in late 1825, the Miramichi continued to be a destination for Irish immigrants in particular, some undoubtedly trying to flee the depression that had struck the British Isles. Two histories of local lumbering enterprises that flourished in the nineteenth and twentieth centuries – John G. Burchill's *A Miramichi Saga* and George Brooks Johnson's *Miramichi Woodsman* – both open with their respective families arriving from County Cork in 1826.[113] The year 1827 saw hundreds more poor Irish migrants arrive in the region, a significant number of them carrying typhus. The Miramichi region's already stressed infrastructure had to construct an expanded quarantine station and to maintain quarantine while providing food and aid.[114]

The Phoenix

As much as the population of the Miramichi did increase in the years after the fire, the rate did not approach that of the rest of the colony or even the county. In 1826 the northern part of Northumberland County was hived off as a new Gloucester County, and its southeastern part was made a new Kent County. This was simultaneously a recognition of Northumberland's growing economic and demographic significance to the colony over the past decade and an understanding that this significance was becoming increasingly distributed beyond the Miramichi. The Northumberland parishes that became Gloucester County tripled in population between 1824 and 1834, and those that became Kent County doubled, whereas the parishes along the Miramichi River and its tributaries saw only 30 per cent growth. In fact, the number of people in the timber-heavy parishes of North Esk and Ludlow decreased in that decade from 1,443 to 1,287 in the case of the former and, more precipitously, from 1,308 to 501 in the case of the latter. Over the same period, Newcastle's population rose from 1,657 to 2,185, and Chatham saw the healthiest increase of anywhere on the Miramichi River, its population climbing from 1,452 to 2,355.[115] As will be shown in chapter 5, the Miramichi region's relatively low growth was tied in part to how New Brunswick's timber economy shifted in the decade after the fire. But it was also tied to the number of residents who quietly moved away from the region but are missing from the relief committee's accounting – and to the number who died in the fire, of course.

In the course of rebuilding after the fire, Miramichiers also rebuilt the rivalry between the north and south sides of the river. Perhaps it was inevitable. Those from Newcastle, Douglastown, and the other destroyed communities on the north side had in many cases lost everything but the lots under their feet; this location was where they had decided to build, so it was where many decided to rebuild. Even Chatham's offer of free lots to displaced survivors may have seemed opportunistic. In any case, even before winter put a halt to construction in 1825, about thirty permanent houses had been built in Newcastle, with preparations made to build double that in the spring. A temporary jail had been built, too.[116] Residents declared that, in line with Governor Douglas's counsel, this would be a more compact, concentrated Newcastle, better than it was before.[117] In December a clearly partisan writer explained in a Halifax newspaper that Newcastle was being resurrected because "[i]t affords tenfold advantages over the village of Chatham in every point of view." It had better anchorage ground, more shelter for vessels, and "water always smoother" than at Chatham.[118]

If it sounds as though Newcastlers were defending their decision to rebuild, that is because they were. Until the fire, Newcastle had been Northumberland County's shiretown, the seat of county government, and after the fire, the people of Chatham felt that their town should take over the role – not unreasonably since at that moment Newcastle did not really exist. On 9 February 1826, two duelling petitions, each bearing the names of thousands of Northumberland County residents, arrived at the legislative assembly. One petition called for Chatham to become the shiretown. Citing Governor Douglas's counsel that the settlements consolidate, the petitioners noted they had set aside lots not only for the displaced people of the north side of the river but also for public buildings to be erected. "[A] close observation of the occurrences of the last season, the general depression in commercial affairs and the almost ruinous state of the timber trade, in particular, show the imperative necessity for promptly adopting such measures as will lead to concentration," they wrote.[119] The second petition, calling for the shiretown to remain in Newcastle, parried all the arguments of the first. Dismayed "that the taking advantage of the present unfortunate crisis endeavours to defraud the people of NewCastle of their just rights," these petitioners noted that Newcastle was a little farther upriver than Chatham and thus the true gateway to the Miramichi River, on which "in an Agricultural and Commercial point of view, the prosperity of Miramichi depends." The pro-Newcastle petition also claimed that the opposing petition had unfairly gathered the support of people along the coast, for whom the shiretown's location "is a matter of no sort of importance." These people, "consisting principally of French," would sign whatever was put in front of them.[120] This is the clearest indication that a component of the two towns' rivalry had been that Newcastle was associated more with Scots and Irish immigrants, whereas Chatham, by its location, was somewhat more associated with the coastal Acadians. Newcastle's status as the shiretown was ultimately retained, but that did not stop its residents from long holding a grudge that Chatham had tried to take it from them.[121] Governor Douglas's hope that the fire might bring the towns together, materially and emotionally, had been in vain. The rivalry had arisen anew from the ashes.

***

Opening the New Brunswick legislature early in 1826, Governor Howard Douglas began by detailing the effects of the "late awful visitation" on several parts of the province, along with the private and public relief efforts still under way to aid the sufferers. His speech then turned to a more general assessment: "I have great pleasure in acquainting you that the general affairs of this Province, though chequered in their well-being by the late awful vicissitudes, are proceeding in a very prosperous condition."[122] When the *London Times* reported on Douglas's speech, it fixed on this reference to the colony's prosperity and commented, "The inhabitants of Halifax appeared thunderstruck at the expressions; they understood the greater proportion of the country was ruined by the late fire; but supposed his Excellency had got hold of an old speech."[123] The newspaper left it at that. It did not ask the awkward follow-up questions: *Was* the country ruined? And if not, why not?

The early work of dispensing relief to the sufferers of the Miramichi Fire and the subsequent work of rebuilding the destroyed communities fell victim to their own success. The weather had cooperated after the fire, staying warm enough to keep the river open for ships all that autumn.[124] On 30 October the warship HMS *Orestes* had appeared with provisions dispatched from Halifax. The *St Lawrence* soon arrived from Quebec carrying supplies donated by the Canadas. Fifteen more vessels out of Saint John, the Bay of Chaleur, Pictou, Antigonish, Halifax, Lunenburg, St John's, and Boston had landed within a short period, all carrying aid for sufferers and all bearing witness to the great early success of the Miramichi and Fredericton relief committees' appeals. Although the Miramichi committee later modestly stated that it would be "as unnecessary as it would be uninteresting, to enter into a minute detail of their proceedings," the members were proud to report that they had distributed the necessities of life to more than 3,000 people for the next six months.[125] Goods had been organized and allocated efficiently: a family of six was initially allotted "a suit of clothes, with shoes to each, 24 yards of osnaburgh [fabric], two pair of blankets, a barrel of flour, one of meal, one of pork or two of fish, six barrels of potatoes, with tea and sugar."[126] The initial fears of widespread starvation and civil collapse evaporated. The relief effort's focus on feeding, clothing, and housing the survivors turned in the months that followed to financially compensating those who had lost property in the fire.

Such a quantity of food and supplies arrived on the Miramichi River's shores in the fall of 1825 that, as early as 21 November, Samuel Cunard, head of the Halifax relief effort and brother of Chatham timber merchant and local committee treasurer Joseph Cunard, stated publicly that no more provisions were presently needed.[127] It is hardly surprising that those who had read in newspapers or heard in sermons apocalyptic descriptions of the Miramichi Fire, and been moved to donate money and supplies, were bewildered by such optimistic reports. What did it mean that many of the survivors were planning to stay, that many trees still stood, that lumbering would apparently go on? There was no scientific, let alone public, knowledge of forest fire dynamics and so no understanding that a fire in mixed forests such as those of the Miramichi leaves many of the trees within their borders unburnt. The obvious conclusion to be drawn was that the original descriptions of the fire had been embellished. But this was a difficult charge to level directly: donors did not want to distrust victims. They would prefer to believe that their charity had brought about this apparent turnaround.

It was left to the people of the Miramichi to admit that there was doubt abroad as to the scale of their misfortune. The editor of the *Chatham Mercury* noted, "To such of our readers as are aware, that in some quarters, the loss by the fire in Miramichi was supposed to be overrated."[128] Similarly, when the Miramichi relief committee published its final report in 1829, it delicately admitted that "an opinion might very naturally arise as the novelty subsided, that more money had been subscribed than the urgency of the case required," and so it explained in detail how so much money and provisions had been usefully dispensed. (The committee also defended financial compensation as a necessary stage in the aid process. It acknowledged that "an opinion has prevailed, particularly in Great-Britain, that when once the more formidable effects of the fire had been subdued, the people might be quickly restored to a situation not much inferior to that which they enjoyed before their dreadful visitation." The committee argued, however, that whereas Britain's existing infrastructure ensured that disasters there were of temporary and limited effect, in an infant colony such as New Brunswick, the survivors of disaster had to rebuild from scratch.)[129] But in 1825 and 1826, this was more than just a matter of the Miramichi's reputation: subscriptions were promises to donate money, so if a feeling grew that the scale of the catastrophe had been exaggerated, subscribers might not pay up. It is impossible to calculate whether the Miramichi relief effort dealt with more delinquent subscriptions than did other charity drives of that period, let alone to calculate whether this delinquency was primarily caused by a belief that the disaster had been overstated or by the contemporary financial crisis, but it is clear that throughout 1826 some subscribers did not follow through on their pledges.[130]

All that the organizers could do was ensure that every bit of charity was well spent – accumulating, in the process, evidence of the scale of disaster. In December 1825 the Miramichi relief committee distributed forms to all survivors that asked them, upon a sworn oath, to compile an itemized list of all the losses sustained "by the fire at Miramichi, N.B. on Friday, 7th October 1825" – thus limiting their range of interest, if not the purported range of the disaster, to that single place and day. By February the committee had compiled what it said was a complete tally of the fire's devastation: 160 dead, 3,078 sufferers, 303 houses and 595 buildings destroyed, 875 livestock dead, £30,000 worth of manufactured timber on 30,000 acres of private property destroyed, and £248,523 in total losses, exclusive of timber on Crown lands.[131]

Such accounting and the relief effort more generally were complicated by the fact that there were two separate New Brunswick groups accepting donations and distributing relief. Besides the Miramichi committee, there was a Fredericton committee that had been convened by Governor Douglas on 8 October to raise funds for the victims of the fire there. This committee consisted of leaders of the colonial establishment and was chaired by Commissioner of Crown Lands and Forests Thomas Baillie.[132] Once Fredericton learned that fire had torched the Miramichi and Oromocto Rivers the same day, this body evolved into a "central committee," which because of its power and connections took responsibility for the major subscription drives in British and American cities as well as legislative grants and the aid flowing directly to the governor. The existence of two relief groups raised two related problems. First, there was the matter of divining and weighing the significance of what motivated relief. On the one hand, it was the accounts of death and devastation on the Miramichi that received all the press and that presumably led people in Glasgow, Quebec City, and Philadelphia to open their wallets, so perhaps the people of the Miramichi deserved disproportionate relief. On the other hand, a fire was a fire, a survivor a survivor; a settler burned out on the Oromocto River on 7 October was as much a victim of the "Miramichi" Fire as was a settler on the Miramichi River. The second problem was that properties in the colony's capital of Fredericton tended to be better established and more valuable, so the crowd there might calculate their town's losses as proportionally greater than those on the Miramichi River. If the relief effort was poorly handled, it could easily drift into accusations of illegitimacy and misappropriation.

The government of the colony moved to forestall any such drama by launching a commission in February 1826 to investigate losses "occasioned by the Fires in the month of October, 1825." The five commissioners – notably including a member of each of the two relief committees – were also to develop a system for the distribution of funds. They travelled that spring through the burnt-over areas of New Brunswick, taking sworn and corroborated statements of losses.[133] Miramichi citizens' anxiety was palpable in the pages of the new local newspaper, the *Chatham Mercury*. If the commissioners found that the damage in the Miramichi – or even its damage relative to other regions – had been overstated, not only would the region see its reputation sullied within the colony and across the Western world, but it would also receive reduced financial aid. So it was a relief when the commissioners announced in June that the total damages in the colony generally and the Miramichi region specifically were just as significant as originally supposed. They calculated total losses at around £225,000, of which £193,000 (86%) occurred on the Miramichi River. Fredericton was said to have almost £27,000 in losses (12%), farmers along the Oromocto River almost £5,500 (2.5%), and farmers in Charlotte County just over £1,100 (0.5%).[134] These figures corresponded quite closely to what newspaper coverage of the disaster had suggested the relative proportion of damage had been.

The commission acknowledged that it was the fire as experienced on the Miramichi River that had drawn the world's attention and that this unique role in attracting charity gave the Miramichi region a unique claim to receiving charity. "The ruling principle in the distribution of every donation, must be the intention of the donor." The commissioners calculated that the Miramichi had already received £11,800 of relief, Fredericton £984, and Oromocto and Charlotte £953. They advised that of the £20,000 more still available to the colony, £18,000 be distributed straightaway, of which people in the Miramichi should receive £15,500, Fredericton £1,700, and Oromocto and Charlotte £800.[135] The *Chatham Mercury*'s editor, James Pierce, could not have been happier. "To say that ample justice has been done to Miramichi, is to say too little; we know that public expectation was carried to a pretty high pitch – and yet we find that all agree in saying, the result is beyond their most sanguine expectations."[136] The Miramichi and its fire had been vindicated.

The commission recommended that distribution of financial aid be handled by local committees whose members knew the local conditions. But it offered strong opinions as to which classes should and should not receive aid. This had been raised as an issue as soon as it became clear just how much charity was flowing in. "The question now arises," the *Halifax Novascotian* had noted, "how this large sum is to be disposed of – it is quite too much to distribute among the lower class of sufferers," as it might pull them out of the lower class. The newspaper's opinion was that the singular nature of this disaster "ought to remove that feeling of stern, though manly independence, which should actuate men upon ordinary occasions."[137] That is, the fire had reduced people of all classes to an equal state of destitution, so even those who had been well off should accept charity. The giving and taking of aid were always awkward matters in a society that assumed a correlation between wealth and goodness, poverty and sin. (Consider that the word "embarrassment" was used most commonly in this era in terms of economic hardship.)[138] It was especially awkward in this case because the conflagration seemed so freighted with religious meaning. If the fire was God's punishment for the excesses of the lumber trade, who was deserving of aid?[139]

The commission separated losses into those suffered by merchants and traders, mechanics, professional men, farmers, lumberers, labourers, tavern keepers, and widows and single women. This was a remarkably tidy classification system, given how many farmers, merchants, and labourers were also engaged in the lumber trade to one degree or another. (What made one farmer-lumberer a "farmer" and another a "lumberer"?) Without explanation, the commissioners then removed the merchants and traders, professional men, and tavern keepers from the list of "proper objects of the charitable donations." They devoted the final sentences of their report to stressing why farmers deserved the most consideration: "Persons of this class beginning in the wilderness, have accumulated their means under severe privations, by hard labour, and slow degrees, and the fruit of years of patient industry, is swept away from them in an instant. They have now the same laborious process to go over again,

126 The Miramichi Fire

under circumstances of infinite disadvantage, arising from the very devastation which has caused their ruin."[140] In making this statement, the commissioners were voicing not only their preference for agriculture but also the widely held belief that forest fires vaporized the soil. The commissioners were in essence arguing that farming remained the proper activity of new settlers even on the marginal farmland of northeastern New Brunswick, although the great fire had made farming a more dubious prospect than ever. The timber trade merited no such consideration. The commission refused outright to compile losses on cut timber or standing wood, owing to the "obvious impracticability of ascertaining it with precision." But it did admit that such losses were immense.[141]

Because receiving charity was such a fundamentally embarrassing thing to admit, there is virtually no published discussion as to the actual distribution of financial aid. The disbursement of funds presumably happened in the second half of 1826, although even that is uncertain. There was a report from November of that year of a shipment of relief funds on its way to the Miramichi, guarded by military escort.[142] In any case, when the Miramichi relief committee implemented the provincial commission's recommendations, it demonstrated that it shared the commission's preference for agriculture. The Miramichi committee's final report, published in 1828, reused the commission's occupational classification system.[143] It also plagiarized the commission's glowing tribute to farmers and then bluntly added, in its own words, that lumberers by comparison had deserved "but little claim" for assistance. Although lumberers had the fourth largest amount of allowable losses (even after losses of timber or standing wood had been disallowed), they were allotted the eighth largest amount of relief. Farmers received not only by far the most relief of any occupation, at £17,000 of the more than £35,000 disbursed, or 47 per cent, but also the most in comparison to its occupation's claimed losses, at £17,000 of £69,000 disbursed, or 24 per cent. By comparison, lumberers were allotted just £1,361, less than 4 per cent of what was awarded and 10 per cent of what they had claimed. Innkeepers received more total aid than lumberers did.[144] It is a powerful testimonial to the agrarian ideal that even in a community built on the timber trade, those who worked in this trade were looked upon as less than fully deserving. It is also telling that there is no public record of anyone complaining that the relief was distributed in this fashion.

The Phoenix

Local historian W.D. Hamilton has compiled the reported losses of a number of Miramichiers, compared these losses to the financial compensation they received, and traced how the disparity between the two affected their life after the fire. The worst cases he documents all involve lumbermen. Consider the case of Samuel Allison, a lumberman living on Boom Road along the Northwest branch of the Miramichi River, who claimed a loss of £608 in the fire but received only £25 in compensation in 1826; he declared bankruptcy later that year. Or lumber operator James Bubar on "the Meadows" (Sunny Corner-Exmoor), also on the Northwest branch, who claimed £1,000, received £160, and promptly left the Miramichi. Or Richard McLaughlin, a large lumber operator (and successful farmer), who claimed £5,153 in losses but received only £257 in compensation. Heavily indebted both to Gilmour and Rankin and to Cunard, McLaughlin gave them everything he had, became homeless, lost his faculties, and died a pauper.[145] These men were not necessarily representative: they lost a lot because they had accumulated a lot and so had farther to fall. But their stories are a valuable reminder that even given an impressive international relief effort, the Miramichi Fire was undeniably a disaster in the lives of many who survived it.

The relief effort had been impressive nonetheless, and there was a great deal of pride in the colony that it had been launched, organized, and dispensed with such alacrity. When in 1827 the writer of a letter to the *Eastport Sentinel* in Maine complained that no American living or working in New Brunswick at the time of the fire had received compensation, the Fredericton central committee thought this "base calumny" so required refutation that it compiled and published as a handbill a list of nineteen US citizens who had received relief.[146] The relief effort's reputation survived and for at least a generation was considered something of a model for responding to disasters in Canada. In May 1845 a fire broke out in the Saint-Roch district of Quebec City, destroying 1,650 wooden houses and displacing some 12,000 people. The Miramichi example was brought up straightaway – and again a year later when the relief effort stalled. *Le Journal de Québec* thundered, "At the time of the Miramichi fire, £150,000 was distributed in *fourteen days*" – a gross overstatement in terms of both speed and amount – "and the committee de Quebec was scarcely able to distribute two-thirds of this sum in *fourteen months*."[147] When six years later an early frost killed the harvest and threatened famine in the eastern townships of Lower Canada, the same newspaper mused that the government must decide whether a relief effort similar to that instituted after the Miramichi Fire was required.[148]

The Miramichi relief effort started to become part of public memory even before its work was complete. After the 1826 disbursement of funds, victims of the fire kept coming forward with petitions for aid. These requests offered incidental critiques of the limits of the original charity. William Murray of Gagetown, southeast of Fredericton, lost his house to the 1825 fire and petitioned for help in 1827 because, "although the County in many sections suffered severely," Gagetown had been outside the general range of relief. He received the £12 he requested.[149] Likewise, James Campbell and Ammon Fowler of Kings County, in the south end of the province, petitioned for a share of the available funds for losses sustained in an August 1825 forest fire.[150] Unstated in such cases is that, in terms of the relief effort, the date of 7 October and the Miramichi had provided useful foci to the devastation, but they had also simplified a complex of fires that had burned over a larger area and a longer period in 1825. Nor did the great fire spell the last of burning forests, and so there was a stream of letters requesting funds from the central committee for losses by fires in 1826 through 1828. The committee was accommodating of such requests, mostly because it still retained some money from the relief effort – which, considering that all the money raised had been only a fraction of the losses sustained, shows how tightly relief funds had been controlled. The central committee ultimately resolved to hold the remaining money in order to help victims of future fires that were sure to come.

This was a reasonable decision but moved ever further away from the donors' original intentions. In 1831 a group of Scottish donors took the Miramichi committee to court in Scotland, demanding that £600 in unspent funds be released and turned over to another charity of their choice: Pictou Academy, a nonsectarian college in Nova Scotia. The plaintiffs claimed that there were "statements circulated here that there was no distress still subsisting attributable to the fires." The Miramichi committee might well have taken this suit as a sign that it was time to fold its operations. But instead, it fought the case. And it won by providing evidence that the funds were still needed by sufferers and still being spent.[151] The Fredericton-based central committee held its own final meeting the following year and emptied the larder, transferring some of its fund to the still-existing Miramichi committee. Of the remainder, "Resolved that the above Balance of £170 be immediately apportioned and distributed among such of the Sufferers

The Phoenix

in Fredericton, whose Losses were the most Severe, and *who still labour under its desolating effects*."[152] The Miramichi Fire charity effort had swept across the Western world in the fall of 1825 with some of the speed and intensity of the fire itself, but its impress, like that of the fire, lasted much longer.

In its final report, the Miramichi Fire relief committee declared that it had overseen the distribution of £37,606 worth of provisions and funds,[153] which suggests that assistance to the entire colony was in the range of £50,000. This is an impressive amount, corresponding to millions of dollars in present-day terms.[154] Still, it represented only a fraction of the colony's economy and, more pertinently, of the losses sustained in the fire. But its significance was much greater. For a time in the fall of 1825, the Miramichi Fire, its victims, and its survivors were the talk of newspapers, sermons, and coffeehouses across the Western world and were the stuff of poetry and song. This outpouring of interest and aid was of great comfort to the people of New Brunswick, particularly to those of the Miramichi region. It united them in a common experience while simultaneously connecting them to the wider world. It reassured the people, many of whom were recent arrivals, that they remained tied to Great Britain and to its other colonies. At any number of points, the charity effort might easily have bred controversy – when the British contribution was unexpectedly small, for example, or when the committees determined which professions merited relief – but there is no record of discord among New Brunswickers. There is in fact no indication that they even noticed such things. Instead, the assistance received was spoken of at the time and in the years to come only with pride – a remarkable thing in itself, given the stigma associated with receiving charity in that era.

***

In 1829 the British journalist Samuel Carter Hall, a famously sanctimonious bore said to have been the model for the villainous Pecksniff in Charles Dickens's *Martin Chuzzlewit*, penned a ten-stanza ballad entitled "The Burning of Miramichi." It is exactly what you would expect. There is a coming darkness, a tempest, fainting wives, heroic husbands, a morning after, and a gentle reminder of a benevolent God. And a benevolent Britain. Hall's poem ends,

> Thine is an awful tale to tell –
> Tried and afflicted! – but thy call

130   *The Miramichi Fire*

Came on our Britain like a spell
That roused thy brethren, one and all;
And soon the ready hand was seen
To heal thy wounds, to calm thy woes –
And from the spot, where thou hadst been,
A nobler town arose![155]

But *was* the post-fire Miramichi nobler? For the death and destruction
to have any meaning whatsoever, it had to be. The phoenix effect –
survivors' desire not just to remake communities that have experienced
disaster but to remake them better than before – virtually required
it. So, for that matter, does our inborn desire for a Cinderella-style
story arc. After experiencing rising fortunes, the Miramichi had been
reduced to cinders, so it seemed only right and proper that it recover
and live happily ever after.

That the Miramichi rose out of it ashes stronger than before became
the standard way of presenting the fire's social effects. In Mrs William
T. Savage's 1865 novel *Miramichi*, for example, a character who
returns to the area in 1828 recounts in a letter, "There is also a mar-
vellous change in the moral aspect of the country. It is ascribed in a
great degree to the deep impression made upon the minds of the
people by the conflagration ... It was a judgment upon the community
for its exceeding wickedness. Nothing short of a grand, widespread
illumination like that, could have penetrated the gross darkness that
hung over the land."[156] And such a reading was rendered not just
long after the fact. A Baptist missionary who had spent time in the
Miramichi in the early 1820s – a time when, he stated, "it was almost
a crime to speak of religion" – reported in 1826 that there was a
newfound interest in the spiritual. The missionary's replacement was
more cautious, saying that morals were still very corrupt and that for
a time in the fire's wake, if anything, "the hearts of the people were
harder than before." But he confirmed that beginning in late 1825
more Miramichiers found religion, and he had soon converted forty-
nine souls. (They were persuaded, perhaps, by his claim that God had
spared Baptists and their property.)[157] Other observers linked moral
improvements not directly to the fire but to the Miramichi's late 1820s
transition away from square timber to sawmilled lumber production,
a transition that will be discussed in the next chapter. Whereas timber
work forced groups of men to live together in proximity in the backwoods for months at a time, resulting in all manner of sin, sawmill

The Phoenix   131

work at the river's mouth meant that men could (or had to) go home to a family every night.[158]

But it was a perceived shift from the timber trade to agriculture that was generally seen as both cause and evidence of the Miramichi's improvement. The calls immediately after the great fire to switch to farming, in order to make full use of ash's and charcoal's fertilizing properties, had failed, but the switch was said to be occurring at a more deliberate pace. The Northumberland Agricultural and Emigrant Society, for example, noted an increased interest in livestock, occasioned by the importation from Scotland of some Ayrshire cattle, and reported the provision of implements and seeds to replace those lost in the fire.[159] When writer John McGregor passed through the Miramichi in 1828, he noted that the depression and the fire "drove the actual settlers to the cultivation of the soil for the means of subsistence; and since that time they have devoted their attention nearly with as much industry to agriculture as to the timber business." In a footnote, he recounted coming down the Southwest branch of the Miramichi River and being "astonished at the unexpected progress made during so short a period in the cultivation of the soil."[160] McGregor reiterated this impression before the 1835 Select Committee on Timber Duties, stating that since the mid-1820s, "the lumberers, even along the banks of the Miramichi, have devoted a great portion of their time to the cultivation of the soil" and were in better straits accordingly. But note that they were still "lumberers." McGregor believed that, whereas previously almost all Miramichiers had been engaged in the timber trade, now only half were – but it was still half.[161] And he was wrong as to the extent of timber's prior dominance: as mentioned previously, even in 1825, only about half of adult men had been involved in the trade.[162] In encouraging Miramichi citizens away from forest work and toward farming, observers had long overstated the hegemony of the former, the weakness of the latter, and the incompatibility of the two. So although the fire and depression did result in an uptick in agriculture concurrent with a slump in timber production, it was not transformational. Farmland was just too marginal and the forests were still too abundant for agriculture to displace the timber trade in the Miramichi.[163]

Robert Cooney was working in a mercantile firm and living only a mile from Newcastle when the Miramichi Fire hit. It is little wonder that when he turned to writing and published *A Compendious History of the Northern Part of the Province of New Brunswick* in 1832, he

132   *The Miramichi Fire*

gave the fire pride of place, devoting fifteen pages to it – more than he gave to the entire eighteenth century. Historian M. Brook Taylor calls Cooney's interpretation of the region's history "unique, for he put at the centre of his account not the arrival of the Loyalists or the conquest of New France but the region's own Great Fire."[164] But that is not really so unique: natural disasters are often portrayed as causing social change and lend themselves to a before-and-after periodization. Cooney's history can be interpreted as chronicling how the fire saved northern New Brunswick, readjusting the region from a path of lumber speculation to a more sensible, substantial agriculture. The author took a few swipes at lumbermen of the pre-fire period, calling them "men of little property and less integrity," but he saved his adjectives for a glowing, full-page tribute to the resurrected Miramichi region:

> A great deal of the scorched and burnt land, saved by the timely application of grass seeds, and other semenal reclaimants, is re-invested with a smiling sward. Newcastle, like a Phoenix, has risen from its ashes; and now blossoms over its original site with renewed beauty. A larger, as well as handsomer Douglastown, has emerged from the ruins of the old one; and Moorfields, Bartibog, Nappan, &c. also display an equal share of the general renovation ... Agriculture is rapidly advancing; every day extends the diffusion of its benignity; and while, by the exercise of its embellishing and provident genius, it labors to reclaim the wilderness; clothe the soil with verdure, and provide a granary for future exigency, it also mildly reproves us for our former negligence.[165]

Yet Cooney could not fully sustain this narrative arc. One would expect him, in depicting Miramichi life before 1825, to have presented a dark and demoralized society, but instead he painted a scene of joyful optimism: "Every heart throbbed with pleasure; present enjoyment inspired coeval happiness; and future prospects opened a pleasant way before us." And in describing contemporary society, just before mentioning agriculture's rapid advance, he noted that "the sphere of our manufacture has been enlarged by the erection of Sawmills."[166] The timber trade was still very much under way and contributing to life.

It is as though Cooney wanted to tell a story of change, but constancy kept leaking through – because, as the next chapter will show,

The Phoenix 133

as destructive as the Miramichi Fire had been, it had not obliterated the Miramichi forests, and every day they recovered a little from what damage they had sustained. It was these factors that led the vast majority of survivors to stay in the region, to rebuild their houses, businesses, towns, and rivalries, and to return to a timber trade that had enriched the region once and might well do so again. And it was this resolve that had so bewildered distant observers, particularly during the relief effort: if the forest fire had been as bad as reported, what was the point of rebuilding a forest industry? It was a messy story from which to take a moral. The Miramichi could never entirely be a phoenix because it had never entirely been ashes.

5

The Barrens and the Birches

*Never to be forgotten – Forgotten – The burnt land – Deadfalls –
The Bartibog settlement reborn – The crisis in the colonies – The
fire next time – Back to business – From timber to lumber – How
the fire worked against itself – The Alexander party – The nature
of succession – A very different growth – Thoreau vs Greeley –
Freshets, fish, and wildlife – A missing history – Firefighting and
fire prevention – Old-growth, new-growth, no-growth – The
Barrens – The loss of centuries – New Brunswick's favourite son –
"On the Limits of the Great Fire" – Evidence on the page and
of the eye – A two-fire solution – Ganong's impact – Ganong's
duality – Nature's variety*

Never far from Miramichiers' minds in those early years of reconstruction, memory of the great fire blazed with special intensity on
its anniversary. James Pierce, the editor of the *Chatham Mercury*,
made sure to reflect on it each time the day came around. In October
1826 he commended the settlements along the Miramichi River for
observing a general fast and thanksgiving and for attending special
church services to honour "the never to be forgotten 7th October."[1]
Two years further on, the day was still being commemorated in this
fashion, and Pierce was still praising the communities for it: "This is
just as it should be – so long as the steps of the 'destroying angel' are
visible to the eye that witnessed his gigantic strides – so long as the
effect of his terrible power awaken mournful recollections in the
bosom of the 'survivor' the day should be celebrated."[2]

So long as the fire's effects were visible. But how long would that
be? Pierce provided an answer the following year: "Long, long will
the traces of that fire be visible, for altho' Newcastle has risen like a
phenix from its ashes, and another Douglastown has emerged from

the ruins of the old one, and time by its mellowing influence, has softened the effects, the once beautiful scenery that ornamented the river and blended its sylvan charms with the bustle of commerce, has not recovered its lost attractions; the trees are still leafless – the forest is yet charred, and the nudity of the one and lividness of the other, preserve the harrowing recollections of that night, to which we advert with mingled feeling of gratitude and awe."[3] Yet just a year later, on the fire's fifth anniversary, Pierce claimed that "the footprints of the destroying angel are hardly visible and the country is fast emerging from the embarrassing effects of that awful and destructive calamity." The steps of the destroying angel, so visible in 1828 and predicted to be long visible in 1829, were hardly visible in 1830. Thanks to the initial aid from Great Britain and America, and thanks above all to the perseverance and industriousness of the local populace, "the black charred forest, so repulsive to the sight, is fast fallen beneath the vigorous stroke of the settler – and its place succeeded by the verdant pasture."[4] Pierce was not suggesting that the forests and settlements of the Miramichi region had healed dramatically between 1829 and 1830: he actually described them in quite similar terms over those two years. Rather, his emphasis changed. In the former, the fire's effects were everywhere. In the latter, societal and natural regeneration predominated. Both were true, and a single observer could choose which reality to accentuate.

If a fire destroys nothing and no one, there is nothing to talk about. If a fire destroys everything and everyone, there is no one to talk about it. But between these two extremes, there are countless permutations of casualties and survivors and of the damaged and the intact, and there are countless possibilities to emphasize one or the other. The Miramichi Fire was portrayed in the fall of 1825 as such an unprecedented natural disaster that it was widely assumed the region was all but obliterated – and as a result, distant readers were bewildered to hear Governor Howard Douglas's claim just a few months later that providence had smiled on the colony.[5] What did it mean that there were so many survivors and that so many decided to stay? What did it mean that they were rebuilding the timber trade and that there were presumably sufficient standing trees to do so? Did the fact that communities survived to commemorate the great fire each year paradoxically prove only that what they were commemorating had been exaggerated?

Those attempting to assess the great fire have, quite naturally, tried to understand it in a single way and to imbue it with a single meaning. That has been true right down to the present. In 1991 the aptly named forest historian Forrest B. Meek, in attempting to prove the Miramichi Fire merited its awesome reputation, went so far as to reduce it to a single number. "If we assume that each acre of forest produced 15,000 feet of timber," he wrote, "a fire which swept over 4,000,000 acres would have destroyed an astounding 6.0 billion feet of timber." With the assistance of a multiplier or two, he concluded that the fire cost the New Brunswick economy $120 million.[6] But such a calculation is utterly misguided. Even if it were possible to determine with confidence the average timber per acre across immense, variable, and unsurveyed mature and old-growth forests such as those of the Miramichi Fire zone, it is ecologically impossible for all those acres to have burned equally, let alone completely. Just attempting such a calculation obscures the reality: that a conflagration such as this one did not, could not, have a simple, let alone single, effect on the great range of forests over which it burned.

This chapter traces the twinned histories of how the great fire affected Miramichi forests over time and how the fire has been remembered. The fire itself was an ephemeral event, one that no one could witness in its entirety. So for those who sought to understand it afterward, the state of the forests provided the most visible evidence of its severity and range. However, the fire, like all forest fires, had burned in some places and not in others, and it had burned in some places more severely than in others. What's more, in burning highly specific vegetation and soil environments, it had produced greatly uneven effects. Its impact was highly dependent on topographical factors, such as whether the fire burned a hill on the upslope or downslope, as well as the grade of that slope. Some species of vegetation were less susceptible to damage from fire, and others flourished in the post-fire landscape; some were fire-resistant and some fire-resilient. In some stands, the same tree species regenerated, whereas in other stands, completely different ones appeared. In some places, the fire left behind seemingly barren wastes that served as highly visible, long-lasting monuments to its destructiveness, whereas in other places, the fire encouraged, via succession, the growth of lush new vegetation that called into question its very presence there. Some landscapes showcased the fire, whereas others concealed it. All were products of it.[7]

This variability grew ever more important in interpreting the Miramichi Fire as the event receded further into the past. For one thing, the variability grew more pronounced as the new growth of

The Barrens and the Birches 137

some trees matured to the point that they were all but indistinguishable from trees that had survived the fire. For another, as the initial grief of mourners subsided, and as survivors themselves died off over time, public memory of the fire increasingly required for fuel not just initial human tragedy but also long-term natural devastation. By the late 1800s, many historical accounts of the fire, often written a great distance from New Brunswick, lamented that the Miramichi forests had been utterly destroyed for a century, if not forever – despite the fact that, almost uninterrupted by the fire, the region had sustained a healthy timber economy throughout the century. It was this growing dissonance that in 1905 allowed William Francis Ganong, the leading scholar of New Brunswick of his day, to produce a revisionist essay that cast serious doubt on the Miramichi Fire's original size and destructiveness. Ganong's interpretation would become the dominant way of remembering – and grounds for forgetting – the fire in the twentieth and now twenty-first centuries.

That time would change the fire's history was evident early on to Miramichi newspaperman James Pierce. Although he himself had drawn attention to how the fire's effects had faded, he was still surprised how quickly "the never to be forgotten 7th October" began to be forgotten. The forests were moving on, more settlers were moving in, and the economy was moving forward. Pierce reported in 1833 that on the fire's eighth anniversary, most commercial activity on the Miramichi River ceased for the day, but the local churches did not open their doors, arousing considerable anger among some citizens.[8] The following year, 8 October was named a colony-wide day of fast and thanksgiving unrelated to, and so conflicting with, remembrance of the fire.[9] Beginning in 1835, just ten years after the communities on the Miramichi River experienced one of the worst forests fires in world history, the anniversary was, in Pierce's words, "passed over without being noticed in the slightest manner."[10]

✳✳✳

Four months after the Miramichi Fire, settlements along the Bartibog River, 15 kilometres east of Newcastle on the north bank of Miramichi Bay, petitioned the colonial legislature for assistance. These small enclaves of recent Irish immigrants had suffered a loss of life and livelihood of a scale initially believed to have occurred throughout the entire Miramichi region. The Bartibog area was said to be the eastern limit of the fire's greatest destruction, and the river itself had offered no refuge from the flames, its waters being too low that autumn to cover a body.[11] The petitioners wrote that twenty of their neighbours had died and that many more were weak and sickly, presumably from the long-term effects of smoke inhalation. They described the surrounding woods as "all either burnt or blownd down in Heaps." In fact, for a distance of 8 miles, there was "not a single Tree to be seen Standing that is fit for any other use than fire wood." Yet their request of the legislature was not for food, provisions, or money to relocate but rather for assistance clearing fallen trees along the road to the Miramichi River. They could recover only if they could reconnect to the wider world.[12]

The Great Road that swung by the Bartibog area on its way between the Miramichi settlements and Bathurst was a critical artery for the colony, ensuring that these petitioners would be heard and that passing travellers would comment often on the state of the Bartibog's forests in the decades that followed. The road superintendent reported in 1828 that although "on the Burnt land many Roots of Large Trees that was blowen down at the time of the Great Fire" still lay on the road, it was now passable for sleighs.[13] This reference to "the Burnt land" foretold the Bartibog's long-lasting condition. In his 1832 *A Compendious History of the Northern Part of the Province of New Brunswick*, Robert Cooney used the "frightful and desolate" Bartibog as a stand-in for all forested areas devastated by the fire:

What was formerly liveried in green, and attired in foliage, is now a barren and miserable heath. The stately pine, the tall birch, and the graceful elm, are no longer visible, for the poplar, the wild cherry, and a variety of degenerate scrubs occupy their place. Where such a succession has not occurred, the intrusion of this dwarfish growth, is either opposed or retarded by large entangled groups of *dead, and fallen, and discolored trees*; some standing in gaunt deformity, their scorched and naked trunks, as well as leafless branches, mocked by every wind; others bowed down as if imploring resuscitation from the sun; and some prostrate on the ground from which they sprung. In short, this extensive district presents a picture so desolate, so black, and so gloomy, that disorder and confusion are the only animating tints in the portrait.[14]

Nor was this a fleeting stage of ecological succession: this hellscape lingered. Abraham Gesner remarked fifteen years after Cooney that the Bartibog, which had once had healthy forests, still retained the "gloomy aspect" with which the Miramichi Fire had left it.[15] As late as 1855 it was noted that although the bridge across the Bartibog River required replacing, there was no available lumber, the forests for many miles having in no way recovered from the fire thirty years earlier.[16] The Bartibog forests' bleakness mixed with their prominence – they were visible both along the Great Road and from ships sailing up Miramichi Bay – meaning that they would be identified as a memorial to the great fire for the remainder of the century.

The enduring effects on the Bartibog tract doubtlessly speaks to damage done by the fire not just to the forests' trees but also to the underlying soil. A severe wildfire is capable of causing dramatic changes to soils and soil hydrology. In obliterating organic matter both atop and within the ground, it can loosen the soil's binding and cause erosion. The loss of groundcover can simultaneously dry the soil out, enhancing its water repellency, and make it more susceptible to raindrops' full impact – both of which in turn can make it more prone to erosion. Although erosion was unlikely to have been a problem given the Bartibog's relatively level topography, it undoubtedly was elsewhere in the Miramichi watershed. But beyond just altering the structure and location of soil, fire also radically transforms its chemical and biological properties. It kills the subsurface microorganisms that constitute the forest's hidden biota, produces nutrient loss as minerals are vaporized from solid to gas and are lost from the system, and raises the soil's pH level. To be sure, fire also deposits ash and charcoal as fertilizer and sets the stage for pioneering early-successional plants to rush in and colonize a site. If it didn't, if fire only killed forests and didn't also create the conditions for their regeneration, there would eventually be no forests. Yet occasionally, a fire *can* be so devastating to a location that the subsoil ecosystem does not recover and the seeds of pioneers are either absent or cannot take root.[17] These are the conditions that produce scenes such as that in the Bartibog forests. Nineteenth-century people did not fully understand this process but recognized that the soil was involved. Indian Commissioner Moses Perley, writing about a Mi'gmaw reserve on the Northwest branch of the Miramichi River in 1841, described a barren tract, 16 square miles in size, as "'burnt land,' it having been swept over by the Great Fire of October 1825, which not only destroyed the vegetable matter on the surface, but actually calcined the sand and gravel to such an extent as to leave the land incapable of bearing anything but Blueberries."[18] Likewise, as reported by agricultural chemist James F.W. Johnston, who had travelled for an entire day through the desolate aftermath of the great fire along the Southwest branch of the Miramichi River, "The substance of the soil is gone, it is said, where the burning has been too severe."[19] And in his monumental 1864 *Man and Nature*, George Perkins Marsh turned to the Miramichi Fire as an example of a fire "of such intensity that it seemed to consume the very soil itself."[20]

In places such as the Bartibog, not only did the great fire kill the trees without replacing them, but it also left them in the way. Deadfalls – trees, whether burnt or not, that had been brought down by the fire's hurricane-like (and perhaps hurricane) winds – were a serious obstacle to Miramichiers attempting to rebuild. Deadfalls had been all but absent in the pre-fire late-successional forests, but now they were everywhere. The charity pamphlet told of large, healthy trees having been snapped in two and thrown 20 feet onto the road.[21] In 1827 James Forein, who carried the mails between the Miramichi communities and the Nepisiguit River, near Bathurst, petitioned the legislature for extra funds, saying that deadfalls resulting from the fire had made his travel difficult in winter and impossible in summer, such that he was forced to take a much longer journey either down the Northwest branch of the Miramichi River or along the coast.[22] The legislature set aside £500 that spring to rebuild bridges and remove deadfalls.[23] Downed timber also hampered the colony's timber industry by making inaccessible both the communities that provisioned lumbermen and the forest interior itself.[24] It was particularly unfortunate that, thanks to its great height and shallow roots, the white pine, the most important timber tree in the Miramichi forests, was particularly susceptible to windthrow, much more so than hardwoods.[25] How much this fact alone affected the post-fire timber economy is unknowable. But it is clear that deadfalls resulting from the fire impeded life in the Miramichi for a very long time. Describing the travails of passing through a "burnt land" littered with windthrows in 1844, James Alexander wrote, "It would be exceedingly difficult to clear a road through woods such as these, which had so recently been burnt" – "recently" being almost two decades earlier.[26]

Yet the very existence of the Bartibog petition in the winter of 1826 signalled that even this area, so devastated by the great fire, was not being forsaken, its residents having found reason to remain. They spoke of it proving to be good farmland before the disaster and of their desire to return to clearing it. (True, the petitioners may have

The Barrens and the Birches   141

emphasized farming over forestry in the belief, likely accurate, that their appeal would be looked on more favourably. They also flattered Governor Douglas by citing his post-fire visit to the Miramichi as great inspiration for their decision to stay.)[27] In Cooney's 1832 book, after describing the Bartibog's deathly landscape, the author then mentioned that there were twenty-three families farming along the shores of its river and two good grist mills in operation.[28] In the decades that followed, the Bartibog settlement never exactly thrived, but neither did it ever fold.[29] That a timber community could suffer indisputably intensive and enduring damage to its forests yet survive shows how difficult it is to assess the Miramichi Fire's impacts.

✳✳✳

The Bartibog represented one end of a spectrum of forest damage, but many forests within the fire zone suffered far less. Indeed, immediately after describing the state of the Bartibog forests in his 1832 book, Cooney remarked that along the Miramichi River and its branches there still stood "a great deal of very excellent white pine" and other timber species.[30] Nor was this a retrospective, revisionist interpretation: accounts closer in time to the fire made the same assessment. In 1831 a Northumberland County committee that included lumbermen Alexander Rankin and James Fraser petitioned the colony to continue leasing small forest lots to individual immigrants, stating "[t]hat although a great quantity of Timber has been cut and exported, and immense Groves totally destroyed by the great Fire of 1825, Yet some valuable Tracts of Wood suitable for the British Market still exist on the River Miramichi and its Branches."[31] In 1827, dispatched by the Colonial Office to seek potential sites for immigration in British North America, Lieutenant Colonel Francis Cockburn and his assistants travelled widely throughout the Miramichi and somehow never even mentioned the great fire.[32] And before all these accounts, there was the evidence of late 1825 itself, provided in reports recognizing that the Miramichi's future "was not altogether blasted," that "the staple article of export of this place is not injured to the extent that was first anticipated, and that the lumberers are again going on with great spirit."[33] Woodsmen had reason to make haste in restarting the timber trade, beyond the desire to make back some of the money they had lost in the fire. The conventional wisdom was that even burnt timber could be salvaged *if* it was cut down and lumbered immediately, before, as "W" (likely Cooney) wrote in the *Chatham Gleaner* in

1831, "the worm finds entrance, and will quickly eat the whole of the sap into holes, and render the timber useless."[34] So some Miramichi lumbermen loaded and shipped lumber within days of the fire and cut still more that winter. The best evidence that vast forests were left standing after the fire was that they were immediately being cut down.

But the fate of the timber harvested in the autumn of 1825 demonstrates what makes it so difficult to establish precisely the environmental and social effects of the Miramichi Fire: they cannot be evaluated in isolation from other factors. As "Civis" (again, Cooney) later recalled in the *Gleaner,* the wood that arrived in Britain that fall received an extremely low price – not because of inferior quality, real or imagined, but because of "depreciation in the home market."[35] The British financial crisis of late 1825 meant that the price of timber had collapsed; the scarcity of money meant that even with a smaller supply available, there was no demand whatsoever.[36] Miramichi ships lay in estuaries fully loaded with unsold wood, waiting for the price to rebound. "We have two of Cunards Miramichi cargoes at the Clyde & two at Leith & cannot sell a stick," one firm reported in October 1826, a full year after the bubble had burst.[37] In fact, the depression had only worsened in 1826, with ramifications that rippled back across the Atlantic.[38] "The year 1825 destroyed our property, and 1826 witnessed the ruin of our credit," according to "Civis."[39] It was not so much, the author argued, that New Brunswick had gotten dragged into Britain's problems but rather that they were both victims of rampant speculation and loose credit, which in the colony had involved the timber trade specifically and in the motherland finance generally. Testifying before the 1835 Select Committee on Timber Duties, writer John McGregor treated the great fire as a convenient dividing line in the Miramichi's history, but he saw the broader economic depression, not the fire, as ultimately responsible for this dramatic change. It was what he dubbed "the Crisis in the Colonies, from 1825 to 1831" that finally convinced should-be farmers throughout the colonies to abandon the timber trade.[40]

Even if there had not been an economic downturn, it would still be impossible to gauge precisely the impact of the 1825 Miramichi Fire because some of the region's forests burned again in 1826. Hot early summer weather and fuels left unburnt in the previous conflagration resulted in June fires up the Northwest branch of the Miramichi River toward the Sevogle River and up its Southwest branch beyond the Cains River. Where these fires touched areas torched the previous

The smoke so dense he could barely see across the Miramichi River, *Chatham Mercury* editor James Pierce wrote, "We were particularly struck with the strong resemblance the day preceding our great calamity in October last, and we doubt not but many persons imagined there was cause to dread a similar result."[41] But there is no record of the 1826 fires causing any loss of life or property. Memory of the 1825 blaze undoubtedly exaggerated the danger and range of the 1826 fires – and then the 1826 fires returned the favour when later travellers who wrote accounts of coming upon the 1825 fire zone confused it with the less-famous fires of a year later. The 1826 fires smudged the map of the 1825 Miramichi Fire once and for all.

Having shipped an all-time high of 417,000 tons of timber in 1825, New Brunswick's timber exports plunged in 1826 to two-thirds of that, staying at approximately that level for the next decade and a half.[42] Historical geographer Graeme Wynn has compiled data showing that the amount of timber licensed to be cut decreased across practically every forest district in New Brunswick between 1824–25 and 1828–29. The crash and recession were certainly the primary causes of this reduction, but the degree to which the decline was spatially differentiated throughout the colony suggests that the Miramichi Fire was also a factor. The Northwest Miramichi district experienced the colony's largest drop in timber production both in real terms (from 42,560 to 7,930 tons) and as a percentage of the total (from 17.2% to just 7.2%).[43] What had been the hottest economic area in New Brunswick decidedly cooled. The fire had destroyed some of the available timber, killed some of the lumbermen, destroyed some of the lumbering infrastructure, and – whether for informed reasons or due to assumptions about the state of the forests – encouraged some in the trade to move on to new timber frontiers, particularly in the northernmost part of the colony.

Yet the Southwest Miramichi district, despite also experiencing a significant drop in timber production between 1824–25 and 1828–29 in real terms (from 43,200 to 27,090 tons), actually saw its percentage of the colony's output rise (from 17.5% to 24.6%), with the result that it became the top timber district in New Brunswick.[44] The Miramichi Fire did not set the Southwest Miramichi district back in the manner that it did the Northwest Miramichi district. What makes the two districts' differing fortunes particularly striking is that it was the Gilmour and Rankin firm out of Newcastle, on the Miramichi River's north bank, that focused more of its operations on the Southwest branch, and the Cunard firm out of Chatham, on the south bank, that held more timber berths on the Northwest branch. Yet in 1828–29 Gilmour and Rankin purchased twice as many timber licences as Cunard.[45] That the company and community that had lost more people and infrastructure in the Miramichi Fire rebounded, whereas the firm and community that had suffered fewer such losses slumped, is compelling evidence that the fire had done considerably less damage to forests on the Southwest branch than on the Northwest branch – whether in terms of the area, quantity, or severity of trees burned or windthrown or in terms of some mix of these factors. Still, considering the innumerable factors, the imprecise data, and simply the vast sizes of the two forest districts involved, this differentiation tells us little about the Miramichi Fire's effects. And it may well distract from the broader point: that even in the years immediately following the fire, the Miramichi experienced only a modest dip in its share of the colony's total timber licences (from 34.7% to 31.8%) and remained New Brunswick's leading timber region.

The Miramichi timber trade persisted because there was still supply – and, eventually, again demand. In May 1826 the *Chatham Mercury* reported that the communal log boom on the Northwest branch of the river had broken from the sheer weight of timber against it. The wood had been recorralled, and the newspaper noted that the harbour had already welcomed eighty square-rigged vessels that spring, ready to load all the timber the Miramichi had to offer.[46] It is true that in the next couple of years merchants shipped less timber and sold even less than that. But Britain and elsewhere still needed wood, and the merchants remained in the business of selling it. If anything, the depression's lower price meant they would have to sell more to reap the same returns.[47]

The late 1820s saw the New Brunswick timber industry begin in earnest a transition from exporting ton-timber (i.e., whole logs simply felled and hewn square) to producing saw-logs (i.e., timber processed into boards, planks, and deals). Nowhere was this transition more pronounced than in Northumberland County. Although woodsmen did not pause to explain why it occurred just then, it was clearly related to the fact that they had run out of the most accessible large white pines – the result of highly selective exploitation of the species earlier in the decade, presumably exacerbated by losses in the great fire. The forest industry subsequently needed to make fuller use of smaller pine, spruce, and other species, so it invested heavily in sawmills to process lumber, which encouraged the turn to smaller trees all the more. Sawmills sprung up throughout the Miramichi, along the Southwest branch of the river in particular, but the most impressive of all was Gilmour and Rankin's new stone sawmill in Millbank, near rebuilt Newcastle. It employed up to 170 men at a time, had twenty-four reciprocating saws and two circular ones, could produce 20,000 feet of planks each day, and was situated, as Robert Cooney put it, "so near the channel, that large vessels can load within pistol shot of it."[48] It was by far the largest sawmill in New Brunswick. Indeed, Allan Gilmour, speaking before the British government's 1835 Select Committee on Timber Duties, proudly stated, "We have upon the River Miramichi, I suppose, the best saw-mill in the country" – that is, all of British North America.[49] Joseph Cunard's Chatham firm had not suffered so much loss in the great fire, nor did it exhibit such showy growth, but it expanded its interests throughout the north of the province, too. Between them, by the mid-1830s, the Gilmour and Rankin firm and the Cunard firm held one-third of the licensed timber area in all of New Brunswick.[50] Rather than being ruined by the one-two punch of the fire and the depression, the Miramichi timber trade had recovered.

Just as the fact that the Miramichi communities initially survived the 1825 fire convinced some early, distant observers that the disaster had been exaggerated in size or ferocity, the fact that the timber trade underlying these communities rebounded only confirmed to later observers the same thing. But it is perfectly reasonable to expect good lumbering after a bad fire. As has been discussed, forest fires destroy only a portion of the forest, leaving many trees undamaged and others scarred but marketable. And it may be, as was reported in the charity pamphlet, that the sheer speed of the fire had limited the damage it could inflict.[51] Contemporary Scottish newspapers, their physical distance from the event inoculating them against a focus only on the immediate tragedy, were unusual in considering what the fire's effects would be on the timber trade's future, and they were confident that it would rebound. According to one, "The branches only of the trees are said to have been burnt, as the gale was too violent to permit the fire to rest on the trunks."[52]

An eyewitness who returned to Scotland shortly after the blaze was equally sanguine, saying the trade would not be materially affected because "[w]herever there was a belt or screen of hard wood, the progress of the fire was arrested."[53] The suggestion that softwood and hardwood stands were differentially damaged is likely sound. Generally speaking, the nature of softwoods' needles, branching, and even bark can mean they catch fire more easily.[54] This distinction was sufficiently understood in 1825 that the charity pamphlet told of a woodsman who, realizing he could not outrun the fire, instead headed for a "green hardwood grove" near his camp. Although the fire passed through it, he was unhurt.[55] But one should not make too much of this variability. Hardwood is wood, and it burns, and if the blaze had touched only softwoods such as pine and spruce, more commentators would surely have said so. What's more, vulnerability to fire varies greatly within both hardwood and softwood species. White pine, for example, has comparatively thick bark that protects it in crown fires, yet it also has a comparatively fragile root system, meaning that it can seemingly survive a fire only to die out afterward, standing vigil as a dead snag for another half-century.[56] Even if softwoods were disproportionately damaged in the great fire, it was only a matter of degree, not kind: many softwood trees survived the blaze, whereas many hardwoods did not. Where one might expect softwoods' relative susceptibility to fire to matter most was in relation to the contemporary belief that the presence of softwoods indicated bad soil. In the early nineteenth century, New Brunswick surveyors typically referred to "fine hardwood land" but spoke of "poor land" only in reference to that of coniferous forests.[57] Yet after the great fire, there is no indication that Miramichiers took solace that the worst damage had happened to the worst land. If anything, they were disappointed that the fire had not cleared better land for them. When in 1831 "W" inspected some of the fire zone to see whether it could be reclaimed as farmland, he regretted to report that "the greater part was covered with the evergreens, and which leads to the consequential inference of the poverty of the soil."[58]

One could legitimately continue considering variables that determined the fire's effects on the forests. Topography, for example, was surely critical, even given the relatively gentle slopes of the Miramichi region. It shaped first what vegetation grew where and then – as determined by a slope's being windward or leeward as well as west- or east-facing – whether the fire travelled slowly or quickly and in what direction.[59] But the inability to know pre-fire stand composition, the fire's exact direction and speed, and a hundred other variables

The Barrens and the Birches

147

makes it impossible to comprehend the fire's effects at anything approaching a granular level. And perhaps it does not matter anyway because it mattered less to the people of the Miramichi than one might suppose. Graeme Wynn concludes that in the late 1820s "the inference from scant evidence is that lumbering was largely confined to the broad areas worked earlier in the decade."[60] A fundamental reason the white pine trade had seemed so charmed was that the tree grew conveniently along waterways and lower slopes, where it could be easily obtained and removed. Whether the Miramichi Fire had missed the most popular timber areas or left many marketable trees in them still standing made no appreciable difference to lumbermen – for now, at least, while there were still pines to harvest. "W" took the analogy of a forest half-full to its logical conclusion, reasoning that the ferocity and scope of the 1825 fire had actually become the region's greatest insurance: "The terrors and disasters which we have experienced in no lenient degree, constitute for the present times, the greatest source of security and happiness to new comers."[61] The forests were somewhat reduced, but that meant only that such a horror could not soon be repeated.

$$* * *$$

And every day that the Miramichi Fire receded into the past, nature worked to cover its traces. There were areas such as the Bartibog where the imprint of the fire long lingered, others where it scarcely left a mark, but also many, many others that immediately began to recover. In 1844 James Alexander reached what he identified as the scene of the great fire when leading a survey team through the wilds between the Gaspereau River and the Southwest branch of the Miramichi River. His description begins as just another Bartibog-like nightmare: "The leafless trunks, grey, and with charred 'butts,' now stood round us and on every side, like ghosts on the margins of the Styx, and we had to cut our way through, and to climb over with considerable exertion the prostrate trees, windfalls, entangled with second growth of birch, fir, &c." Progress through the snarls grew more and more difficult, the men tripped and fell hard with their loads, the branches ripped their clothes and footwear to shreds, and their supplies dwindled. "If this goes on," one of Alexander's party was heard to say, "we shall be killed." Defeated, some of the party received permission to quit the expedition and raft down the Cains River to safety while Alexander and the others carried on. But even as Alexander sought to pin his troubles on a landscape ravaged by fire, he captured the riot of life underway there – including the "second growth of birch, fir, &c." mentioned above. Blueberries, which thrive after fire, were plentiful. There were miles of young alder to fight through, new cherry trees, and the "ladylike" birches that grew around a scorched "parent" tree. The depleted survey team finally reached the Great Road between Fredericton and Chatham, where their wild appearance scared off a group of children gathering blueberries along the road. Alexander's description of the expedition appeared in his 1849 *L'Acadie*, which contains a sketch titled "View on the Miramichi." It is a typical sylvan scene, with not a hint of desolation.[62]

The fire that destroys a forest often creates another. It releases the nutrients contained in the plants it burns, delivering a much-needed pulse to stimulate growth. It kills microorganisms in the soil, but in doing so it reduces competition for the nutrients that remain. Seeds already present in the soil have evolved to await just this moment: some species require the heat shock of fire as a germination cue, and some even require smoke. Fireweed, raspberries, blueberries, and other plants would have made their appearance throughout the Miramichi Fire zone in 1826. Many such first responders are nitrogen-fixing, restoring organic nitrogen to a soil depleted of it by fire. Within a few more years, the sprouts of broadleaved pioneer shrubs and trees such as alder, pin cherry (or fire cherry), yellow birch, and aspen – all species that thrive where there is bare soil, direct sunlight, and little competition – would have shot up. They in turn would have provided shade for balsam fir and other species that would in later decades grow through their canopy and crowd them out.[63] This is the standard model for post-fire ecological succession in this part of the world. But its initial stages occurred even more quickly and dramatically than was normal because, after the cool, post-Tambora decade of 1815 to 1825, a warm period beginning in 1825 resulted in exceptional pent-up forest growth. In eastern North America, the period from 1827 to 1835 experienced the most persistently above-average tree ring growth of the past three centuries.[64]

Observers were amazed both by the speed with which burned forests began to grow back and by the composition of these forests. Because fire creates new environmental conditions above and below ground, it can, for example, wipe out the advantages enjoyed by slow-growing, shade-tolerant species and accommodate the rise of fast-growing, shade-intolerant species. As early as 1832, the author of *A Subaltern's*

Figure 5.1 "View on the Miramichi," 1849.

Furlough told of passing through woods burned in the summer of 1825 – in Nova Scotia, notably, not New Brunswick – and being struck that after a fire "a different growth of wood springs up from that which the ground formerly produced; thus a hard timber is frequently succeeded by a soft one, and maple or birch shoot out from amongst the roots of the pine."[65] Throughout northeastern New Brunswick, early-successional trees such as balsam fir, poplar, and yellow birch flourished in the decades after the fire, whereas late-successional, fire-sensitive species such as beech and spruce declined.[66] To be sure, fire was only one agent of this change: widespread land clearing and logging were two other settler introductions that, in intentionally removing forests, also unintentionally remodelled them. But the fact that the great fire came on the heels of the peak logging boom made 1825 a doubly transformative year.

Some saw the trading of an old forest for a new one as a good deal. In describing the Miramichi Fire zone in 1855, surveyor Alexander Monro noted that it was now a much better forest for agriculture: what had been softwood, with needles that did not provide good manuring, was now principally hardwood, with leaves that did.

150 *The Miramichi Fire*

"Hence the land ... being stript by fire, in some places, almost to its subsoil, is now mantled with a growth of trees of the average height of about thirty feet, and will no doubt, if these are allowed to attain the size of forest timber, become much better fitted for agricultural operations, than it ever has been hitherto, at least for many past centuries."[67] And it was not as if the new forest was good only for clearing: it held promise for the lumberman, too. New Brunswick was exporting more yellow birch than pine by 1869, for instance.[68] Although many mid-century travellers noted the forest changes underway in the Miramichi region, the best summary may be that of Nova Scotian geologist Sir John W. Dawson in the 1868 edition of his magnum opus *Acadian Geology*:

> The pine woods of Miramichi, destroyed by the great fire above referred to, have been followed by a second growth principally composed of white birch, larch, poplar, and wild cherry. When I visited this place, twenty years after the great fire, the second growth had attained to nearly half the height of the dead trunks of the ancient pines, which were still standing in great numbers; and in 1866 I found that the burnt woods were replaced by a dense and luxuriant forest principally of white birch and larch ... This is an instructive illustration of the fact, that after a great forest fire an extensive region may in less than half a century be re-clothed with different species from those by which it was originally covered.[69]

That new and different forests sprung from the fire's ashes drew the Miramichi into a contemporary scientific controversy as to how succession occurred. On the one hand, writing in 1831, "W" deduced that among the principal agents of this process were birds led "into the burnt woods in pursuit of the insects which infest the decaying trees, and there depositing the stones and seeds of trees which pass their bodies undigested." (He was right, of course: birds – as well as other animals, wind, and water – do indeed promote seed dispersal.) On the other hand, given that young shoots appeared within two years of the fire, "W" was also "tempted to believe that trees are *indigenous* to this soil, and will spring up without seminal origin."[70] The emergence of new species where they had not been seen before convinced some nineteenth-century observers that in certain circumstances, such as after fire, plants generated spontaneously. (They were wrong, of course: trees need seeds.)

In 1860 the American nature writer Henry David Thoreau penned the essay "The Succession of Forest Trees" expressly to counter the theory of spontaneous regeneration; it would be his most-read work during his lifetime. Nature did not require such contrivances, he argued: all it needed was a seed.[71] Having published Thoreau's essay, *New-York Weekly Tribune* editor Horace Greeley stirred up publicity for it by publishing a letter to Thoreau in rebuttal. Greeley led with this evidence: "In the great Pine forest which covers (or recently covered) much of Maine, New-Brunswick, &c. a long summer drouth has sometimes been followed by a sweeping fire, which swept a district forty miles long by ten to twenty broad as with the besom of destruction ... The very next season, up springs a new and thick growth of White Birch – a tree not before known there. Not a pine or other fir – nothing but miles on miles of deciduous trees, almost entirely White Birch."[72] How could you account for this occurrence? Thoreau replied dryly that pine, by which Greeley presumably meant white pine, was not actually as common in Maine as its fame would suggest. Rather, it was well known that pine principally grew in small "veins" throughout the region. Birch, by contrast, was ubiquitous. It was hardly a surprise that birch's fine, winged seeds scattered and took root in the aftermath of fire – or that they were already present in the soil, ready to do so. It is a small irony that Thoreau, a man still taunted around Concord, Massachusetts, with the nickname "Burnt Woods" for having let a blaze get out of control seventeen years earlier, understood better than most anyone of his day the degree to which life carried on after a fire.[73]

The fire had environmental effects that in turn produced their own unexpected effects. For instance, a survivor who returned to Scotland reported in late 1825 that there was sure to be a decline in timber exports from the Miramichi the following year because 1,000 stone (6,350 kilograms) of hay had burned, and less hay meant less feed for oxen, which meant less timber hauled, which meant less timber shipped.[74] Similarly, the fact that the fire had stripped so much vegetation from the forest floor, allowing rain and melting snow to feed more quickly into rivers, contributed to the spring 1826 freshet being an exceptionally strong one not just in the Miramichi region but across the entire Northeast – with the result that it produced New England's highest spring flooding in at least thirty-five years.[75] On the Miramichi tributaries, the freshet was also exceptionally early, so much so that lumber parties had not yet hauled all their winter's worth of cut timber to the riverbanks and so missed the chance to float some of it down to Chatham and Newcastle.[76] Pierce, the *Chatham Mercury*'s editor, traced the roots of this problem step-by-step back to its source and concluded, "The effects of the fire will probably be longer felt in this respect than in any other."[77] He was right and he was wrong: although subsequent springs also brought huge freshets, they occurred at more opportune times, allowing all cut timber to be brought downriver.[78]

Given that early accounts of the Miramichi Fire were universal in discussing fish and wildlife – their behaviour during the blaze and their appearance in death – the fact that *no* subsequent commentator described the fire's effects on animal populations is nothing short of extraordinary. Did some species suffer greater mortality in the fire than others? Were some populations more resilient afterward? How did the changing concentration of existing faunal and floral species and the introduction of new species reshape the ecology of the Miramichi region? How, in turn, did this altered ecology affect people's ability to feed themselves? Fires actually tend not to have much of an immediate, direct effect on wildlife populations: animals can move, so most escape. But over time, indirect effects resulting from habitat change can be profound.[79] For example, the number of woodpeckers likely soared at first, as they exploited dead standing timber, but over time they would have given way to birds that flourish in new, shrubby growth. (Perhaps that is why in the early 1840s surveyor James Alexander, when approaching what he described as the Miramichi Fire zone, made no mention of birdsong but said that "the woodpeckers with their sharp and strong beaks would interrupt the dead silence around.")[80] Game such as caribou and marten that thrive in late-successional forest environments would not have fared so well, whereas species such as white-tailed deer and moose that relish the chewy vegetation of an early-successional forest would have benefited. More than a century later, eminent New Brunswick biologist Bruce S. Wright called the Miramichi Fire "the greatest single factor in the status of big game in the province for the next one hundred years." Whereas Robert Cooney claimed in 1832 that the moose was extinct in northern New Brunswick – blaming hunters and making no mention of the fire – Wright credited the fire with the moose's return. It had transformed the landscape from a near-continuous forest to a patchier one that mixed open areas with sheltering

The Barrens and the Birches   153

timber, an "ideal moose habitat." The return of the moose in turn attracted wolves. Beaver also appreciated the new aspens rising along the rivers.[81] Wright surely overestimated the impact of the 1825 fire, giving too great a weight to that single event at the expense of the long-term process of ecological disturbance brought about by settler agriculture and forestry. But at least he was making connections that no one had previously made. When James Alexander noted in 1844 that "[b]lueberries were now very numerous in these open and burnt woods, which, when the berries were ripe, would attract bears and flocks of pigeons," he might have mused about whether the fire meant there were more bears and more pigeons. Instead, he moved on.[82]

Later in the nineteenth century the Miramichi River would gain fame for having the most abundant Atlantic salmon run in the world, but the great fire undoubtedly obliterated the 1825 run, killing not just many mature and young fish but also, thanks to the temporarily elevated water temperature, all eggs already deposited.[83] As a result, the 1826 and 1827 salmon fisheries were essentially nonexistent.[84] But even as the catches remained low well into the 1830s, blame fell on the forest industry rather than the fire. Newspaperman James Pierce believed – correctly – that timber driving likely disturbed salmon spawning beds but thought that overfishing by lumbermen was the real culprit: "It is notorious that lumbering parties have cured from 10 to 50 barrels … and what they were unable to consume themselves, they *made an article of food for their Cattle!*" It speaks to the historical importance of small-town newspapers as papers of record that a reader wrote, and the paper published, an impassioned letter to the editor in agreement a full twenty-four months later.[85] Pierce was right to attribute the problem to the timber industry, although like others he underrated the significance of sawdust and other timber debris in choking fish stocks.[86] In the decade prior to the Miramichi Fire, the rise of the timber industry had already reduced the salmon population and fishery to just a fraction of what they had been in the late 1700s. Yet the colony had responded with regulations that targeted not lumbermen but fishermen – including a ban on traditional Indigenous fishing methods in 1824.[87]

So settler colonial policies were putting pressure on Indigenous subsistence even before the fire disturbed fish and game populations. The Mi'gmaq of the Miramichi region simply must have had a great deal of difficulty feeding themselves in the years after the great fire. But since they were not beneficiaries of the charity effort – which in itself demonstrates how little they were noticed and cared for in the colony – there is nothing in the written record of how the fire affected them. In the late 1830s a New Brunswick Indian commissioner reported that in the Miramichi there were approximately 400 Mi'gmaq living hand to mouth because their hunt had been ruined by the great fire.[88] The game population did recover, such that by the 1860s a British writer would once again blame local moose extermination on "Indian hide hunters."[89] But how Mi'gmaq survived the great fire, and how often they did not, is unknown. There is a hole where that history should be.

***

The great fire might be expected to have changed settlers' attitudes and actions toward fire in the Miramichi region and even farther afield. "[T]o tell you the truth," survivor Isaac Hanselpecker said two decades later, "it makes me feel kind a nervous, when I see a fallow burning ever since."[90] The New Brunswick legislature passed bills in 1826 that improved the Fredericton fireward system and required that in the colony's principal towns, the walls behind fireplaces must be stone or brick rather than wood. For their part, Chatham and a rebuilding Newcastle instituted new firefighting measures. The Miramichi communities bought hoses, various tools, and fire engines – Chatham's, at least, coming all the way from Great Britain – and more citizens were tapped as firewards.[91] These actions took place in the context of the early nineteenth century's adoption of civic firefighting across the Western world, but there can be no doubt that the Miramichi Fire focused New Brunswickers' minds.[92] Of course, preparation did not guarantee results. In the winter of 1831 a Chatham home caught fire, and one of the firewards ran toward it, as he would later recount, with "a mixture of joy and pride ... that in a few minutes the real utility of a good Engine, and the Company belonging to it, would for the first time in Chatham be clearly manifested." But no one could get the frozen engine working. Part of the town burned to the ground.[93] On the whole, however, firefighting does seem to have gotten better organized after the great fire. When in 1834 a blaze on the Northwest branch of the river approached the Miramichi settlements – burnt leaves falling on Chatham – the inhabitants, in the words of the *Chatham Gleaner*, "adopted every precautionary measure. Puncheons were filled with water, ladders placed on many of the houses, and all easily ignited materials removed; the Firewards

The Barrens and the Birches

caused the breaks to be dammed up, to afford a supply of water, and a watch to be set during the night."[94]

Yet some people clearing land nearby chose that very moment to set fire to piles of brushwood. (The *Gleaner*'s editor demanded "*summary punishment* for such aggressors.")[95] Settlers' experience with wildland and urban fires did not diminish their need of fire. It cooked their food, warmed their houses, and cleared their land.[96] Fire was too indispensable a tool for settlers to pretend they could do without it – and too unruly to imagine they could ever fully control it. So although caution increased, there were limits to the degree to which behaviour changed. In 1851 agricultural chemist James F.W. Johnston observed that the effects of the 1825 fire were visible, in the form of blackened trees, all day as he travelled along the Southwest branch of the Miramichi River. He then came upon a place being cleared by fire and spoke approvingly of the group of farmers keeping watch for sparks that might carry toward their fields. Such an immediate juxtaposition implied that Miramichiers, or maybe North Americans generally, had grown more respectful of forest fire than they used to be. But only a few pages earlier, Johnston had remarked that, at a farm he visited, "[a]dvantage had been taken of the extreme drought to burn up some stumps," and the fire had swiftly gotten out of control.[97] Settlers needed fire, and so they would sometimes continue to burn in the best – that is, the worst – possible conditions for it.

Nor did the Miramichi Fire, as a silver lining, result in New Brunswick implementing laws that protected forests from fire. In fact, Commissioner of Crown Lands and Forests Thomas Baillie soon introduced a watered-down timber-leasing system with lower stumpage fees, which meant less government revenue and less protection of forests.[98] It would take the next great forest fire of the nineteenth century to convince North Americans that such events were grave and preventable threats to life and livelihood. On 8 October 1871, the same night as the Great Chicago Fire, 1,500 people died in a forest fire in and around Peshtigo, Wisconsin.[99] The Peshtigo Fire, and a rash of major American forest fires in subsequent decades, led professional foresters and the broader public to call for stricter regulation of forested land, tougher punishment for those who caused fires, and improved fire suppression technologies and methods. New Brunswick, modelling its efforts on Ontario initiatives that were themselves modelled on American ones, in 1885 finally passed a Fire Act "to prevent the destruction of woods, forests, and other properties by fires" and

156 *The Miramichi Fire*

in 1897 introduced a fire ranger system.[100] These initiatives began a century of strict forest fire suppression policies, where all fires were seen as bad ones. The Peshtigo Fire can reasonably be said to have had a far greater impact on New Brunswick forest fire policy than the Miramichi Fire ever did. As a result, it may well have had a greater impact on New Brunswick's forests.

∗∗∗

The story of the Miramichi timber trade in the decades after 1825 was one of instability but also resilience.[101] The industry began the transition from whole timber to processed lumber in the ashes of the fire and at the height of an economic crisis, yet it came out the other side. It would never again see a boom time like 1825, but neither would it see the depths of 1826. Communities returned to greater normalcy more quickly than expected because lumbermen returned to many of the same tracts depleted of the largest white pine, this time bringing downriver smaller pines and spruce, now more often to make deals, planks, and boards to ship to Britain. The trade continued to be shaken by outside forces: the 1830s alone saw cholera ships, the threatened end to the colonial timber preference, and another severe depression. When Britain did reduce the preferential tariff in 1842, the New Brunswick timber trade was hard hit. Exports declined, prices fell, and timber operations failed. An overextended Joseph Cunard struggled for five years before finally declaring bankruptcy – news that, if true, a Halifax paper cried, "will be equal, in its consequences to Miramichi, to the great fire of 1825!"[102] The statement was more accurate than intended. Like the fire, Cunard's insolvency and subsequent departure rattled the region, laying bare the fragile nature of the industry on which society depended. But like the fire, it was not the region's death knell. In the decades that followed, the Miramichi timber trade survived and from time to time thrived thanks to new American markets, new lumber products – including, by the 1880s, pulp and paper – and new trees.[103]

Over time the Miramichi forests increasingly differed in structure and composition from those that existed in 1825. Some tracts were still untouched and largely unchanged, but many more near waterways had been worked over by lumbermen, in many cases repeatedly. Still other stands had been cleared for settlement and farming. Colonists' fires, first and foremost among them the Miramichi Fire, had obliterated the soil in some places, such that little to no regrowth had occurred. In still other places, the forest had largely grown back, concealing the original devastation, although with a different mix from what had been there before. The number and average size of remaining white pine had declined, more because of relentless timber exploitation than fire, but the numbers of fire-sensitive, late-successional species such as beech and particularly eastern hemlock had also decreased. By comparison, the young growth of shorter-lived species such as balsam fir, poplar, and birch – smaller even in maturity than those they replaced – had increased.[104] Banks pine (or jack pine), for example, had been absent altogether from descriptions of the Miramichi forests in the early nineteenth century, but by the 1870s they had grown so thick in groves throughout the Southwest Miramichi district that "it is almost impossible to press one's way through them."[105]

In the process of recording New Brunswick's surface geology in 1887, the Geological Survey of Canada's Robert Chalmers – a native of Belledune, near Bathurst – tried his hand at mapping the Miramichi Fire's range based on existing forest conditions. He had the fire burning almost exclusively on the north side of the Miramichi River, a rough 45 by 60 kilometre rectangle – 2,700 square kilometres or 1,000 square miles – from Heath Steel nearly to Burnt Church and from the Nepisiguit River to Newcastle. There is every reason to question Chalmers's estimate. Although an inveterate amateur botanist, he was not an expert on fires or forests, he had no way of distinguishing the 1825 fire from subsequent ones, and his cartographic reconstruction was the only published mention he ever made of the fire. But his description of this area's forests, based on a boots-on-the-ground survey, is plain enough: "This tract is now covered with a new growth of trees usually in groves consisting of red pines, black and white spruce, birch, maple, beech, poplar, cherry, hacmatac [larch], etc. Clumps of the original forest here and there escaped destruction."[106]

The sheer variety of contemporaneous Miramichi forests – old-growth, new-growth, no-growth – gave writers great latitude in describing them, which circled back to growing disagreement as to the great fire's extent and ferocity. It even allowed commentators to be inconsistent within a single account. Writing in 1847, Abraham Gesner declared that in 1825 the Miramichi had been "visited by a most awful and calamitous fire that consumed the forests like stubble, and ... involved the whole population in ruin and distress. From the great annual exports also, the timber is growing scarce." But if the forests were consumed, how had there been subsequent great exports? Gesner

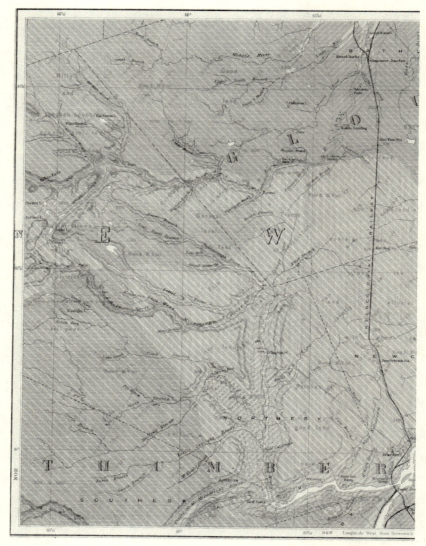

Figure 5.2 Robert Chalmers's estimate of the Miramichi Fire zone *(in light grey)*, 1888.

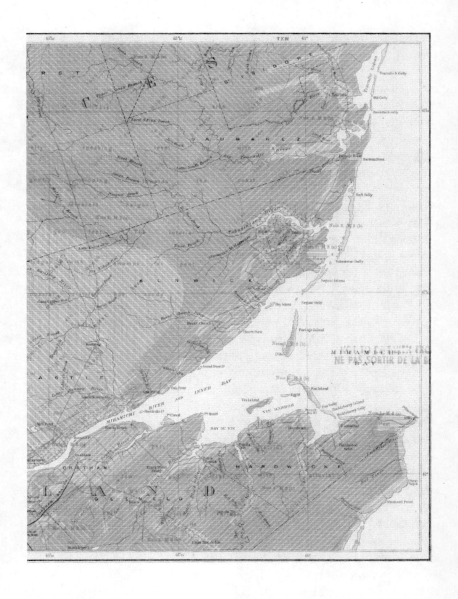

160   *The Miramichi Fire*

repeated the contradiction later. "[M]uch of its timber had been removed," he wrote, "and a still greater quantity was destroyed" by the fire, yet in the very next sentence he stated that some of the timber in the burnt country had been cut into lumber and that "from the vast extent of the pine tracts, great exports are still made."[107] Nova Scotia politician George R. Young came to the same conclusions after touring New Brunswick in 1849. "The great fire of 1824 [*sic*] cut off the supply for twenty years on the Eastern side of that fine Province," Young wrote, and future trade had been confined to lumber. Nonetheless, he added, "[t]heir command of logs is boundless."[108] If attempting to square such contradictions, one might conclude that the writers meant that trees once marketable whole, as timber, had been sufficiently damaged that they now had to be sawn and sold as lumber – that this might in fact have been a prime motivation for the Miramichi industry's transition to sawn lumber.[109] But if the forests still provided a livelihood, where was the evidence of "ruin and distress"? How was the timber both "growing scarce" and "boundless"? The various Miramichi forests allowed for various interpretations of their present health and of the past fire – even within the space of sentences.

But in the last third of the nineteenth century, one interpretation of the great fire came to dominate because one area came to define it more than any other: the Bartibog. Life returned to the Bartibog River east of Newcastle, as it did to the rest of the Miramichi, but it retained more visible evidence of the fire than did most places. New trees did not grow up and cover dead ones there, presumably because the blaze had incinerated the soil's organic matter on which regrowth depended. Succession stalled. And because the site of this sterility was alongside the road between Newcastle and Bathurst, one of the colony's main arteries, its desolation remained a monument to the Miramichi Fire. Scottish writer Rev. Norman MacLeod described the scene vividly in "Fire in the Woods," an 1861 essay that would be reprinted widely, including in British and Canadian school readers, for the remainder of the century:

> The road from Newcastle to Bathurst ... passes for five or
> six miles through a district called the Barrens. The scene which
> meets the eye of the traveller is perhaps unequalled. Far as the
> eye can reach upon every side, there is nothing but desolation ...
> All is a barren waste! The trees are not black now, but white,
> and bleached by sun and rain; and far to the horizon, round and

round, nothing is discovered but one vast and apparently boundless forest of the white skeleton trunks of dead lifeless trees! That immense tract is doomed to remain barren, perhaps, for ever, – at least for many years to come.[110]

This route of desolation became sufficiently well known that in *Ocean to Ocean*, the account of Sandford Fleming's expedition through Canada in 1872, when author George M. Grant sought to describe the scrubby pine region east of Edmonton, Alberta, he trusted that his readers would understand a comparison to "the country between Bathurst and Miramichi, New Brunswick, that was burnt over by the great Miramichi fire."[111]

The Barrens became synonymous with the Bartibog area, which became synonymous with the Miramichi Fire's entire range. As the fire faded deeper into the past, and as more of its survivors passed on, accounts of it shifted from its immediate human toll to its long-term environmental toll. And the farther authors were from the Miramichi, the more likely they were to speak of the region's desolation. So a character in James DeMille's 1871 novel *Fire in the Woods* claims that the Miramichi Fire "ruined the timber of all that country, turned fertile districts into barren wastes, and annihilated in one night all the resources of a great commerce."[112] Others called the Miramichi "a barren desert to this day" and "a blackened desert," with "hundreds of square miles ... left bare as the Sahara."[113] "Cowering under the effects of that paralysing blow, the earth seemed powerless to reclothe her nakedness, except in tattered shreds and patches," in the words of sportsman and travel writer Arthur P. Silver.[114] These statements spoke to the surprising longevity of real, visible evidence of the fire. (Or fires; the course of decades meant the authors had no real way to be certain they were describing areas burned in 1825 or *only* in 1825.) But they also spoke to authors' difficulty in chronicling the fire without the assistance of surviving witnesses – and to their freedom to do so without the encumbrance of surviving witnesses.[115]

Moreover, these statements spoke to a post-Peshtigo consensus that protecting North America's forests first and foremost meant preventing forest fires. In the late nineteenth century, those in the forest industry grew increasingly worried that the continent's forests were being depleted, so they sought to develop systematic and efficient ways to ensure the forests' permanence; the resultant forest conservation movement eventually spread to other resources, sparking the first iteration of North American environmentalism.[116] In advocating large-scale, scientific, planned modern forestry, professional foresters and large timber companies could and did find fault with earlier forestry practices, but fire was a particularly useful foil because it directed the blame for forest loss beyond the forest industry. In the words of US chief forester Gifford Pinchot in 1899, of "all of the foes which attack the woodlands of North America, no other is so terrible as fire."[117] Foresters in Canada and the United States built a case against fire that relied as much on its lasting impact as on its immediate destruction, and the Miramichi Fire was sufficiently catastrophic and distant in time – yet also well enough remembered – to assist with that. As early as the 1840s, commentators had spoken of the Miramichi having "never since recovered" from the fire, but this interpretation increased markedly toward the end of the 1800s.[118] Now, it was said that the Miramichi would long be unsuited for forestry *or* agriculture, that it demonstrated "how a country may be utterly devastated by ravages from fire, without hope of restoration to its former condition for many generations."[119] When *Scientific American* published an article on "Historic Forest Fires" in 1904, it began with a paragraph about the Miramichi Fire and then immediately noted, "In the majority of such forest fires as this the destruction of the timber is a more serious loss by far than that of the cattle and buildings, for it carries with it the impoverishment of a whole region for tens or even hundreds of years afterward. The loss of the stumpage value of the timber at the time of the fire is but a small part of the damage to the neighborhood."[120] This account came about as close as one could to saying that a forest fire's true victims were not those who died in it or survived it but rather latter-day lumbermen.

An apocalyptic reading of the Miramichi Fire's effects was useful in that it extended the event's significance and the lessons one might take from it. The only problem was that it did not conform well to reality. The Miramichi at the turn of the twentieth century was still a forestry region, and a forested one, and it had never stopped being so. When, for example, a photographer with the William Notman & Son studio of Montreal took a series of shots along the Miramichi River in 1908, he again and again captured forests. Perhaps they were not as impressive as settlers would have seen a century earlier, but they were substantial, seemingly healthy forests.[121] It was this growing disjuncture between the Miramichi region as it was supposed to be and as it was that lay the groundwork for a paradigm shift in

Figure 5.3 *Salmon Fishing on Miramichi River,* NB, c. 1908.

thinking about the Miramichi Fire. It provided the opportunity for someone with sufficient authority to offer a new, revisionist interpretation arguing that talk of the fire had always been overheated.

✳✳✳

"Everything which concerns New Brunswick interests me," wrote William Francis Ganong.[122] He was born in 1864 of the chocolate Ganongs, the family that in the 1870s opened what is now Canada's oldest candy company in little St Stephen, New Brunswick. But rather than join the family business, he became enamoured with studying the geography and history of his home province. Beginning at age eighteen, Ganong spent almost all of the next fifty summers canoeing, hiking, mapping, surveying, photographing, and documenting the wilds of New Brunswick; the rest of his year was spent poring over its documentary record. Even after beginning in 1895 what would be a long career as a professor of botany at Smith College in Massachusetts, rising to the presidency of the Botanical Society of America, much of his scholarly life remained dedicated to the province of his birth. He

Figure 5.4 Dr. William Francis Ganong, Renous River Region, Northumberland County, New Brunswick, 1904.

became its foremost botanist, historical geographer, *and* physical geographer, as well as a leading scholar on the Acadian era, early cartography, place names, and the Maliseet and Mi'gmaw languages. A recent biographer states, "No one before or since has studied the natural and physiographic history of the province in such detail."[123]

Ganong initially intended to gather his research into a single, comprehensive history of New Brunswick. But he came to the conclusion, as he later told the Royal Society of Canada, that "[a] history of mine would be cold, scientific, precise, classified, complete; but it would lack the life and form and colour which should distinguish a history for the people."[124] He was a strict empiricist, a lover of facts and their compilation, and he knew that his strengths were not as a theorist or stylist.[125] So he took to writing short pieces that could accumulate and aggregate into a portrait of the province. In this manner, he published 1,000 pages of New Brunswick history in the *Transactions of the Royal Society of Canada*. But the principal destination for his work was the *Bulletin of the Natural History Society of New Brunswick*, where, beginning in 1896, he wrote a long series of essay-length "Notes" on the province's natural history and physiography – "Remarkable Sounds in the Bay of Fundy," "On a Division of New Brunswick into Physiographic Districts," "On an Unusual Frost-Effect of 1901 on the Tobique," and "The Morphology of New Brunswick Waterfalls" – and, over the next two decades, on 134 other topics that struck his fancy. Ganong contributed almost one-third of the *Bulletin*'s content during those decades.[126]

That it took Ganong ten years and ninety "Notes" to get around to writing about the Miramichi Fire is surprising given that it would seem a natural topic for him. In a previous essay, he had called this forest fire "the worst the province has ever suffered" and had mused that knowing the extent of such fires could have economic application by helping to determine the rate of natural reforestation.[127] But Ganong may have felt that he did not know the Miramichi region particularly well. Having initiated annual field trips in 1880, he travelled the Miramichi River only twice in the next quarter-century, paddling the Southwest branch in 1890 and the Northwest branch in 1903.[128] It was the latter trip that presumably inspired him to finally turn to the fire, and in February 1905 he gave a lecture to the provincial Natural History Society "On the Limits of the Great Fire of Miramichi of 1825," which he published in revised form in the Society's *Bulletin* a year later. It was an essay of only 3,500 words, but it was the most sustained historical examination of the disaster since it had occurred eight decades earlier.

In ascertaining the range of the great fire, Ganong began by running through the contemporary documentary sources available to him, "accounts proceeding from eye-witnesses or others in a position to know": a newspaper article of 11 October 1825 headlined "Fire and Hurricane," the charity pamphlet, Robert Cooney's 1832 *A Compendious History*, John McGregor's 1832 *British America*, James F.W. Johnston's 1851 *Notes on North America*, and S.W. Fullom's 1863 *The Life of General Sir Howard Douglas*. Although they mentioned different districts that had burned, they were in general agreement that the fire measured in the thousands of square miles, with 6,000 square miles the standard figure. Ganong then focused on later accounts "compiled with a genuine regard for the truth" that confirmed the earlier accounts while fleshing out some more details: Peter Fisher's 1838 *Notitia of New Brunswick*, Abraham Gesner's 1847 *New Brunswick*, and Alexander Monro's 1855 *New Brunswick*.[129]

Next, he turned to "tradition," relying exclusively on his long-time "valued correspondent" P.H. Welch, an experienced lumber scaler and woodsman. After seeing a newspaper article summarizing Ganong's lecture to the Natural History Society, Welch had written Ganong, concerned that he was woefully underestimating the fire's range.[130] (As so often happens, the act of presenting scholarship generates information from the public that would have been helpful while preparing it. I hope that will happen with the publication of this book.) Based on a conversation with an eyewitness forty years earlier and on his own long-time understanding, Welch believed that the fire started just east of Fredericton and swept northeast through the Miramichi all the way to Tracadie Beach, that a spur jumped the main river below Chatham and so laid waste to the land on the south side of Miramichi Bay as well, and that the fire also jumped the Southwest branch of the Miramichi River and burned as far southeast as the Gaspereau River. Ganong made a cursory attempt to confirm Welch's details from a few published sources – such as noting that James Edward Alexander, in his 1849 *L'Acadie*, spoke of coming across the fire's effects when nearing the Gaspereau. But beyond that, he did not measure any source against any other and simply allowed this inventory of opinions to accumulate.

Then, three-quarters of the way through his essay, Ganong changed directions. Believing "that an observant and well-informed lumberman thoroughly acquainted with the Miramichi country would probably know, in part from the ages of the trees growing there, the approximate limits of the great fire," he sought out the opinion of Ernest Hutchison of Douglastown. Hutchison was as close to Miramichi royalty as it was possible to be. His father, Richard, had been born in Mearns, Scotland, the town that had given birth to Gilmour, Pollok, & Co. Richard Hutchison went to work for that firm at age fourteen, joined its Miramichi operation Gilmour and Rankin, and worked his way up to partner. It would later be said of Richard that he "lacked the elements of touch and sympathy with his fellow creatures" – or, more bluntly, that he had "a turkey-buzzard's eye for mortgages on poor people's farms." By the end of his life, Richard was the sole owner of what was left of Gilmour and Rankin, and he passed this down to his son, Ernest. Like his father, Ernest tried his hand at politics, but he withdrew in 1890 to oversee full-time what was now the firm of "E. Hutchison, Lumber Merchant."[131]

Hutchison was delighted to receive Ganong's question because he had long thought the Miramichi Fire's size exaggerated. He replied to Ganong once and then again and again and again – at least ten times in all. The first thing one had to do, he argued, was throw out the early reports entirely, on the grounds that since the first was probably recycled ad nauseam in the press, "all printed statements including Cooneys without doubt originated at same source."[132] Once those sources were set aside, it was obvious to Hutchison that although small fires undoubtedly burned over a great area on that famous day, intensive fire was largely limited to Newcastle and its environs on the north side of the Miramichi River. He based this belief on two things. First, there was the evidence of "old trees" still standing and still being cut within the fire's reputed boundaries. There were simply too many healthy, mature trees still throughout the region, and the "growth of trees on certain districts preclude the assumption that these districts were destroyed by the fire."[133] But Hutchison actually passed by this first point quickly and focused more on a second, which he returned to repeatedly in his letters: since the wind was coming from the northwest, the fire could not possibly have swept down the Southwest branch of the Miramichi River – that is, swept toward the northeast – and therefore could not possibly have done the damage in that area as some accounts suggested. He wrote,

[A]s no one disputes the wind was NorthWest all must recognize the self evident fact that the fire swept across or at right angles to the course of the river not down the river.

You will see that I really judge by known actual facts not by what any one might have imagined. Now I did know a most estimable woman who at the time was a girl of 12 years of age and should have known about it and she assured me that a whole district in which she with her parents at the time resided was burned and that they nearly lost their lives when as a matter of fact I convinced her afterwards that fright and anxiety with what she had heard of other places had so warped her judgments or memory that she was entirely wrong.

As Robbie Burns says, 'And nail it wi' scripture.'[134]

Mansplaining on the Miramichi. You almost have to admire a person so self-assured as to be able to talk the survivor of a disaster out of what happened to her.

Hutchison was born and had lived all his life in Douglastown, on the Miramichi River's north shore, and he recalled as a boy having heard eyewitnesses describe the fire that descended on that side of the river. His Miramichi Fire was one based on how it had been experienced in the Miramichi settlements. He ignored or did not know that a number of contemporary reports had the wind blowing from the southwest and west prior to its arrival on the Miramichi River and that the wind likely shifted as a cold front came through. Hutchison did understand that, as he told Ganong, "[t]he case presents great difficulty as even the persons whom I knew who saw the fire had very different versions of it and only knew what happened within a mile or two of their own location."[135] But he did not see that his was also a localized interpretation of it.

Ganong gave Hutchison's opinion great deference in his essay. After all, as he wrote, it was judgment grounded on "the unassailable testimony of the age of trees standing on the areas in question." He summarized Hutchison's belief that, based on the presence of "abundant and old logs," it was simply impossible for the fire to have burned extensively to the south or southwest of the Miramichi settlements. He quoted Hutchison that "[b]lack spruce ... does not make logs fit to cut much more than 100 years, and I have counted 265 rings on a black spruce" – as if the survival of an individual tree proved the fire could not have passed through an area. As for the other, more dominant strand of Hutchison's argument – the matter of wind direction – Ganong made no mention of it whatsoever.[136]

Having catalogued a wide range of evidence and opinions, Ganong then pulled them all together and analyzed their meaning in his essay's final paragraph. His conclusion was that "two quite distinct ideas are associated with the name Great Fire of Miramichi." On the one hand, it referred to a "general fire, or series of fires" that on 7 October 1825 blazed extensively across a range of 6,000 to 8,000 square miles of New Brunswick, a "great triangle" whose vertices were near Fredericton in the colony's southwest, Belledune on its north coast, and Richibucto on its east coast. Fires within this vast area burned in irregular patches, occasionally uniting, but they also left vast tracts unburnt, "especially in the river valleys." On the other hand, the great fire referred specifically to the fire that burned with special ferocity,

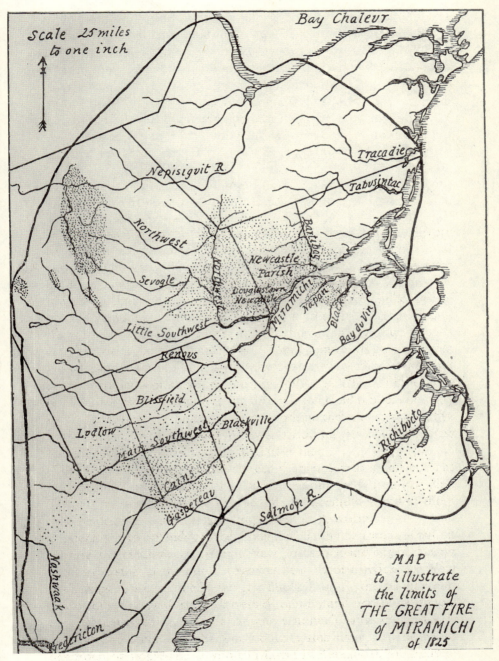

Figure 5.5 "Map to Illustrate the Limits of the Great Fire of Miramichi of 1825," 1906.

and at great cost to life and property, across some 400 square miles in Newcastle Parish and vicinity.[137] This more intensive "special fire," he called the "Great Fire proper." His essay ends, "If we keep in mind this double use of the name Great Fire, the subject of the limits become fairly plain."[138] Accompanying Ganong's essay was his hand-drawn map of these two distinct Miramichi fires.[139]

It is difficult to overstate just how influential Ganong's interpretation has been in shaping how the Miramichi Fire has been remembered, and forgotten, over the past century. Historians have referenced and accepted it whenever writing about the fire; often it is the only source cited. J. Clarence Webster reproduced Ganong's argument and map in his 1928 *An Historical Guide to New Brunswick*.[140] Esther Clark Wright praised Ganong in the acknowledgments of her 1945 *The Miramichi* and, when discussing the fire, stated that Cooney's estimate "exaggerates the extent. Actually, it has been computed by more careful investigators"; following Ganong, she gave just its tight dimensions close to the Miramichi settlements.[141] Graeme Wynn accepts Ganong's interpretation unreservedly in his doctoral dissertation, even reproducing Ganong's map, which helps to explain why in his 1981 *Timber Colony* the fire merits only a single paragraph – much of it devoted to quoting Cooney's purple prose.[142] The map has continued to be reproduced this century as the authoritative representation of the Miramichi Fire in local and academic histories and was even featured on the website of the New Brunswick Department of Natural Resources for years.[143]

The most remarkable thing about the enduring significance of Ganong's interpretation is that it supplanted all the contemporary nineteenth-century accounts of the great fire without disproving them or even really challenging them. Given that, it is worth considering how Ganong constructed his argument. After documenting as many written sources as he could find, he trusted a single correspondent, Welch, to speak to tradition, and another, Hutchison, to speak to a knowledge of trees, forests, and fire. He did not hear from other lumbermen, settlers, local history buffs, or Mi'gmaq. As for the sources that he did consult, he did little to assess them individually and did not openly favour one over another but rather accepted them all equally. Such is evident in the very existence of his two-fire theory. In a winter 1905 lecture, Ganong had argued more assertively that the fire's size had been exaggerated. It was only after Welch wrote him protesting a newspaper report of the talk, headlined "The Great

Miramichi Fire of 1825 Reviewed by Prof. Ganong, Who Finds Area Burned Was 400 Square Miles," that Ganong developed a putatively more noncommittal viewpoint.[144] The author's desire to appeal to all positions can also be seen in his map. Ganong sent Welch and Hutchison blank maps and asked them to shade in where they understood the fire to have burned. Welch returned his with red running along both sides of the Southwest branch of the Miramichi River, through the Miramichi settlements on the north side of the main river, and all the way to Tracadie; Hutchison returned his with a single red quadrilateral that blanketed just the settled parts of Newcastle and North Esk Parishes. Ganong essentially merged the two interpretations to make his map and added a few elements from other sources, such as Cooney's to the fire burning in Richibucto. Ganong's map is a palimpsest, a visual expression of his essay's practice of seemingly accepting all available sources, no matter how conflicting, as all contributing to a single understanding of the fire's size.

Or, rather, a dual understanding – for the only way to reconcile the original, expansive interpretations of the fire, such as Cooney's, with the narrow, revisionist one of Hutchison was to contend that they were not talking about the same thing. But Ganong's resolution – his two-fire theory – requires that within the boundaries of the extensive fire, there were large areas that did not burn intensively. How could one map those? Ganong's method seems to have been to assume that unless there was express documentary evidence that an area had burned badly, it had not. Put another way, his interpretation required that the fire burned intensively only in places where, coincidentally, there were people to report it having done so. The flaw in this logic is obvious: absence of evidence is not evidence of absence. Yet that was exactly the argument Hutchison had made explicitly and repeatedly in his letters to Ganong. For example, on no evidence, Hutchison wrote, "I think that all or nearly all of these fires were near settled districts and destroyed them but each district was the victim of a separate fire."[145] Since less-populated and less-travelled areas – such as the entire Northwest branch of the Miramichi River – would be unable to provide the documentary evidence that Hutchison (and Ganong) required, the damage they sustained was bound to be under-represented, resulting in great blank spaces on Ganong's map.

There was one other New Brunswicker whose authority Ganong could have relied on in his essay, a person who more than anyone combined a scientific and situated knowledge of the province's

The Miramichi Fire

environment and history: himself. But he never called on his own expertise. Having travelled the back roads and rivers of his home province for decades, he had developed a strong opinion about forest fires. In his 1899 "The Forestry Problem in New Brunswick," he argued that forestry itself was not the problem, or at least not his concern. "I do not now refer to defects in forest regulations, systems of cutting, stumpage, etc., for I know nothing about this subject." To critique management practices would require imagining a forest that might exist if practices were different, and Ganong was constitutionally incapable of such counterfactual thinking. He was an empiricist who trusted what he saw, and what he saw were the effects of fire:

> But there is one deadly enemy of our forests whose worst visitations can *never* be entirely recovered from, and that is the great forest fires. It is not only the timber they destroy that makes these fires so bad, for in a generation or two it may be partially restored, but it is the *permanent* injury they do to much of our soil whereby its capacity to produce trees for the future is *permanently* lessened or even practically destroyed.

Thin soil covered much of the province's forest land, and when fire killed the vegetation that was holding this soil together, rain washed it away, leaving behind nothing but rocks.

> An awful example of this practically *permanent* destruction is to be found in an area many miles square on the upper Lepreau river; the still standing rampikes and great stumps show how fine a forest once clothed this land, which now is but a stony desert that not for generations, and perhaps *never*, can again bear trees.[146]

Ganong spoke of fire's effects in the language of absolutes, of "nevers" and "permanents." Yet the Lepreau landscape resulted from a fire that, as he noted elsewhere, had burned less than thirty years earlier.[147] It was thin soil from which to cultivate talk of permanence.

William Francis Ganong was not unique in his prejudice against fire in forests; this was the overwhelming attitude of his day.[148] Nor was Ganong uniquely unaware of the dynamics of forest succession or the role fire can play in that process; the science behind the former was still in its infancy and the science behind the latter did not yet

Figure 5.6 Dr. William Francis Ganong, Banksian [Jack] Pine, Portage Road along Portage Brook, Northumberland County, New Brunswick, 1902.

exist. Thoreau notwithstanding, it was only in the 1890s that a few European scientists began to make serious advances in understanding succession by studying plants not in isolation but in relation to their environment, doing so by way of the new field of ecology. Ganong was more than just familiar with this work; he was an early, vocal advocate for moving beyond what he called "local Botany" and toward a more comprehensive, integrated ecology.[149] But as he wrote in *Science* in 1904, he also recognized that the experiment- and systems-based studies that this new science required "can not be made by busy teachers who can give to them only a vacation leisure and a scanty

174 *The Miramichi Fire*

equipment" – teachers such as himself, presumably. He downplayed his own observational work as ecology of the "get-rich-quick" variety.[150] Ganong knew that a more informed understanding of nature was just over the horizon – but he also knew that knowing this to be the case did not help him see it.

In the very first line of his Miramichi Fire essay, Ganong stated that he had been drawn to the topic by "observations upon the extensive burnt country at the head of the northwest and other branches of the Miramichi."[151] That the most-obvious artifacts of the fire first attracted his notice was only natural; this was the same reason commentators had long identified barrens such as those seen in the Bartibog area with the fire. The problem was that Ganong associated forest fires *only* with such highly visible long-term damage. But the fact that other forests were substantial now did not in itself mean that they had not burned eighty years earlier. It just meant that the Miramichi forests were healthy, ecologically diverse, and resilient, and as a result they had in most cases grown fully back, if in different form. I picture Ganong paddling the Northwest branch of the Miramichi River in the summer of 1903 and struggling to make the historical record conform to what his eyes were telling him. Both the writers of the early nineteenth century who had offered varying measures of the Miramichi Fire's size and ferocity and the writers of the late nineteenth century who had begun to exaggerate its long-term devastation gave him the grounds for revisionism. But really, his argument was with nature. Without noticing that he was doing so, he was using nature against itself. He was using its restorative power to discredit its destructive power.

✳✳✳

In his 1832 *The Forest, or Rambles in the Woodland*, British author Jefferys Taylor devoted 200 pages to classifying and describing trees and timbering before, on the final page, turning to the greatest threat the forest faces: fire. His book's very final sentences read, "[T]he fires amongst the American forests are the most awfully terrific. A hundred miles of country were seen on fire at once, in the year 1825, on the north side of the Miramichi river. I suppose, that we Europeans can scarcely form an idea of such a spectacle as this … If these fires occur much oftener, North America, vast as is its natural supply, will no longer export timber as it has hitherto done; and we may then think more of the value of our small, but better protected British Forests."[152]

To a nineteenth-century Western world built on a reliable wood supply, the Miramichi Fire was a cautionary tale. It demonstrated for the first time the vulnerability of the seemingly inexhaustible North American forests and of the communities that drew their living from them. It was, for a time, a world-historical event.

Compare this perception to a more recent depiction of the fire. In the early twenty-first century, the American Red Cross's website disasterrelief.org contained information about historical natural disasters. Its list of forest fires began, as most such lists do, with the 1825 blaze. There was even a helpful accompanying map of the United States, with Maine and New Jersey singled out. The site's creators presumably confused a fire that torched the state of Maine and the neighbouring British colony of New Brunswick with one that torched Maine and the town of New Brunswick, New Jersey.[153] This error seems a fitting illustration of how the Miramichi Fire has been simultaneously remembered and forgotten.

It is no surprise, of course, that memory of the fire has faded across the past two centuries. Survivors passed on. More history kept getting made. New and fresh tragedies drew public attention. Conversely, there was not another forest fire of the kind that observers like Taylor had dreaded, at least until the Peshtigo Fire in 1871, so the Miramichi Fire's early significance as a wake-up call weakened. And as the Red Cross map suggests, the international border also played a part. Natural disasters, and perhaps all historical events, undergo a process of spatial and temporal consolidation as they move into the past: boundaries become firmer. But in this case, the two core areas were on two sides of an international border, so the areas drew apart and consolidated separately. That the fire on the Canadian side resulted in far more deaths and damage ensured that it became known by a Canadian name, and it also meant that Canadians lost track of its American dimension, whereas Americans – always ten times more numerous than Canadians and always ten times more interested in America than in Canada – lost interest in it altogether.[154]

But nature's aliveness also played an integral part in how memory of the fire faded. Year by year, season by season, even day by day, the Miramichi ecosystem was constantly changing, making it difficult enough for observers to come to terms with the region's current state, let alone determine what had once happened there: the ground was moving beneath their feet. More specifically, the forests grew back, papering over – very nearly literally – evidence of the disaster and

Figure 5.7 American Red Cross map of the Miramichi Fire, c. 2000.

ensuring that future writers unwittingly papered over it too. As a result, what arguably is the most famous historical event to have ever taken place in New Brunswick does not even appear in some histories of it. The case of the Miramichi Fire suggests why more environmental history work is needed to reclaim the significance of the natural world to human affairs through time and why much more remains to be uncovered.

6

Conclusion

Boring history – What we learned – Climate changes past and future – Fossil-fuelled

One summer, early in my research into the Miramichi Fire, I found myself bouncing along the teeth-jarring forestry roads of the Miramichi region in a four-wheel-drive with University of New Brunswick Forestry and Environmental Management research assistant Chris Norfolk at the wheel.[1] I had exhaustively researched the fire in archives, libraries, and online by that point – or thought I had before the proliferation of digital sources drew me back to more online research and then more – and I had come to see William Francis Ganong's 1906 interpretation as key to how the fire was subsequently remembered and forgotten. But I wondered whether I could find out more in the woods themselves. Forest fires leave material traces of their passing on the trees that survive them. When a fire burns through the bark, it kills the cambium tissue underneath, leaving a fire scar and, often, a residue of charcoal. Since trees grow a new ring each year, it is possible to date when fire struck such wounded trees.[2] I wondered whether it was possible to find fire scars and charcoal in 1825 tree rings, particularly in areas that, according to Ganong's map of the fire, were not supposed to have badly burned.

I approached David MacLean, who was then the dean of forestry at the University of New Brunswick, and learned that the provincial Department of Natural Resources and Energy periodically runs a Forest Development Survey of a wide sample of forest stands in the province, taking core samples from a small number of somewhat representative trees in those stands. Among other things, the surveys record the tree's age. What if, I asked, we extracted from the database all the cored trees alive in 1825 – there turned out to be about

150 such trees surveyed in the whole province – to determine which of these trees in northeastern New Brunswick were beyond what Ganong considered the fire's intensive range and then visited some of those stands not to find the specific surveyed trees necessarily but on the assumption that where there was already evidence of one tree in a stand predating 1825, there may well be others? The dean's reply: "We?"

That was what had me driving those Miramichi backroads. To be sure, I also simply wanted to revisit the scene of the crime: I had spent plenty of time in the relevant libraries, archives, museums, and graveyards, but I wanted to better understand the fire by being on the ground where it occurred. In some ways, New Brunswick is much the same as it was in 1825. The province is still more than four-fifths forest-covered, and the forest industry is still the leading industry, employing about 24,000 people – coincidentally, almost the exact number it employed in 1825, albeit now amid a population ten times the size.[3] Driving deep into the Miramichi interior, knowing that there may well be no other humans within a 20-kilometre radius, you can almost convince yourself that you are seeing the same natural world of two centuries ago. But of course you aren't: this is only superficially the same place. Mi'gmaq still live in the area, on and off the reserves they were pushed onto in the early 1800s, but they no longer occupy the interior as they once did. There are no caribou here anymore, or grey wolf, or wolverine. As for the woods themselves, after 200 years of land clearing, settler fires, and unremittent logging, less than 2 per cent of the Acadian forest is more than 100 years old. The forest composition has changed, too. Early-successional spruce and balsam fir have become much more prevalent within the Miramichi watershed, particularly along bodies of water, where they are estimated to have increased from 35 per cent of the trees in 1800 to 77 per cent today.[4] There has been an associated drop in white pine and a sharp reduction in eastern hemlock, American beech, and ash, too. There is also considerably less diversity. Whereas nine dominant tree species made up 95 per cent of the 1800 forest, today only six do. Forest ecologist Donna Crossland concludes, "With the exception of the Carolinian forest in southern Ontario, perhaps no other forest region in Canada has lost more of its character than the Acadian forest."[5] The nature that we see today in the Miramichi, that we think of as natural, is almost as much a product of our culture as Irving gas stations.

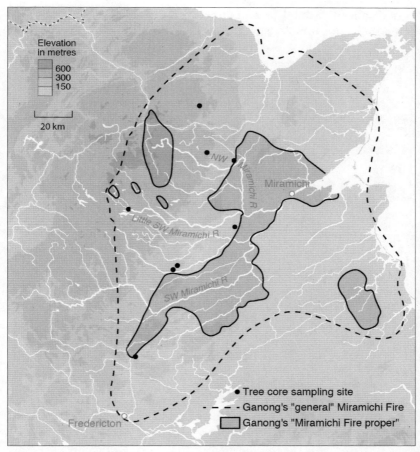

Figure 6.1 Tree core sampling project by Chris Norfolk and Alan MacEachern.

But perhaps there were a few relics of the past to be found. The process that Chris Norfolk and I used was to map the Forest Development Survey's pre-1825 trees and then to target selected stands based on age (the older the better), species (seeking variety since we were unsure which trees would both scar most and survive longest), and location (distributed outside Ganong's intensive burn area and moderately accessible). Next, we obtained aerial photos of these stands, drove as close to a stand as the roads allowed, and started walking. We slogged through swamps, ate and were eaten by mosquitoes, fell periodically in thick brush, and sometimes even followed the surveyors' thread that the survey team had left behind, until we came to what we hoped was the chosen stand. We then looked for what looked to be old trees. These trees were not necessarily the largest ones since it is often the wizened, inaccessible trees that have so long escaped the axe and saw, but we did come across some so large that they had outgrown the industrial feller buncher. We then used an increment borer – an auger that you screw manually into the tree – to remove long, cigarette-like cores from the cardinal points of the trees we chose. This was all new to me, and I learned a lot. For instance, I saw that we had underestimated the size of Miramichi trees: our 50-centimetre borer could not always take us to the centre of the trees we found. I also learned that a borer biting through wood sounds disconcertingly like a scream, and also that white pine's soft heartwood – so squishy that it repeatedly plugged the borer – demonstrates why the tree was once known as pumpkin pine. We took the samples back to the forestry lab, looked at them under the microscope, and found no trace of a fire scar or charcoal from 1825. Not one.

This was not really a surprise. Even while travelling throughout northeastern New Brunswick, Chris and I realized how quixotic our research plan was. We were looking for trees that were within the fire's perimeter but outside Ganong's estimate, that were in an area likely to burn (not a bog, for example), that *did* burn, that were scarred, that were old enough in 1825 to have survived the fire (in effect, at least twenty years old or so), and that were not only still standing almost two centuries later but were also still alive (since dead trees rot from the middle, making tree-ring dating next to impossible). And even if we had found such trees with such scars, that would not have disproved Ganong's interpretation since the trees were outside his intensive fire zone but within his extensive one.[6]

"Next time," I told Chris, "we'll core every tree in the province, just to be sure."

"We might have done better looking for human survivors," he replied. How would you do that, I wondered: aerial surveys searching for bald heads? I imagined coring heads for knowledge, making your way through the thick bark, beyond the harder cambium, to the soft pumpkiny mass below. It was time to head home.

Nonetheless, the research trip was a success. Beyond what I learned about dendrochronology, geography, and forest ecology – and what I hope Chris learned about environmental and climate history – our

Conclusion 181

method of using the Forest Development Survey was more effective than even we had expected. We cored what turned out to be a number of very old trees, including a 278-year-old eastern hemlock and a 341-year-old red pine – quite unusual in a small province that has been logged extensively for so long. And we may have just missed more. There were times that we broke through dense brush and came upon an empty clearing where the stand we were looking for should have been. We were not the only ones using the survey to find old trees: the Department of Natural Resources and Energy was flagging the same data as evidence that the stand was overmature, so it was such stands that the province gave companies licences to remove. New Brunswick has been managing Crown-owned lands so studiously and intensively in recent decades that, with about 2 per cent of the province's trees cut down systematically each year, even in the face of extensive conservation, there are fewer and fewer trees from the 1800s. This was likely my last chance to find trees that had survived the Miramichi Fire.

And, of course, humans are also having less direct but no less real effects on the Miramichi forests through anthropogenic climate change. I know that, of late, it seems every work of climate history, or environmental history, or history, or nonfiction turns, toward the end, to a discussion of climate change. That is to the good: we need to turn more conversations toward it, sooner rather than later. But I will not try to convince you that a massive wildfire in a quiet corner of the world 200 years ago offers direct parallels to, let alone direct lessons for, our present and pending experience of the climate crisis. Yes, the number of acres burned in Canadian wildfires has doubled since the 1970s and is predicted to double again by 2050 and again by 2100, so Canadians will face many more of the kinds of disasters that struck Kelowna in 2003, Slave Lake in 2011, and Fort McMurray in 2016.[7] But the story is more complex in eastern Canada, where wetter conditions are likely to protect forests from the worst fires. In the Acadian forest specifically, large, stand-replacing wildfires are rare, and it is expected that they will continue to be, notably even more so in northern than in southern New Brunswick. The greater change will be in forest composition. Warmer and wetter conditions will promote deborealization of the province: warm-adapted species such as maple, oak, pine, and beech will enjoy a longer growing season and grow faster, whereas cold-adapted species such as spruce, fir, poplar, and birch will face more disease, insects, and competition. The Miramichi

182   *The Miramichi Fire*

forests will become less and less what they were in 1825.[8] Miramichiers and New Brunswickers, and all Canadians for that matter, should feel blessed to be missing – for the near future at least – the worst, most catastrophic effects of climate change that are being experienced elsewhere. The downside is that we may be blind to the change that is coming and is already here.

But it is not the case that fossil fuels, in helping to erase the landscape of the Miramichi Fire, have suddenly become a part of the fire's story. The history of burning wood was always built on the burning of fossil fuels. In the late eighteenth and early nineteenth centuries, all of Europe was troubled by what was being called "the death of the forest." It was forest depletion in Britain that led to the first widespread use of a fossil fuel – coal – for heat there, which encouraged the improvement of the steam engines that were first used to pump water from coal mines, which helped to power the Industrial Revolution, which fostered economic activity that put even more pressure on European forests, which resulted in reliance on timber colonies such as New Brunswick.[9] Fossil fuels were a new injection in the world system, and they have powered all the other changes that we have experienced across the past two centuries. They have allowed for the precipitous growth of the economy, population, food production, and so much else.[10] They have also produced a sharp rise in the atmospheric concentration of greenhouse gases such as carbon dioxide, which over the long span of the earth's history corresponds closely to temperature changes. Whereas the carbon dioxide level was around 200 parts per million (ppm) during the last ice age, it rose slowly for millennia until by 1825 it was about 284 ppm. As I write this, it is 415 ppm. Put another way, atmospheric carbon dioxide concentration has risen one and a half times as much in the past 200 years as it had in the previous 12,000.[11]

And a full one-third of the rise since 1825 has happened in the twenty-first century. The increase is accelerating. This fact is a healthy reminder that not just the history described in this book but the book itself has been built on the burning of fossil fuels. The online research, utilizing technology whose development was predicated on a fantastic rise in resource extraction at the front end and in energy availability at the back end, was fossil-fuelled. The plane that flew me to New Brunswick and the four-wheel-drive that carried me around the Miramichi were fossil-fuelled. The civilizational wealth that has allowed for a sharp rise in the number of academic historians over

Conclusion 183

the past century means that my career, my life are fossil-fuelled. I was able to dive into the history of a past forest fire to a degree that earlier scholars could not because, fundamentally, my curiosity was fossil-fuelled. As we make the complicated but necessary turn away from fossil fuels, we will undoubtedly discover how much we took for granted. But in developing alternative systems, we will need to remember that the goal is not just – "just" – for humans to survive but for us to thrive and that expressions of our humanity, such as curiosity, must be nurtured, too. Otherwise, future disasters will not only be as immense as the Miramichi Fire but also as difficult to chronicle and learn from.

Acknowledgments

When I pushed open the front door of the Miramichi Natural History Museum almost twenty years ago, it was like entering a cabinet of curiosities. It was a single large overflowing room. On display were a stuffed puma, spider monkey, bear, caribou, moose, skunk, and – the museum's showpiece – eight-legged cat. There were collections of swords, rocks, boomerangs, shells, bugs, and butterflies from around the world, military uniforms from more than a century of wars, posters advertising boxing matches and Tom Thumb, Mi'gmaw woven baskets, and maps of Canada. And there were two visibly freaked-out summer students on their first morning of work. What had they gotten themselves into? After looking through some old timber company ledgers that I had permission to see – nothing there – I said goodbye to the students with what was likely an irritating mix of cheerfulness and pity, relieved that I had escaped their fate.

But I hadn't. I spent the next sixteen years not writing this book as I curated my own cabinet of curiosities about the Miramichi Fire. Thank you to all those who helped me to assemble it and to those who helped me to stop assembling and to start writing.

Thank you to Yolanda House, Cody P. Miller, and Suzanne Moulton for research assistance early on in New Brunswick and Maine. Thank you to the staff at the Public Archives of New Brunswick, the New Brunswick Museum, the Newcastle Public Library, the Weldon and Taylor Libraries at Western University, Library and Archives Canada, the Internet Archive, and Canadiana Online. Thank you to Chris Norfolk and David MacLean for indulging this historian's foray into dendrochronology. Thank you to Martin E. Alexander, Bill Bensen, Yves Bergeron, Ted Binnema, Dan Casavant, Jane Cook, Greg

Cunningham, Teresa Devor, Harold Dolan, Margaret Eaton, James R. Fleming, George Gilmore, Tom Griffiths, Jason Hall, Idris Hughes, Will Knight, Ed MacDonald, Josh MacFadyen, Christof Mauch, Paul Mayewski, Shawn McCarthy, Mike McDonald, Mark McLaughlin, Robert McNeil, Alex Mosseler, Jeff Patch, Tom Peace, Liza Piper, Daniel Rück, John Sadler, Valerie Sherrard, Anne Skoczylas, Victoria Slonosky, Ian Steele, Neville Thompson, Bill Turkel, Doug Underhill, Conevery Bolton Valencius, Greg Watling, Bill Wicken, and D. Murray Young for their material assistance in helping me to understand the Miramichi Fire, the Miramichi, fire, and a host of related topics. Thank you to Professor Toru Tanaka, who, more than anyone, taught me how to survive in academe. Thank you to the Faculty of Social Science and the Department of History at Western University and to the Forest History Society for research support. A special thank you to Stephen J. Pyne, who at a critical moment told me, "You can have it," and to Graeme Wynn, who always let me have it – encouragement, differences of interpretation that helped to hone my argument, and even the research index cards from his doctoral dissertation.

As much as I would like to acknowledge individually all the scholars and friends who have provided encouragement over the years, if I start, I might never stop. So allow me to give thanks in groups. Thank you to all my fellow travellers in NICHE: Network in Canadian History & Environment; this book is better and appears years later because of you. Thank you to students, staff, and faculty in the Department of History at Western University; it is a privilege to work with you every day. Thank you to the directors, staff, and the 2016 cohort of Carson Fellows at the Rachel Carson Center for Environment and Society at Ludwig-Maximilians-Universität; my fellowship term there gave this manuscript the boost and feedback it needed. Thank you to the many audiences who have listened to presentations based on this research and have provided invaluable questions and advice.

Thank you to the staff at McGill-Queen's University Press for believing in the manuscript and making it a book. Thank you to Jeannie Prinsen for first-rate copy editing, as always. Thank you to Eric Leinberger for first-rate maps, as always. Thank you to Canada's Awards for Scholarly Publications Program and to Western University's J.B. Smallman Research Fund for publication support.

Finally, thank you to my family. [End with a sentence or two more eloquent, touching, and true than anything that has ever been written.]

APPENDIX

Some of the Dead

In the course of researching this book, I compiled a list of 130 named or specified individuals said to have died in the Miramichi Fire or likely to have died because of it (e.g., people who died in the Miramichi region in mid-October 1825). The list necessarily relies on second-hand accounts, many of them long after the fact, and is far from authoritative. What is most striking is the list's size: 130 represents more than 80 per cent of the official death toll of 160. Even if only half of the names are accurate, or 40 per cent of the death toll, it is impossible to imagine that, even with an infinite amount of historical research, one could name 40 per cent of the individuals – the surveyed population, new immigrants, itinerant lumbermen, and Mi'gmaq – residing in the Miramichi in October 1825. This fact suggests either that the official death toll is low, that the fire's victims have been better remembered than its survivors, or that some combination of the two is in play.

Dead	Names (and ages)	Details	Source
2	Ann (11 months) and William Hervey (2.5 years), children of William and Sarah ABRAMS	Of Newcastle, buried 20 and 24 November respectively	Extract of letter from a mercantile house "to their friends here," cited in unknown newspaper, [1825], J.C. Webster papers, F452, NBM; Anglican Church Burial Registers, 1822–1970, 7, NPL; gravestone, St Paul's Anglican Church, Miramichi
2	Mr and Mrs William BARCLAY	Died "in a canoe crossing the river" (see next item in list)	Personal communication with John Sadler, 2011
1	Frances BARKLEY	Died in the river near Middle Island	"Cooney manuscript," W.F. Ganong papers, F399–402 S223, NBM
1	John BIGGS (also "some of Biggs family")	However, it is elsewhere said Biggs died on 6 October and was buried on 7 October (see Mullin, *Cemeteries of the Parish of Newcastle*, 176)	Fraser, *Gretna Green*, 53
4	Peter BLACKLOCK, wife, and 2 children		Baxter, "Bartibogue Fort," 9
1	Pierre BOUDREAU (1 month)	Of Petit Rocher, Northumberland County	Pierre Boudreau, September 1825 to 29 October 1825, Ancestry.ca
1	William BRANDEN		*Saint John Daily Telegraph*, 18 November 1892; New Brunswick Newspaper Vital Statistics database, PANB
8	Wife and 7 children of Calvin CAMP		*Saint John Courier*, 15 August 1829; New Brunswick Newspaper Vital Statistics database, PANB
1	CARROLL	On Big Bartibog River, suffocated in his well	"Cooney manuscript," W.F. Ganong papers, F399–402 S223, NBM
7	John F. CORBETT, wife, and 5 children (one named J. Stokes Corbett)	Of Newcastle	*Chatham Mercury*, 13 June, 20 June, and 4 July 1826; Maria Corbett (38), buried 9 October, and John Corbett (38), buried 20 October, Anglican Church Burial Registers, 1822–1970, 6, NPL
1	Agnes CURREN (33)	Of Chatham, buried 8 October	Anglican Church Burial Registers, 1822–1970, 5, NPL

No.	Name	Notes	Source
1	DONNAN	His widow received cash in relief to re-establish business	Miramichi Fire relief committee records, RS660B, PANB
1	Lady Jane ERSKINE (31)	Died 10 October, Miramichi; given that "Lady Jane Erskine" was also the name of a nineteenth-century ambassador to Munich, the name (and/or her relationship to Miramichi) is suspect	Lady Jane Erskine, 1794 to 10 October 1825, Ancestry.ca
1	ESTEY son		Hamilton, *Old North Esk Revised*, 22
1	Margaret FITZGERALD (11)	Of Northumberland (now Kent) County, died 16 October	New Brunswick Cemeteries database, PANB
2	Mr and Mrs FLEMING	On Big Bartibog River	"Cooney manuscript," W.F. Ganong papers, F399–402 S223, NBM
2	Unnamed children of William and Ann FORSYTH	Died October 1825, "possibly" in the Miramichi Fire	Hamilton, *Old North Esk on the Miramichi*, 164
9	David GOODFELLOW, his wife (perhaps Janet McCurrie), their daughter Catherine (wife of William Luke), and Catherine's 5 children	Hamilton reports David dying from a "cold," having stood in the Miramichi River for an extended period to avoid the flames. He is reported to be dead four days after the fire in the *London Times* article.	Hamilton, "Goodfellow, Alexander," *Dictionary of Miramichi Biography*; Hamilton, *Old North Esk on the Miramichi*, 181; letter from Miramichi, 11 October 1875, *London Times*, 19 November 1825; Janet McCurrie, 30 December 1857 to 7 October 1825, Ancestry.ca; "Cooney manuscript," W.F. Ganong papers, F399–402 S223, NBM
3	"Mrs. GREEN and her 2 children"	On Big Bartibog River	"Cooney manuscript," W.F. Ganong papers, F399–402 S223, NBM
1	HAMILTON daughter		St Andrew's Cemetery, Miramichi, Findagrave.com; see Baxter, "Bartibogue Fort," 9, on Simon Hamilton's dying daughter
1	Margaret HESKET (40)	Of North Esk, buried 24 November	Anglican Church Burial Registers, 1822–1970, 7, NPL
7	Ann JACKSON (41), children William (15), Robert (12), John (13), Joseph (9), Margaret (6), and Anthony (10 months)	Of Chatham	Anglican Church Burial Registers, 1822–1970, 6, NPL; gravestone, St Paul's Anglican Church, Miramichi

Dead	Names (and ages)	Details	Source
1	Marie Angelique JULIEN (20)	Of Northumberland (now Gloucester) County, died 8 October	New Brunswick Cemeteries database, PANB
1	Hugh KELL	Said to have died in the Miramichi Fire	Hugh Kell, d. 7 October 1825, Ancestry.ca
2	KILPATRICK man and wife	"There is now a fence around their graves on the road out to George Creighton's"	Baxter, "Scraps of Local History," 48
4	William KIRKPATRICK, wife, son, and daughter	As stated in the *London Times*, "this is the old man whose mill Mr. Gilmour turned, and whose cleanly house he admired so much"	letter from Miramichi, 11 October 1875, *London Times*, 19 November 1825; Mullin, *Cemeteries of Parish of Newcastle*, 176; Baxter, "Bartibogue Fort," 9
1	Amelia LEDDEN (8 months)	Of Chatham, buried 8 October	Anglican Church Burial Registers, 1822–1970, 6, NPL; given as "Amelia Mary Leydon," 4 February to 8 October 1825, Ancestry.ca
6	David LOCKHART, father, mother, sister, and 2 children		letter from Miramichi, 11 October 1875, *London Times*, 19 November 1825
3	James LYON, wife, and child	His sons received cash in relief	Miramichi Fire relief committee records, RS 660B, PANB; letter from Miramichi, 11 October 1875, *London Times*, 19 November 1825
6	Eleanor, George, Hanagh, James, Thomas, and a sixth LYONS		James Lyons, d. 8 October 1825, Ancestry.ca
1	Alexander MACBEAN (22)	Of Alnwick Parish, Northumberland County	Alexander MacBean, c. 1803 to October 1825, Ancestry.ca
1	MAHAR	His widow received cash in relief	Miramichi Fire relief committee records, RS 660B, PANB
1	Thomas MILLER	Drowned crossing the Miramichi River on 7 October	*Chatham Mercury*, 13 June 1826

3	Mrs MURRAY and her 2 children	Bathurst Road, 2 miles from Miramichi River	Baxter, "Bartibogue Fort," 9
4	Mother and 3 sisters of John NEVILLE	Reference is made to "Mrs. Naval, her four children, and a hired man," on Big Bartibog River, in "Cooney manuscript," F.W. Ganong papers, F399–402 S223, NBM	New Brunswick Genealogical Society, Miramichi Branch, *Cemeteries of the Parish of Alnwick*, 242
2	"Old NEWLANDS" and nephew		letter from Miramichi, 11 October 1875, *London Times*, 19 November 1825
1	James NOWLAN	Died in river; since reference is made to his grandchildren, he may be the "Old Newlands" cited above	"Cooney manuscript," F.W. Ganong papers, F399–402 S223, NBM
2	2 children of Patrick O'LEARY		*Moncton Times*, 10 February 1881; New Brunswick Newspaper Vital Statistics database, PANB
1	Richard POMEROY (39)	Died 7 October, Northumberland County	Richard Pomeroy, 8 July 1784 to 7 October 1825, Ancestry.ca_
1	Mrs George PRICE	Of Bedeque, Prince Edward Island	Haslam, *Wrights of Bedeque*, 3–4
1	Richard PRICE (40)	Of Ludlow, Northumberland County, died 15 October	Hamilton, "Price, Richard," *Dictionary of Miramichi Biography*; Richard E. Price, 30 December 1784 to 15 October 1825, Ancestry.ca
1	Donald RAMSAY	Losses sustained in the fire were paid to "the estate of Donald Ramsay"	Hamilton, *Old North Esk on the Miramichi*, 395
1	Richard RIMMER	"Some gimlets in his pocket suggesting he was a ship's carpenter, & from appearance of corpse, was in water all winter"	*Chatham Mercury*, 13 June 1826
2	David (15) and William (17) RUSSELL	Of Chatham, description of David's death in "Cooney manuscript," F.W. Ganong papers, F399–402 S223, NBM	"People Who Perished the Night of the Fire of 1825," in Miramichi Historical Society files, Miramichi Fire file, NPL; David Russell, 1810–1825, Ancestry.ca; William Russell, 1808–1825, Ancestry.ca

Dead	Names (and ages)	Details	Source
6	Robert SCOB, wife, and 4 children	There is a reference to victim "Robert Scott" in Miramichi Fire relief committee records, RS 660B, PANB	letter from Miramichi, 11 October 1875, *London Times*, 19 November 1825
6	Father, mother, eldest brother, and 3 sisters of STODDART	Uncertain if this is the same family listed below	*London Times*, 30 November 1825
1	David STOTHART		Miramichi Fire relief committee records, RS 660B, PANB
6	John STOTHART (40), wife Ellen, 3 sisters Ellen, Jennie, and Mary, and brother David	Family of Scots who immigrated in 1815 and opened store in Douglastown	Stothart manuscript, in Miramichi Historical Society files, Miramichi Fire file, NPL; Ellen, d. 6 October 1825, Ancestry.ca
1	Thomas TAYLOR	Lived on the Little Bartibog River, a mile from its mouth, the only named person said to have been in the woods, disappeared, and assumed to have died	"Cooney manuscript," F.W. Ganong papers, F399–402 S223, NBM
1	Mrs URE	"Confined in backwoods of Newcastle"	"People Who Perished the Night of the Fire of 1825," in Miramichi Historical Society files, Miramichi Fire file, NPL
1	Rev. John URQUHART	Died of complications from fire and scarlet fever	Haslam, *Wrights of Bedeque*, 43–4
1	Davenport WALKER (19)	Of Chatham, buried 12 October	Anglican Church Burial Registers, 1822–1970, 6, NPL
1	Thomas WALSH	His child received cash in relief of sufferers	Miramichi Fire relief committee records, RS 660B, PANB
1	Jane WRIGHT (10)	Of Newcastle, buried 23 October	Anglican Church Burial Registers, 1822–1970, 7, NPL

NBM/New Brunswick Museum; NPL/Newcastle Public Library; PANB/Provincial Archives of New Brunswick

Notes

PROLOGUE

1 Canada, Statistics Canada, "Population Ecumene of Canada."
2 Hamilton, *Old North Esk on the Miramichi*, 569.
3 Hamilton, "Jackson, John."
4 This account is according to American artist William Edward West, who in 1822 chatted with Byron while painting what would be the last portrait of the poet. Lovell, ed., *His Very Self and Voice*, 299.
5 Thoreau, *Week on the Concord and Merrimack*, 395.

CHAPTER ONE

1 Marsh, *Man and Nature*, 28.
2 Burton, *Emigrant's Manual*, 41.
3 Pyne, *Fire in America*, 56. See also Holbrook, *Burning an Empire*, 54.
4 For example, see Hough, *Report on Forestry*, 228; Guthrie, *Great Forest Fires*, 4; Omi, *Forest Fires*, 335–6; Tymstra, *Chinchaga Firestorm*, 62; and Struzik, *Firestorm*, 7.
5 Dick, *Celestial Scenery*, 265.
6 Horace Greeley, "Are Plants Ever Spontaneously Generated? Letter to H.D. Thoreau," *New-York Weekly Tribune*, 2 February 1861, reprinted in Dean, "Henry D. Thoreau and Horace Greeley," 632.
7 MacLeod, "Fire in the Woods," 674–5, reprinted in, for example, Daniel, ed., *Battersea Series*, 228.
8 Dalhousie College and University, "Examination Papers, 1884–5."
9 MacKinnon, *Sketch Book*, 67.
10 MacNutt, *New Brunswick*, 216; Fingard, "1820s," 263, 267; Wynn, *Timber Colony*, 47; Ganong, "Note 90: On the Limits." I do not include

194 *Notes to pages 6–14*

Pyne, *Awful Splendour*, in this discussion because, as he mentions, his description of the fire at pages 127–32 relies heavily on my unpublished essay "The Meaning of the Miramichi Fire."

11 Jardine, "Miramichi Fire"; Doucette, "Miramichi Fire"; Manny and Wilson, *Songs of Miramichi*, 145–9.

12 Ives, *Joe Scott*, 277.

13 Both now have vast literatures. Some useful starting points on the field of environmental history, internationally and nationally, are Hughes, *What Is Environmental History?*; McNeill and Mauldin, eds, *Companion to Global Environmental History*; MacDowell, *Environmental History of Canada*; MacEachern, "Forum: The Landscape"; and MacEachern and Turkel, eds, *Method and Meaning*. Some useful starting points on the field of social memory (aka collective or cultural memory), internationally and nationally, are Halbwachs, *On Collective Memory*; Nora, *Realms of Memory*; Nora, "Between Memory and History"; Pasts Collective, eds, *Canadians and Their Pasts*; and Opp and Walsh, eds, *Placing Memory and Remembering Place*. There is surprisingly little yet written at the confluence of these two fields, but see Uekötter, ed., "Environment and Memory."

14 Thoreau, 5 February 1855, *Journal of Henry David Thoreau*, vol. 7, 215.

15 Nora, "Between Memory and History," esp. 7–8.

16 Throughout this book, I follow the invaluable Gespe'gewa'gi Mi'gmawei Mawiomi, *Nta'tugwaqanminen*, for the spelling of Mi'gmaw words.

17 See the story of John Neptune in chapter 3.

18 See https://archive.org, http://canadiana.ca, https://news.google.com/newspapers, https://www.hathitrust.org, http://www.biographi.ca/en/index.php, http://ourroots.ca, https://ancestry.ca, and https://www.biodiversitylibrary.org. Many open-access databases welcome online donations; if you use them regularly, please support their work.

19 See "British Library Newspapers, Part 1: 1800–1900," Gale: A Cengage Company, https://www.gale.com/c/british-library-newspapers-part-i.

20 If you are interested in a source for which there is no link or the link is broken, I would encourage you to search for it online anyway. The great majority of sources cited here are beyond copyright protection and so may have been digitized (or their URLs may have been changed rather than the sources removed) since this book was published.

CHAPTER TWO

1 Finan, *Journal of a Voyage*, 191, 1, 93; Williams, "Bulk Carriers."

Notes to pages 15–21

2 Latham, *Timber*, 138.
3 Williams, "Bulk Carriers"; Marcil, "Wood, Charles." Wood had built a somewhat smaller ship, the *Columbus*, a year earlier on the same principle. It had made it safely to England, but the owners elected to return it to Canada rather than have it dismantled, only to see it flooded and go down on the return voyage.
4 Finan, *Journal of a Voyage*, 93.
5 Defebaugh, *History of the Lumber Industry*, vol. 2, 73.
6 Finan, *Journal of a Voyage*, 100.
7 Defebaugh, *History of the Lumber Industry*, vol. 2, 73.
8 Finan, *Journal of a Voyage*, 109, 108.
9 *Quebec Gazette*, reprinted in *Fredericton New Brunswick Royal Gazette*, 26 July 1825. Deals are pieces of lumber 3 to 3.5 inches thick and 9 to 11 inches wide. As applied to timber, 1 ton is equivalent to 40 cubic feet.
10 Mitchell, *Dendrologia*, 186.
11 For example, see Bellin and Jefferys, *New Chart*.
12 Bouchette, *British Dominions*, vol. 2, 131.
13 Rayburn, *Naming Canada*, 187.
14 Chadwick, *Water, Science, and the Public*.
15 Mosseler, Lynds, and Major, "Old-Growth Forests"; Aubé, "Pre-European Settlement Forest Composition"; Aubé, "Historical Influence of Forest Exploitation"; Wynn, *Timber Colony*, 12.
16 Loucks, "Forest Classification"; Zelazyny, *Our Landscape Heritage*. Coincidentally, the more broadly known environmental term "bioregion" was also coined by a Canadian, 1970s counterculture poet Allen van Newkirk. Unlike Loucks, who went on to have a distinguished teaching career, van Newkirk went on to stick up a Toys "R" Us. See "Surreal Life."
17 Zelazyny, *Our Landscape Heritage*; Loucks, "Forest Classification."
18 Mosseler, Lynds, and Major, "Old-Growth Forests," S48, S68.
19 Ibid., S55.
20 Crossland, "Defining a Forest Reference Condition," 76. Graeme Wynn wrote, "Almost all descriptions of the New Brunswick landscape in the mid-1820's are so general, that they might have been written with equal accuracy at almost any time in the first half of the nineteenth century." Wynn, "Assault on the New Brunswick Forest," 74. But understanding of that landscape has been sharpened by works of historical ecology this century, such as Aubé, "Pre-European Settlement Forest Composition"; Aubé, "Historical Influence of Forest Exploitation"; and Mosseler, Lynds, and Major, "Old-Growth Forests." Crossland's extraordinary thesis uses documentary historical accounts, surveyors' witness tree records, square

196 — *Notes to pages 21–2*

timber harvest data, and ecosystem archaeology to reconstruct forests of the early nineteenth century for comparison with today's forests. Her subject area is less than 50 kilometres southeast of the communities at the mouth of the Miramichi River – they are within the same ELC ecodistrict – so although her findings do not relate strictly to the Miramichi watershed, they are highly applicable to my work.

21 Crossland, "Defining a Forest Reference Condition," 111, 245, 250, passim.

22 This is not to say that the Miramichi's forests were disease-free. For example, they experienced periodic attacks by spruce budworm, a thrice-misnamed species that would be better called "fir foliage insect." Such outbreaks, which typically last eight to twelve years, can kill great swaths of forests yet leave them standing, making them susceptible to fires that typically occur three to nine years afterward. There is known to have been a spruce budworm infestation in the Miramichi region in the early nineteenth century – it has been dated to as early as 1802 and as late as 1817 – so in the twentieth and twenty-first centuries, forestry scientists have increasingly assumed that the outbreak produced dead and dried wood that fuelled the 1825 fire. This may well be true, although the story has lent itself to a *post hoc ergo propter hoc* argument: there was a budworm outbreak, then a fire, so the outbreak must have caused the fire or at least contributed greatly to its severity. J.R. Blais has a New Brunswick (and northern Maine) outbreak beginning in 1802. Blais, "Trends in the Frequency." Others date it to 1806. See Aubé, "Historical Influence of Forest Exploitation," esp. 216. On the relationship between budworm outbreaks and fire generally, see Fleming, Candau, and McAlpine, "Exploratory Retrospective Analysis"; and Flieger, "Forest Fire and Insects."

23 Aubé, "Pre-European Settlement Forest Composition," 1173–4; Wynn, *Timber Colony*, 14–16; Crossland, "Defining a Forest Reference Condition," 245.

24 That is, "irrevocably altered" at least on any timescale that is meaningful to us. For example, see Green, "Pollen Evidence"; and Warner, Tolonen, and Tolonen, "Postglacial History of Vegetation."

25 Gespe'gewa'gi Mi'gmawei Mawiomi, *Nta'tugwaqanminen*, 8–10. The boundaries between historic Mi'gmaq districts are not precise, and the Miramichi region is sometimes instead said to be part of the Signigtewa'gi district, along New Brunswick's eastern shore. On Mi'gmaq history, *Nta'tugwaqanminen* is an exceptional, collaborative modern work, but see

Notes to pages 22–6

also, for comparison, Paul, *We Were Not the Savages*; and Upton, *Micmacs and Colonists*.

26 Gespe'gewa'gi Mi'gmawei Mawiomi, *Nta'tugwaqanminen*, 35–6, 59, 111. See also Ganong, "Origin of the Major Canadian Place-Names."

27 For distinct perspectives on this incident and its meaning, see Gespe'gewa'gi Mi'gmawei Mawiomi, *Nta'tugwaqanminen*, 108–11; Spray, "Davidson, William"; and Hamilton, *Old North Esk on the Miramichi*, 14–19, 23–7.

28 See Wicken, *Colonization of Mi'kmaw Memory*; Reid, "Empire"; and Colley, *Captives*.

29 Mosseler, Lynds, and Major, "Old-Growth Forests," S52. Crossland, "Defining a Forest Reference Condition," 227, notes that at nearby Kouchibouguac National Park, because of the frequency of fires during the twentieth century, the average fire return interval was estimated to be 210 years, whereas from 250 to 9,000 years ago, it was 2,900 years.

30 John Wentworth to Principal Officers and Commissioners of His Majesty's Navy, 20 March 1790, 11–16, Sir John Wentworth letterbook, RG1, vol. 49, Nova Scotia Archives. Thanks to Bill Wicken for sharing this reference. See Fingard, "Wentworth, Sir John." For a broader history of the British North American timber trade, see Lower, *Great Britain's Woodyard*.

31 Cooney, *Compendious History*, 48–51.

32 Wynn, *Timber Colony*, 20.

33 Ibid., 28–9. Very little of the British North America figure came from New Brunswick and little of that from the Miramichi.

34 Ibid., 29–31.

35 Potter, "British Timber Duties," is a very useful encapsulation of the issue. Opponents of colonial preference would later claim that the differential duty was so absurdly high that timber was shipped from the Baltic to the Miramichi, where it was reshipped and imported to England. *London Times*, 14 June 1844.

36 Great Britain, *Report from the Select Committee*, 173. Bliss had already published *On the Timber Trade*, a book defending the duties.

37 Wynn, *Timber Colony*, 33.

38 Cooney, *Compendious History*, 57–8.

39 *Chatham Mercury*, 28 March 1826. The "Richibuctos" were in fact a group of Mi'gmaq living along the Richibucto River on the colony's east shore, 60 kilometres southeast of the Miramichi region.

40 Anderson, *History of Scottish Forestry*, 116.

198 *Notes to pages 27–9*

41 MacKinnon, *Over the Portage*, 28–9.

42 See Rankin, *History of Our Firm*; and Fay, "Mearns and the Miramichi."

43 Spray, "Rankin, Alexander"; Hamilton, "Rankin, Alexander." Gilmour Sr was married to an Elizabeth Pollok, and Rankin is said to have been related to the Polloks.

44 However, Lucille Campey points out that it was precisely during downturns in the British economy that emigration demand was at its highest but timber demand at its lowest. Campey, "Scottish Trading and Settlement Patterns," 16.

45 MacKinnon, "Doak, Robert."

46 Henry Bliss, 7 July 1835, in Great Britain, *Report from the Select Committee*, 167.

47 Campey, "Scottish Trading and Settlement Patterns," 21.

48 Mannion, *Irish Settlements in Eastern Canada*, 20–1; Spray, "Irish in Miramichi," 56–7.

49 See chart of immigration to Miramichi in Hamilton, *Old North Esk Revised*, 20. In 1823 alone, 4,700 Irish arrived in New Brunswick. In 1824, with Britain's passing of a more stringent Passenger Act that required passengers to be better fed during the crossing, the number dipped to 2,000. Spray, "Reception of the Irish," 14.

50 Spencer, *History of Early Boiestown*.

51 John McGregor, 30 June 1835, in Great Britain, *Report from the Select Committee*, 131.

52 Spray, "Cunard, Joseph"; Blakeley, "Cunard, Sir Samuel."

53 New Brunswick, *Journal of the House of Assembly*, 1825, 97. I define the Miramichi region here as Northumberland County minus Carleton, Beresford, Saumarez, and Wellington Parishes.

54 See Wynn, *Timber Colony*, 82. Nonetheless, they did develop skills in their trade. There is a lovely letter from the 1840s in which the co-owner of a New Brunswick lumber company wrote his partner with instructions for buying axes from a Connecticut company: "not quite so round on the edge as those they made for us in the Spring the weight and shape in every other respect were good." He wrote with the knowledge, care, and discrimination of a baseball player selecting a bat. Willard Broad to William Fowler, 18 July 1830, Broad & Fowler Co. Ltd papers, 1826–39, MS1 A2 MC2466, Provincial Archives of New Brunswick (PANB).

55 Neeson, *History of Irish Forestry*; McCracken, *Irish Woods since Tudor Times*.

56 Jonsson, *Enlightenment's Frontier*, 148; Davis, *Samuel Johnson Is Indignant*.

Notes to pages 29–33   199

57 Gilpin, *Observations, Relative Chiefly to Picturesque Beauty*, 117.

58 See Smout, ed., *People and Woods in Scotland*, particularly Stewart, "Using the Woods."

59 Anderson, *History of Scottish Forestry*, 119. However, Scottish forest historians agree that increased pressure on the forests that remained, such as during the Napoleonic Wars, tended to result in better management because the resource was more highly valued. See Stewart, "Using the Woods," 123; Smout, ed., *Scottish Woodland History*, 17; and Smout, MacDonald, and Watson, *History of the Native Woodlands of Scotland*, 162–3.

60 Pyne, *Vestal Fire*, 373. That the Parliament felt obliged to do so is an indication, of course, that such burning was taking place.

61 Ibid., 169–70; Evans, *Irish Folk Ways*, 147–8.

62 By the early 1800s, 90 per cent of County Clare's potatoes were being grown on burnt land. Evans, *Irish Folk Ways*, 147.

63 Pyne, *Vestal Fire*, 358. See also Anderson, *History of Scottish Forestry*, 95, 136; and Smout, MacDonald, and Watson, *History of the Native Woodlands of Scotland*, 115.

64 See Guevara-Murua et al., "Observations of a Stratospheric Aerosol *Veil*."

65 Oppenheimer, *Eruptions that Shook the World*, 295–311. Tambora was much larger than the better-known Krakatoa seventy years later. Winchester, *Krakatoa*, 5, goes far too far in justifying the subject of his book when he lumps Tambora among earlier eruptions that are "quite lost in antiquity, with rather little direct effect on human society."

66 On the international climatic repercussions of Tambora, and on 1816 more generally, see Post, *Last Great Subsistence Crisis*; Harington, ed., *Year without a Summer?*; Fagan, *Little Ice Age*, esp. ch. 10; and Klingaman and Klingaman, *Year without Summer*. For Canada's experience of 1816, see Harington, ed., *Year without a Summer?*; MacEachern, "Big Chill"; and MacEachern and O'Hagan, "Canada's Year without a Summer." Other major eruptions in this era included Soufriere in 1812, Mayon in 1814, Vesuvius in 1818, Kluchev in 1821, and Galunggung in 1822. See Eddy, "Before Tambora." New Brunswick historian Peter Fisher noted that the colony had been cooling for several years prior to 1816. Fisher, *Sketches of New-Brunswick*, 17.

67 Fisher, *Sketches of New-Brunswick*, 18; Fagan, *Little Ice Age*, 176.

68 Houle, Moore, and Povencher, "Ice Bridges on the St. Lawrence."

69 On the late 1810s as a period of continued cold, see Harington, ed., *Year without a Summer?*, esp. 127, 255–6, 266–78; Briffa et al., "Influence of Volcanic Eruptions"; and Fagan, *Little Ice Age*.

70 Kendall, *History of the Town of Houlton, Maine*, 28.

71 "Canada, at this day, is an exact picture of ancient Germany," Edward Gibbon said, arguing that agriculture would produce beneficial climate change. Gibbon, *History of the Decline and Fall*, 219.

72 Fleming, *Historical Perspectives on Climate Change*, is particularly useful here because he not only outlines the intellectual history of the majority argument, that clearing moderated climate (esp. 24–8), but also documents the continuing presence of a minority who believed that it did not do so (see 55). See also Zilberstein, *Temperate Empire*.

73 Fisher, *Sketches of New-Brunswick*, 18.

74 Bouchette, *British Dominions*, vol. 2, 142. See also Fisher, *Sketches of New-Brunswick*, 17–18.

75 Harington, ed., *Year without a Summer?*.

76 On fires of the Maine–New Brunswick border, see *Baltimore Niles' Weekly Register*, 1 September 1821; Wynn, "Assault on the New Brunswick Forest," 359; and Davis, *International Community on the St. Croix*, 118, citing *Eastport Sentinel*, 13 August 1821. On the Tobique and Cains fires, see "W," "Forests of New-Brunswick, No. 4," *Chatham Gleaner and Northumberland Schediasma*, 20 September 1831. The Cains River, 50 kilometres from Newcastle-Chatham, is within the Miramichi watershed.

77 On how the subsistence crisis spurred emigration from Europe, see Post, *Last Great Subsistence Crisis*; and Fagan, *Little Ice Age*, 174.

78 Crossland found that at her site southeast of the Miramichi River, nine species together had comprised 95 per cent of the total forest composition in about 1800, whereas six do today. Crossland, "Defining a Forest Reference Condition," 113, 144.

79 *Fredericton New Brunswick Royal Gazette*, 30 March 1824, cited in Wynn, *Timber Colony*, 35.

80 Cooney, *Compendious History*, 247. Likewise, "W," writing a series on New Brunswick forests for the *Chatham Gleaner and Northumberland Schediasma*, called the white pine "the monarch of the forest" on 27 September 1831. Then again, Cooney worked at the *Gleaner* in 1831 and was almost certainly "W."

81 Abrams, "Eastern White Pine Versatility," 967. Based on witness tree research, Crossland estimates that in the early nineteenth century pine – white *and* red – represented only 7 per cent of the trees in her study area. Crossland, "Defining a Forest Reference Condition," 144.

82 Wynn, "Assault on the New Brunswick Forest," 84.

83 Bliss, *On the Timber Trade*, 30.

Notes to pages 36–7

84 Wynn, *Timber Colony*, 35. Wynn refers solely to "pine," but this term was largely synonymous with white pine. Red pine, as Allan Gilmour told the Select Committee on Timber Duties in 1835, was a relatively rare and commercially insignificant species. Allan Gilmour, 21 July 1835, in Great Britain, *Report from the Select Committee*, 236.

85 Wynn, *Timber Colony*, 35.

86 Timber licences in the era required that any pine cut be "large enough to square 12 inches" – that is, able to produce a piece of timber 30.5 centimetres to a side – which meant only pines with a minimum diameter of 48 centimetres, bark included. The trees also had to be straight and true, as well as "free from knotty tops, plugs, rots, rotten or concase knots, decayed sap and worm holes." See Crossland, "Defining a Forest Reference Condition," 169, 201.

87 Springer, *Forest Life and Forest Trees*, 52–3.

88 Crossland, "Defining a Forest Reference Condition," ch. 4, esp. 184, 199.

89 Beavan, *Sketches and Tales*, 81. Crossland notes that white pine and eastern hemlock appeared 6 to 7 per cent more frequently along rivers than in inland forests in early surveyors' witness tree records. She also notes that what makes the historic riparian forests of the region of greatest interest – that these were the first areas cleared for the timber trade and settlement – also makes them the most difficult to reconstruct. Crossland, "Defining a Forest Reference Condition," 125.

90 Levinge, *Echoes from the Backwoods*, 284.

91 Cox et al., *This Well-Wooded Land*, 81.

92 Browne, *Sylva Americana*, 242. Writing in 1832, D.J. Browne did not call the white pine yellow, however, because he knew that the two-leaf yellow pine is distinct from the five-leaf white one.

93 Henry Warburton, 7 August 1835, in Great Britain, *Report from the Select Committee*, 373.

94 The fungus that presents itself as dry rot had always existed in Great Britain, but ironically, it was likely the increased use of Baltic timber in the late eighteenth century that produced an epidemic. Dry rot became an important public issue in 1782 when the bottom fell out of HMS *Royal George*, resulting in the deaths of 800 men. In 1838 it was discovered that coating ship's timber with creosote prevented dry rot. An exciting environmental history of dry rot is waiting to be written. Until then, see Money, *Carpet Monsters and Killer Spores*.

95 In Great Britain, *Report from the Select Committee*, see witnesses W. Parker, 26 June 1835 (92); John White, 14 July 1835 (204); Sir Robert Smirke, 17 July 1835 (231); and Warburton, 7 August 1835 (373).

202   *Notes to pages 37–43*

96 Stuart, *Three Years in North America*, vol. 1, 154–5.

97 Bliss, *On the Timber Trade*, 29.

98 For example, see Richard Norman, 19 June 1835, in Great Britain, *Report from the Select Committee*, 53.

99 Henry Warburton, 7 August 1835, in ibid., 362–3. Warburton speaks of this practice in 1835 as "the custom of late," so it is unclear whether the same was done in the years before the Miramichi Fire.

100 Bliss, *On the Timber Trade*, 65.

101 Fisher, *Sketches of New-Brunswick*, 57. See also Condon, "Fisher, Peter."

102 Wynn, "Assault on the New Brunswick Forest," 354.

103 Wynn, *Timber Colony*, 79.

104 MacNutt, "Politics of the Timber Trade," 51.

105 See timber licence, 1824, Timber and Sawmill records, RS 663 F1, PANB; and Crossland, "Defining a Forest Reference Condition," 178.

106 Spray, "Reception of the Irish," 11–26.

107 This paragraph draws heavily on Wynn, *Timber Colony*, 57–78.

108 Ibid., 85, 75.

109 New Brunswick, *Journal of the House of Assembly*, 1824, 101.

110 John McGregor, 30 June 1835, in Great Britain, *Report from the Select Committee*, 123. See also Bumsted, "MacGregor, John." McGregor's name can be found spelled as "Mac," "Mc," and "M'." I use "Mc" throughout since that is the spelling on the title page of his two books that I cite.

111 John McGregor, 30 June 1835, in Great Britain, *Report from the Select Committee*, 123.

112 Wynn, *Timber Colony*, 47.

113 [Hunter?], *Letters from Nova Scotia and New Brunswick*, 156.

114 "Civis," "Letter 4," letter to the editor, *Chatham Gleaner and Northumberland Schediasma*, 25 August 1829. By the time Cooney published *A Compendious History*, he had censored himself, saying that borrowers needed only to assure merchants that they had landed upon "a capital chance, or a fine grove." Cooney, *Compendious History*, 97.

115 John McGregor, 30 June 1835, in Great Britain, *Report from the Select Committee*, 122.

116 See [Hunter?], *Letters from Nova Scotia and New Brunswick*, 155; and Wynn, "'Deplorably Dark and Demoralized Lumberers'?"

117 Johnston, *Notes on North America*, vol. 1, 36–7. See also Wynn, "Johnston, J.F.W."

118 New Brunswick, *Journal of the House of Assembly*, 1825, 97.

119 *Chatham Mercury*, 28 March 1826.

120 "Civis," "Letter 4," letter to the editor, *Chatham Gleaner and Northumberland Schediasma*, 25 August 1829.

Notes to pages 44–7   203

121 McGregor, *Historical and Descriptive Sketches*, 167–8.

122 Springer, *Forest Life and Forest Trees*, 152.

123 John McGregor, 30 June 1835, in Great Britain, *Report from the Select Committee*, 121. See also McGregor, *Historical and Descriptive Sketches*, 167.

124 *Fredericton New Brunswick Royal Gazette*, 13 August 1822. See also MacKinnon, *Over the Portage*, 55–7. On riots of the early nineteenth century in New Brunswick generally, consult See, *Riots in New Brunswick*.

125 Lieutenant Governor Howard Douglas to Earl Bathurst, 30 December 1826, Colonial Office records, CO188, vol. 33, 218–19, Library and Archives Canada (LAC); Douglas to Bathurst, 8 March 1826, Colonial Office records, CO188, vol. 34, 101, LAC.

126 Cited in Holbrook, *American Lumberjack*, 66.

127 *Chatham Mercury*, 4 April 1826.

128 Levinge, *Echoes from the Backwoods*, 78–9; Crossland, "Defining a Forest Reference Condition," 176, 182; Parenteau, "New Brunswick Forest Heritage," 6.

129 Buckingham, *Canada, Nova Scotia*, 408.

130 Henry Bliss, 7 July 1835, in Great Britain, *Report from the Select Committee*, 167.

131 Allan Gilmour, 21 July 1835, in ibid., 247.

132 See Wynn, *Timber Colony*, 84; and New Brunswick, *Journal of the House of Assembly*, 1825, 97.

133 Uranophilus, *Almanack for … 1826*, n.p.

134 McGregor, *Historical and Descriptive Sketches*, 168.

135 I have misplaced the exact location of this anecdote in the George Patterson papers, MG1, vols 741–4, Nova Scotia Archives. Sue me.

136 Hamilton, *Old North Esk on the Miramichi*, 175–6. The poem appears in *Saint John Daily Sun*, 5 May 1899. On the poem's author, see Hamilton, "Parker, Hedley S. Vicars."

137 The remainder of this paragraph draws heavily on Gespe'gewa'gi Mi'gmawei Mawiomi, *Nta'tugwaqanminen*, 135–8; as well as Wicken, *Colonization of Mi'kmaw Memory*, 111; Upton, *Micmacs and Colonists*, 99–100; and Hamilton, *Old North Esk on the Miramichi*, 23–6.

138 In 1841 a New Brunswick census of Indigenous people counted a population of 158 living on what were now just two reserves – Eel Ground and Red Bank – on the Northwest branch of the Miramichi River. Perley, *Reports on Indian Settlements*, 8.

139 This is not to say that Mi'gmaq submitted meekly to such treatment. Gespe'gewa'gi Mi'gmawei Mawiomi, *Nta'tugwaqanminen*, 137, for example, tells of Mi'gmaq people retaliating against white incursions by

204   *Notes to pages 48–51*

sabotage and stealing, whereas William C. Wicken details their political and legal responses. Wicken, *Colonization of Mi'kmaw Memory*, 114–16.

140 Wynn, "Assault on the New Brunswick Forest," 102; "Appendix: Extracts from the Sketches of New Brunswick," in *Narrative of the Late Fires*, 16–17.

141 See Wynn, *Timber Colony*, 34, 47.

142 Rees, *New Brunswick's Early Roads*, 13.

143 New Brunswick, *Journal of the House of Assembly*, 1825, 97.

144 Hamilton, "Pierce, James A."

145 Ibid.; Hamilton "Clarke, Christopher."

146 Hamilton, "Caie, James."

147 *Fredericton New Brunswick Royal Gazette*, 13 September 1825.

148 Cooney, *Compendious History*, 63–4.

149 *Halifax Novascotian*, 2 and 9 November 1825.

150 Ralph Waldo Emerson's brother William was aboard a ship sailing westward across the Atlantic at that moment. His ship caught a terrible storm, and he would later write of being "compelled to sit in the cabin, and tranquily to make up what I deemed my last accounts with this world." He realized that he did not want to go to the bottom a clergyman, so he renounced the ministry when he arrived home. He became a lawyer. Rusk, *Life of Ralph Waldo Emerson*, 113.

151 *London Times*, 21 October 1825; *Lancaster Gazette*, 29 October 1825; and Williams, "Bulk Carriers," 380–1.

CHAPTER THREE

1 *Narrative of the Late Fires*, 5.

2 Ludlum, *Country Journal*, 63. See also United States, *Meteorological Register*. The average for Fort Sullivan, Maine, in 1825 was a full 2.5 degrees Fahrenheit higher than it was the previous three years.

3 West, *Journal of a Mission*, 218; *Narrative of the Late Fires*, 5. In Maine that July, G.W. Pierce wrote his sister, "My room is warm and uncomfortable, and the heat has been so oppressive for these some days … Even at this moment it is nearly 80 degrees though so early as 9 o clock – the thermometer here stood as high as 100 twice this week." G.W. Pierce to sister, 15 July 1825, MMN 28365, Maine Memory Network.

4 However, Siveright has the temperature reach that level by noon only twice in August and not at all in September and October. Thanks to Victoria Slonosky for sharing her transcriptions of Siveright's observations, the originals of which may be found in "John Liveright's [*sic*] Thermometrical Journals," McCord family papers, P001–838, McCord

Notes to pages 51–4

Museum. See Slonosky, "Historical Climate Observations in Canada"; also Pinhey weather diary, file 6 (1821–28), Hamnett K. Pinhey papers, MG24 114, Library and Archives Canada (LAC).

5 Frederick Dibblee diary, 17 September 1825, MC1721 M51, Provincial Archives of New Brunswick (PANB). See also "Extracts from Rev. Frederick Dibblee's Diary."

6 See evidence from Bedford, Maine, in Harington, ed., *Year without a Summer?*, 137.

7 George Coffin journal, 21 and 22 September 1825, 1, 4, and 5 October 1825, A21 R20, Maine State Archives (MSA). On the historical relationship between the two regions generally, see Hornsby and Reid, eds, *New England and the Maritime Provinces*.

8 Irish, *Report of the State of the Land Office*, 8.

9 George Coffin journal, 7 October 1825, A21 R20, MSA.

10 On fire behaviour and ecology, see Scott et al., *Fire on Earth*; Pyne, Andrews, and Laven, *Introduction to Wildland Fire*; Chandler et al., *Fire in Forestry*, vol. 1; and Omi, *Forest Fires*.

11 *Narrative of the Late Fires*, the pamphlet distributed across North America and Europe that autumn to raise money for survivors, is a uniquely important and uniquely problematic source. Although it offers by far the most comprehensive contemporary account of the blaze, one might discount it as untrustworthy since it was created with the express goal of eliciting sympathy and so had every incentive to exaggerate the scale of the disaster. Certainly, that is worth keeping in mind when considering it. However, only about a quarter of the pamphlet's content was written specifically for it. The remainder of the text is a compendium of newspaper articles, extracts from survivors' letters, the text of a speech by Governor Douglas, reports from relief committees, a description of Northumberland County, and so on. One does not sense when reading the pamphlet that its author thought the disaster *needed* to be embellished but rather that the facts – as imperfectly known as they were – would speak for themselves.

12 *Almanack for ... 1825.*

13 *Montreal Herald*, 6 October 1825. Having just arrived in Montreal from Sault Ste Marie, surveyor J.L. Tiarks wrote in his journal on 6 October, "The weather is again as hot as before, every body is astonished by the unusual state of the season." The next day was "as hot as before." J.L. Tiarks journal, file xxxii(3), MG24 H64, LAC.

14 Benjamin B. Crawford diary, 1825, vol. 7 (1824–25), MC1115, PANB.

15 Fullom, *Life of General Sir Howard Douglas*, 244. See also Jno. B. Hamilton, "New Brunswick and Its Scenery," 1874, Louise Manny papers, F198, New Brunswick Museum (NBM).

206   *Notes to pages 55–6*

16 "Incidents of the Great Miramichi Fire: An Old Narrative," *Newcastle Union Advocate*, 6 October 1897, Louise Manny papers, F198, NBM.

17 Cited in Lincoln, "Through Flame and Tempest," 451. Because of drought, the price of Quebec potatoes rose that fall, a time of year when the price traditionally plummeted. *Quebec Gazette*, 6 October 1825. See also Fyson, "Eating in the City," 121.

18 Benjamin B. Crawford diary, 1825, vol. 7 (1824–25), MC1115, PANB. Coffin calls the 14 and 17 September rains "very hard." George Coffin journal, 21 and 22 September 1825, 1, 4, and 5 October 1825, A21 R20, MSA. See also *Narrative of the Late Fires*, 5; and "W," "Forests of New-Brunswick, No. 4," *Chatham Gleaner and Northumberland Schediasma*, 20 September 1831.

19 George N. Smith, Miramichi, to Thomas Baillie, 20 October 1825, *Montreal Gazette*, 16 December 1825.

20 *Narrative of the Late Fires*, 5.

21 Cooney, *Compendious History*, 67.

22 For example, see Gesner, *New Brunswick*, 191; and especially DeMille, *Fire in the Woods*, 219. It would take well over a century's distance from the event before a commentator felt free, in the process of encouraging readers to recognize a forest fire's warning signs, to say that those who died in the Miramichi Fire had only themselves to blame. That is the thesis of Cooke, "Biggest Fire."

23 Cited in *Montreal Gazette*, 16 December 1825.

24 Governor Howard Douglas to Earl Bathurst, 17 October 1825, *London Times*, 19 December 1825, reprinted in *Chatham Mercury*, 28 February 1826.

25 Cooney, *Compendious History*, 67.

26 "I.P." to "My Dear Father," 17 October 1825, reprinted in *London Times*, 16 November 1825. See also Isaac Paley to Mr Dyson, 14 October 1825, New Brunswick, Original Correspondence, Secretary of State, Offices and Individuals, 1825, Colonial Office records, CO188, vol. 32, LAC.

27 *Greenoch Advertiser*, 19 November 1825, reprinted in *London Times*, 24 November 1825.

28 Fuller, *Forest Fires*, 42. People of the time understood this phenomenon, if imperfectly. In describing the Miramichi Fire, John McGregor explained that once a fire starts, "the surrounding air becomes highly rarified; and the wind consequently increases till it blows a perfect hurricane." McGregor, *British America*, vol. 2, 265. See also Bouchette, *British Dominions*, vol. 2, 135.

Notes to pages 56–7

29 Cited in *Montreal Gazette*, 16 December 1825. Smith has darkness fall at 8:00 P.M., whereas the charity pamphlet says 7:00 P.M. *Narrative of the Late Fires*, 6.

30 *Narrative of the Late Fires*, 6.

31 Ibid., 5–6; Isaac Paley to Mr Dyson, 14 October 1825, New Brunswick, Original Correspondence, Secretary of State, Offices and Individuals, 1825, Colonial Office records, CO 188, vol. 32, LAC; and "Incidents of the Great Miramichi Fire: An Old Narrative," *Newcastle Union Advocate*, 6 October 1897, Louise Manny papers, F198, NBM.

32 Cited in Montreal *Gazette*, 16 December 1825; Governor Howard Douglas to Earl Bathurst, 17 October 1825, *London Times*, 19 December 1825, reprinted in *Chatham Mercury*, 28 February 1826; *Eastport Sentinel*, 22 October 1825, reprinted in *Canadian Courant and Montreal Advertiser*, 9 November 1825; *London Times*, 11 November 1825.

33 *Edinburgh Weekly Journal*, 16 November 1825; *Inverness Journal and Northern Advertiser*, 18 November 1825.

34 McGregor, *Historical and Descriptive Sketches*, 169; McGregor, *British America*, vol. 2, 265–6.

35 The American meteorologist who discovered the cyclonic nature of hurricanes, W.C. Redfield, studied the Miramichi Fire as potential evidence of large fires creating their own cyclonic winds. Redfield, "Some Account of Violent Columnar Whirlwinds." On winds and fire, see also Thomas and McAlpine, *Fire in the Forest*, 74–7; and Brotak and Reifsnyder, "Investigation of the Synoptic Situations." In 1851 agricultural chemist James F.W. Johnston recounted being told by a Mr Rankin of the Miramichi that the wind from the southwest blew the fire beyond the region all the way to Burnt Church on the Atlantic Coast. Only then did the wind turn, such that the fire headed back inland "and by the way licked up the towns of Douglastown and Newcastle." Johnston, *Notes on North America*, vol. 2, 35; Wynn, "Johnston, J.F.W." Burnt Church's name has nothing to do with the Miramichi Fire, by the way. It was named after the British lay waste to the French settlement there during the Seven Years' War (1756–63).

36 Smith, cited in *Montreal Gazette*, 16 December 1825; "I.P.," *London Times*, 16 November 1825. See also McGregor, *British America*, vol. 2, 265.

37 See *Fredericton New Brunswick Royal Gazette*, 18 October 1825; *Halifax Novascotian*, 19 October 1825; and *Narrative of the Late Fires*, 10. Reference to a hurricane is also made in *Edinburgh Weekly Journal*, 16 November 1825; *Stanstead British Colonist and Saint Francis Gazette*, 24 November 1825; *Fredericton New Brunswick Royal Gazette*,

208 *Notes to pages 58–9*

22 November 1825; and Captain Walton of the Ship "James," Miramichi, letter, 11 October 1825, *London Times*, 24 November 1825. "Walton" is identified as "Walter" in *London Observer*, 27 November 1825.

38 *Narrative of the Late Fires*, 6, 11. See also Cooney, *Compendious History*, 69.

39 Bouchette, *British Dominions*, vol. 2, 135.

40 See Pérez, *Winds of Change*, 32, 34; Poey, "Chronological Table"; Lehman, "Meteorological Observations"; Bossak, "Early 19th Century U.S. Hurricanes," 31; and *Baltimore Niles' Weekly Register*, 29 October 1825. If there was a hurricane, it was clearly not a major one. A standard source, Ludlum, *Early American Hurricanes*, does not list any hurricane in 1825 or, for that matter, any significant hurricane hitting Maine, let alone New Brunswick, between 1788 and 1839.

41 Petition of Gilmour, Rankin & Co. and William Abrams, 20 February 1828, Legislative Assembly and Sessional Records, S36 P31, microfilm F17182, RS24, PANB.

42 Scott et al., *Fire on Earth*, 332.

43 Fisher, *Notitia of New Brunswick*, 127. Many decades later, James B. Pollard reported that he had been on Prince Edward Island on the night of the great fire when embers landed on the island's west coast, more than 20 kilometres from the fire's easternmost range. He also recalled, "During the nights of the conflagration a bright light was seen from Charlottetown to illuminate the western sky, the brilliancy of which made an indelible impression on the then youthful mind of the writer." Pollard, *Historical Sketch*, 61. See also "I.P.," *London Times*, 16 November 1825; "Extract of a letter from a gentleman to his brother," Miramichi, 10 October 1825, cited in unknown newspaper, [1825], J.C. Webster papers, F452, NBM. In 1917 ninety-nine-year-old William Henry Best recalled that leaves from the fire had reached his home in Kings County in southern New Brunswick. Cited in "Recollections of Canada's Greatest Forest Fire," 1410. Reference to an August 1825 Kings County forest fire is also made in Petition of James Campbell, 7 May 1827, Delancey-Robinson collection, vol. 1, file 3, MG24 L6, LAC.

44 MacLeod, "Fire in the Woods," 674.

45 Captain Walton of the Ship "James," Miramichi, letter, 11 October 1825, *London Times*, 24 November 1825.

46 *Narrative of the Late Fires*, 20.

47 Johnston, *Notes on North America*, vol. 2, 35.

48 Manny and Wilson, *Songs of Miramichi*, 147; Curtis, *Currents in the Stream*, 198.

Notes to pages 59–63 209

49 Scott et al., *Fire on Earth*, 331–2; Fuller, *Forest Fires*, 36; Pyne, *Fire in America*, 25.

50 Cooney, *Compendious History*, 69.

51 *Narrative of the Late Fires*, 6; McGregor, *Historical and Descriptive Sketches*, 169; Governor Howard Douglas to Governor General of British North America Earl of Dalhousie, 15 October 1825, cited in Lower Canada, *Journal of the House of Assembly*, 1826, 25; *London Times*, 24 December 1825.

52 This incident is reconstructed from *Newcastle Union Advocate*, June 1902, reprinted in *Newcastle Northumberland News*, 8 October 1980; Amos, "Can Newydd," stanzas 11–12; Cooney, *Compendious History*, 68; Boyd, "Preston, Richard." Amos's ballad, written and published in Wales to raise money for victims of the fire, claims that the black worshippers were unhurt because God protected them. Cooney credited "Mr. Wright and others" with attempting to raise the alarm.

53 *Narrative of the Late Fires*, 6.

54 Ibid.; "I.P.," *London Times*, 16 November 1825; Cooney, *Compendious History*, 68.

55 *Fredericton New Brunswick Royal Gazette*, 18 October 1825.

56 "I.P.," *London Times*, 16 November 1825.

57 *Narrative of the Late Fires*, 7; *Halifax Novascotian*, 19 October 1825, reprinted in *Montreal Gazette*, 9 November 1825.

58 *Halifax Novascotian*, 26 October 1825.

59 Cited in Hamilton, *Old North Esk on the Miramichi*, 138.

60 Mrs Ann Dawkins (daughter of Howard Douglas), "Memories of the Past," 64, Ann Dawkins papers, R3671-0-X-E, MG24 C43, LAC.

61 "I.P.," *London Times*, 16 November 1825; letter from Miramichi, 11 October 1825, *London Times*, 19 November 1825.

62 *Edinburgh Caledonian Mercury*, 5 December 1825.

63 Captain Walton of the Ship "James," Miramichi, letter, 11 October 1825, *London Times*, 24 November 1825.

64 *Saint John New Brunswick Courier*, 22 October 1825; *Narrative of the Late Fires*, 21, 28; West, *Journal of a Mission*, 239; Cooney, *Compendious History*, 79.

65 Manners, *Conflagration*, 14. A different poem with the same name appears at the end of *Narrative of the Late Fires*, 47–8. Manners's poem is discussed in Dahl, "American School of Catastrophe."

66 *Boston Patriot*, n.d., reprinted in *Eastport Sentinel*, 24 December 1825.

67 *London Times*, 30 October 1825.

68 *Narrative of the Late Fires*, 21; *Boston Columbian Centinel*, 21 September 1825; Beavan, *Sketches and Tales*, 82–3.

69 *Narrative of the Late Fires*, 22; *Halifax Novascotian*, 26 October 1825; McGregor, *British America*, vol. 2, 269; Gesner, *New Brunswick*, 192.

70 *Quebec Gazette*, 10 November 1825.

71 Cooney, *Compendious History*, 71.

72 Captain Walton of the Ship "James," Miramichi, letter, 11 October 1825, *London Times*, 24 November 1825.

73 *Bristol Mercury*, 21 November 1825. The *Lancaster Gazette*, 26 November 1825, states that "Redpath" was G. Smith, the *Canada*'s master and owner. Coincidentally, a New York newspaper mentioned in mid-October that the *Canada* was late in arriving in that city and "anxiously looked for," the assumption being that because of the storm, it "had probably found it necessary to stand off from the coast." Cited in *Charleston Courier*, 17 October 1825.

74 *Halifax Novascotian*, 26 October 1825; *Narrative of the Late Fires*, 8.

75 Jardine, "Miramichi Fire."

76 Amos, "Can Newydd."

77 "I.P.," *London Times*, 16 November 1825.

78 Cooney, *Compendious History*, 73.

79 Local historian W.D. Hamilton concludes, "There would be nothing to be gained by attempting to prove or disprove the fire stories, but it is evident that folklore has taken over from fact when the same story is told about individuals in different families, living at different places on the Miramichi, some of whom would not have been born in time to experience the events of 1825." Hamilton, *Old North Esk on the Miramichi*, 45.

80 Manny, "Miramichi Fire," CBC broadcast, 1957, Miramichi Historical Society files, Miramichi Fire file, Newcastle Public Library (NPL).

81 Chatham Parish baptisms, transcribed by New Brunswick Genealogical Society, Miramichi, 2004, 18–19, Anglican Church Baptism Registers, 1822–38, NPL. The likely reason for the high number of baptisms is discussed in the next chapter.

82 "People Who Perished the Night of the Fire of 1825," typescript, Miramichi Historical Society files, Miramichi Fire file, NPL.

83 Mrs C.F. Fraser. "Story of the Great Fire at Miramichi," *Newcastle Union Advocate*, 3 November 1897, Louise Manny papers, F198, NBM.

84 *Narrative of the Late Fires*, 3.

85 MacLean, *Young Men and Fire*, 124.

86 *Narrative of the Late Fires*, 7. The *Halifax Novascotian*, 19 October 1825, also called the blaze "unparalleled in the History of North America."

Notes to pages 65–70

211

87 Jardine, "Miramichi Fire."

88 *Narrative of the Late Fires*, 22.

89 *Halifax Acadian Recorder*, reprinted in *Narrative of the Late Fires*, 31; ibid., 22–3. Cooney noted that fires still blazed in the woods on 8 October, and the Welsh charity ballad by Amos went further, saying that the fire lasted two more months, destroying the whole country. Cooney, *Compendious History*, 75; Amos, "Can Newydd." One source has the fire lasting considerably longer still. According to Fred McClement, "Between 1825 and 1837 [*sic*] the Miramichi fires in Maine and New Brunswick levelled an incredible 3,000,000 acres and killed more than 100 settlers." McClement, *Flaming Forests*, 51.

90 "Un embrasement épouvantable dans les bois toul a l'entour … Nous ne voyons de nos fenêtres qu'une affreuse solitude, et la fumée des bois adjacents enveloppe la ville dans une obscurité presque totale." Report from Fredericton, 10 October 1825, in *La bibliothèque canadienne* (Montreal), November 1825, 198. S.W. Fullom has the fire burning for several more days there. Fullom, *Life of General Sir Howard Douglas*, 251.

91 McGregor, *Historical and Descriptive Sketches*, 169; McGregor, *British America*, vol. 2, 266; Alexander, *L'Acadie*, vol. 2, 185.

92 Chandler et al., *Fire in Forestry*, vol. 1, 97. On the characteristics of flame fronts, see Scott et al., *Fire on Earth*, 324–6. Thanks to one of the press's anonymous readers for assistance with this paragraph. In what I hope is taken as a tribute rather than plagiarism, the final sentence is that reader's.

93 Johnston, *Notes on North America*, vol. 2, 35; Cooke, "Biggest Fire," 20; Manny and Wilson, *Songs of Miramichi*, 147; Curtis, *Currents in the Stream*, 198.

94 Fuller, *Forest Fires*, 89.

95 McGregor, *Historical and Descriptive Sketches*, 168; McGregor, *British America*, vol. 2, 265. Joseph Bouchette borrowed liberally from McGregor's 1828 writing for his 1831 book but, extending the fire's range greatly, stated that the fire devastated a tract "upwards of 300 miles in extent." Bouchette, *British Dominions*, vol. 2, 135.

96 McGregor, *Historical and Descriptive Sketches*, 172; McGregor, *British America*, vol. 2, 268. Bouchette retained McGregor's 1828 use of "fire" when writing in 1831. Bouchette, *British Dominions*, vol. 2, 137.

97 *Chatham Mercury*, 28 February 1826.

98 Baillie, *Account of the Province*, frontispiece.

99 Jack, "Expedition to the Headwaters," 147–8, 118.

100 *Halifax Novascotian*, 2 November 1825.

101 *Montreal Herald*, 13 October 1825.

212   *Notes to pages 70–2*

102 George Coffin journal, 8 October 1825, A21 R20, MSA.

103 George Coffin journal, 9 October 1825, A21 R20, MSA. The following
     day he claimed to be unable to see more than 30 or 40 feet distant.
     Likewise, at Long Reach in southern New Brunswick, diarist Benjamin
     Crawford noted that 9 October was "smoky and so thick you cannot see
     five rods [25 metres]," and he called the air of 10 October "very thick."
     Benjamin B. Crawford diary, 1825, vol. 7 (1824–25), MC1115, PANB.

104 *Narrative of the Late Fires*, 22–3.

105 Ibid. Elsewhere in the pamphlet, it was said that an "immense number"
     of cattle suffocated from the smoke. Ibid., 28.

106 *Montreal Herald*, 10 October 1825; *Portland Eastern Argus*, 14 October
     1825; *London Times*, 19 November 1825. The word "smog" was not
     coined until the early twentieth century.

107 The widespread occurrence of smoke was well demonstrated by the
     Baltimore Gazette, 20 October 1825, which reprinted a series of short
     articles from Massachusetts, New York, and Maine, including one from
     a Boston newspaper that on 13 October stated, "The same appearance
     extended a great distance, both along the sea coast and the interior, and
     was first observed at points remote from each other, at about the same
     time."

108 *Montreal Herald*, 10 October 1825; *Portland Eastern Argus*, 21 October
     1825.

109 *Portland Eastern Argus*, 14 October 1825.

110 *Hampshire Telegraph*, reprinted in *London Times*, 17 October 1825;
     Thornes, *John Constable's Skies*, 44; *Trois-Rivières Le constitutionnel*,
     6 June 1870, 2.

111 See Tymstra, *Chinchaga Firestorm*, ch. 2.

112 *Canadian Courant and Montreal Advertiser*, 29 October 1825, reprinted
     in *Stanstead British Colonist and Saint Francis Gazette*, 10 November
     1825, and in *Baltimore Niles' Weekly Register*, 5 November 1825;
     Baltimore Gazette, 20 October 1825.

113 US newspaper, reprinted in *Canadian Courant and Montreal Advertiser*,
     26 October 1825. See Campanella, "'Mark Well the Gloom.'"

114 *Portland Advertiser*, n.d., reprinted in *Baltimore Gazette*, 20 October
     1825. See also *Portland Eastern Argus*, 14 October 1825; *Montreal
     Herald*, 10 October 1825; and *Eastport Sentinel*, 15 October 1825.

115 *Portland Eastern Argus*, 21 October 1825.

116 *Quebec Gazette*, 13 October 1825; *Canadian Courant and Montreal
     Advertiser*, 15 October 1825; *London Times*, 19 November 1825. On
     9 October the Earl of Dalhousie, governor general of British North

Notes to pages 72–4   213

America, jotted down in his journal that the smoke shrouding his Quebec City home "proceeds from fires in the woods." He was not surprised by its presence – that was common – only its magnitude. But within a week, he was marvelling at the reports of smoke hanging in the air all the way from York (Toronto) to Quebec City. Earl of Dalhousie, 9 and 16 October 1825, *Dalhousie Journals*, vol. 3, 29, 32.

117 *Montreal Herald*, 13 October 1825.

118 *Montreal Gazette*, 16 November 1825.

119 *Fredericton New Brunswick Royal Gazette*, 18 October 1825. This article appears subsequently in, for example, *Saint John New Brunswick Courier*, 22 October 1825; *Toronto Upper Canada Gazette*, 27 October 1825; *Quebec Gazette*, 27 October 1825; *Montreal Herald*, 29 October 1825; and *London Examiner*, 13 November 1825. *Edinburgh Weekly Journal*, 16 November 1825, carries part of the account, beginning midway through. In 1905 Clarence Ward gave William Francis Ganong a copy of this account, saying it was prepared as a circular by agent William J. Bedell for Robert Rankin, younger brother of Alexander Rankin of Gilmour & Rankin. When Ganong published an excerpt, he said it was the work of Alexander Rankin himself. See Clarence Ward to Ganong, 30 March 1905, W.F. Ganong papers, S218, F76–1, 5, NBM; and Ganong, "Note 90: On the Limits," 410.

120 *Halifax Novascotian*, 19 October 1825.

121 *Narrative of the Late Fires*, 8. These dimensions were also used in Fisher, *Notitia of New Brunswick*, 126.

122 *Eastport Sentinel*, 22 October 1825. But the report also warned that "the whole mischief is not yet known." See also, for example, Boston *Palladium*, 25 October 1825; *New York Albion*, 5 November 1825; *Baltimore Niles' Weekly Register*, 5 November 1825; and *Canadian Courant and Montreal Advertiser*, 9 November 1825.

123 Jardine, "Miramichi Fire," stanza 12; Amos, "Can Newydd," stanzas 6 and 19.

124 Captain Walton of the Ship "James," Miramichi, letter, 11 October 1825, *London Times*, 24 November 1825. Other British newspapers call him "Captain Walter."

125 *Greenoch Advertiser*, 19 November 1825, reprinted in *London Times*, 24 November 1825.

126 William Butterfield, "Memoirs of a Maine Pioneer," Dan Casavant personal collection. Thanks to Casavant for sharing this source with me.

127 *Eastport Sentinel*, 17 June 1826; *Washington Daily National Journal*, 20 June 1826; *Chatham Mercury*, 27 June 1826.

214   *Notes to pages 74–7*

128 For example, see Crown Land Maps and Plans, RS656 1C 40 1 Hunter 1832 map, RS656 2B 12 1 Jouett 1835 map, RS656 2B 1 1 Jouett 1837 map, and RS656 2B Boies 1837 map, PANB; and Timber and Sawmill records, RS663 E13 1832 map and RS663 E1 3 Peters 1835 map, PANB.

129 R.C. Minette, Survey of the Line of Road from Miramichi to Bathurst, 1828, PANB; Report of John Young, Superintendent of the Great Road, 2 January 1828, Legislative Assembly and Sessional Records, S36 M3.6, RS24, PANB. See also Rees, *New Brunswick's Early Roads*.

130 "W," "Forests of New-Brunswick, No. 4," *Chatham Gleaner and Northumberland Schediasma*, 20 September 1831.

131 Cooney, *Compendious History*, 69; Cooney, *Autobiography of a Wesleyan*, 55.

132 For example, see Buckingham, *Canada, Nova Scotia*, 431; Levinge, *Echoes from the Backwoods*, 40–1; Gesner, *New Brunswick*, 87; Marsh, *Man and Nature*, 28; Defebaugh, *History of the Lumber Industry*, vol. 1, 222; Flexner with Flexner, *Pessimist's Guide to History*, 113–14.

133 Gesner, *New Brunswick*, 78–9, 192, 194.

134 Alexander, *L'Acadie*, vol. 2, 184; Russell, "Gesner, Abraham."

135 Johnston, *Notes on North America*, vol. 2, 34–5. He also told of seeing the visible effects of the fire all day while travelling along the Southwest branch of the Miramichi River on the road from Nelson to Chatham. Ibid., vol. 1, 95.

136 Monro, *New Brunswick*, 202; Swanick, "Monro, Alexander."

137 Thomas Baillie to Earl Bathurst, 31 October 1825, New Brunswick, Original Correspondence, Secretary of State, Offices and Individuals, 1825, Colonial Office records, CO188, vol. 32, 143–5, LAC. Baillie's map does not accompany the letter in either the LAC microfilmed copy or the original in Britain's National Archives.

138 MacNutt, "Baillie, Thomas"; Young, *Colonial Office*, 65. See Young on the Colonial Office generally, as well as Thompson, *Earl Bathurst*.

139 George Coffin journal, 11 October 1825, A21 R20, MSA; New Brunswick Agricultural and Emigrant Society minute book, 21 October 1825, Delancey-Robinson collection, vol. 3, MG24 L6, LAC. Two years later, reporting on a visit to the Miramichi, Baillie spoke of having been better able to inspect the land "than on my former visit on account of the then State of the Woods." Thomas Baillie to Governor Howard Douglas, 8 November 1827, Baillie general correspondence, file 2d5, Surveyor General records, RS637, PANB.

140 George N. Smith to Thomas Baillie, 20 October 1825, reprinted in *Montreal Gazette*, 16 December 1825.

Notes to pages 78–80   215

141 George Baillie to Governor Howard Douglas, 16 December 1825, Douglas papers, cited in notes of Murray Young, correspondence with author, 2003.

142 For example, see Baillie, *Account of the Province*, 84, 89.

143 Descriptions of the Fredericton fire appear throughout the Miramichi Fire record, but see in particular *Narrative of the Late Fires*, 43–4; Governor Howard Douglas to Earl Bathurst, 3 October 1825, New Brunswick, Original Correspondence, Secretary of State, Despatches, 1825, Colonial Office records, CO 188, vol. 31, part 1, 178–80, LAC; *Quebec Gazette*, 27 October and 14 November 1825; *La bibliothèque canadienne* (Montreal), November 1825, 197–9; and Fullom, *Life of General Sir Howard Douglas*, 246. See also Hill, *Fredericton, New Brunswick*, 339; and Baird, *Seventy Years*, 21.

144 *Narrative of the Late Fires*, 43.

145 See ibid.; Governor Howard Douglas, cited in *Fredericton New Brunswick Royal Gazette*, 25 October 1825, reprinted in *London Times*, 17 December 1825; *Montreal Gazette*, 9 November 1825; and *La bibliothèque canadienne* (Montreal), November 1825, 197–9.

146 That December, Colonial Secretary Earl Bathurst received a petition from Irish emigrants to Charlotte County complaining that all available land had already been granted, with the exception of timber reserves. They asked whether some of the reserves could be granted them on the grounds "[t]hat the dreadful fires which have prevailed in said province at different times, & more particularly that of last Summer [*sic*] have destroyed all timber on the reserves, in the county of Charlotte, for naval purposes." Sam and Robert Thomson to Earl Bathurst, 21 December 1825, New Brunswick, Original Correspondence, Secretary of State, Offices and Individuals, 1825, Colonial Office records, CO 188, vol. 32, 224–5, LAC.

147 In mid-September, a forest fire burned for a week in the mountains to the east of Poultney and Ira, Vermont. *Baltimore Niles' Weekly Register*, 24 September 1825.

148 *Narrative of the Late Fires*, 8. There were fires far beyond that, too. Based on reports from Detroit that the prairies were on fire, a South Carolina newspaper concluded, "Thus from New Brunswick to Lake of the Woods, our country has been as it were, guarded on the north by a wall of fire." *Charleston Courier*, 12 December 1825. See also George Back's 1825 painting *Upper Part of the Mackenzie River, Woods on Fire*, National Gallery of Canada. When discussing the Miramichi Fire in 1837, R. Montgomery Martin wrote, "During the greater part of the year 1825 I was on the coast of Eastern Africa and Madagascar ... where I found the temperature dreadfull hot, although on board ship ... and I observed

216 Notes to pages 81–3

forest fires on different parts of the shore, from Patta and Lamoo, near the equator, down to Mozambique." Martin, *History of Nova Scotia*, 128.

149 Cooney, *Compendious History*, 65–6.

150 *Narrative of the Late Fires*, 8. Whereas the pamphlet stated that fires burned on the western part of the Nova Scotia peninsula that August and September, Cooney – using otherwise much the same language – stated that they occurred on the eastern part in July and August. Cooney, *Compendious History*, 65. Both may well have been correct. Methodist minister Robert Lusher recounted a "Providential Escape" from fire in the woods near Liverpool, southwest of Halifax, shortly before the Miramichi conflagration. *Wesleyan Methodist Magazine* (London), August 1826, reprinted in *Boston Zion's Herald*, 4 October 1826. In 1826 British soldier and author E.T. Coke passed through the "leafless forests" that resulted from 1825 fires as he made his way from Windsor, northwest of Halifax. Coke, *Subaltern's Furlough*, 404.

151 *Quebec Gazette*, 12 September 1825; *Saint John New Brunswick Courier*, 1 October 1825; Sandham, *Ville-Marie*, 105. Almost £500 was raised to help fifty-nine sufferers, as catalogued in *Montreal Herald*, 31 December 1825.

152 Report from Montreal, 10 October 1825, in *Halifax Novascotian*, 2 November 1825. See also *Montreal Herald*, 26 September 1825. *Canadian Courant and Montreal Advertiser*, 12 October 1825, spoke of the probability of the local fires having been "caused by persons under the most depraved circumstances." More perceptively, the *Montreal Gazette*, 15 October 1825, stated that "whether the cause is accidental or designed, there is great blame to attach somewhere."

153 See in particular *Quebec Gazette*, 13, 17, and 24 October 1825; *Canadian Courant and Montreal Advertiser*, 29 October 1825, reprinted in *Stanstead British Colonist and Saint Francis Gazette*, 10 November 1825; *Baltimore Niles' Weekly Register*, 5 November 1825; and *Boston Recorder & Telegraph*, 28 October 1825.

154 *Potsdam St. Lawrence American*, n.d., cited in *Baltimore Niles' Weekly Register*, 5 November 1825.

155 *Canadian Courant and Montreal Advertiser*, 29 October 1825, reprinted in *Stanstead British Colonist and Saint Francis Gazette*, 10 November 1825.

156 *Montreal Courier*, n.d., reprinted in *British Farmer's Magazine* (London), 1843–44, 510.

157 Sellar, *History of the County of Huntingdon*, 373, 474–5, 329, also 252, 262, 374, 415, 422, 430. Sellar is remembered for having also written historical fiction that has been mistaken as fact, but there is no indication

Notes to pages 83–4

that he embellished this historical work. See Brisson and Bouchard, "Haut-Saint-Laurent Wilderness"; and Hill, *Voice of the Vanishing Minority*, 169–71.

158 Hallowell report, 31 August 1825, in *Portsmouth New Hampshire Gazette*, 6 September 1825; *Providence Rhode-Island American*, 9 September 1825.

159 Norridgewock report, 6 September 1825, in *Newport Rhode-Island Republican*, 15 September 1825. A local history of the nearby town of Industry recalled how the 1825 fire season was exacerbated by the worst drought the town had ever seen: "[W]ells were either dry or yielded a limited and uncertain supply, and springs which had previously been considered 'never-failing' now absolutely refused to yield a single drop. A fire in the woods, dreaded as it naturally is at any time, becomes infinitely more dreadful when it occurs during a great scarcity of water, – when our homes are threatened by the fire fiend without any means at command to defend them." Hatch, *History of the Town of Industry*, 218.

160 Loring, *History of Piscataquis County*, 231–2; *History of Penobscot County*, 400. On page 421, this section of the latter book is said to have been written by "Mr. Soule."

161 Bangor report, 8 September 1825, in *Middletown Sentinel and Witness*, 21 September 1825. The 30-mile figure was repeated in, for example, *Saint John New Brunswick Courier*, 1 October 1825. See also Lehman, "Meteorological Observations," 345.

162 *Augusta Chronicle*, 28 September 1825; *Baltimore Niles' Weekly Register*, 24 September 1825; *Halifax Novascotian*, 26 October 1825.

163 *Baltimore Niles' Weekly Register*, 17 September 1825.

164 *Kennebec Gardiner Chronicle*, report, 11 October 1825, in *Boston Columbian Centinel*, 15 October 1825. On Maine's September weather, see *Boston Columbian Centinel*, 17 September 1825; and *Danville North Star*, 4 October 1825.

165 *Eastport Sentinel*, 22 October 1825; *Edinburgh Magazine & Literary Miscellany*, December 1825, 749.

166 *Baltimore Niles' Weekly Register*, 22 October 1825; *Quebec Gazette*, 27 October 1825; *Hallowell American Advocate*, 29 October 1825; *Canadian Courant and Montreal Advertiser*, 2 November 1825. Numerous articles state that twenty-one houses and twenty-five barns were lost in these towns.

167 *Concord Patriot*, 12 December 1825.

168 *Halifax Acadian Recorder*, reprinted in *Narrative of the Late Fires*, 32. See also *New York Albion*, 5 November 1825, reprinted in *Canadian Courant and Montreal Advertiser*, 12 November 1825.

218 *Notes to pages 85–90*

169 Late in the century, Maine forest commissioner Charles E. Oak reportedly established that the Maine and New Brunswick fires were distinct and, in the words of historian John Francis Sprague, "spread from opposite directions." Sprague, "Forests, Forest Fires," 117.

170 "W," "Forests of New-Brunswick, No. 4," *Chatham Gleaner and Northumberland Schediasma*, 20 September 1831.

171 Greenleaf, *Map of ... Maine.*

172 Governor Howard Douglas, cited in *Fredericton New Brunswick Royal Gazette*, 25 October 1825, reprinted in *London Times*, 17 December 1825.

173 *Halifax Novascotian*, 19 October 1825; *Saint John New Brunswick Courier*, 29 October 1825, reprinted in *Montreal Herald*, 16 November 1825.

174 However, Susanna Moodie states that the Miramichi Fire was "supposed to have been kindled by lightning." Moodie, *Flora Lyndsay*, 341. Lightning-caused October forest fires are extremely rare in northeastern New Brunswick. Patch, "Analysis of Lightning Fire Frequency."

175 Amos, "Can Newydd," stanza 14.

176 McGregor, *British America*, vol. 2, 265.

177 Alexander, *L'Acadie*, vol. 2, 185. See also Johnson, *Fire and Vegetation Dynamics*, 50.

178 Fisher, *Notitia of New Brunswick*, 129; Buckingham, *Canada, Nova Scotia*, 430.

179 *Montreal Herald*, 29 October 1825, reprinted in *Halifax Novascotian*, 30 November 1825.

180 *Quebec Gazette*, 3 November 1825. The *Gazette* recommended that Montreal newspapers establish regular correspondents on the other planets.

181 *Montreal Gazette*, 8 October 1825. Other descriptions of the comet include *Saint John New Brunswick Courier*, 24 September 1825; *Montreal Herald*, 13 October 1825; and *Canadian Courant and Montreal Advertiser*, 12 October 1825. See also Bortle, "Bright-Comet Chronicles."

182 *Baltimore Niles' Weekly Register*, 22 October 1825.

183 *La bibliothèque canadienne* (Montreal), November 1825, 198.

184 Bouchette, *British Dominions*, vol. 2, 135. Damp moss or rolled cedar bark was commonly set alight to create a smoky fire that kept insects away. Crossland, "Defining a Forest Reference Condition," 57–8.

185 *Eastport Sentinel*, 13 August 1821, cited in Davis, *International Community on the St. Croix*, 118; Pyne, *Fire in America*, 56.

186 Alexander, *L'Acadie*, vol. 2, 186–7. Andrew Spedon was blunter still: "Such an alarming and destructive calamity has been considered by the

Notes to pages 90–4   219

reflective Christian as a divine chastisement for the sins of the people. The inhabitants being chiefly lumbermen, and generally destitute of moral and religious influence, had become at length regardless of the laws of both God and man. Drunkenness and gambling triumphed over virtue ... Newcastle was a second Sodom in profanity; the infant country had become old in iniquity." Spedon, *Rambles among the Blue-Noses*, 43.

187 Baillie, *Account of the Province*, 117. See also Whitney, *From Coastal Wilderness to Fruited Plain*, 133.

188 Benjamin Smith diaries, F582, Archives of Ontario.

189 *Narrative of the Late Fires*, 5, 14; *Edinburgh Weekly Journal*, 16 November 1825.

190 Cruickshank, *Practical Planter*, 6.

191 *London Examiner*, 13 November 1825.

192 Fisher, *Notitia of New Brunswick*, 129. Indigenous people were commonly portrayed as incendiaries in the era. In John Galt's 1839 poem "Fire in the Forest," a group of settlers sit around a nighttime campfire in the woods. "A sullen savage left his trodden path, / And at their fire, uncourteous stoop'd to light / His quench'd cigar, to dare the gath'ring night. / They saw him soon, unspeaking still, resume / The Indian track, and vanish in the gloom, / Though in the dark they long beheld afar, / The crimson radiance of his fir'd cigar, / And sparks, like fire-flies, ever and anon / Stream from the star which then red-twinkling shone." Almost immediately, a wildfire roars their way. Galt, *Demon of Destiny*, 71.

193 For example, see Jack, "Remarks Concerning Forest Fires," 214–15.

194 Berton, *Acts of ... New Brunswick*, 48; Webb, "Development of Forest Law."

195 See Hazen Hindle and Hazen, *Keepers of the Flame*.

196 Willis, "Pedlar Karl," 2.

197 Simcoe, *Diary*, 7 July 1792, 115.

198 Johnston, *Notes on North America*, vol. 2, 12.

199 George Coffin journal, 11 October 1825, A21 R20, MSA.

200 Irish, *Report of the State of the Land Office*, 11.

201 George Coffin journal, 4 October 1825, A21 R20, MSA.

202 Irish, *Report of the State of the Land Office*, 15.

203 *Bangor Register*, 15 September 1825. Neptune was said to have dictated his letter to a "St. Johns indian," and the *Register* published it "*verbatim et literatim.*" For broader context on this episode, see Freland, "Tribal Dissent or White Aggression?" esp. 150–1.

204 *Richmond Enquirer*, 18 November 1825.

205 "The dense smoke ... is now accounted for in the most natural and simple manner." *Boston Patriot*, 17 October 1825, reprinted in *Philadelphia Aurora and Franklin Gazette*, 21 October 1825.

Notes to pages 94–100

206 *History of Penobscot County*, 620.

207 Ibid., 622. This account of the affair is the most complete. The author blames Irish's "obnoxious deputy" – presumably Chase – for having inflamed tensions with the illegal timber trespassers.

208 *History of Penobscot County*, 425.

209 "How Maine Got Birch Trees," *New York Times*, 14 August 1899.

CHAPTER FOUR

1 *Chatham Mercury*, 21 February 1826.

2 Spray, "Abrams, William"; Hamilton, "Abrams, William."

3 Extract of letter from a mercantile house "to their friends here," cited in unknown newspaper, [1825], J.C. Webster papers, F452, New Brunswick Museum (NBM); gravestone, St Paul's Anglican Church, Miramichi, New Brunswick.

4 "I.P.," *London Times*, 16 November 1825. Paley refers to them as the "Abrahams."

5 *Chatham Mercury*, 3 July 1827.

6 *Chatham Mercury*, 13 June 1826.

7 Hamilton, "Ledden, James."

8 *Halifax Novascotian*, 19 October 1825; *Chatham Mercury*, 11 July 1826.

9 MacKinnon, *Over the Portage*, 74; Hamilton, "Ledden, James."

10 Dyer, "Phoenix Effect."

11 Solnit, *Paradise Built in Hell*, 8, 9. Solnit admits that this heady optimism is temporary; Klein, *Shock Doctrine*, is a useful counterpoint to Solnit's book, showing how, in the longer term, states use upheaval to further a neoliberal agenda.

12 That is, knowledge of the existence of lemonade may make you more liable to buy lemons. Mauch, "Phoenix Syndrome"; Rosario, "Making Progress."

13 *Narrative of the Late Fires*, 9.

14 "I.P.," *London Times*, 16 November 1825.

15 Letter from Miramichi, 11 October 1825, *London Times*, 19 November 1825.

16 Hamilton, "Rankin, Alexander."

17 Extract of letter from a mercantile house "to their friends here," cited in unknown newspaper, [1825], J.C. Webster papers, F452, NBM.

18 "I.P.," *London Times*, 16 November 1825; Hamilton, "Smith, John"; Hamilton, "Key, Alexander."

Notes to pages 100–1

19 Petition of John Fraser and others of the Church of Scotland in Newcastle, 3 March 1828, Legislative Assembly and Sessional Records, S36 P95, 59, RS24, Provincial Archives of New Brunswick (PANB).

20 Governor Howard Douglas, cited in *Fredericton New Brunswick Royal Gazette*, 25 October 1825, reprinted in *London Times*, 17 December 1825.

21 *Narrative of the Late Fires*, 9. Cooney offers much the same information, paraphrased, in *Compendious History*, 79. See also Halttunen, "Humanitarianism and the Pornography of Pain."

22 *Narrative of the Late Fires*, 10.

23 Cooney's claim in *Compendious History*, 75, that it rained heavily on the night of the fire is contradicted by the 1825 evidence. The charity pamphlet stated that the fire extinguished itself before morning "without the agency of rain," and a letter from Chatham stating that "[r]ain has at last come" was written only on 10 October. *Narrative of the Late Fires*, 22, 26. See also *Halifax Novascotian*, 19 October 1825. When George Coffin described the weather on his arrival in Fredericton on 10 October as "showery," it was his first mention of rain in ten days. Two days later, he reported that "a very seasonable rain had caused the fire to subside" in a burnt-over area near the capital. George Coffin journal, 10 and 12 October 1825, A21 R20, MSA. A cold spell then set in, and by 17 October all of New Brunswick was blanketed with snow. See George Coffin journal, 17 October 1825, A21 R20, Maine State Archives (MSA); *Halifax Novascotian*, 2 November 1825; "I.P.," *London Times*, 16 November 1825; and *Greenoch Advertiser*, 19 November 1825, reprinted in *London Times*, 24 November 1825. One might assume that Cooney added the nighttime rain for dramatic purposes, as a way of showing the speed with which the Miramichi Fire had done all its damage – except that Cooney is unusual in also saying that fires still blazed in the morning. In any case, he was likely the fount for accounts in the late nineteenth and twentieth centuries that claimed it rained or even snowed on the night of 7 October. For example, see "Observer," letter to the editor, *Saint John Daily Telegraph*, December 1871, Louise Manny papers, F198, NBM; and MacKinnon, *Sketch Book*, 71.

24 *Narrative of the Late Fires*, 10.

25 Captain Walton of the Ship "James," Miramichi, letter, 11 October 1825, *London Times*, 24 November 1825.

26 "Extract of a letter from a gentleman to his brother," Miramichi, 10 October 1825, cited in unknown newspaper, [1825], J.C. Webster papers, F452, NBM. The charity pamphlet also noted that the Miramichi

222   *Notes to pages 101–3*

region had been dealing with a yellow fever outbreak, which contributed markedly to the fire's impact. *Narrative of the Late Fires*, 27.

27 Chatham Parish burials, transcribed by Appolline Savage for New Brunswick Genealogical Society (NGBS), Miramichi, 2008, 4–11, Anglican Church Burial Registers, 1822–1970, Newcastle Public Library (NPL).

28 Chatham Parish baptisms, transcribed by NGBS, Miramichi, 2004, 18–19, Anglican Church Baptism Registers, 1822–38, NPL.

29 *Halifax Novascotian*, 19 October 1825; *Narrative of the Late Fires*, 19.

30 Letter from Halifax, *Boston Recorder & Telegraph*, 28 October 1825; *Baltimore Niles' Weekly Register*, 5 November 1825; *Baltimore Gazette*, 3 November 1825. An 18 October letter from Halifax published in Edinburgh claimed that 500 named individuals were known to have died, and "it is feared that not less than 2,000 have fallen victim." *Edinburgh Magazine & Literary Miscellany*, December 1825, 747. The *London Times*, 12 November 1825, also discussed fear of a rising body count.

31 *Halifax Novascotian*, 26 October 1825, reprinted in *Saint John New Brunswick Courier*, 29 October 1825, and in *Eastport Sentinel*, 5 November 1825. It is unclear whether "100 to 120" and "thirty to forty" refer only to victims in lumbering parties or to victims overall. For growing relief about a lower body count, see also *Halifax Free Press*, 25 October 1825, reprinted in *Montreal Herald*, 16 November 1825.

32 For example, see "I.P.," *London Times*, 16 November 1825; *Halifax Free Press*, 18 October 1825, cited in unknown newspaper, [1825], J.C. Webster papers, F452, NBM; *Quebec Gazette*, 27 October 1825; and *New York Albion*, 29 October 1825.

33 *Narrative of the Late Fires*, 28.

34 Governor Howard Douglas to John Bainbridge, Agent for New Brunswick, 26 October 1825, cited in *London Times*, 17 December 1825.

35 Letter from Miramichi, 11 October 1825, *London Times*, 19 November 1825.

36 Jardine, "Miramichi Fire," stanza 2, puts the death toll at 200.

37 *Halifax Novascotian*, 19 October 1825. See also *Narrative of the Late Fires*, 29.

38 *Greenoch Advertiser*, 19 November 1825, reprinted in *London Times*, 24 November 1825. This witness put the death toll at about 300.

39 *Narrative of the Late Fires*, 28, 31.

40 "General Abstract of the Loss Sustained by the Fire at Miramichi on Friday, 7th October, 1825," Raymond Paddock Gorham papers, MC211 4/9/13, PANB. Its main conclusions were published in *Chatham Mercury*, 28 February 1826.

Notes to pages 103–5 223

41 *Saint John New Brunswick Courier*, 15 August 1829, New Brunswick Newspaper Vital Statistics database, PANB. Historian Murray Young likewise notes that Governor Douglas visited Oromocto shortly after the 7 October fire and wrote of loss of life there. Young, "Great Fires of 1825," 8.

42 The 1841 New Brunswick Indian commissioners' report has a table listing the "Persons" who have settled on or occupy Indian reserves. These "Persons" are white settlers; the Mi'gmaq reserve population is given separately. Perley, *Reports on Indian Settlements*, 15.

43 One purported Mi'gmaw story published in 1955 has it that the Mi'gmaq and a white man who treated them kindly were spared from the conflagration. Wallis and Wallis, *Micmac Indians of Eastern Canada*, 476–7. As previously mentioned, lumber company owner Alexander Rankin was associated with this legend, his house having escaped the flames.

44 *Chatham Mercury*, 25 April 1826.

45 Discussions of their inquests are in *Chatham Mercury*, 13 June, 20 June, and 4 July 1826.

46 *Report of the Miramichi Committee*. A counternarrative developed that 500 died in the Miramichi Fire. John McGregor championed this figure as "the lowest computation" in his 1828 and 1832 descriptions of the fire, which were influential (and occasionally plagiarized) throughout the nineteenth century. McGregor, *Historical and Descriptive Sketches*, 172; McGregor, *British America*, vol. 2, 268–9. Others who cited this figure included Bouchette, *British Dominions*, vol. 2, 137; Buckingham, *Canada, Nova Scotia*, 431; Warburton, *Hochelaga*, 320–1; Alexander, *L'Acadie*, vol. 2, 185; and Hodgins, *Geography and History*, 87. Today, descriptions of the Miramichi Fire typically give its death toll as 160, 200, or 500 – never making clear from where these figures are derived – but 160 remains dominant. There are outliers. Ed Struzik puts the death toll of the 1825 "Miramachi" fires at 1,200. Struzik, *Firestorm*, 7.

47 *Halifax Free Press*, 18 October 1825, reprinted in *Edinburgh Magazine & Literary Miscellany*, December 1825, 748–9. Writing in 1832, Cooney employed the relief committee's numbers but added, "[I]t grieves us to believe, that there has been a greater sacrifice of both life and property, than even the rigid enquiries of the committee have been able to ascertain." Cooney, *Compendious History*, 86. In the appendix, I have compiled a list of 130 named or specified individuals said to (or likely to) have died in the fire.

48 "Official Session," Chatham, 11 October 1825, Provincial Secretary correspondence, 32e/1825 file, RS13, PANB. For the committee as ultimately

224 *Notes to pages 105–8*

constituted, see *Report of the Miramichi Committee*, 1. For more on the relief effort, see MacEachern, "Popular by Our Misery."

49 Some of the very wealthiest and poorest may have been saved by topography. Timber baron Allan Gilmour's house in Newcastle was said to have escaped the flames because it was situated high on a hill, such that the hurricane blew the flames around it. Yet others "in low situations" in Newcastle also survived when the flames passed over. *Narrative of the Late Fires*, 25; extract of letter from a mercantile house "to their friends here," cited in unknown newspaper, [1825], J.C. Webster papers, F452, NBM.

50 The jail's prisoners were released during the blaze. An often repeated anecdote about the fire, first appearing in the charity pamphlet, told of "a coloured girl … imprisoned in the jail for making away with an illegitimate child" who died after returning to the jail in search of safety. *Narrative of the Late Fires*, 18. See also *Newcastle Union Advocate*, June 1902, reprinted in *Newcastle Northumberland News*, 8 October 1980.

51 *Narrative of the Late Fires*, 20.

52 *Fredericton New Brunswick Royal Gazette*, 18 October 1825.

53 *London Times*, 12 November 1825.

54 *Chatham Mercury*, 13 June 1826.

55 Letter from a Gentleman, Miramichi, to his brother in Halifax, 10 October 1825, cited in *Narrative of the Late Fires*, 27. Likewise, a report that "Clothes, Beds, Blankets, Household Furniture, and goods of all kinds" were pillaged during the Fredericton fire is at least ambiguous: were some of those goods needed to clothe, take care of, and house the injured and homeless? *Fredericton New Brunswick Royal Gazette*, 18 October 1825.

56 Boyle, *Chronology of the Eighteenth and Nineteenth Centuries*, 665.

57 Miramichi relief committee, 26 April 1826, cited in MacKinnon, *Over the Portage*, 13. However, according to a poem of the early twentieth century, men working in the backwoods were exploited terribly by merchants that winter: "That was not the worst, / For the men of the woods, / They doubled the price / On provisions and goods. / … I was told by a man / That on the south shore / Gave ten thousand shingles / For a barrel of flour." Poem by an "Old man in Whitneyville," 1911, published as "The Miramichi Fire," 1943, unknown newspaper, Miramichi Historical Society files, Miramichi Fire file, NPL.

58 *Halifax Novascotian*, 26 October 1825.

59 Mulcahy, *Hurricanes and Society*, 193. The British allocation of £100,000 in 1831 was a highly unusual case, in which the citizens of Barbados and

the Windward Islands invoked Parliament's even more extraordinary allocation of £120,000 following a 1780 hurricane. In 1812 the US Congress gave $50,000 for provisions to assist sufferers of a Venezuelan earthquake, but this was the only case of officially sanctioned federal government foreign disaster relief for most of the nineteenth century. Matthew Mulcahy's discussion of British and American responses to eighteenth-century natural disasters offers the most useful international context for the Miramichi case. There are few sources dealing with relief efforts in British North America prior to 1825, but see [Hanway], *Motives for a Subscription*; and Sabine, *Sermon in Commemoration*.

60 *Narrative of the Late Fires*, 10–11.

61 *Halifax Free Press*, 18 October 1825, cited in unknown newspaper, [1825], J.C. Webster papers, F452, NBM.

62 Earl of Dalhousie, 9 October 1825, *Dalhousie Journals*, vol. 3, 34.

63 For example, see *Fredericton New Brunswick Royal Gazette*, 18 October 1825; *Saint John New Brunswick Courier*, 22 October 1825; *Toronto Upper Canada Gazette*, 27 October 1825; *Quebec Gazette*, 27 October 1825; *Montreal Herald*, 29 October 1825; *Montreal Gazette*, 29 October 1825; *Canadian Courant and Montreal Advertiser*, 29 October 1825; *Stanstead British Colonist and Saint Francis Gazette*, 10 November 1825; and *London Examiner*, 13 November 1825.

64 *Halifax Novascotian*, 2 November 1825. Murdoch's biographer credits him with authorship of both the pamphlet and the poem "The Conflagration" that closes it. Girard, *Lawyers and Legal Culture*, esp. 157–8. He may well be right but offers no evidence. It is worth noting that Murdoch reprinted the pamphlet's description of the fire later in life without claiming it as his own. Murdoch, *History of Nova-Scotia*, 539.

65 See *Narrative of the Late Fires*; *Report of the Miramichi Committee*; and *Report of the Commissioners*. Specific donations and events mentioned here are from *Montreal Gazette*, 2 November 1825; *Boston Christian Watchman*, 5 May 1826; *Saint John New Brunswick Courier*, 29 October 1825; *Halifax Novascotian*, 2 November 1825; *Quebec Gazette*, 14 November 1825; and *Montreal Herald*, 5 November 1825.

66 Bremner, *American Philanthropy*, 40–3, 53–4; Curti, *American Philanthropy Abroad*.

67 *Montreal Gazette*, 12 November 1825. Conversion from 1830 British pounds to US dollars is from the website MeasuringWorth.

68 *New York Albion*, reprinted in *Canadian Courant and Montreal Advertiser*, 10 December 1825.

226   *Notes to pages 110–13*

69 *Montreal Herald*, 30 November 1825; Curti, *American Philanthropy Abroad*, 13–14.
70 *Boston Zion's Herald*, 16 November 1825.
71 *Salem Gazette*, 18 November 1825.
72 *Eastport Sentinel*, 22 and 29 October 1825.
73 *Boston Columbian Centinel*, 9 November 1825.
74 Manners, *Conflagration*.
75 *Canadian Courant and Montreal Advertiser*, 10 December 1825.
76 *Boston Columbian Centinel*, 9 February 1826, reprinted in *Hartford Courant*, 21 February 1826.
77 *Narrative of the Late Fires*, 37, 45.
78 Word of the fire reached continental Europe about the same time. New Brunswicker Edward Jarvis was in Paris little more than a month after the fire when he began reading about it in the press. Edward Jarvis to John Boyd, Saint John, 19 January 1826, in "Chronicles of the Jarvis Family," Edward Jarvis papers, vol. 1, MG24 B13, Library and Archives Canada (LAC). Likewise, a search of Austrian Newspapers Online, Austrian National Library, for the keyword "Miramichi" yields eighteen newspaper articles from the fall of 1825. There was no organized relief in continental Europe for sufferers of the fire.
79 *Edinburgh Caledonian Mercury*, 5 December 1825; *London Times*, 17 January 1826.
80 *London Times*, 12 and 15 November 1825. Such subscription campaigns had been common in Britain since the late eighteenth century. One observer noted, "There is scarcely a newspaper but records some meeting of men of fortune for the most salutary purposes." Cited in Mulcahy, *Hurricanes and Society*, 148.
81 Amos, "Can Newydd."
82 *Liverpool Mercury*, 9 December 1825. Liverpool's mayor received some bad press for not having called a public meeting until he had official word of the fire's scale. He stated in defence that he would not have been opposed to a grant of £5,000. Edinburgh had its own urban "great fire" in November 1824, and there was discussion of sending surplus funds from that relief effort to the Miramichi. It was ultimately decided that doing so might set a bad precedent, making future charity drives more difficult. *Edinburgh Caledonian Mercury*, 28 November 1825. On the Edinburgh fire, see Ewen, *Creating the British Fire Service*, 30–50.
83 *Aberdeen Journal*, 16 November 1825.
84 *London Times*, 24 December 1825.

Notes to pages 113–16

85 Reade, *Hard Cash*, 83. Financial bubbles and scandals were staples of Victorian fiction. The 1825 bubble is said to have been Charles Dickens's model for the one that bankrupted Nicholas Nickelby's father: "A mania prevailed, a bubble burst, four stock-brokers took villa residences at Florence, four hundred nobodies were ruined, and among them Mr. Nickleby." Dickens, *Life and Adventures of Nicholas Nickleby*, 6.

86 Sinclair, *Sir Gregor MacGregor*.

87 Neal, "Financial Crisis of 1825."

88 *London Times*, 23 December 1825.

89 *Edinburgh Caledonian Mercury*, 3 December 1825.

90 The Colonial Office gave £1,000, he noted. George Baillie to Governor Howard Douglas, 16 December 1825, Douglas papers, cited in notes of Murray Young, correspondence with author, 2003.

91 *London Times*, 17 January 1826.

92 Young, "Douglas, Sir Howard"; Spray, "Early Northumberland County." See also, more generally, Young, *Colonial Office*, 202–40.

93 For example, see [Hunter?], *Letters from Nova Scotia and New Brunswick*, 156–8; and debates between "Argus" and "CD" in *Chatham Gleaner and Northumberland Schediasma*, March-April 1834. For more on the depression's effects on the New Brunswick and Upper Canada forest economies, see Wynn, "Assault on the New Brunswick Forest," 362–7; and McCalla, "Forest Products."

94 McGregor, *Historical and Descriptive Sketches*, 155.

95 *Fredericton New Brunswick Royal Gazette*, 8 November 1825, reprinted in *Narrative of the Late Fires*, 38–43. On Douglas's visit, see also Young, "Great Fires of 1825"; and the reminiscences of his daughter Ann Dawkins. "Memories of the Past," Ann Dawkins papers, R3671-0-X-E, MG24 C43, LAC.

96 Fullom, *Life of General Sir Howard Douglas*, 253. Later in his biography, S.W. Fullom noted that Douglas performed so well in crisis because it was so familiar to him: "It is remarkable his career … embraced the range of human catastrophes; for he experienced the perils of battle, storm, shipwreck, and famine; faced pestilence at Walcheren, revolt in Belgium, and fire in New Brunswick; and now destiny made him a witness of earthquake." Ibid., 335. Others might have concluded he was jinxed.

97 Cited in *Narrative of the Late Fires*, 38–43.

98 Chatham Parish baptisms, transcribed by NGBS, Miramichi, 2004, 22, Anglican Church Baptism Registers, 1822–38, NPL; Manny, *Ships of Miramichi*, 16.

228 *Notes to pages 116–18*

99 *Chatham Mercury*, 21 February 1826.

100 What the people of the Miramichi would do next was a subject of interest on both sides of the Atlantic. In the Colonial Office, Earl Bathurst received a letter from "R. Stennett, Artist" in late November 1825 requesting they meet. This letter writer seems to have been the same R. Stennett who had recently created *Aldiborontiphoskyphorniostikos: A Round Game for Merry Parties*. Stennett wrote Bathurst that whereas others' attention was focused on charity for the Miramichi, "Your acumen will readily seize on one point likely to pass unnoticed by the British public, yet of vital importance; I allude to the Demolition of the standing timber, that Staple commodity which principally created and sustained those commercial establishments which are now annihilated, and which never will use them again." If Bathurst would give him but fifteen minutes, he would share "a modification of a comprehensive Plan for the relief of Indigence couched in a form with Statistics and other Notes," and Bathurst could expect "cordial adoption of my sentiments and advocation of the plan in Parliament next session." Alas, the world would never learn of Stennett's plan, as Bathurst declined to meet with him. R. Stennett to Earl Bathurst, 24 November 1825, New Brunswick, Original Correspondence, Secretary of State, Offices and Individuals, 1825, Colonial Office records, CO188, vol. 32, 222–4, LAC.

101 *Chatham Mercury*, 28 March 1826.

102 *Chatham Mercury*, 13 June 1826; Fredericton relief committee minute book, 9 February 1826, Delancey-Robinson collection, vol. 1, file 1, MG24 L6, LAC; *London Times*, 12 November 1825.

103 *Chatham Mercury*, 4 July 1826.

104 New Brunswick Agricultural and Emigrant Society minute book, 17 February 1827, Delancey-Robinson collection, vol. 3, MG24 L6, LAC.

105 *Narrative of the Late Fires*, 40.

106 Ganong, "Note 118: On the Physiographic Characteristics," 204.

107 For example, a young man petitioned for land on Prince Edward Island in 1828 on the basis that he was "a grat suffer at the fire in Mirimachi." Petition of Roderick McNeill, 1828, series 4, file 40, 1828, petition 707, RG5, Public Archives and Record Office of Prince Edward Island.

108 Hamilton, *Old North Esk on the Miramichi*, 47, also 92, 111, 162; Ganong, *History of Caraquet and Pokemouche*, 58.

109 See City of Pembroke, "History of Pembroke."

110 *Chatham Mercury*, 28 February 1826.

111 *Report of the Miramichi Committee*, 6.

Notes to pages 118–20   229

112 H.G. Clopper note, 27 December 1828, Delancey-Robinson collection, vol. 1, file 2, MG24 L6, LAC.

113 Burchill, *Miramichi Saga*; Johnson, *Miramichi Woodsman*.

114 Petition of Justices of Northumberland County, 29 February 1828, Legislative Assembly and Sessional Records, s36 P82, RS24, PANB; *London Times*, 10 September 1827; Arbuckle, *North West Miramichi*, 42.

115 New Brunswick, *Journal of the House of Assembly*, 1825, 97; New Brunswick, *Journal of the House of Assembly*, 1835, appendix, xciii. I ignore here the fact that part of Alnwick Parish joined Gloucester County, whereas the rest remained in Northumberland County. On boundaries, see Wynn, "New Brunswick Parish Boundaries"; and Hale, "New Brunswick Counties."

116 The following summer, the *Chatham Mercury*, 27 June 1826, reported on an attempted escape at the jail, calling it no surprise since the jail was far too small for the thirty-five prisoners it held. "[W]e doubt if the black hole at Calcutta could be much worse to endure than our own County Gaol at this sultry season."

117 Petition of Northumberland County inhabitants to maintain Newcastle as the shiretown, 9 February 1826, Legislative Assembly and Sessional Records, s34 P44, RS24, PANB.

118 Report from Miramichi, 2 December 1825, in *Halifax Acadian Recorder*, 17 December 1825.

119 Petition of Northumberland County inhabitants to establish Chatham as the shiretown, 9 February 1826, Legislative Assembly and Sessional Records, s34 P45, RS24, PANB.

120 Petition of Northumberland County inhabitants to establish Newcastle as the shiretown, 9 February 1826, Legislative Assembly and Sessional Records, s34 P44, RS24, PANB. The pro-Newcastle petition is identified as having 1,433 signatures; the pro-Chatham one has many more. In the same file, there are also pro-Newcastle petitions signed by residents of North Esk, Carleton, and Ludlow Parishes. That same spring, Saumarez and Beresford Parishes, on the coast north of outer Miramichi Bay, petitioned to become a separate county, claiming that it would be impossible to turn to agriculture if its settlers had to carry seeds and implements each spring all the way from the shiretown, whether Newcastle or Chatham. The petitioners wished to make clear, however, that "they are not in the smallest degree influenced by any recent opinion taken up since the late and much to be lamented misfortune that befell their brethren of Miramichi." Petition of Saumarez and Beresford Parishes, 1826, Legislative Assembly and Sessional Records, s34 P44, RS24, PANB.

230 *Notes to pages 120–4*

121 As a Newcastle resident wrote to the local newspaper five years later, "When our once thriving little town was a ruin – when our fortunes – our prospects – and our hopes – were buried in the wreck of our property – I thought the exertions, then made, by the people of Chatham, locally to disenfranchise us – to tear from us – for their own aggrandizement, our corporate privilege, an act of refined cruelty." "Homo," letter to the editor, *Chatham Gleaner and Northumberland Schediasma*, 5 January 1830.

122 Governor Howard Douglas, 19 January 1826, in New Brunswick, *Journal of the House of Assembly*, 1826, 1–4. In the same month, the *Saint John New Brunswick Courier* likewise stated that providence had smiled on the colony and that "no other tract of country in the British colonies of North America can vie with ours in the number and rapidity of improvements." Cited in Wynn, "Assault on the New Brunswick Forest," 358.

123 *London Times*, 6 March 1826.

124 *Halifax Novascotian*, 14 December 1825. The weather in early December was said to be as warm as May or June. Report from Miramichi, 2 December 1825, in *Halifax Acadian Recorder*, 17 December 1825.

125 *Report of the Miramichi Committee*, 12. In May 1826 those granted supplies were told to pick them up by 1 June, when the relief stores would be shut down for good. *Chatham Mercury*, 23 May 1826.

126 *Narrative of the Late Fires*, 45.

127 See Cunard to H.G. Otis, Boston, 21 November 1825, reprinted in *Canadian Courant and Montreal Advertiser*, 10 December 1825.

128 *Chatham Mercury*, 2 May 1826.

129 *Report of the Miramichi Committee*, 16, 14–15.

130 See Fredericton relief committee minute book, 9 February, 20 June, and 21 June 1826, Delancey-Robinson collection, vol. 1, file 1, MG24 L6, LAC. The Fredericton committee threatened to publish the list of delinquents and noted that, eight months following the fire, the £30 subscription by Judge John Murray Bliss – of the same family as Henry Bliss, co-chair of the London relief committee – was yet to be paid. Subscription figures also muddy the waters as to how quickly the relief effort petered out. For example, if the citizens of a place immediately subscribed £100 and ultimately gave £100, it is not clear how much of the final amount came from the original subscriptions and how much from subsequent donations.

131 *Chatham Mercury*, 28 February 1826. A copy of the committee's handbill enumerating the losses is in Louise Manny papers, F21–2, NBM.

132 *Narrative of the Late Fires*, 43–4.

133 A public notice appears, for example, in *Chatham Mercury*, 14 March 1826. The commission's form for reporting losses is in Louise Manny papers, F21–4, NBM.

Notes to pages 124–7   231

134 *Report of the Commissioners*, 5.
135 Ibid., 4–11, quotation at 9. Put another way, Miramichi was to receive 86 per cent of the total relief (exactly in line with its losses), Fredericton 8.5 per cent (somewhat less than its losses), and Oromocto and Charlotte together 5.5 per cent (considerably more their losses). The report noted that some individuals did not come forward to report their loss and that others came forward just to have their loss counted but without any wish to obtain relief. Ibid., 6, 9.
136 *Chatham Mercury*, 18 July 1826.
137 *Halifax Novascotian*, 23 November 1825.
138 So, for example, a Miramichi newspaper reported in 1830 that the region was "fast emerging from the embarrassing effects of that awful and destructive calamity." *Chatham Gleaner and Northumberland Schediasma*, 12 October 1830. Likewise, in a letter to the editor, "Civis" blamed "our embarrassment" after 1825 as much on financial speculation as on the fire itself. "Civis," "Letter 6," letter to the editor, *Chatham Gleaner and Northumberland Schediasma*, 22 September 1829.
139 Remarkably, decency even limited how much donors should give. According to George Manners, the British consul in Massachusetts, affluent Bostonians had been ready to send larger sums to the Miramichi, but these donations were "very properly declined, by the Committee appointed to conduct the Subscription, lest their acceptance should have excited unpleasant and disadvantageous feelings in the bosoms of those whose means were not so adequate to the manifestations of their equally humane dispositions." Donors' sensitivities were judged of greater consequence than recipients' needs. Manners, *Conflagration*, 18.
140 *Report of the Commissioners*, 12.
141 Ibid., 4. The central committee had compiled data on the value of manufactured timber lost. See form for survivors to itemize losses, Delancey-Robinson collection, vol. 1, file 2, MG24 L6, LAC.
142 *Chatham Mercury*, 14 November 1826.
143 It did make three small changes: adding a class of wounded, aged, and infirm men; including "orphans" with widows and single women; and replacing "tavern-keepers" with "innkeepers."
144 *Report of the Miramichi Committee*, 23–4, 26.
145 Hamilton, *Old North Esk on the Miramichi*, 61, 80, 344, passim.
146 *Eastport Sentinel*, 7 July 1827; *Following List of Citizens*, also published in *Chatham Mercury*, 6 November 1827.
147 "Quoi, lors de l'incedie de Miramichi, £150,000 ont été distribués en *quatorze jours*, et le comité de Québec a pu à peine distribuer les

232   *Notes to pages 128–30*

deux tiers de cette somme en *quatorze mois." Le journal de Québec,* 14 July 1846. See also *Le journal de Québec,* 3 July 1845.

148 *Le journal de Québec,* 17 April 1852.

149 Harry Peters, on behalf of William Murray, to H.G. Clopper, central committee, 6 October 1827, Delancey-Robinson collection, vol. 1, file 2, MG24 L6, LAC. Peters's petition is worded so that it is not entirely clear that the fire occurred on or about 7 October – or was even a forest fire.

150 Petitions of James Campbell, 7 May 1827, and Ammon Fowler, 19 [?] May 1827, Delancey-Robinson collection, vol. 1, file 3, MG24 L6, LAC.

151 *Ewing &c. v. M'Gavin,* no. 331, in Shaw, et al., *Cases Decided in the [Scotland] Court of Session,* vol. 9, 622–4, quotation at 622. Exacerbating the donors' irritation was that so much had been raised elsewhere – that their contribution was not as crucial as they had supposed when they made it. But the judge concluded that after such a disaster, "however large the contributions in other quarters may have been," it was still within the discretion of those to whom the charity had been given to determine its use. The case was cited as precedent in Scottish charity law through at least the 1840s. See *Highland Destitution,* 26.

152 Fredericton relief committee minute book, 23 July 1832, Delancey-Robinson collection, vol. 1, file 1, MG24 L6, LAC.

153 *Report of the Miramichi Committee,* 21.

154 Just how many millions is difficult to determine. The website MeasuringWorth permits comparison of 1825 British figures with those of today but warns of the numerous ways one can make such a calculation. If attempting to determine the cost of a project such as the building of a bridge – or perhaps the rebuilding of a community – one might use a deflator of gross domestic product, in which case £50,000 in 1825 is equivalent to about £4 million today. However, if one takes into account that the overall past economy was much smaller and thus calculates the earlier value in terms of its percentage of the overall (British) economy, £50,000 in 1825 is equivalent to about £213 million today.

155 Hall, "Burning of Miramichi." See also Crowe, "Man Who Was Pecksniff."

156 Savage, *Miramichi,* 201–2.

157 Charles Miller, letter, 26 July 1826, *American Baptist Magazine* (Boston) 6, no. 9 (1826): 280–1; David James, letter, [1826], *American Baptist Magazine* (Boston) 6, no. 12 (1826): 371–2; David James, letter, 1 February 1827, *American Baptist Magazine* (Boston) 8, no. 5 (1828): 203–5. The fire was interpreted as a call for religious recommitment far beyond the Miramichi. See the Irish tract by MacGregor, *Fire in the Forest of New Brunswick.*

Notes to pages 131–6

158 Lower, *Settlement and the Forest Frontier*, 37n23.

159 *Chatham Mercury*, 16 January 1827 and 15 January 1828.

160 McGregor, *British America*, vol. 2, 262. Others who spoke of a shift to agriculture include Bouchette, *British Dominions*, vol. 2, 132; and "Observer," letter to the editor, *Chatham Gleaner and Northumberland Schediasma*, 4 June 1833.

161 John McGregor, 30 June 1835, in Great Britain, *Report from the Select Committee*, 127, 126.

162 Wynn, *Timber Colony*, 84.

163 Wynn, "'Deplorably Dark and Demoralized Lumberers'?"; MacKinnon, *Over the Portage*, 21–2.

164 Taylor, *Promoters, Patriots, and Partisans*, 74–5.

165 Cooney, *Compendious History*, 62, 87–8. And it had not taken until 1832 to effect this transformation. Three years earlier, Cooney had written much the same thing in much the same terms. See *Chatham Gleaner and Northumberland Schediasma*, 13 October 1829, reprinted in *New-Brunswick Religious and Literary Journal* 1, no. 40 (1829): 318–19.

166 Cooney, *Compendious History*, 64, 87.

CHAPTER FIVE

1 *Chatham Mercury*, 10 October 1826.

2 *Chatham Mercury*, 7 October 1828.

3 *Chatham Gleaner and Northumberland Schediasma*, 18 October 1829. Pierce shuttered the *Mercury* in March of that year and launched the *Gleaner* a few months later.

4 *Chatham Gleaner and Northumberland Schediasma*, 12 October 1830. Governor Howard Douglas was even faster than Pierce in saying that nature was recovering. In his 1827 speech opening the legislative assembly, Douglas gave thanks that "[t]he traces of the dreadful conflagration are rapidly disappearing," and the reply to the address concurred. Governor Howard Douglas, 8 February 1827, and reply, 12 February 1827, in New Brunswick, *Journal of the House of Assembly*, 1827, 4, 13.

5 Cited in Wynn, "Assault on the New Brunswick Forest," 358.

6 Meek, *Lumbering in Eastern Canada*, 57.

7 Works that have been particularly helpful to discussion of post-fire ecology in this chapter include Scott et al., *Fire on Earth*; Pyne, Andrews, and Laven, *Introduction to Wildland Fire*; Chandler et al., *Fire in Forestry*, vol. 1; Omi, *Forest Fires*; Wallace, ed., *After the Fires*; Aubé, "Pre-European Settlement Forest Composition"; and Mosseler, Lynds, and Major, "Old-Growth Forests."

234 Notes to pages 137–40

8 *Chatham Gleaner and Northumberland Schediasma*, 8 October 1833.

9 *Chatham Gleaner and Northumberland Schediasma*, 7 October 1834.

10 *Chatham Gleaner and Northumberland Schediasma*, 13 October 1835 and 10 October 1837.

11 See "W," "Forests of New-Brunswick, No. 4," *Chatham Gleaner and Northumberland Schediasma*, 20 September 1831. "W" stated that the fire produced "a vast amphitheatre of blackened, dead, and useless forest trees – daily falling, encumbering the land, and rendering it almost impassable for man or beast."

12 Petition of Great and Little Bartibog Rivers settlers, 7 February 1826, Legislative Assembly and Sessional Records, s34 p35, microfilm f17170, rs24, Provincial Archives of New Brunswick (panb). On the Great Roads, see Rees, *New Brunswick's Early Roads*.

13 Report of John Young, Superintendent of the Great Road, 2 January 1828, Legislative Assembly and Sessional Records, s36 m3.6, microfilm f17181, rs24, panb.

14 Cooney, *Compendious History*, 118.

15 Gesner, *New Brunswick*, 194.

16 David Crocker, "Newcastle to Tabusintac," in "Appendix: Reports on Great Roads and Bridges," in New Brunswick, *Journal of the House of Assembly*, 1855, cccli.

17 On fire and soils, see Scott et al., *Fire on Earth*, 157–64; Pyne, Andrews, and Laven, *Introduction to Wildland Fire*, 193–6; and Omi, *Forest Fires*, 174–6. See also Colpitts et al., *Forest Soils of New Brunswick*.

18 Perley, *Reports on Indian Settlements*, cxii.

19 Johnston, *Notes on North America*, vol. 1, 95. Johnston elsewhere noted that "the soil itself is permanent injured" by fires such as the Miramichi one: "The clouds of ashes borne away by the wind are an actual robbery by nature." Ibid., vol. 2, 36.

20 Marsh, *Man and Nature*, 28.

21 *Narrative of the Late Fires*, 21.

22 Petition of James Forein, 1 May 1827, Legislative Assembly and Sessional Records, s35 p123, microfilm f17176, rs24, panb.

23 Bill to appropriate a part of the public revenue, March 1827, Legislative Assembly and Sessional Records, S35 B67, microfilm f17174, rs24, panb.

24 *Halifax Novascotian*, 2 November 1825.

25 Abrams, "Eastern White Pine Versatility"; Foster and Aber, eds, *Forests in Time*, 56–7.

Notes to pages 140–2

26 Alexander, *L'Acadie*, vol. 2, 142. The author took pains to note that these woods in south-central New Brunswick were the product of an 1827 fire, not the Miramichi Fire.

27 Petition of Great and Little Bartibog Rivers settlers, 7 February 1826, Legislative Assembly and Sessional Records, S 34 P 35, microfilm F 17170, RS 24, PANB.

28 Cooney, *Compendious History*, 119.

29 That the Bartibog River divided two parishes, the colony's census units, makes it all but impossible to know the Bartibog area's population.

30 Cooney, *Compendious History*, 120.

31 Petition of Northumberland County committee, 1831, Timber and Sawmill records, RS 663A, PANB.

32 *Emigration*, 85–92; McKenna, "Cockburn, Sir Francis."

33 *Halifax Novascotian*, 26 October 1825; Report from Miramichi, 2 December 1825, in *Halifax Acadian Recorder*, 17 December 1825.

34 "W," "Forests of New-Brunswick, No. 3," *Chatham Gleaner and Northumberland Schediasma*, 13 September 1831. "W" went so far as to claim that the effect of fire on standing timber was "superficial" as long as it was dispatched quickly. In the twentieth century, timber salvage after hurricane-caused blowdowns was sometimes shown to cause more damage to forests than the hurricane itself, but pre-industrial forestry was incapable of that great an effect. Foster and Aber, eds, *Forests in Time*, 253–4.

35 "Civis," "Letter 5," letter to the editor, *Chatham Gleaner and Northumberland Schediasma*, 8 September 1829.

36 For example, see *Chatham Mercury*, 22 August 1826; and George Brown, Liverpool, to John Ward & Sons, 24 October and 2 December 1825, John Ward & Sons Company papers, F1 S47, New Brunswick Museum (NBM).

37 Bainbridge & Brown to John Ward & Sons, 20 October 1826, Ward & Sons Company papers, F1 S47, NBM, cited in Blakeley, "Cunard, Sir Samuel." Early in 1826 *Blackwood's Edinburgh Magazine* ran a bit of social satire in which a citizen notes that the wood merchant "Mr. Sapling" had bought a new pair of trousers, having been much in need of them what with things "very shabby thereabouts, after the fire at Miramichi." "Excerpts from the Diary of an Old Citizen," 274.

38 The opening of the Erie Canal stands as another contemporaneous event with long-term repercussions. Less than three weeks after the Miramichi Fire, bonfires blazed along the mountaintops of upstate New York to celebrate that passenger and freight traffic could now move easily from the

236   *Notes to pages 142–5*

Hudson River to Buffalo and, therefore, from the Atlantic Ocean to the Great Lakes. The Erie Canal pulled population and trade westward in the decades that followed, helping to develop the Midwest at the expense of Atlantic colonies such as New Brunswick. Bernstein, *Wedding of the Waters*.

39 "Civis," "Letter 5," letter to the editor, *Chatham Gleaner and Northumberland Schediasma*, 8 September 1829. See also article from unidentified Saint John newspaper, 27 May 1826, reprinted in *Washington Daily National Journal*, 20 June 1826.

40 John McGregor, 30 June 1835, in Great Britain, *Report from the Select Committee*, 120, 125–6, 132.

41 *Chatham Mercury*, 27 June 1826. See also *Eastport Sentinel*, 17 June 1826; and *Washington Daily National Journal*, 20 June 1826.

42 Graeme Wynn notes, however, that "the data on New Brunswick timber exports are incomplete, intractable, and at times, contradictory." Wynn, *Timber Colony*, 34–5, 192n20 (quotation).

43 Wynn, *Timber Colony*, 37, also 38 for a map of the forest districts; Wynn, "Assault on the New Brunswick Forest," 102. In all the colony, only the small timber-producing districts of Oromocto and Upsalquitch saw increases in this era, and they were small ones. The Tobique district in northwestern New Brunswick experienced a decline almost as great as that of the Northwest Miramichi district, but this was the case at least in part because the colony placed a moratorium on settlement and timber operations there while the border with the United States was being determined.

44 Wynn, "Assault on the New Brunswick Forest," 106.

45 Wynn, *Timber Colony*, 128.

46 *Chatham Mercury*, 23 May 1826.

47 *Chatham Mercury*, 8 January 1828; Wynn, *Timber Colony*, 48.

48 Cooney, *Compendious History*, 106; Wynn, *Timber Colony*, 126; Spray, "Rankin, Alexander." A listing of Northumberland County's fifteen sawmills in 1831 may be found in New Brunswick, Miscellanea – Memoranda & Correspondence Concerning the Administration of Crown Lands, 1825–33, MGII CO193, vol. 3, Library and Archives Canada.

49 Gilmour stated its construction cost to be upward of £15,000. Allan Gilmour, 21 July 1835, in Great Britain, *Report from the Select Committee*, 237. In the course of arguing that large mills such as Gilmour and Rankin's could never recoup their investment, one letter provides useful detail as to the economics of running a sawmill in this era. "Philopater,"

letter to the editor, *Chatham Gleaner and Northumberland Schediasma*, 25 October 1831.

50 Wynn, *Timber Colony*, 125.

51 *Narrative of the Late Fires*, 22, but conversely, *Halifax Acadian Recorder*, reprinted in *Narrative of the Late Fires*, 31.

52 *Edinburgh Weekly Journal*, 16 November 1825. See also *Inverness Journal and Northern Advertiser*, 18 November 1825.

53 *Greenoch Advertiser*, 19 November 1825, reprinted in *London Times*, 24 November 1825.

54 Not specifically referencing the Miramichi Fire, "W" wrote in 1831, "fire seldom ravages in the hard wood, owing to the absence of materials of a highly inflammable nature, which tend to increase its fury; consequently so soon as it may have passed through a spruce swamp, and arrived at a ridge covered with deciduous growth, an obstacle is opposed to its further progress." "W," "Forests of New-Brunswick, No. 3," *Chatham Gleaner and Northumberland Schediasma*, 13 September 1831. This assessment by "W" was reproduced – with small changes and without attribution – in Fowler, *Journal of a Tour*, 273, which was in turn plagiarized by Atkinson, *Historical and Statistical Account*, 137. It can feel as though all nineteenth-century writing about New Brunswick forests can be traced back to "W" – Robert Cooney.

55 *Narrative of the Late Fires*, 19.

56 Scott et al., *Fire on Earth*, 141–3; Chandler et al., *Fire in Forestry*, vol. 1, 158; Wessels, *Reading the Forested Landscape*, 28–9.

57 Crossland, "Defining a Forest Reference Condition," 110.

58 "W," "Forests of New-Brunswick, No. 4," *Chatham Gleaner and Northumberland Schediasma*, 20 September 1831.

59 Scott et al., *Fire on Earth*, 311–13. Doyle, "Early Postfire Forest Succession," is useful in detailing how small changes in variables can produce different forests.

60 Wynn, "Assault on the New Brunswick Forest," 106.

61 "W," "Forests of New-Brunswick, No. 4," *Chatham Gleaner and Northumberland Schediasma*, 20 September 1831.

62 Alexander, *L'Acadie*, vol. 2, 184–201, sketch at 162. The author's wife, Eveline Marie Alexander, was a noted amateur artist who created the illustrations for at least one of her husband's others books, but there is no indication in *L'Acadie* that these sketches are hers.

63 On early post-fire succession, see Scott et al., *Fire on Earth*, 131–6; Pyne, Andrews, and Laven, *Introduction to Wildland Fire*, 193–6; Crossland,

238   *Notes to pages 148–52*

"Defining a Forest Reference Condition," 60–2; and Wynn, "Assault on the New Brunswick Forest," 28–30.

64 D'Arrigo, Jacoby, and Cook, "Impact of Recent North Atlantic Anomalies," 2322.

65 Coke, *Subaltern's Furlough*, 118–19.

66 Crossland, "Defining a Forest Reference Condition," 71, 32, 61, passim; Aubé, "Pre-European Settlement Forest Composition," 1159–60.

67 Monro, *New Brunswick*, 203.

68 Crossland, "Defining a Forest Reference Condition," 193. Two turn-of-the-century pieces on Maine's having become "the paper-birch state" thanks to its 1825 fires are "Paper Birch," *Press Bulletin of U.S. Forest Service*, cited in Bigelow, ed., *Nature-Study Review*, 168; and "How Maine Got Birch Trees," *New York Times*, 14 August 1899.

69 Dawson, *Acadian Geology*, 51; Dawson, "On the Destruction and Partial Reproduction," 267; Eakins and Eakins, "Dawson, Sir John William." For earlier reports of the forests' recovery, see Johnston, *Notes on North America*, vol. 2, 38; Monro, *New Brunswick*, 203; and Mountain Shepherd, "Wonderful Fire of Miramichi," 6.

70 "W," "Forests of New-Brunswick, No. 4," *Chatham Gleaner and Northumberland Schediasma*, 20 September 1831.

71 Thoreau, "Succession of Forest Trees." See also Egerton, "History of Ecological Sciences"; and Walls, *Henry David Thoreau*, esp. 471–2.

72 Horace Greeley, "Are Plants Ever Spontaneously Generated? Letter to H.D. Thoreau," *New-York Weekly Tribune*, 2 February 1861, reprinted in Dean, "Henry D. Thoreau and Horace Greeley," 632–3.

73 Henry David Thoreau, "Mr. Thoreau's Reply," *New-York Weekly Tribune*, 2 February 1861, reprinted in Dean, "Henry D. Thoreau and Horace Greeley," 633–4. On Thoreau's fire, see Schofield, "Burnt Woods"; and Walls, *Henry David Thoreau*, 171–4.

74 *Greenoch Advertiser*, 19 November 1825, reprinted in *London Times*, 24 November 1825.

75 Perley, "Spring Freshet of 1826." On fire and hydrologic processes, see Chandler et al., *Fire in Forestry*, vol. 1, 184–91.

76 *Chatham Mercury*, 28 March 1826 and 2 May 1826.

77 *Chatham Mercury*, 17 April 1827.

78 For example, see *Chatham Mercury*, 22 May 1827, 23 October 1827, and 15 July 1828.

79 On fire and fauna, see Scott et al., *Fire on Earth*, 147–55; Chandler et al., *Fire in Forestry*, vol. 1, 203–53; and Pyne, Andrews, and Laven, *Introduction to Wildland Fire*, 190–1.

Notes to pages 152–5

80 Alexander, *L'Acadie*, vol. 2, 122; Crossland, "Defining a Forest Reference Condition," 74; Scott et al., *Fire on Earth*, 149.

81 Wright, *Moose of New Brunswick*, 11, 14, 30–1; Cooney, *Compendious History*, 231.

82 Alexander, *L'Acadie*, vol. 2, 184, 187.

83 Dunfield, *Atlantic Salmon*, 100–1. See also Thomas, *Lost Land of Moses*.

84 *Chatham Mercury*, 27 June 1826 and 24 July 1827.

85 *Chatham Gleaner and Northumberland Schediasma*, 9 February 1830 and 7 February 1832.

86 Allardyce, "'Vexed Question of Sawdust.'"

87 Dunfield, *Atlantic Salmon*, 99.

88 Cited in Upton, *Micmacs and Colonists*, 103. In an 1841 census, Commissioner Moses Perley counted 198 Mi'gmaq living in the Eel Ground, Red Bank, and Renous settlements in the Miramichi interior and another 201 on the coast at Burnt Church. Perley, *Reports on Indian Settlements*, cix. Governor Douglas had set up the Indian commissioner system in 1826, and the legislative assembly voted £200 toward assisting "aged and distressed Indians" in 1827, but there is no indication that these acts were related in any way to the great fire.

89 Richard Lewes Dashwood, cited in Wright, *Moose of New Brunswick*, 31.

90 Cited in Beavan, *Sketches and Tales*, 84.

91 Bill to guard against destruction by fire in Fredericton and St Andrew's, 22 February 1826, Legislative Assembly and Sessional Records, S34 B50, RS24, PANB; New Brunswick, *Journal of the House of Assembly*, 1826, 110; *Fredericton New Brunswick Royal Gazette*, 29 April 1828; Public Works reports re firewards, 1829 and 1831, Northumberland County Council records, file F8d1 and F8d2, RS153, PANB.

92 See Greenberg, *Cause for Alarm*; and Ewen, *Creating the British Fire Service*.

93 *Chatham Gleaner and Northumberland Schediasma*, 25 January and 1 February 1831.

94 *Chatham Gleaner and Northumberland Schediasma*, 13 August 1834.

95 *Chatham Gleaner and Northumberland Schediasma*, 29 July 1834; see also 13 August 1834. Seven years later, settlers again cleared land while fire raged in the woods. See *Chatham Gleaner and Northumberland Schediasma*, 17 August 1841.

96 Robert Young, for example, reported that in the spring and summer of 1826, mere months after the Miramichi Fire, his brother in Pockshaw (now Pokeshaw), northern New Brunswick, employed recent Irish immigrants to help him cut down and burn 28 acres of trees to make way for

240 *Notes to pages 155–61*

crops. Notes of Lieutenant Colonel Cockburn, 26 April 1827, *Emigration*, 86.

97 Johnston, *Notes on North America*, vol. 1, 96, 92.

98 Wynn, *Timber Colony*, 142–6.

99 Gess and Lutz, *Firestorm at Peshtigo*.

100 Webb, "Development of Forest Law"; Gibson, *History of Forest Management*, 4; Fellows, *New Brunswick's Natural Resources*, 51. On fire and the rise of forest conservation in the late nineteenth century, see Pyne, *Awful Splendour*, 140–6; Pyne, *Fire in America*, 184–98; and Gillis and Roach, *Lost Initiatives*.

101 On this era for New Brunswick generally, see Wynn, *Timber Colony*, 42–53.

102 *Halifax Sun*, 30 November 1847, reprinted in *Wilmington Journal*, 7 January 1848. Hearing the news, a mob gathered in Chatham and threatened to loot Cunard's store – and to kill him. The timber baron, on horseback and with pistols in his boots, is said to have yelled, "Now show me the man who will shoot Cunard!" and returned home without incident. See Spray, "Cunard, Joseph"; and Hamilton, "Cunard, Joseph."

103 To be sure, there was also much more competition. After 1825, the heart of the British North American and then Canadian timber industry moved to the Ottawa Valley and the Great Lakes basin and eventually British Columbia, never returning to the Miramichi.

104 See Aubé, "Pre-European Settlement Forest Composition," 1159–60; Mosseler, Lynds, and Major, "Old-Growth Forests," S53; and Crossland, "Defining a Forest Reference Condition," 71, passim.

105 Bailey and Jack, *Woods and Minerals*, 30.

106 Chalmers, *Report on the Surface Geology*, and accompanying map; Brookes, "Robert J. Chalmers." Chalmers was an inveterate amateur botanist and a long-time contributor to the natural history societies of both the Miramichi region and New Brunswick.

107 Gesner, *New Brunswick*, 93, 188.

108 George R. Young, "Appendix 30: Report on the Subject of the Halifax and Quebec Railroad," in Nova Scotia, *Journal of the House of Assembly*, 1849, A30–279. See also Beck, "Young, George Renny."

109 On this question, see Wynn, "Assault on the New Brunswick Forest," 108–9.

110 MacLeod, "Fire in the Woods," 674–5. This passage is also cited in Rankin, *History of Our Firm*, 298–9. See also Hamilton, "MacLeod, Norman."

111 Grant, *Ocean to Ocean*, 161.

Notes to pages 161–2

112 DeMille, *Fire in the Woods*, 223.

113 Moore, *Universal Assistant*, 80; Louis Bubier, cited in Lincoln, "Through Flame and Tempest," 451; Silver, *Through Miramichi*, 11, repeated in Silver, *Farm-Cottage, Camp and Canoe*, 232.

114 Silver, *Through Miramichi*, 11, repeated in Silver, *Farm-Cottage, Camp and Canoe*, 233.

115 Silver was one of a number of writers in the late nineteenth century who got the fire's year or day wrong. See *Barnes's New Brunswick Almanack … 1880*, 42; and Merivale, "On Some Features of American Scenery," 648.

116 On forest conservation and the rise of a broader conservation movement, see Gillis and Roach, *Lost Initiatives*; and Barton, *Empire Forestry*. On forest conservation and fire, see Pyne, *Fire in America*, 191–6, 260–72; and Pyne, *Awful Splendour*, 140–60.

117 Cited in Pyne, *Fire in America*, 194.

118 Ware, *Account of the River St. John*, 11; plagiarized by Atkinson, *Historical and Statistical Account*, 80.

119 Hay, "South Tobique Lakes," 479. See also, for example, "Forest Preservation," *Saint John Globe*, 1 March 1901. The degree to which this was a new stance is evident in the 1882 discussion of the Miramichi Fire by the man sometimes called the father of American forestry, the first chief of the US Division of Forestry, Franklin B. Hough. His encyclopedic *Report on Forestry*, submitted to Congress, included a section on "The Great Historical Forest Fires of North America," which began with "The Great Miramichi Fire of 1825." Following an extended description of the Canadian component of the blaze exclusively, Hough ended by noting that "the second growth that sprang up consisted chiefly of white birch, poplar, and wild cherry. In portions of Maine that were overrun by fire during the same year, and at or about the same time, pine and spruce timber were succeeded by white pine, with some white birch and poplar. The pine in this interval of fifty-five years has grown into a dense forest, now of much greater value than the original forest growth." Whereas the mast and ton-timber trades had required the largest trees, the sawmill and, by this point, pulp and paper trades could prosper with many smaller trees. By the calculus of America's leading forester, the forest was better than ever after this fire. It is difficult to imagine any forester writing such a thing just a few years later. Consider Yale forestry professor Ernest Bruncken's 1900 caustic description of an early-successional forest: "Where the comparatively valueless poplars and white birches or the despised jack pine" – despised! – "have taken the place of white pine,

242 *Notes to pages 162–7*

there is a distinct loss of natural wealth." Hough, *Report on Forestry*, 231; Bruncken, *North American Forests and Forestry*, 94.

120 "Historic Forest Fires," 23.

121 See twenty-one images from this series in the McCord Museum's online photography collection under the keywords "Miramichi" and "1908."

122 Ganong, "Plan for a General History," 91.

123 Guitard, *Lost Wilderness*, 22. See also Rees, *New Brunswick Was His Country*; Wynn, "W.F. Ganong, A.H. Clark"; New Brunswick Museum, "William Francis Ganong's Field Trips."

124 Ganong, "Plan for a General History," 91.

125 Rees, *New Brunswick Was His Country*, 93; Wynn, "W.F. Ganong, A.H. Clark," 6, 8. Ganong's description of Bald Head as the most "mountain-like mountain" in New Brunswick hints at his literary abilities, I think.

126 Rees, *New Brunswick Was His Country*, 7. Ganong's series of "Notes" for the *Bulletin of the Natural History Society of New Brunswick* is listed in Guitard, *Lost Wilderness*, 205–10.

127 Ganong, "Note 46: Great Forest Fires," 434.

128 Ganong's trips are listed in Guitard, *Lost Wilderness*, appendix A, 202.

129 Robert Chalmers's 1887 map of the fire, made while doing work for the Geological Survey of Canada, is conspicuous in its absence from this list. Not only was Chalmers a still-living, long-time member of the Natural History Society of New Brunswick, but Ganong had often cited the geologist on other matters. He had even cited this very map and its accompanying text on matters of geology. But Ganong apparently did not think highly of Chalmers's work. His references to it usually involved corrections or differences of opinion, and although Ganong was invariably professional, he could not hide exasperation when once calling a claim by Chalmers "quite incomprehensible to me." Ganong, "Note 33: The Physiographic History," 319.

130 P.H. Welch to Ganong, 16 March 1905 and undated, W.F. Ganong papers, S217 F39–16–1, NBM; *Saint John Telegraph*, 4 March 1905.

131 Hamilton, "Hutchison, David Alexander Ernest"; Hamilton, "Hutchison, Richard"; Rankin, *History of Our Firm*, 62–3.

132 Ernest Hutchison to Ganong, 1 April 1905, W.F. Ganong papers, S217 F17–22–1, NBM.

133 It was this opinion, which Ganong presumably shared in his talk, which was then described in the *Saint John Telegraph*, that led Welch to write Ganong in disagreement: "As to the growth of the wood, 50 years ago when I was a small boy I gathered blue berries on ground completely

Notes to pages 167–72

burned to the ground and 5 years ago I scaled lumber cut on same ground that measured 20 feet long and 12 inches at the small end." P.H. Welch to Ganong, 16 March 1905, W.F. Ganong papers, S217 F39–16–1, NBM.

134 Ernest Hutchison to Ganong, 1 April 1905, W.F. Ganong papers, S217 F17–22–1, NBM. Quoting Burns's "Death and Doctor Hornbrook" here is ironic given that the verse reads in full, "Some books are lies from end to end, / And some great lies were never penned: / Even ministers, they have been known, / In holy rapture, / A rousing fib at times to vend, / And nail it with Scripture."

135 Ernest Hutchison to Ganong, April 1905, F.W. Ganong papers, S217 F17–22–3, NBM.

136 Ganong, "Note 90: On the Limits," 416.

137 Ganong wrote, "[E]xtending from the Square Forks of Sevogle and Mullins Stream easterly to the Bartibog, and beyond in a narrow tongue to near Grand Dune, and from Tomogonops and Portage River south to the Miramichi, which it crossed below Chatham to devastate Napan and even Black River, though possibly the fires south of the river originated separately." Ganong, "Note 90: On the Limits," 417–18.

138 Ibid., 418–19.

139 Ibid., 419.

140 Webster, *Historical Guide to New Brunswick*, 58–60.

141 Wright, *Miramichi*, 38.

142 Wynn, "Assault on the New Brunswick Forest," 361–2; Wynn, *Timber Colony*, 47.

143 Hamilton, *Old North Esk on the Miramichi*, 44–5; Guitard, *Lost Wilderness*, 194; New Brunswick, "Great Miramichi Fire."

144 *Saint John Telegraph*, 4 March 1905; P.H. Welch to Ganong, 16 March 1905, W.F. Ganong papers, S217 F39–16–1, NBM. The *Telegraph* article opens with reference to "[t]he following paper" by Ganong and is written in the first person, so it presumably captures the essence of Ganong's argument, although it may have been shortened for publication.

145 Ernest Hutchison to Ganong, April 1905, W.F. Ganong papers, S217 F17–22–3, NBM; Ernest Hutchison to Ganong, 1 April 1905, W.F. Ganong papers, S217 F17–22–2–1, NBM.

146 Ganong, "Note 23: The Forestry Problem," 228, emphasis added.

147 Ganong, "Note 12: On the Physiography," 61–2. In 1869 the Saxby Gale, a tropical cyclone, had windthrown a great number of trees, which, dead and drying out, were then susceptible to a large fire. Ganong stated that nearby granite hills were "stripped forever of their covering" and so lie "white and grinning, the very naked skeleton of the land." Ibid., 62.

244   *Notes to pages 172–7*

148 Indeed, in 1906 New Brunswick science, state, and industry came together to promote forest conservation via fire protection. The result was a Forest Domain Act that ordered a provincial forest survey, a Forestry Convention in 1907 to address critical issues in the industry, and the creation of a School of Forestry at the University of New Brunswick in 1908. In the decades that followed, New Brunswick was fiercely committed to managing fires. Stephen J. Pyne writes, "What is striking is not simply the tempo but also the thoroughness of the endeavour … A province with 1 percent of Canada's landmass and a dwindling population of fires became a national paragon of fire protection." Pyne, *Awful Splendour*, 232–5, quotation at 235.

149 Ganong, "Article 1: An Outline of Phytobiology," 3–5. "Phytobiology" was a neologism of Ganong's, intended to replace a number of other words for this developing new science, including "'Oekeologie,' which many recommend but, nobody uses." Ibid., 4. His attempt to popularize "phytobiology" in the 1895 *Botanical Gazette* was unceremoniously shot down. Ganong, "Term Phytobiology," 38. Ganong read the work of Eugenius Warming, Oscar Drude, and others in German while completing his doctorate in Munich. On this period in ecology and the growing understanding of succession, see Worster, *Nature's Economy*, chs 10 and 11.

150 Ganong, "Cardinal Principles of Ecology," 494, 493.

151 Ganong, "Note 90: On the Limits," 410.

152 Taylor, *Forest*, 205–6.

153 The American Red Cross site no longer exists but is archived – with the map link broken, unfortunately – at the Internet Archive, http://web.archive.org/web/20050310050329/http://www.disasterrelief.org/Library/WorldDis/firestuff/imagepages/fire32.html.

154 Mid-twentieth-century American fire historian Stuart Holbrook downplayed it as "a Canadian fire" before discussing it solely in terms of its impact in Maine. Holbrook, *Burning an Empire*, 59. Stephen J. Pyne is unusual in writing about the fire on both sides of the border, but it is worth noting that he does so separately, in two distinct national histories. Pyne, *Fire in America*, 56–7; Pyne, *Awful Splendour*, 127–32.

CHAPTER SIX

1 As of this writing, Chris is the director of Forest Planning and Stewardship in New Brunswick's Department of Natural Resources and Energy Development.

Notes to pages 177–82 245

2 Useful introductions are Basquill, *Practitioner's Guide to Sampling Fire History*; and http://www.madlabsk.ca, a showcase of the work of the Mount Allison Dendrochronology Lab, which in 2014 moved to the University of Saskatchewan and was renamed the Mistik Askiwin Dendrochronology Lab.

3 Contemporary statistics are from Brunswick News, *Forestry in New Brunswick*. See also Wynn, *Timber Colony*, 84.

4 Aubé, "Pre-European Settlement Forest Composition."

5 Crossland, "Defining a Forest Reference Condition," 190, 132–3, 113, 138 (quotation).

6 Of course, the opposite is also true: perhaps the entire areas surrounding the trees we cored had been destroyed, and ours were the only ones to escape burning or scarring.

7 See Struzik, *Firestorm*; and Pyne, *Awful Splendour*.

8 In writing this section, I have benefited particularly from Boulanger et al., "Fire Regime Zonation"; Taylor et al., "Rapid 21st Century Climate Change"; D'Orangeville et al., "Northeastern North America"; and Fundy Biosphere Reserve, "Forests of the Future."

9 Radkau, *Age of Ecology*, 10–21.

10 Malm, *Fossil Capital*; Pomeranz, *Great Divergence*.

11 There is so much good and bad information being produced about climate change that it is hard to know where to start. A good jumping-off point is NASA, "Global Climate Change."

Bibliography

ARCHIVES

Archives of Ontario (Toronto)
  Benjamin Smith diaries, F582
Austrian National Library
  Austrian Newspapers Online, http://anno.onb.ac.at/
Dan Casavant personal collection (Waterville)
  William Butterfield, "Memoirs of a Maine Pioneer"
Library and Archives Canada (Ottawa)
  Ann Dawkins papers, MG24 C43
  Colonial Office records, CO188, vols 31–4
  Delancey-Robinson collection, MG24 L6, http://heritage.canadiana.ca/
    view/oocihm.lac_mikan_100836
  Edward Jarvis papers, MG24 B13
  Hamnett K. Pinhey papers, MG24 I14
  J.L. Tiarks journal, MG24 H64
  New Brunswick, Miscellanea, MG11 CO193, vol. 3
  Peter Winkworth Collection of Canadiana, R9266–3280
Maine Memory Network (Portland)
  G.W. Pierce to sister, 15 July 1825, MMN 28365, https://www.maine
    memory.net/media/pdf/28365.pdf
Maine State Archives (Augusta)
  George Coffin journal, A21 R20
McCord Museum (Montreal)
  McCord family papers, P001–838

248 *Bibliography*

National Gallery of Canada (Ottawa)
George Back, *Upper Part of the Mackenzie River, Woods on Fire*, water-colour,1825,https://www.gallery.ca/collection/artwork/upper-part-of-the-mackenzie-river-woods-on-fire
New Brunswick Museum (Fredericton)
J.C. Webster papers, F452
John Ward & Sons Company papers, FI S47
Louise Manny papers, F21–2, F21–4, F198
W.F. Ganong papers, S217–18, S223
W.F. Ganong photo collection, 1987.17.1218.202, 1987.17.1219.187
Newcastle Public Library (Miramichi)
Anglican Church Baptism Registers, 1822–38
Anglican Church Burial Registers, 1822–1970
Miramichi Historical Society files, Miramichi Fire file
Nova Scotia Archives (Halifax)
George Patterson papers, MGI, vols 741–4
Sir John Wentworth letterbook, RGI, vol. 49
Provincial Archives of New Brunswick (Fredericton)
Benjamin B. Crawford diary, 1825, MCI115
Broad & Fowler Co. Ltd papers, 1826–39, MSI A2 MC2466
Crown Land Maps and Plans, RS656
Frederick Dibblee diary, MC1721 M51
Legislative Assembly and Sessional Records, RS24
Miramichi Fire relief committee records, RS660A, RS660B
New Brunswick Cemeteries database, https://archives.gnb.ca/Search/Cemeteries
New Brunswick Newspaper Vital Statistics database, https://archives.gnb.ca/Search/NewspaperVitalStats
Northumberland County Council records, RS153
Provincial Secretary correspondence, RS13
Raymond Paddock Gorham papers, MC211
Surveyor General records, RS637
Timber and Sawmill records, RS663, RS663A
Public Archives and Record Office of Prince Edward Island
Petition of Roderick McNeill, 1828, RG5

GOVERNMENT SOURCES

Canada, Statistics Canada. "The Population Ecumene of Canada: Exploring the Past and Present." Geography Working Paper Series.

Bibliography

Great Britain. *Report from the Select Committee on Timber Duties.* London: House of Commons, 1835. http://www.canadiana.ca/view/oocihm.9_01807.

Lower Canada. *Journal of the House of Assembly.* 1825–26. http://eco.canadiana.ca/view/oocihm.9_00938_36/2?r=0&s=1.

New Brunswick. "Great Miramichi Fire: The Largest Fire Ever in Eastern North America." Natural Resources website. 2009. https://web.archive.org/web/20090401160515/http://www.gnb.ca/0249/miramichi_fire-e.asp.

– *Journal of the House of Assembly.* 1820–50. http://eco.canadiana.ca/view/oocihm.9_00951.

New Brunswick Museum. "William Francis Ganong's Field Trips around the Province of New Brunswick." Virtual exhibit. 2004. http://website.nbm-mnb.ca/CAIN/english/william_ganong/.

Nova Scotia. *Journal of the House of Assembly.* 1849. http://eco.canadiana.ca/view/oocihm.9_00946_99/2?r=0&s=1.

United States. *Meteorological Register for the Years 1822, 1823, 1824, and 1825, from Observations by the Surgeon of the Army at the Military Posts of the United States.* Prepared by Joseph Lovell, Surgeon General of the US Army. Washington, DC: E. DeKrafft, 1826. https://archive.org/details/meteorologicalroostatgoog.

NEWSPAPERS AND MAGAZINES

Aberdeen Journal, 1825
American Baptist Magazine (Boston), 1826–28, https://hdl.handle.net/2027/iau.31858046357665.
Augusta Chronicle, 1825
Baltimore Gazette, 1825
Baltimore Niles' Weekly Register, 1821, 1825–26
Bangor Register, 1825
Boston Christian Watchman, 1826
Boston Columbian Centinel, 1825
Boston Palladium, 1825
Boston Patriot, 1825
Boston Recorder & Telegraph, 1825
Boston Zion's Herald, 1825–26
Bristol Mercury, 1825
British Farmer's Magazine (London), 1843–44, https://archive.org/details/britishfarmersmooviigoog

250 Bibliography

Canadian Courant and Montreal Advertiser, 1825, https://news.google.
    com/newspapers?nid=_axFR9aDTfoC
Charleston Courier, 1825
Chatham Gleaner and Northumberland Schediasma, 1829–36
Chatham Mercury, 1826–28, https://news.google.com/newspapers?
    nid=RoGtuAMwyXEC
Concord Patriot, 1825
Danville North Star, 1825
Eastport Sentinel, 1821, 1825–27
Edinburgh Caledonian Mercury, 1825
Edinburgh Magazine & Literary Miscellany, 1825
Edinburgh Weekly Journal, 1825
Fredericton New Brunswick Royal Gazette, 1822, 1824–25, 1828, https://
    news.google.com/newspapers?nid=YFjsv_pBGBYC
Greenoch Advertiser, 1825
Halifax Acadian Recorder, 1825, https://novascotia.ca/archives/
    newspapers/results.asp?nTitle=Acadian+Recorder
Halifax Free Press, 1825
Halifax Novascotian, 1825
Halifax Sun, 1847
Hartford Courant, 1826
Hallowell American Advocate, 1825
Inverness Journal and Northern Advertiser, 1825
Kennebec Gardiner Chronicle, 1825
La bibliothèque canadienne (Montreal), 1825, http://collections.banq.
    qc.ca/ark:/52327/2270873
Lancaster Gazette, 1825
Le journal de Québec, 1845–46, 1852, http://collections.banq.qc.ca/
    ark:/52327/2644732
Liverpool Mercury, 1825
London Examiner, 1825
London Observer, 1825
London Times, 1825–26
Middletown Sentinel and Witness, 1825
Moncton Times, 1881
Montreal Gazette, 1825
Montreal Herald, 1825
Newcastle Northumberland News, 1980
Newcastle Union Advocate, 1897, 1902

Bibliography

New-Brunswick Religious and Literary Journal (Saint John), 1829
Newport Rhode-Island Republican, 1825
New York Albion, 1825
New York Times, 1899
New-York Weekly Tribune, 1860–61
Philadelphia Aurora and Franklin Gazette, 1825
Portland Advertiser, 1825
Portland Eastern Argus, 1825
Portsmouth New Hampshire Gazette, 1825
Potsdam St. Lawrence American, 1825
Providence Rhode-Island American, 1825
Quebec Gazette, 1825, https://news.google.com/newspapers?nid=F_tUK
    v7nyWgC
Richmond Enquirer, 1825
Saint John Daily Sun, 1899, https://news.google.com/newspapers?
    nid=aqlVkmm33-oC
Saint John Globe, 1901
Saint John New Brunswick Courier, 1825
Saint John Telegraph, 1905
Salem Gazette, 1825
Stanstead British Colonist and Saint Francis Gazette, 1825, https://news.
    google.com/newspapers?nid=HDshCWvjkbEC
Toronto Upper Canada Gazette, 1825
Trois-Rivières Le constitutionnel, 1870, http://collections.banq.qc.ca/
    ark:/52327/2743970
Washington Daily National Journal, 1826
Wesleyan Methodist Magazine (London), 1826
Wilmington Journal, 1848

PUBLISHED SOURCES

Abrams, Marc D. "Eastern White Pine Versatility in the Presettlement
    Forest." *Bioscience* 51, no. 11 (2001): 967–79.
Alexander, James Edward. *L'Acadie, or Seven Years' Explorations in
    North America.* Vol. 2. London: H. Colburn, 1849. https://archive.org/
    details/lacadieorsevenyeo2alex_o.
Allardyce, Gilbert. "'The Vexed Question of Sawdust': River Pollution
    in Nineteenth Century New Brunswick." *Dalhousie Review* 52, no. 2
    (1972): 177–90.

Bibliography

An Almanack for the Year of Our Lord 1825 ... Calculated for the Meridian of Saint John, N.B. Saint John, NB: Henry Chubb, 1824. https://archive.org/details/cihm_28751.

Amos, Dafydd . "Can Newydd yn rhoddi hanes am y tan dinystriol a fu yn Ngogledd America, Hydref 1825." Caerfyrddin/Carmarthen: Jonathan Harris, [1825?]. https://books.google.ca/books/about/Can_newydd_yn_rhoddi_hanes_am_y_tan_diny.html?id=1_GLNQEACAAJ&redir_esc=y.

Anderson, Mark L. *A History of Scottish Forestry: From the Industrial Revolution to Modern Times.* Vol. 2. London: Nelson, 1967.

Arbuckle, Doreen Menzies. *The North West Miramichi.* Ottawa: Westboro Printers, 1978.

Atkinson, Christopher W. *A Historical and Statistical Account of New Brunswick, BNA.* Edinburgh: Anderson & Bryce, 1844. https://archive.org/details/historicalstatisooatki.

Aubé, Melanie. "Historical Influence of Forest Exploitation on the Miramichi Human Ecosystem." PhD diss., University of New Brunswick, 2012.

– "The Pre-European Settlement Forest Composition of the Miramichi River Watershed, New Brunswick, as Reconstructed Using Witness Trees from Original Land Surveys." *Canadian Journal of Forest Research* 38, no. 5 (2008): 1159–83.

Bailey, L.W., and Edward Jack. *The Woods and Minerals of New Brunswick.* Fredericton, NB: Daily Telegraph, 1876. https://www.biodiversitylibrary.org/bibliography/39736#.

Baillie, Thomas. *An Account of the Province of New Brunswick.* London: J.G. & F. Rivington, 1832. https://archive.org/details/cihm_21383.

Baird, William. *Seventy Years of New Brunswick Life: Autobiographical Sketches.* Fredericton, NB: St Anne's Point Press, 1890. https://archive.org/details/seventyyearsnewoobairgoog.

Barnes's New Brunswick Almanack for the Year of Our Lord 1880. Saint John, NB: Barnes, 1880. https://archive.org/details/cihm_27676/.

Barton, Greg. *Empire Forestry and the Origins of Environmentalism.* Cambridge, UK: Cambridge University Press, 2002.

Basquill, Sean. *A Practitioner's Guide to Sampling Fire History in the Acadian Forest.* Halifax: Parks Canada, 1988.

Baxter, J. McG. "The Bartibogue Fort." *Proceedings of the Natural History Association of Miramichi* 5 (1907): 5–9. https://archive.org/details/proceedingsofnat17natu/page/n251.

– "Scraps of Local History." *Proceedings of the Natural History Association of Miramichi* 7 (1913): 30–57. https://archive.org/details/proceedingsofnat17natu/page/30.

Bibliography

Beavan, Frances. *Sketches and Tales Illustrative of Life in the Backwoods of New Brunswick, North America.* London: G. Routledge, 1845. http://eco.canadiana.ca/view/oocihm.26449/90?r=0&s=1.

Beck, J. Murray. "Young, George Renny." *Dictionary of Canadian Biography.* http://www.biographi.ca/en/bio/young_george_renny_8E.html.

Bellin, Jacques Nicolas, and Thomas Jefferys. *New Chart of the Coast of New England, Nova Scotia, New France or Canada, with the Islands of Newfoundl'd, Cape Breton, St. John's &c.* London: Edw. Cave, 1746. http://nscc.cairnrepo.org/islandora/object/nscc%3A126.

Bernstein, Peter L. *Wedding of the Waters: The Erie Canal and the Making of a Great Nation.* New York: W.W. Norton, 2006.

Berton, George F.S. *The Acts of the General Assembly of Her Majesty's Province of New Brunswick.* Fredericton, NB: John Simpson, 1838. https://hdl.handle.net/2027/coo.31924018090823.

Bigelow, Maurice A., ed. *The Nature-Study Review* 4, no. 5 (1908). https://archive.org/details/naturestudyrevie04amer/page/140.

Blais, J.R. "Trends in the Frequency, Extent, and Severity of Spruce Budworm Outbreaks in Eastern Canada." *Canadian Journal of Forest Research* 13, no. 4 (1983): 539–47.

Blakeley, Phyliss R. "Cunard, Sir Samuel." *Dictionary of Canadian Biography.* http://www.biographi.ca/en/bio/cunard_samuel_9E.html.

Bliss, Henry. *On the Timber Trade.* London: J. Ridgway, 1831. https://archive.org/details/ontimbertradeooblis.

Bortle, John E. "The Bright-Comet Chronicles." *International Comet Quarterly* (1998). http://www.icq.eps.harvard.edu/bortle.html.

Bossak, Brian H. "Early 19th Century U.S. Hurricanes: A GIS Tool and Climate Analysis." PhD diss., Florida State University, 2003.

Bouchette, Joseph. *The British Dominions in North America.* Vol. 2. London: H. Colburn & R. Bentley, 1831. https://archive.org/details/britishdominiono1boucgoog.

Boulanger, Yan, Sylvie Gauthier, David R. Gray, Héloïse Le Goff, Patrick Lefort, and Jacques Morissette. "Fire Regime Zonation under Current and Future Climate over Eastern Canada." *Ecological Applications* 23, no. 4 (2013): 904–23.

Boyd, Frank S., Jr. "Preston, Richard." *Dictionary of Canadian Biography.* http://www.biographi.ca/en/bio/preston_richard_8E.html.

Boyle, Henry. *The Chronology of the Eighteenth and Nineteenth Centuries ... to the Close of the Year 1825.* London: Sherwood, Gilbert, and Piper, 1826. https://hdl.handle.net/2027/hvd.32044088056361.

Bibliography

Bremner, Robert H. *American Philanthropy*. 1960. 2nd ed. Chicago: University of Chicago Press, 1988.

Briffa, K.R., P.D. Jones, F.H. Schweingruber, and T.J. Osborn. "Influence of Volcanic Eruptions on Northern Hemisphere Summer Temperatures over the Past 600 Years." *Nature* 393, no. 6684 (1998): 450–5.

Brisson, Jacques, and Andre Bouchard. "The Haut-Saint-Laurent Wilderness at the Time of Settlement Based on Sellar's History – Part II: Forests and Wetlands." *Chateauguay Valley Historical Society Annual Journal*, no. 39 (2006): 29–45.

Brookes, Ian A. "Robert J. Chalmers: Pioneer Surficial Geologist." *Geoscience Canada* 35, nos 3–4 (2008). https://journals.lib.unb.ca/index.php/GC/article/view/11272/12016.

Brotak, E.A., and W.E. Reifsnyder. "An Investigation of the Synoptic Situations Associated with Major Wildland Fires." *Journal of Applied Meteorology* 16, no. 9 (1977): 867–70.

Browne, D.J. *The Sylva Americana, or A Description of the Forest Trees Indigenous to the United States, Practically and Botanically Considered.* Boston: William Hyde and Co., 1832. https://archive.org/details/sylvaamericanaoroobrow.

Bruncken, Ernest. *North American Forests and Forestry.* New York and London: Putnam, 1900. https://archive.org/details/northamerican foroobrun.

Brunswick News. *Forestry in New Brunswick*. Newspaper insert. September 2018.

Buckingham, James S. *Canada, Nova Scotia, and the Other British Provinces in North America.* London: Fisher, Son, & Co., 1841. https://archive.org/details/cihm_43017.

Bumsted, J.M. "MacGregor, John." *Dictionary of Canadian Biography*. http://www.biographi.ca/en/bio/macgregor_john_8E.html.

Burchill, John G. *A Miramichi Saga*. Miramichi, NB: Miramichi Press, 1992.

Burton, John Hill. *The Emigrant's Manual: Australia, New Zealand, America, and South Africa.* Edinburgh: William and Robert Chambers, 1851. https://catalog.hathitrust.org/Record/009038394.

Campanella, Thomas J. "'Mark Well the Gloom': Shedding Light on the Great Dark Day of 1780." *Environmental History* 12, no. 1 (2007): 35–58.

Campey, Lucille. "Scottish Trading and Settlement Patterns in British North America during the Early Nineteenth Century." *British Journal of Canadian Studies* 15, nos 1–2 (2002): 14–26.

Chadwick, E. Michael P. *Water, Science, and the Public: The Miramichi Ecosystem*. Ottawa: National Research Council of Canada, 1995.

Chalmers, Robert. *Report on the Surface Geology of North-Eastern New Brunswick*. Montreal: Dawson Brothers, 1888. https://archive.org/details/cihm_08571; map at https://geoscan.nrcan.gc.ca/starweb/geoscan/servlet.starweb?path=geoscan/downloade.web&search1=R=107662.

Chandler, Craig, Phillip Cheney, Philip Thomas, Louis Trabaud, and Dave Williams. *Fire in Forestry*. Vol. 1, *Forest Fire Behavior and Effects*. New York: John Wiley & Sons, 1983.

City of Pembroke. "History of Pembroke." 2019. http://www.pembroke.ca/city-hall/history-of-pembroke/.

Coke, E.T. *A Subaltern's Furlough*. London: Saunders and Otley, 1833. https://archive.org/details/asubalternsfurlo2cokegoog.

Colley, Linda. *Captives: Britain, Empire, and the World, 1600–1850*. New York: Anchor, 2004.

Colpitts, Marc C., Sherif H. Fahmy, John E. MacDougall, Tom T.M. Ng, Bryce G. Mclnnis, and Vincent F. Zelazny. *Forest Soils of New Brunswick*. Fredericton, NB: Agriculture and Agri-Food Canada and Natural Resources Canada, 1995. http://sis.agr.gc.ca/cansis/publications/surveys/nb/nb9538/index.html.

Condon, Ann Gorman. "Fisher, Peter." *Dictionary of Canadian Biography*. http://www.biographi.ca/en/bio.php?id_nbr=3383.

Cooke, Ronald J. "The Biggest Fire." *Rod and Gun in Canada*, September 1963, 18, 20.

Cooney, Robert. *The Autobiography of a Wesleyan Methodist Missionary*. Montreal: E. Pickup, 1856. https://archive.org/details/cu31924029471764.

– *A Compendious History of the Northern Part of the Province of New Brunswick, and of the District of Gaspé, in Lower Canada*. Halifax: Joseph Howe, 1832. https://archive.org/details/compendioushisto00coon.

Cox, Thomas R., Robert S. Maxwell, Phillip Drennon Thomas, and Joseph J. Malone. *This Well-Wooded Land: Americans and Their Forests from Colonial Times to the Present*. Lincoln and London: University of Nebraska Press, 1985.

Crossland, Donna R. "Defining a Forest Reference Condition for Kouchibouguac National Park and Adjacent Landscape in Eastern New Brunswick Using Four Reconstructive Approaches." MSc thesis, University of New Brunswick, 2006. https://www.collectionscanada.gc.ca/obj/thesescanada/vol2/002/MR49667.PDF.

256   *Bibliography*

Crowe, Julian. "The Man Who Was Pecksniff: Samuel Carter Hall (1800–1889)." http://www.wildflowersplanted.co.uk/HistoryNotes/SCHallV2.pdf.

Cruickshank, Thomas. *The Practical Planter*. Edinburgh and London: William Blackwood and T. Cadell, 1830. https://archive.org/details/practicalplanter00crui.

Curti, Merle. *American Philanthropy Abroad*. New Brunswick, NJ: Rutgers University Press, 1963.

Curtis, Wayne. *Currents in the Stream*. Fredericton, NB: Gooselane, 1988.

Dahl, Curtis. "The American School of Catastrophe." *American Quarterly* 11, no. 3 (1959): 380–90.

Dalhousie College and University. "Examination Papers, 1884–5: Faculty of Arts." In *Calendar of Dalhousie College and University*, iii–xciv. 1885. https://archive.org/details/calendardalhous08univgoog.

Daniel, Evan, ed. *The Battersea Series of Standard Reading Books for Boys*. Bk 4. London: Edward Stanford, 1891. https://archive.org/details/batterseaseries06danigoog.

D'Arrigo, Rosanne, Gordon C. Jacoby, and Edward R. Cook. "Impact of Recent North Atlantic Anomalies on Surrounding Land Areas Based on Dendroclimatic Evidence." *Geophysical Research Letters* 19, no. 23 (1992): 2321–4.

Davis, Harold A. *An International Community on the St. Croix, 1604–1930*. Orono: University of Maine at Orono, 1974.

Davis, Lydia. *Samuel Johnson Is Indignant*. New York: Picador, 2002.

Dawson, Sir John W. *Acadian Geology: The Geological Structure, Organic Remains and Mineral Resources of Nova Scotia, New Brunswick and Prince Edward Island*. 1855. 2nd ed. London: Macmillan and Co., 1868. http://online.canadiana.ca/view/oocihm.12530/1?r=0&s=1.

– "On the Destruction and Partial Reproduction of Forests in British North America." *Edinburgh New Philosophical Journal* 42 (1847): 259–71. https://archive.org/details/edinburghnewphi11unkngoog/page/n270.

Dean, Bradley. "Henry D. Thoreau and Horace Greeley Exchange Letters on the 'Spontaneous Generation of Plants.'" *New England Quarterly* 66, no. 4 (1993): 630–8.

Defebaugh, James Elliott. *History of the Lumber Industry of America*. Vols 1–2. Chicago: American Lumberman, 1907. https://archive.org/details/historyoflumberio1defeuoft and https://archive.org/details/historylumberino1defegoog.

Bibliography

DeMille, James. *Fire in the Woods.* [1871?]. Reprint, Boston: Lee and Shepard, 1893. https://archive.org/details/fireinwoodsoodemi.

Dick, Thomas. *Celestial Scenery, or The Wonders of the Planetary System Displayed.* New York: Harper & Brothers, 1838. https://archive.org/details/celestialsceneryoodick.

Dickens, Charles. *The Life and Adventures of Nicholas Nickleby.* 1839. Reprint, New York: George Routledge & Sons, 1879. https://archive.org/details/worksdicko8dickuoft.

D'Orangeville, L., L. Duchesne, D. Houle, D. Kneeshaw, B. Côté, and N. Pederson. "Northeastern North America as a Potential Refugium for Boreal Forests in a Warming Climate." *Science* 352, no. 6292 (2016): 1452–5.

Doucette, Long Joe. "The Miramichi Fire." c. 1825. On the album *The Folk Songs of Maine*, collected and recorded by Edward "Sandy" Ives. Folkways Records, 1959. https://www.youtube.com/watch?v=Bw DkjEgpKpA.

Doyle, Kathleen M. "Early Postfire Forest Succession in the Heterogeneous Teton Landscape." In Linda L. Wallace, ed., *After the Fires: The Ecology of Change in Yellowstone National Park,* 235–78. New Haven, CT, and London: Yale University Press, 2004.

Dunfield, R.W. *The Atlantic Salmon in the History of North America.* Ottawa: Department of Fisheries and Oceans, 1985. http://www.dfo-mpo.gc.ca/Library/28322.pdf.

Dyer, Christopher L. "The Phoenix Effect in Post-Disaster Recovery: An Analysis of the Economic Development Administration's Culture of Response after Hurricane Andrew." In Susanna M. Hoffman and Anthony Oliver-Smith, eds, *The Angry Earth: Disaster in Anthropological Perspective,* 278–300. New York: Routledge, 1999.

Eakins, Peter R., and Jean Sinnamon Eakins. "Dawson, Sir John William." *Dictionary of Canadian Biography.* http://www.biographi.ca/en/bio/dawson_john_william_12E.html.

Earl of Dalhousie. *The Dalhousie Journals.* Vol. 3. Ed. Marjory Whitlaw. Ottawa: Oberon, 1982.

Eddy, John A. "Before Tambora: The Sun and Climate, 1790–1830." In C.R. Harington, ed., *The Year without a Summer? World Climate in 1816,* 11. Ottawa: Canadian Museum of Nature, 1992. https://archive.org/details/yearwithoutsumme1992hari/page/10.

Egerton, Frank. "History of Ecological Sciences, Part 39: Henry David Thoreau, Ecologist." *Bulletin of the Ecological Society of America* 92, no. 3 (2011): 251–75.

Bibliography

Emigration: Appendix to Report of Lieutenant Colonel Cockburn, on the Subject of Emigration. London: House of Commons, 1828. http://eco. canadiana.ca/view/oocihm.48628.

Evans, E. Estyn. *Irish Folk Ways.* London and New York: Routledge, 1957.

Ewen, Shane. *Creating the British Fire Service, 1800–1978.* London: Palgrave Macmillan, 2009.

"Excerpts from the Diary of an Old Citizen." *Blackwood's Edinburgh Magazine* 19, no. 108 (1826): 272–4. https://hdl.handle.net/2027/ mdp.39015030603792.

"Extracts from Rev. Frederick Dibblee's Diary." Compiled by Jo Edkins. http://www.gwydir.demon.co.uk/jo/genealogy/earlydib/frederickdiary. htm.

Fagan, Brian. *The Little Ice Age: How Climate Made History, 1300–1850.* New York: Basic Books, 2000.

Fay, C.R. "Mearns and the Miramichi: An Episode in Canadian Economic History." *Canadian Historical Review* 4, no. 4 (1923): 316–20.

Fellows, Edward S. *New Brunswick's Natural Resources: 150 Years of Stewardship.* Fredericton, NB: Natural Resources and Energy, 1987.

Finan, P. *Journal of a Voyage to Quebec in the Year 1825, with Recollections of Canada, during the Late American War, in the Years 1812–13.* Newry, Northern Ireland: Alexander Peacock, 1828. https:// archive.org/details/cihm_35638.

Fingard, Judith. "The 1820s: Peace, Privilege, and the Promise of Progress." In Phillip A. Buckner and John G. Reid, eds, *The Atlantic Region to Confederation: A History*, 263–83. Toronto: University of Toronto Press, 1994.

– "Wentworth, Sir John." *Dictionary of Canadian Biography.* http://www. biographi.ca/en/bio/wentworth_john_1737_1820_5E.html.

Fisher, Peter. *Notitia of New Brunswick, for 1836, and Extending into 1837.* Saint John, NB: H. Chubb, 1838. https://archive.org/details/ notitianewbrunsoogoog.

– *Sketches of New-Brunswick.* Saint John, NB: Chubb & Sears, 1825. https://archive.org/details/sketchesofnewbruoofish.

Fleming, James Rodger. *Historical Perspectives on Climate Change.* New York and Oxford: Oxford University Press, 1998.

Fleming, Richard A., Jean-Noel Candau, and Rob S. McAlpine. "Exploratory Retrospective Analysis of the Interaction between Spruce Budworm (SBW) and Forest Fire Activity." n.d. https://www.research gate.net/publication/228813964.

Bibliography

Flexner, Stuart, with Doris Flexner. *The Pessimist's Guide to History*. New York: Quill, 2000.

Flieger, B.W. "Forest Fire and Insects: The Relation of Fire to Insect Outbreak." In *Proceedings: 10th Tall Timbers Fire Ecology Conference 1970*, 107–14. Tallahassee, FL: Tall Timbers Research Station, 1970. http://talltimbers.org/wp-content/uploads/2014/03/Flieger1970_op.pdf.

The Following List of Citizens of the United States Who Were Sufferers by the Awful Conflagration at Miramichi, on the 7th October, 1825. Fredericton, NB: n.p., 1827. https://archive.org/details/cihm_53204.

Foster, David R., and John D. Aber, eds. *Forests in Time: The Environmental Consequences of 1,000 Years of Change in New England*. New Haven, CT, and London: Yale University Press, 2004.

Fowler, Thomas. *The Journal of a Tour through British America to the Falls of Niagara*. Aberdeen: L. Smith, 1832. https://archive.org/details/cihm_46810.

Fraser, James Andrew. *Gretna Green: A History of Douglastown, New Brunswick, Canada, 1783–1900*. Chatham, NB: Miramichi Press, 1969.

Freland, Jacques. "Tribal Dissent or White Aggression? Interpreting Penobscot Indian Dispossession between 1808 and 1835." *Maine History* 43, no. 2 (2007): 124–70.

Fuller, Margaret. *Forest Fires: An Introduction to Wildland Fire Behaviour, Management, Firefighting, and Prevention*. New York: John Wiley & Sons, 1991.

Fullom, S.W. *The Life of General Sir Howard Douglas*. London: John Murray, 1863. https://archive.org/details/lifeofgeneralsiroofulluoft.

Fundy Biosphere Reserve. "Forests of the Future in the Fundy Biosphere Reserve." 2018. http://www.fundy-biosphere.ca/en/home/forests-of-the-future.html.

Fyson, Donald. "Eating in the City: Diet and Provisioning in Early Nineteenth-Century Montreal." MA thesis, McGill University, 1989.

Galt, John. *The Demon of Destiny; and Other Poems*. Greenock: W. Johnston and Son, 1839. https://archive.org/details/demonofdestinyoogalt.

Ganong, William Francis. "Article 1: An Outline of Phytobiology." *Bulletin of the Natural History Society of New Brunswick*, no. 12 (1894): 3–15. https://www.biodiversitylibrary.org/item/35561.

– "Cardinal Principles of Ecology." *Science* 19, no. 482 (1904): 493–8.

– *History of Caraquet and Pokemouche*. Ed. Susan Brittain Ganong. Saint John, NB: New Brunswick Museum, 1948. https://cdm22007.contentdm.oclc.org/digital/collection/p22007coll8/id/330735/rec/2.

- "Note 12: On the Physiography of the Basin of the Mahood (Lepreau) Lakes." *Bulletin of the Natural History Society of New Brunswick*, no. 16 (1898): 57–63. https://www.biodiversitylibrary.org/item/35256.
- "Note 23: The Forestry Problem in New Brunswick." *Bulletin of the Natural History Society of New Brunswick*, no. 18 (1899): 227–30. https://www.biodiversitylibrary.org/item/35256.
- "Note 33: The Physiographic History of the Nepisiguit River." *Bulletin of the Natural History Society of New Brunswick*, no. 19 (1901): 314–19. https://www.biodiversitylibrary.org/item/196184.
- "Note 46: Great Forest Fires in New Brunswick." *Bulletin of the Natural History Society of New Brunswick*, no. 20 (1902): 434–5. https://www.biodiversitylibrary.org/item/196088.
- "Note 90: On the Limits of the Great Fire of Miramichi of 1825." *Bulletin of the Natural History Society of New Brunswick*, no. 24 (1906): 410–18. https://www.biodiversitylibrary.org/item/196097.
- "Note 118: On the Physiographic Characteristics of Cains River." *Bulletin of the Natural History Society of New Brunswick*, no. 28 (1910): 201–10. http://www.biodiversitylibrary.org/item/196095.
- "The Origin of the Major Canadian Place-Names Fundy and Miramichi." *Transactions of the Royal Society of Canada* ser. 3, vol. 20, sec. 2 (1926): 15–35.
- "A Plan for a General History of the Province of New Brunswick." In *Proceedings and Transactions of the Royal Society of Canada*, ser. 2, vol. 1, 91–102. Ottawa: John Durie & Son, 1895. http://www.biodiversitylibrary.org/item/40773.
- "The Term Phytobiology." *Botanical Gazette* 20, no. 1 (1895): 38. https://www.biodiversitylibrary.org/page/27556610.

Gesner, Abraham. *New Brunswick with Notes for Emigrants*. London: Simmonds and Ward, 1847. https://archive.org/details/newbrunswick witoogesngoog.

Gespe'gewa'gi Mi'gmawei Mawiomi. *Nta'tugwaqanminen: Our Story – The Evolution of the Gespe'gewa'gi Mi'gmaq*. Halifax and Winnipeg: Fernwood, 2016.

Gess, Denise, and William Lutz. *Firestorm at Peshtigo: A Town, Its People, and the Deadliest Fire in American History*. New York: Henry Holt and Company, 2002.

Gibbon, Edward. *History of the Decline and Fall of the Roman Empire*. Vol. 1. London: W. Strahan and T. Cadell, 1776. https://archive.org/details/historyofdecline01gibb_0.

Bibliography

Gibson, J. Miles. *The History of Forest Management in New Brunswick.* Vancouver: H.R. Macmillan Lecture, University of British Columbia, 1953.

Gillis, R. Peter, and Thomas R. Roach. *Lost Initiatives: Canada's Forest Industries, Forest Policy, and Forest Conservation.* New York and Westport: Greenwood, 1986.

Gilpin, William. *Observations, Relative Chiefly to Picturesque Beauty, Made in the Year 1776, on Several Parts of Great Britain.* Vol. 2. London: R. Blamire, 1789. https://archive.org/details/obserrelativeo2gilpiala.

Girard, Philip. *Lawyers and Legal Culture in British North America: Beamish Murdoch of Halifax.* Toronto: Osgoode Society for Canadian Legal History and University of Toronto Press, 2011.

Grant, George M. *Ocean to Ocean: Sandford Fleming's Expedition through Canada in 1872.* Toronto: J. Campbell, 1873. https://archive.org/details/oceantooceanoogranuoft.

Green, David G. "Pollen Evidence for the Postglacial Origins of Nova Scotia Forests." *Canadian Journal of Botany* 65, no. 6 (1987): 1163–79.

Greenberg, Amy S. *Cause for Alarm: The Volunteer Fire Department in the Nineteenth-Century City.* Princeton, NJ: Princeton University Press, 1998.

Greenleaf, Moses. *Map of the Inhabited Part of the State of Maine.* Portland, ME: Shirley & Hyde, 1829. http://www.davidrumsey.com/maps880040-24208.html.

Guevara-Murua, A., C.A. Williams, E.J. Hendy, A.C. Rust, and K.V. Cashman. "Observations of a Stratospheric Aerosol *Veil* from a Tropical Volcanic Eruption in December 1808: Is This the *Unknown ~1809* Eruption?" *Climate of the Past* 10, no. 5 (2014): 1707–22.

Guitard, Nicholas. *The Lost Wilderness: Rediscovering W.F. Ganong's New Brunswick.* Fredericton, NB: Goose Lane, 2015.

Guthrie, John D. *Great Forest Fires of America.* Washington, DC: Forest Service, US Department of Agriculture, 1936. https://hdl.handle.net/2027/umn.31951d01394395b.

Halbwachs, Maurice. *On Collective Memory.* Ed. and trans. Lewis A. Coser. Chicago: University of Chicago Press, 1992.

Hale, Wallace. "New Brunswick Counties." Provincial Archives of New Brunswick. https://archives.gnb.ca/exhibits/forthavoc/html/Counties.aspx.

Hall, S.C. "The Burning of Miramichi." *The Religious Magazine, or Spirit of the Foreign Theological Journals and Reviews,* June 1829, 518–19. https://books.google.ca/books?id=AEgZAQAAIAAJ&pg=PA518.

Bibliography

Halttunen, Karen. "Humanitarianism and the Pornography of Pain in Anglo-American Culture." *American Historical Review* 100, no. 2 (1995): 303–34.

Hamilton, W.D. "Abrams, William (1785–1844)." *Dictionary of Miramichi Biography*. 1997. New ed. 2013. https://archives.gnb.ca/Search/Hamilton/DMB/SearchResults.aspx?culture=en-CA&action=0&page=1.

– "Caie, James (1805–1864)." *Dictionary of Miramichi Biography*. 1997. New ed. 2013. https://archives.gnb.ca/Search/Hamilton/DMB/SearchResults.aspx?culture=en-CA&action=0&page=132.

– "Clarke, Christopher (1796–1834)." *Dictionary of Miramichi Biography*. 1997. New ed. 2013. https://archives.gnb.ca/Search/Hamilton/DMB/SearchResults.aspx?culture=en-CA&action=0&page=174.

– "Cunard, Joseph (1799–1865)." *Dictionary of Miramichi Biography*. 1997. New ed. 2013. https://archives.gnb.ca/Search/Hamilton/DMB/SearchResults.aspx?culture=en-CA&action=0&page=229.

– "Goodfellow, Alexander (1794–1867)." *Dictionary of Miramichi Biography*. 1997. New ed. 2013. https://archives.gnb.ca/Search/Hamilton/DMB/SearchResults.aspx?culture=en-CA&action=0&page=386.

– "Hutchison, David Alexander Ernest (1847–1918)." *Dictionary of Miramichi Biography*. 1997. New ed. 2013. https://archives.gnb.ca/Search/Hamilton/DMB/SearchResults.aspx?culture=en-CA&action=0&page=481.

– "Hutchison, Richard (1812–1891)." *Dictionary of Miramichi Biography*. 1997. New ed. 2013. https://archives.gnb.ca/Search/Hamilton/DMB/SearchResults.aspx?culture=en-CA&action=0&page=482.

– "Jackson, John (1785–1862)." *Dictionary of Miramichi Biography*. 1997. New ed. 2013. https://archives.gnb.ca/Search/Hamilton/DMB/SearchResults.aspx?culture=en-CA&action=0&page=489.

– "Key, Alexander (1795–1851)." *Dictionary of Miramichi Biography*. 1997. New ed. 2013. https://archives.gnb.ca/Search/Hamilton/DMB/SearchResults.aspx?culture=en-CA&action=0&page=531.

– "Ledden, James (1780–1860)." *Dictionary of Miramichi Biography*. 1997. New ed. 2013. https://archives.gnb.ca/Search/Hamilton/DMB/SearchResults.aspx?culture=en-CA&action=0&page=552.

– *The Old North Esk on the Miramichi*. 1979. Enlarged ed. Saint John, NB: Miramichi Books, 2004.

– *Old North Esk Revised*. Fredericton, NB: Micmac-Maliseet Institute, University of New Brunswick, 1988.

Bibliography

263

- "Parker, Hedley S. Vicars (1856–1935)." *Dictionary of Miramichi Biography*. 1997. New ed. 2013. https://archives.gnb.ca/Search/Hamilton/DMB/SearchResults.aspx?culture=en-CA&action=0&page=788.
- "Pierce, James A. (1804–1867)." *Dictionary of Miramichi Biography*. 1997. New ed. 2013. https://archives.gnb.ca/Search/Hamilton/DMB/SearchResults.aspx?culture=en-CA&action=0&page=814.
- "Price, Richard (1783–1825)." *Dictionary of Miramichi Biography*. 1997. New ed. 2013. https://archives.gnb.ca/Search/Hamilton/DMB/SearchResults.aspx?culture=en-CA&action=0&page=827.
- "Rankin, Alexander (1788–1852)." *Dictionary of Miramichi Biography*. 1997. New ed. 2013. https://archives.gnb.ca/Search/Hamilton/DMB/SearchResults.aspx?culture=en-CA&action=0&page=841.
- "Smith, John (1784–1861)." *Dictionary of Miramichi Biography*. 1997. New ed. 2013. https://archives.gnb.ca/Search/Hamilton/DMB/SearchResults.aspx?culture=en-CA&action=0&page=940.

Hamilton, Thomas. "MacLeod, Norman, D.D. (1812–1872)." *Dictionary of National Biography, 1885–1900*, vol. 35, 217–18. New York: Macmillan & Co., 1893. https://archive.org/details/DictionaryOfNationalBiographyVolume35/page/n229.

[Hanway, Jonas]. *Motives for a Subscription towards the Relief of the Sufferers at Montreal in Canada*. London: n.p., 1766. https://archive.org/details/cihm_39604.

Harington, C.R., ed. *The Year without a Summer? World Climate in 1816*. Ottawa: Canadian Museum of Nature, 1992. https://archive.org/details/yearwithoutsumme1992hari.

Haslam, Doris Muncey. *The Wrights of Bedeque, Prince Edward Island: A Loyalist Family*. Summerside, PEI: D.M. Haslam, 1978.

Hatch, William Collins. *A History of the Town of Industry, Franklin County, Maine*. Farmington, ME: Press of Knowlton, McCleary & Co., 1893. https://archive.org/details/historyoftownofio1hatc.

Hay, G.U. "The South Tobique Lakes." *Bulletin of the Natural History Society of New Brunswick*, no. 20 (1902): 472–82. https://biodiversitylibrary.org/page/49570211.

Hazen Hindle, Margaret, and Robert M. Hazen. *Keepers of the Flame: The Role of Fire in American Culture, 1775–1925*. Princeton, NJ: Princeton University Press, 1992.

Highland Destitution: First Report of the Edinburgh Section of the Central Board for the Relief of Destitution in the Highlands and Islands

264   *Bibliography*

of Scotland, for 1848. Edinburgh: William Blackwood & Sons, 1848. https://hdl.handle.net/2027/nyp.33433075943526.

Hill, Isabel Louise. *Fredericton, New Brunswick, British North America*. Fredericton, NB: York-Sunbury Historical Society, 1968.

Hill, Robert. *Voice of the Vanishing Minority: Robert Sellar and the Huntingdon Gleaner, 1863–1919*. Montreal and Kingston: McGill-Queen's University Press, 1998.

"Historic Forest Fires." *Scientific American*, 9 July 1904, 23. https://archive.org/details/scientific-american-1904-07-09.

History of Penobscot County, Maine. Cleveland, OH: Williams, Chase, & Co., 1882. https://archive.org/details/historyofpenobscoowill.

Hodgins, J. George. *Geography and History of the British Colonies*. Toronto: MacLear and Co., 1860. https://archive.org/details/geographyhistoryoohodg.

Holbrook, Stuart. *The American Lumberjack*. New York: Collier, 1962.

– *Burning an Empire: The Story of American Forest Fires*. New York: Macmillan, 1943.

Hornsby, Stephen J., and John G. Reid, eds. *New England and the Maritime Provinces: Connections and Comparisons*. Montreal and Kingston: McGill-Queen's University Press, 2005.

Hough, Franklin B. *Report on Forestry, Submitted to Congress by the Commissioner of Agriculture*. Washington, DC: Government Printing Office, 1882. https://hdl.handle.net/2027/hvd.32044102819224.

Houle, Daniel, Jean-David Moore, and Jean Povencher. "Ice Bridges on the St. Lawrence River as an Index of Winter Severity from 1620 to 1910." *Journal of Climate* 20, no. 4 (2007): 757–64.

Hughes, J. Donald. *What Is Environmental History?* 2nd ed. Malden, MA: Polity, 2016.

[Hunter, William?]. *Letters from Nova Scotia and New Brunswick, Illustrative of Their Moral, Religious, and Physical Circumstances, during the Years 1826, 1827, and 1828*. Edinburgh: Waugh and Innis, 1829. https://archive.org/details/cihm_48436.

Irish, James. *Report of the State of the Land Office, for the Year 1825*. Portland, ME: A.W. Thayer, 1825. https://books.google.ca/books?id=TvgUAAAAYAAJ.

Ives, Edward D. *Joe Scott: The Woodsman-Songmaker*. Urbana: University of Illinois Press, 1978.

Jack, Edward. "An Expedition to the Headwaters of the Little South-West Miramichi." Ed. and annot. W.F. Ganong. *Acadiensis* 5 (1905): 116–51. https://archive.org/details/acadiensisquarteo5jackuoft.

Bibliography

- "Remarks Concerning Forest Fires in New Brunswick." In Franklin B. Hough, *Report on Forestry, Submitted to Congress by the Commissioner of Agriculture*, 213–15. Washington, DC: Government Printing Office, 1882. https://hdl.handle.net/2027/hvd.32044102819224.

Jardine, John. "The Miramichi Fire." c. 1825. *Music to the Ear*. Virtual Museum of Canada. http://www.virtualmuseum.ca/edu/ViewLoitDa.do?method=preview&lang=EN&id=1428.

Johnson, Edward A. *Fire and Vegetation Dynamics: Studies from the North American Boreal Forest*. Cambridge, UK: Cambridge University Press, 1992.

Johnson, George Brooks. *Miramichi Woodsman*. Richmond, VA: Whittet & Shepperson, 1945.

Johnston, James F.W. *Notes on North America, Agricultural, Economical, and Social*. Vols 1–2. Edinburgh and London: William Blackwood and Sons, 1851. https://archive.org/details/notesofnorthamer01john and https://archive.org/details/notesnorthamer02johnrich.

Jonsson, Fredrik Albritton. *Enlightenment's Frontier: The Scottish Highlands and the Origins of Environmentalism*. New Haven, CT: Yale University Press, 2013.

Kendall, Joseph. *History of the Town of Houlton, Maine from 1803 to 1883*. Haverhill, MA: C.C. Morse and Son, 1884.

Klein, Naomi. *The Shock Doctrine: The Rise of Disaster Capitalism*. Toronto: A.A. Knopf, 2007.

Klingaman, W.K., and N.P. Klingaman. *The Year without Summer: 1816 and the Volcano that Darkened the World and Changed History*. New York: St Martin's, 2013.

Latham, Bryan. *Timber: Its Development and Distribution, a Historical Survey*. London: George C. Harrap & Co., 1957.

Lehman, George F. "Meteorological Observations Made on the Island of Tinicum ... for the Year 1825." *American Journal of the Medical Sciences* 2, no. 4, art. 13 (1828): 345–75. https://hdl.handle.net/2027/msu.31293021817105.

Levinge, R.G.A., Capt. *Echoes from the Backwoods, or Sketches of Transatlantic Life*. London: J. & D.A. Darling, 1849. http://www.canadiana.ca/view/oocihm.45515.

Lincoln, Jesse E. "Through Flame and Tempest." *The Youth's Companion* 67, 11 October 1894, 451–2. https://hdl.handle.net/2027/njp.32101079674980.

Loring, Amasa, Rev. *History of Piscataquis County, Maine, from its Early Settlement to 1880*. Portland, ME: Hoyt, Fogg, and Donham, 1880. https://archive.org/details/cu31924028809592.

Loucks, O.L. "A Forest Classification for the Maritime Provinces." *Proceedings of the Nova Scotian Institute of Science* 25, part 2 (1962): 85–167. https://dalspace.library.dal.ca/handle/10222/13605.

Lovell, Ernest, Jr, ed. *His Very Self and Voice: Collected Conversations of Lord Byron.* New York: Macmillan, 1954.

Lower, A.R.M. *Great Britain's Woodyard: British America and the Timber Trade, 1763–1867.* Montreal and Kingston: McGill-Queen's University Press, 1973.

– *Settlement and the Forest Frontier in Eastern Canada.* Ed. W.A. Mackintosh and W.L.G. Joerg. Toronto: Macmillan, 1936.

Ludlum, David. *The Country Journal New England Weather Book.* Boston: Houghton Mifflin, 1976.

– *Early American Hurricanes, 1492–1870.* Boston: American Meteorological Society, 1963.

MacDowell, Laurel Sefton. *An Environmental History of Canada.* Vancouver: UBC Press, 2012.

MacEachern, Alan. "The Big Chill: Two Centuries Ago, Much of the World Was Left in the Cold during What Became Known as the Year without a Summer." *Canada's History*, August-September 2016, 52–5. https://www.canadashistory.ca/explore/environment/the-big-chill.

– "Popular by Our Misery: The International Response to the 1825 Miramichi Fire." In Claire E. Campbell and Robert Summerby-Murray, eds, *Land and Sea: Environmental Histories of Atlantic Canada*, 161–80. Fredericton, NB: Acadiensis, 2012.

– ed. "Forum: The Landscape of Canadian Environmental History." *Canadian Historical Review* 95, no. 4 (2014): 545–630.

MacEachern, Alan, and Michael O'Hagan. "Canada's Year without a Summer." NICHE: Network in Canadian History & Environment, 2016. http://niche-canada.org/yearwithoutasummer/.

MacEachern, Alan, and William J. Turkel, eds. *Method and Meaning in Canadian Environmental History.* Toronto: Nelson, 2009. http://niche-canada.org/method-and-meaning/.

MacGregor, Duncan. *Fire in the Forest of New Brunswick.* Dublin: J.&M. Porteous, [1826?]. https://hdl.handle.net/2027/uc1.31175035489429.

MacKinnon, John. *A Sketch Book Comprising Historical Incidents, Traditional Tales, and Translations.* Saint John, NB: Barnes & Co., 1915. https://archive.org/details/sketchbookcomprioomackuoft.

MacKinnon, William R., Jr. "Doak, Robert." *Dictionary of Canadian Biography.* http://www.biographi.ca/en/bio/doak_robert_8E.html.

Bibliography 267

– *Over the Portage: Early History of the Upper Miramichi.* 1984. Rev. ed. Fredericton, NB: New Ireland, 2000.

MacLean, Norman. *Young Men and Fire.* Chicago: University of Chicago Press, 1992.

MacLeod, Norman, Rev. "Fire in the Woods." *The Good News* 1, no. 22 (1861): 673–6. http://eco.canadiana.ca/view/oocihm.8_06044_22.

MacNutt, W.S. "Baillie, Thomas." *Dictionary of Canadian Biography.* http://www.biographi.ca/en/bio/baillie_thomas_9E.html.

– *New Brunswick, a History: 1784–1867.* Toronto: Macmillan of Canada, 1963.

– "The Politics of the Timber Trade in Colonial New Brunswick, 1825–40." *Canadian Historical Review* 30, no. 1 (1949): 47–65.

Malm, Andrea. *Fossil Capital: The Rise of Steam Power and the Roots of Global Warming.* London: Verso, 2016.

Manners, George. *The Conflagration: A Poem Written and Published for the Benefit of the Sufferers by the Recent Disastrous Fires in the Province of New Brunswick.* Boston: Ingraham & Hewes, 1825. http://archive.org/details/cihm_48670.

Mannion, John. *Irish Settlements in Eastern Canada: A Study of Cultural Transfer and Adaptation.* Toronto: University of Toronto Press, 1974.

Manny, Louise. *Ships of Miramichi.* Saint John, NB: New Brunswick Museum, 1960.

Manny, Louise, and James Reginald Wilson. *Songs of Miramichi.* Fredericton, NB: Brunswick, 1968.

Marcil, Eileen. "Wood, Charles." *Dictionary of Canadian Biography.* http://www.biographi.ca/en/bio/wood_charles_7E.html.

Marsh, G.P. *Man and Nature, or Physical Geography as Modified by Human Action.* New York: Charles Scribner, 1864. https://archive.org/details/manandnatureorpoomarsgoog.

Martin, R. Montgomery. *History of Nova Scotia, Cape Breton, the Sable Islands, New Brunswick, Prince Edward Island, the Bermudas, Newfoundland, &c. &c.* London: Whittaker & Co., 1837. https://archive.org/details/cihm_46128.

Mauch, Christof. "The Phoenix Syndrome: Natural Catastrophes in American History and Culture." *Jadavpur University Journal of History* 30 (2014–15): 19–38.

McCalla, Douglas. "Forest Products and Upper Canadian Development, 1815–46." *Canadian Historical Review* 68, no 2 (1987): 159–98.

McClement, Fred. *The Flaming Forests.* Montreal: McClelland and Stewart, 1969.

McCracken, Eileen. *The Irish Woods since Tudor Times: Distribution and Exploitation*. Newton Abbot, UK: David & Charles, 1971.

McGregor, John. *British America*. Vol. 2. Edinburgh: W. Blackwood, 1832. https://archive.org/details/britishamericaino2macg.

– *Historical and Descriptive Sketches of the Maritime Provinces*. London: Longman, Rees, Orme, Brown, and Green, 1828. https://archive.org/details/cihm_38031.

McKenna, Ed. "Cockburn, Sir Francis." *Dictionary of Canadian Biography*. http://www.biographi.ca/en/bio/cockburn_francis_9E.html.

McNeill, J.R., and Erin Stewart Mauldin, eds. *A Companion to Global Environmental History*. Chichester and Hoboken, UK: Wiley Blackwell, 2012.

MeasuringWorth. http://measuringworth.com.

Meek, Forrest B. *Lumbering in Eastern Canada: Compilation of Selected Lumbering Districts within Eastern Canada during the 18th & 19th Centuries*. Clare, MI: White Pine Historical Society and Edgewood Press, 1991.

Merivale, Herman. "On Some Features of American Scenery." *Littell's Living Age* 99, no. 128 (1868): 643–56. https://hdl.handle.net/2027/uiug.30112107852482.

Mitchell, James. *Dendrologia, or A Treatise of Forest Trees, with Evelyn's Silva*. Rev. ed. London: Keighley, 1827. https://archive.org/details/dendrologiaaorato1evelgoog.

Money, Nicholas P. *Carpet Monsters and Killer Spores: A Natural History of Toxic Mold*. Oxford, UK: Oxford University Press, 2004.

Monro, Alexander. *New Brunswick*. Halifax: Richard Nugent, 1855. https://archive.org/details/newbrunswickwitoomonrgoog.

Moodie, Susanna. *Flora Lyndsay, or Passages in an Eventful Life*. New York: DeWitt and Davenport, 1854. http://www.gutenberg.org/files/27373/27373-h/27373-h.htm.

Moore, Richard. *The Universal Assistant and Complete Mechanic*. Whitby, ON: J.S. Robertson, 1879. https://archive.org/details/cihm_11146/page/n81.

Mosseler, A., J.A. Lynds, and J.E. Major. "Old-Growth Forests of the Acadian Forest Region." *Environmental Review* 11, no. S1 (2003): S47–S77.

Mountain Shepherd. "The Wonderful Fire of Miramichi." *The Independent* 13, no. 643 (1861): 6.

Mulcahy, Matthew. *Hurricanes and Society in the British Greater Caribbean, 1624–1783*. Baltimore, MD: Johns Hopkins University Press, 2006.

Bibliography

Mullin, Katie. *Cemeteries of the Parish of Newcastle, Northumberland County, Province of New Brunswick, Canada*. Miramichi, NB: New Brunswick Genealogical Society, Miramichi Branch, 2003.

Murdoch, Beamish. *A History of Nova-Scotia, or Acadie*. Halifax: J. Barnes, 1867. https://archive.org/details/cihm_37228.

A Narrative of the Late Fires at Miramichi, New-Brunswick. Halifax: P.J. Holland, 1825. https://archive.org/details/cihm_37196.

NASA. "Global Climate Change: Vital Signs of the Planet." https://climate.nasa.gov/.

Neal, Larry. "The Financial Crisis of 1825 and the Restructuring of the British Financial System." *Review – Federal Reserve Bank of St. Louis*, May-June 1998, 53–76. https://files.stlouisfed.org/files/htdocs/publications/review/98/05/9805ln.pdf.

Neeson, Eoin. *A History of Irish Forestry*. Dublin: Liliput, 1991.

New Brunswick Genealogical Society, Miramichi Branch. *Cemeteries of the Parish of Alnwick, Northumberland County, Province of New Brunswick, Canada*. Miramichi, NB: New Brunswick Genealogical Society, Miramichi Branch, 2006.

Nora, Pierre. "Between Memory and History: *Les Lieux de Mémoire*." *Representations*, no. 26 (1989): 7–24.

– *Realms of Memory: Rethinking the French Past*. 3 vols. English ed. Trans. Arthur Goldhammer. Ed. Lawrence D. Kritzman. New York: Columbia University Press, 1996–98.

Omi, Philip N. *Forest Fires: A Reference Handbook*. Santa Barbara, CA: ABC-CLIO, 2005.

Opp, James, and John C. Walsh, eds. *Placing Memory and Remembering Place in Canada*. Vancouver: UBC Press, 2010.

Oppenheimer, Clive. *Eruptions that Shook the World*. Cambridge, UK: Cambridge University Press, 2011.

Parenteau, Bill. "The New Brunswick Forest Heritage: A History of the Forest Industry, 1780–1930." Unpublished manuscript, 1996.

Pasts Collective, eds. *Canadians and Their Pasts*. Toronto: University of Toronto Press, 2013.

Patch, Jeff. "Analysis of Lightning Fire Frequency by Ecodistrict." Unpublished report to New Brunswick Department of Natural Resources and Energy, 1998.

Paul, Daniel N. *We Were Not the Savages: Collision between European and Native American Civilizations*. 1993. 3rd ed. Halifax: Fernwood, 2006.

Pérez, Louis A., Jr. *Winds of Change: Hurricanes and the Transformation of Nineteenth-Century Cuba*. Chapel Hill and London: University of North Carolina Press, 2001.

Perley, Moses. *Reports on Indian Settlements, &c.* [Fredericton, NB?]: J. Simpson, 1842. http://leg-horizon.gnb.ca/e-repository/monographs/31000000049445/31000000049445.pdf.

Perley, Sidney. "The Spring Freshet of 1826." In *Historic Storms of New England*, 194–7. 1891. Reprint, Carlisle, MA: Commonwealth Editions, 2001.

Poey, Andres. "A Chronological Table, Comprising 400 Cyclonic Hurricanes Which Have Occurred in the West Indies and in the North Atlantic within 362 Years, from 1493 to 1855." *Journal of the Royal Geographical Society* 25 (1855): 291–328. https://archive.org/details/jstor-1798124.

Pollard, James B. *Historical Sketch of the Eastern Regions of New France ... also Prince Edward Island: Military and Civil.* Charlottetown, PEI: Coombs, 1898. https://archive.org/details/historicalsketchoopolluoft.

Pomeranz, Kenneth. *The Great Divergence: China, Europe, and the Making of the Modern World Economy.* Princeton, NJ: Princeton University Press, 2000.

Post, J.D. *The Last Great Subsistence Crisis in the Western World.* Baltimore, MD: Johns Hopkins University Press, 1977.

Potter, J. "The British Timber Duties, 1815–60." *Economica* 22, no. 86 (1955): 122–36.

Proulx, Annie. *Barkskins.* New York: Scribner, 2016.

Pyne, Stephen J. *Awful Splendour: A Fire History of Canada.* Vancouver: UBC Press, 2007.

– *Fire in America: A Cultural History of Wildland and Rural Fire.* Princeton, NJ: Princeton University Press, 1982.

– *Vestal Fire: An Environmental History, Told through Fire, of Europe and Europe's Encounter with the World.* Seattle and London: University of Washington Press, 1997.

Pyne, Stephen J., Patricia L. Andrews, and Richard D. Laven. *Introduction to Wildland Fire.* 1984. 2nd ed. New York: John Wiley & Sons, 1996.

Radkau, Joachim. *The Age of Ecology: A Global History.* Trans. Patrick Camiller. New York: Polity, 2014.

Rankin, John. *A History of Our Firm: Being Some Account of the Firm of Pollok, Gilmour, and Co. and Its Offshoots and Connections, 1804–1920.* 2nd ed. Liverpool: Henry Young and Sons, 1921. https://archive.org/details/historyofourfirmoorankuoft.

Rayburn, Alan. *Naming Canada: Stories about Canadian Place Names.* 1994. Rev. ed. Toronto: University of Toronto Press, 2001.

Bibliography

Reade, Charles. *Hard Cash*. London: Chatto and Windus, 1863. https://archive.org/details/in.ernet.dli.2015.91926.

"Recollections of Canada's Greatest Forest Fire." *Canadian Forestry Journal* 13, no. 11 (1917): 1409–10. http://eco.canadiana.ca/view/oocihm.8_06922_91/38?r=0&s=1.

Redfield, W.C. "Some Account of Violent Columnar Whirlwinds, Which Appear to Have Resulted from the Action of Large Circular Fires." *Edinburgh Philosophical Journal* 27, no. 54 (1839): 369–79. https://archive.org/details/edinburghnewphil27edin.

Rees, Ronald. *New Brunswick's Early Roads: The Routes that Shaped the Province*. Halifax: Nimbus, 2012.

– *New Brunswick Was His Country: The Life of William Francis Ganong*. Halifax: Nimbus, 2016.

Reid, John G. "Empire, the Maritime Colonies, and the Supplanting of Mi'kma'ki/Wulstukwik, 1780–1820." *Acadiensis* 38, no. 2 (2009): 78–97.

Report of the Commissioners for Ascertaining the Losses Occasioned by the Late Fires in New Brunswick. Fredericton, NB: G.K. Lugrin, 1826. https://archive.org/details/cihm_48084.

The Report of the Miramichi Committee Appointed for the Distribution of the Subscriptions Made for the Relief of the Sufferers by the Great Fire, on the 7th October, 1825. Miramichi, NB: James A. Pierce, 1828. https://archive.org/details/cihm_91975.

Rosario, K. "Making Progress: Disaster Narratives and the Art of Optimism in Modern America." In L.J. Vale and T.J. Campanella, eds, *The Resilient City: How Modern Cities Recover from Disaster*, 27–54. Oxford: Oxford University Press, 2005.

Rusk, Ralph L. *The Life of Ralph Waldo Emerson*. 1949. Reprint, New York: Columbia University Press, 1957.

Russell, Loris S. "Gesner, Abraham." *Dictionary of Canadian Biography*. http://www.biographi.ca/en/bio/gesner_abraham_9E.html.

Sabine, James, Rev. *A Sermon in Commemoration of the Benevolence of the Citizens of Boston*. St John's, NL: John Ryan, 1818. https://archive.org/details/cihm_41487.

Sandham, Alfred. *Ville-Marie, or Sketches of Montreal, Past and Present*. Montreal: George Bishop & Co., 1870. https://archive.org/details/cihm_12998.

Savage, Mrs William T. *Miramichi*. Boston: Loring, 1865. https://archive.org/details/miramichioosavagoog.

Schofield, Edmund A. "Burnt Woods: Ecological Insights into Thoreau's Unhappy Encounter with Forest Fire." *Thoreau Research Newsletter* 2, no. 3 (1991): 1–8.

Bibliography

Scott, Andrew C., David M.J.S. Bowman, William J. Bond, Stephen J. Pyne, and Martin E. Alexander. *Fire on Earth: An Introduction.* West Sussex, UK: Wiley Blackwell, 2014.

See, Scott W. *Riots in New Brunswick: Orange Nativism and Social Violence in the 1840s.* Toronto: University of Toronto Press, 1993.

Sellar, Robert. *History of the County of Huntingdon and the Seigniories of Chateaugay and Beauharnois.* Huntingdon, QC: Canadian Gleaner, 1883. https://archive.org/details/historyofcountyooosellrich.

Sherrard, Valerie. *Three Million Acres of Flame.* Toronto: Boardwalk Books, 2007.

Shaw, Patrick, Alex Dunlop, Mark Napier, and J.M. Bell. *Cases Decided in the [Scotland] Court of Session from Nov. 12, 1830 to July 9, 1831.* Vol. 9. Edinburgh: J. Shaw and Co., 1831. https://archive.org/details/casesdecidedincooshawgoog.

Silver, Arthur P. *Farm-Cottage, Camp and Canoe in Maritime Canada.* London: G. Routledge & Sons, 1908. https://archive.org/details/farmcottagecampoosilv.

– *Through Miramichi with Rod and Rifle.* Halifax: Holloway Bros, 1890.

Simcoe, Elizabeth. *The Diary of Mrs. John Grave Simcoe.* Ed. J. Ross Robertson. Toronto: W. Briggs, 1911. https://archive.org/details/diaryofmrsjohngroosimcuoft.

Sinclair, David. *Sir Gregor MacGregor and the Land That Never Was.* London: Headline, 2003.

Slonosky, Victoria. "Historical Climate Observations in Canada: 18th and 19th Century Daily Temperature from the St. Lawrence Valley, Quebec." *Geoscience Data Journal* 1, no. 2 (2014): 103–20. https://doi.org/10.1002/gdj3.11.

Smout, T.C., ed. *People and Woods in Scotland: A History.* Edinburgh: Edinburgh University Press, 2003.

– ed. *Scottish Woodland History.* Edinburgh: Scottish Cultural Press, 1997.

Smout, T.C., Alan R. MacDonald, and Fiona Watson. *A History of the Native Woodlands of Scotland, 1500–1920.* Edinburgh: Edinburgh University Press, 2005.

Solnit, Rebecca. *A Paradise Built in Hell: The Extraordinary Communities That Arise in Disaster.* New York: Penguin, 2009.

Spencer, Grace MacMillan. *A History of Early Boiestown.* Boiestown, NB: Central New Brunswick Woodsmen's Museum, 1987.

Spedon, Andrew. *Rambles among the Blue-Noses.* Montreal: John Lovell, 1863. https://archive.org/details/cihm_40289.

Sprague, John Francis. "Forests, Forest Fires, Fish and Game." *Sprague's Journal of Maine History* 11, no. 3 (1923): 115–26. https://archive.org/details/spraguesjournal002spra/page/n447.

Spray, William A. "Abrams, William." *Dictionary of Canadian Biography*. http://www.biographi.ca/en/bio/abrams_william_7E.html.

– "Cunard, Joseph." *Dictionary of Canadian Biography*. http://www.biographi.ca/en/bio/cunard_joseph_9E.html.

– "Davidson, William." *Dictionary of Canadian Biography*. http://www.biographi.ca/en/bio/davidson_william_4E.html.

– "Early Northumberland County, 1765–1823: A Study in Local Government." MA thesis, University of New Brunswick, 1963.

– "The Irish in Miramichi." In P.M. Toner, ed., *New Ireland Remembered: Historical Essays on the Irish in New Brunswick*, 55–62. Fredericton, NB: New Ireland, 1988.

– "Rankin, Alexander." *Dictionary of Canadian Biography*. http://www.biographi.ca/en/bio/rankin_alexander_8E.html.

– "Reception of the Irish in New Brunswick." In P.M. Toner, ed., *New Ireland Remembered: Historical Essays on the Irish in New Brunswick*, 9–26. Fredericton, NB: New Ireland, 1988.

Springer, John S. *Forest Life and Forest Trees*. New York: Harper and Brothers, 1851. https://archive.org/details/forestlifeforestoospri.

Stennett, R. *Aldiborontiphoskyphorniostikos: A Round Game for Merry Parties, with Rules for Playing the Game*. New York: S. King, 1825. https://www.loc.gov/item/21003058/.

Stewart, Mairi. "Using the Woods, 1600–1850 (2): Managing for Profit." In T.C. Smout, ed., *People and Woods in Scotland: A History*, 105–27. Edinburgh: Edinburgh University Press, 2003.

Struzik, Edward. *Firestorm: How Wildfire Will Shape Our Future*. Washington, DC: Island, 2017.

Stuart, James. *Three Years in North America*. Vol. 1. Edinburgh: Robert Cadell, 1833. https://archive.org/details/threeyearsinnoro3stuagoog.

"Surreal Life." *Detroit Metro Times*, 25 January 2005. http://www.detroitartistsworkshop.com/van-newkirk-allen-surreal-life/.

Swanick, Eric L. "Monro, Alexander." *Dictionary of Canadian Biography*. http://www.biographi.ca/en/bio/monro_alexander_12E.html.

Taylor, Anthony R., Yan Boulanger, David T. Price, Dominic Cyr, Elizabeth McGarrigle, Werner Rammer, and John A. Kershaw Jr. "Rapid 21st Century Climate Change Projected to Shift Composition and Growth of Canada's Acadian Forest Region." *Forest Ecology and Management* 405 (2017): 284–94.

274   *Bibliography*

Taylor, M. Brook. *Promoters, Patriots, and Partisans: Historiography in Nineteenth-Century English Canada.* Toronto: University of Toronto Press, 1989.

Taylor, Jefferys. *The Forest, or Rambles in the Woodland.* New York: Betts & Anstice, 1832. https://archive.org/details/forestorramblesoo taylgoog.

Thomas, Peter. *Lost Land of Moses: The Age of Discovery on New Brunswick's Salmon Rivers.* Fredericton, NB: Goose Lane, 2001.

Thomas, Peter A., and Robert S. McAlpine. *Fire in the Forest.* Cambridge, UK: Cambridge University Press, 2010.

Thompson, Neville. *Earl Bathurst and the British Empire.* Barnsley, UK: Leo Cooper, 1999.

Thoreau, Henry David. *The Journal of Henry David Thoreau.* Vol. 7. 1906. Ed. Bradford Torrey and Francis Allen. New York: Dover, 1962.

– "The Succession of Forest Trees." *New-York Weekly Tribune,* 6 October 1860.

– *A Week on the Concord and Merrimack Rivers.* New York: Penguin, 1849. https://archive.org/details/weekonconcordmer1849thor.

Thornes, John E. *John Constable's Skies: A Fusion of Art and Science.* Birmingham, UK: University of Birmingham Press, 1999.

Tymstra, Cordy. *The Chinchaga Firestorm.* Edmonton: University of Alberta Press, 2014.

Uekötter, Frank, ed. "Environment and Memory." Special issue, *Global Environment* 6, no. 11 (2013).

Upton, L.F.S. *Micmacs and Colonists: Indian-White Relations in the Maritimes, 1713–1867.* Vancouver: UBC Press, 1979.

Uranophilus. *An Almanack for the Year of Our Lord, 1826.* Saint John, NB: Henry Chubb, 1825. https://archive.org/details/cihm_28752.

Wallace, Linda L., ed. *After the Fires: The Ecology of Change in Yellowstone National Park.* New Haven, CT, and London: Yale University Press, 2004.

Wallis, W.D., and R.S. Wallis. *The Micmac Indians of Eastern Canada.* Minneapolis: University of Minnesota Press, 1955. https://books.google. ca/books/about/The_Micmac_Indians_of_Eastern_Canada.html? id=vv-UWbD4bCEC&redir_esc=y.

Walls, Laura Dassow. *Henry David Thoreau: A Life.* Chicago: University of Chicago Press, 2017.

Warburton, George. *Hochelaga, or England in the New World.* London: H. Colburn, 1846. https://archive.org/details/hochelagaorenglo6 warbgoog.

Bibliography

Ware, Edmund. *An Account of the River St. John, with Its Tributary Rivers and Lakes*. Fredericton, NB: Sentinel Office, 1841. https://archive.org/details/cihm_21809.

Warner, B.G., K. Tolonen, and M. Tolonen, "A Postglacial History of Vegetation and Bog Formation at Point Escuminac, New Brunswick." *Canadian Journal of Earth Sciences* 28, no. 10 (1991): 1572–82.

Webb, Horace. "The Development of Forest Law in New Brunswick." MSc thesis, University of New Brunswick, 1924.

Webster, J. Clarence. *An Historical Guide to New Brunswick*. Fredericton, NB: New Brunswick Tourist Association, 1928.

Wessels, Tom. *Reading the Forested Landscape: A Natural History of New England*. Woodstock, VT: Countryman, 1997.

West, John. *A Journal of a Mission to the Indians of the British Provinces*. London: L.B. Seeley and Son, 1827. https://archive.org/details/journalofmission00west.

Whitney, George G. *From Coastal Wilderness to Fruited Plain: A History of Environmental Change in Temperate North America from 1500 to the Present*. Cambridge, UK: Cambridge University Press, 1994.

Wicken, William C. *The Colonization of Mi'kmaw Memory and History, 1794–1928: The King v. Gabriel Sylliboy*. Toronto: University of Toronto Press, 2012.

Williams, David M. "Bulk Carriers and Timber Imports: The British North American Trade and the Shipping Boom of 1824–5." *Mariner's Mirror* 54, no. 4 (1968): 373–82.

Willis, Nathaniel P. "Pedlar Karl." In *Inklings of Adventure*, 1–22. London: Saunders and Otley, 1836. https://archive.org/details/inklingsadventu00willgoog.

Winchester, Simon. *Krakatoa: The Day the World Exploded*. New York: Perennial, 2003.

Worster, Donald. *Nature's Economy: The Roots of Ecology*. San Francisco: Sierra Club Books, 1977.

Wright, Bruce S. *The Moose of New Brunswick: A Report to the Minister of Lands and Mines, New Brunswick*. Fredericton, NB: Northeastern Wildlife Station, 1956.

Wright, Esther Clark. *The Miramichi: A Study of the New Brunswick River and the People Settled along It*. Sackville, NB: Tribune, 1945.

Wynn, Graeme. "The Assault on the New Brunswick Forest, 1780–1850." PhD diss., University of Toronto, 1974.

- "'Deplorably Dark and Demoralized Lumberers'? Rhetoric and Reality in Early Nineteenth-Century New Brunswick." *Journal of Forest History* 24, no. 4 (1980): 168–87.
- "Johnston, J.F.W." *Dictionary of Canadian Biography*. http://www.biographi.ca/en/bio.php?id_nbr=3990.
- "New Brunswick Parish Boundaries in the pre-1861 Census Years." *Acadiensis* 6, no. 2 (1977): 95–105. https://journals.lib.unb.ca/index.php/Acadiensis/article/viewFile/11441/12191.
- "Population Patterns in Pre-Confederation New Brunswick." *Acadiensis* 10, no. 2 (1981): 124–38. https://journals.lib.unb.ca/index.php/acadiensis/article/view/11176/11912.
- *Timber Colony: A Historical Geography of Early Nineteenth Century New Brunswick*. Toronto: University of Toronto Press, 1981.
- "W.F. Ganong, A.H. Clark and the Historical Geography of Maritime Canada." *Acadiensis* 10, no. 2 (1981): 5–28.
Young, D.M. *The Colonial Office in the Early Nineteenth Century*. London: Longmans, 1961.
- "Douglas, Sir Howard." *Dictionary of Canadian Biography*. http://www.biographi.ca/en/bio/douglas_howard_9E.html.
Young, Murray. "The Great Fires of 1825." *The Officers' Quarterly* 13, no. 1 (1997): 7–11.
Zelazyny, Vincent Frank. *Our Landscape Heritage: The Story of Ecological Land Classification in New Brunswick*. Fredericton, NB: New Brunswick Department of Natural Resources, 2007. https://www2.gnb.ca/content/gnb/en/departments/erd/natural_resources/content/ForestsCrownLands/content/ProtectedNaturalAreas/OurLandscapeHeritage.html.
Zilberstein, Anya. *A Temperate Empire: Making Climate Change in Early America*. Oxford, UK: Oxford University Press, 2016.

Index

Abbott, James, 97
Abrams, Sarah, 96–7
Abrams, William, 46, 58, 96–7
Acadian Forest Region, 18–19, 24, 178, 181
Acadians, 22, 26, 120
agriculture, 33–4, 46, 116–17, 125–6, 131–2
Alexander, James, 75, 147–8, 152–3
Allison, Samuel, 127
American Red Cross, 175
Amos, Dafydd, 64, 73, 87, 112

Bacon, Samuel, 101
Baillie, George, 77–8, 113
Baillie, Thomas, 51, 69, 93, 123, 155; description of fire, 76–8
Baillie, William, 77
Bainbridge, John, 112, 117
Barrens, the, 160–1
Baron of Renfrew, 14–16, 49
Bartibog River: and fire, 60, 72, 75, 103, 108, 132; settlement along, 28, 137–41, 160
Bathurst, Earl, 76, 112, 114
Beaubears Island, 22, 32
Black River, 72, 102

Bliss, Henry, 25, 27, 36–8, 45, 112
Boies, Thomas, 28, 73–4, 107
Boiestown, 28, 73–5
Bouchette, Joseph, 17, 34
Bubar, James, 127
Bubier, Louis, 55
Burchill, John G., 118
Burnt Land Brook, 75
Butterfield, William, 73–4

Caie, James, 48
Cains River, 34, 73–5, 142, 147
Camp, Calvin, 103
Campbell, James, 128
Chalmers, Robert, 157–9, 242n129
charity pamphlet. See *Narrative of the Late Fires at Miramichi, A* (1825)
Charlotte County, 80, 85, 124
Chase, Ezekiel, 52, 93–4
Chatham, xi, 27–8, 44, 119–20, 154; deaths in, 103; fire in, 57, 61, 66, 70–1, 99; relief committee, 105; rivalry with Newcastle, 29, 44, 120
Chatham Fire Company, 48
Chatham Mercury, 26, 96–7, 116, 134, 143. *See also* Pierce, James

278   Index

Chicago Fire (1871), 65, 155

"Civis," 42–3, 142. *See also* Cooney, Robert

climate change, 33, 181–3

Cockburn, Francis, 141

Coffin, George, 50–2, 55, 70, 93–5

Collins, Enos, 111

Cooney, Robert, 35, 131–2, 165; description of fire, 55, 59–61, 64, 67; on fire's effects, 138, 141; on fire's range, 75, 81, 85; on Miramichi, 26, 48. *See also* "Civis"; "W"

Corbett, John F., 104

Cort, John, 23

Crawford, Benjamin, 54–5

Crossland, Donna, 20–1, 36, 178, 195n20

Cunard, Joseph, xii, 28, 156, 240n102. *See also* Joseph Cunard & Co.

Cunard, Samuel, 122

Curtis, Wayne, 59, 67

Dalhousie, Earl of, 109

Davidson, William, 23

Dawson, John W., 150

DeMille, James, 161

dendrochronology. *See* tree core sampling project

Dibblee, Frederick, Rev., 51

Dick, Thomas, 4

digital sources and tools, 12–13, 194n18, 194n20

Dixon, Thomas, 110

Doak, Robert, 27, 29

Doaktown, 27

Douglas, Howard, 44, 48, 51, 78, 108, 114; description of fire, 56–7, 87, 100; on Chatham-Newcastle rivalry, 29, 115, 120;

on fire's effects, 102, 121; visit to Miramichi, 115–17

Douglastown (Gretna Green), 27, 48; and Miramichi Fire, 60–1, 72, 99, 102; rebuilding of, 116, 132, 134

dry rot, 201n94

Ecological Land Classification, 19–20

ecoregions, 19–20

Emerson, William, 204n150

environmental history, 7–8, 98, 194n13

Erie Canal, 235n38

Finan, P., 14–16

firefighting, 154–5

Fisher, Peter, 34, 38–9, 59, 88, 91

Forein, James, 140

forest conservation, 155, 161–2, 244n148

Forest Development Survey, 177, 181

forest fires: attitudes to, 91–3, 155; earlier in 1825, 81, 83, 128; post-1825, 74, 128, 142–3, 154; pre-1825, 34, 89

forest fires beyond the Miramichi, 78–81, 215nn147–8; in Charlotte County, 80, 85; around Fredericton, 66, 78, 109, 129, 211n90, 215n143; in Gaspé, 80–1; around Montreal, 81–2; in Maine, xiii, 52, 71–2, 83–7, 93–5; in Nova Scotia, 81, 216n150; along Oromocto River, 80, 85; in Vermont, 80

forests: effects of fire, 68, 146–7; growth, 33, 148; post-fire succession and composition, 147–51, 156–60, 172–3, 175–6, 233n7; white pine (*Pinus strobus*), 35–8,

140, 146–7. *See also* Miramichi; New Brunswick; timber trade
Fowle, John, 93–4
Fowler, Ammon, 128
Fredericton, 51, 93, 124, 154. *See also* forest fires beyond the Miramichi

Ganong, William Francis, 163–5; on ecology, 173–4, 244n149; on forest fires, 172–3; "On the Limits of the Great Fire of Miramichi of 1825," 6, 165–6, 168–74; two-fire theory of, 168–71, 177
Gaspereau River, 75, 147, 166
Gesner, Abraham, 75, 138–9, 157–60
Gespe'gewa'gi, 22
Gillis, Duffy, 46–7
Gilmour, Allan, Sr, 26, 45, 145
Gilmour, James, 46
Gilmour, Pollok, & Co., 26, 58, 166
Gilmour, Rankin, & Co., 58, 144–5, 166
Gilpin, William, 29
Grant, George M., 161
Great Britain: and British North American timber trade, 14–15, 23–5, 37–8, 77–8, 156, 182; Colonial Office, 56, 76–8, 114; financial crisis of 1825, 113–14, 142; forest fires, 30–1, 45; forests, 29, 182; and Miramichi settlement, 9, 26, 45; and Miramichi timber trade, 22–3; relief effort, 107–8, 111–15
Great Roads, 138–9, 148
Greeley, Horace, 4, 151
Greenleaf, Moses, 85–6
Gretna Green. *See* Douglastown

Hall, Samuel Carter, 129–30
Halliburton, Brenton, 111
Hamilton, W.D., 7, 118, 127
Hanselpecker, Isaac, 154
hurricane, 57–8, 207n35
Hutchison, Ernest, 166–8, 170–1
Hutchison, Richard, 166

immigration: from Great Britain, xiv, 26, 35, 45, 73; from Ireland, 28, 41, 118, 137–8; from Scotland, 27–8; and knowledge of forests and fire, 29–32
Irish, James, 50–2, 93–5

Jack, Edward, 69
Jackson family, xiii–xiv
Jardine, John, 6–7, 63; "The Miramichi Fire" ballad (1825), 6, 63, 65, 73, 102
Johnson, George Brooks, 118
Johnston, James F.W., 42–3, 92; description of fire, 59, 67, 76; on fire's effects, 92, 140, 155
Joplin, William, 108–9
Joseph Cunard & Co., 28–9, 38, 142, 144–5, 156. *See also* Cunard, Joseph
Julien, John, 23, 47

land clearing, 33–4, 90–2
Ledden, James, 97
Ledden, W., 97
lieux de mémoire, 8
Lord Byron, xiii–xiv
Loucks, Olie, 19–21
Ludlow Parish, 75, 103, 119

MacGregor, Gregor, 113
MacKinnon, John, 4–6
MacKinnon, William R., Jr, 7

280 Index

MacLean, David, 177
MacLeod, Norman, Rev., 4, 160
Maine, 110, 161; and New Brunswick border dispute, 50–2, 93. See also forest fires beyond the Miramichi
Manners, George, 62, 110–11
Manny, Louise, 59, 64, 67
Marsh, George Perkins, 3, 140
Mauch, Christof, 98
McGregor, John, 41, 87; description of fire, 57, 66, 68; on post-fire period, 114–15, 131, 142; on timber trade, 41–4, 46
McLaughlin, Richard, 127
meadow hay, 93–4, 151
Meek, Forrest B., 136
Mi'gma'gi, 22, 47
Mi'gmagiji'j, 22
Mi'gmaq, 11, 21–4, 47, 178, 239n88; blamed for fire, 91; fire's effects on, 104, 153–4; population, 239n88
Miller, Thomas, 104
Miramichi: forests, 20–1, 24–5, 35; name, xi, 22; population, 23, 29–31, 43, 119; reputation, 43–6; settlement, 26, 32, 39–40; society, 38, 41–7. See also forests; immigration; New Brunswick; timber trade
Miramichi Fire: accounts in Britain, 12, 111–12; arrival in Miramichi, 59–61; as apocalyptic, 63–4; blame, 52–3; blamed on careless-ness, 91; blamed on comet, 89; blamed on divine punishment, 90; blamed on land agents, 93–5; blamed on land clearing, 90; blamed on lightning, 87; blamed on lumbermen, 89–90; blamed on

Mi'gmaq, 91; blamed on sponta-neous combustion, 87–8; breadth of flames, 67; commemoration of, 134–5, 137; deaths, 100–4, 187–92, 223n48; duration, 65–6, 211n89; effects, 99; effects on ani-mals, 63, 152–4; effects on atti-tude to fire, 154–5; effects on fish, 62, 153; effects on forests, 131–3, 135–7, 140–2, 162, 241n119; effects on waterways, 151–2; as exaggerated, 76–7, 121–2, 135, 145; financial losses from, 58, 123–4, 126–7; fire or fires, 67–9; folklore, 64–5, 210n78, 224n50; height of flames, 66–7; in history, 6, 131–3, 162, 165–70, 174; igni-tion, 52; outmigration after, 117–18; people's behaviour during, 34–5, 55–6, 59, 61–2; in popular memory, 6–7, 175; range, xiii, 3, 68–70, 72–6, 80, 157, 165–71; smoke, 55–6, 59, 66, 70–2, 143; speed, 59–60, 66, 145; spotting, 59–60, 71, 208n43; threat of social disorder after, 105–6; winds, 57–8, 140, 168, 207n35
"Miramichi Fire, The," ballad (1825). See Jardine, John
Miramichi River: 17–19, 153, 162–3, 165; fire's effects on Northwest branch, 72, 75, 77, 102, 139, 143–4; fire's effects on Southwest branch, 73, 77, 140, 142–4, 147; Northwest branch, 23, 142; Southwest branch, 28, 131, 142; Welastuguji'j, 22
Monro, Alexander, 76, 149–50
Mosseler, Alex, 24
Murdoch, Beamish, 109, 225n64
Murray, William, 128

Index

Nappan River, 72, 75, 103, 108, 132

Narrative of the Late Fires at Miramichi, A (1825), 106, 109, 205n11; on deaths, 100, 102–3; descriptions of fire, 57–8, 61, 65–8, 99, 140, 145–6; on fire's cause, 90; on fire's range, 73, 80, 84. *See also* Murdoch, Beamish; relief effort

Nashwaak River, 60, 76

Nelson Parish, 48, 103, 105

Nepisiguit River, 75, 140, 157

Neptune, John, 94

New Brunswick, 6, 13, 178; forest composition in future, 181–2; forest composition in past, 20; forest composition today, 18–21, 178. *See also* forests; timber trade

New Brunswick, Department of Natural Resources and Energy, 19, 170, 178, 181

New Brunswick Agricultural and Emigrant Society, 117

Newcastle, xi, 27–8; deaths in, 102–3; fire in, 61, 67, 99; rebuilding of, 107, 119–20, 132, 134; rivalry with Chatham, 29, 44, 120

Nora, Pierre, 8–9

Norfolk, Chris, 177, 179–8

North Esk Parish, 43, 103, 119

Northumberland Agricultural and Emigrant Society, 46, 116–17, 132

Northumberland County, xi, 17, 29, 119–20, 144

Oromocto River, 80, 85, 103, 123–4, 223n41

Ottawa Valley, 118, 240n103

Paleo-Indians, 21

Paley, Isaac, 56–7, 61, 64, 99

Perley, Moses, 139, 239n88

Peshtigo Fire (1871), 4, 155–6, 161

Petrie, Dr James, 100

phoenix effect, 98, 130

Pierce, James, 48, 96, 124–5, 134–5, 137, 152. *See also Chatham Mercury*

Pinchot, Gifford, 162

Post, J.D., 33

Poyais, Republic of, 113

Preston, Richard, 61

Proto-Eastern Algonquin, 21

Proulx, Annie, 7

Pyne, Stephen J., 4, 31–2

Quebec City, 14–16, 33, 70–2, 108–9, 121, 127

Rankin, Alexander, 27, 29, 46, 99–100

Reade, Charles, 113

Redpath, John, 63

relief effort: in British North America, 109; distribution of aid, 121, 126; Fredericton committee, 108, 117, 123, 128, 230n130; in Great Britain, 111–15; international, 107–8, 129, 224n59; Miramichi committee, 103–4, 108, 118, 123, 126, 128–9; as model, 127–8; New Brunswick commission to determine losses and distribution of aid, 124–6; request for aid, 108; Scottish lawsuit (1831), 128; in United States, 62, 110–11, 127. *See also Narrative of the Late Fires at Miramichi, A* (1825)

Restigouche, 73

Index

Richibucto, 41, 73, 168
Rimmer, Richard, 104
rivalry, Chatham-Newcastle, 29, 44, 115–16, 119–20, 229n120
Roberts, W.C., 82
Roman Catholic chapel, Nelson, 48, 100

Savage, Mrs William T., 130
Select Committee on Timber Duties (1835), 25, 27, 37, 41–2, 45; on post-1825 period, 131, 142, 145
Sellar, Robert, 82–3
Sevogle River, 28, 142
Sherrard, Valerie, 7
Silver, Arthur P., 161
Simcoe, Elizabeth, 92
Singer, John S., 36
Siveright, John, 51
Smith, Benjamin, 90
Smith, George N., 55–7
Smith, John, 100
social memory, 7–8, 194n13
Solnit, Rebecca, 98
spruce budworm, 196n22
St Paul's Anglican Church, xi–xii, 64, 101
Stennett, R., 228n100
Strawberry Marsh, 61, 99
Stuart, James, 37

Tambora eruption (1815), xiv, 33, 199nn65–6
Taylor, Jefferys, 174
Taylor, M. Brook, 132
Thoreau, Henry David, xiv, 4, 7, 151
timber trade, xiv, 26, 29–30, 40–1, 44–5, 156; British North

America, 14–17, 23–4; duties, 25–6, 58, 156; financial crisis's effect on, 114, 142–3; fire's effect on, 131, 136, 141–7, 150–1, 162; licenses, 39, 201n86; "mania," 41–2, 114; Miramichi, 24, 26, 36–8, 47–8; New Brunswick, 17, 25–6; reputation of, 38, 42–6; sawmills, 40, 130, 132, 144–5, 160. *See also* forests; Great Britain; Miramichi; New Brunswick
Tobique River, 34, 41, 75–6
tree core sampling project, 177–80
Tuchman, Barbara, 12

"W," 74–5, 85, 141–2, 146–7, 150. *See also* Cooney, Robert
Walton, Captain, 63, 73
Warburton, Henry, 37–8
weather: after the fire, 100–1, 221n23; before the fire, 51–2, 54–5, 81; pre-1825, 32–4; post-1825, 148
Webster, J. Clarence, 170
Welch, P.H., 166, 170–1, 242n133
Wentworth, John, 23–4
William Notman & Son, 162–3
Willis, Nathaniel P., 92
Wilson, James, 59, 67
Wood, Charles, 15, 195n3
Wright, Bruce S., 152–3
Wright, Esther Clark, 170
Wynn, Graeme, 6, 143, 147, 170

Year of the Burnings (1814), 31
Year Without a Summer (1816), 33, 199n66
Young, George R., 160